Philippe Palanque and Fabio Paternò (Eds)

Formal Methods in Human-Computer Interaction

Springer

Philippe Palanque
LIS-FROGIS, University of Toulouse 1, Place Anatole France,
31042 Toulouse Cedex, France

Fabio Paternò
CNUCE-CNR, Via S. Maria 36, 56126 Pisa, Italy

Series Editor

S.A. Schuman, BSc, DEA, CEng
Department of Mathematical and Computing Sciences
University of Surrey, Guildfoid. Surrey GU2 5XH, UK

ISBN-13: 978-3-540-76158-7   e-ISBN-13: 978-1-4471-3425-1
DIO:10.1007/978-1-4471-3425-1

British Library Cataloguing in Publication Data
Formal methods in human-computer interaction.   (Formal
   approaches to computing and information technology)
   1.Human-computer interaction   2.User interfaces (Computer Systems)
   I.Palanque, Philippe   II.Paterno, Fabio
   004'.019
   ISBN 3540761586

Library of Congress Cataloging-in-Publication Data
Formal methods in human-computer interaction / Philippe Palanque and Fabio Paternò, eds.
      p.   cm.   - -   (Formal approaches to computing and information technology)
   Includes bibliographical references and index.
   ISBN 3-540-76158-6 (paperback : alk. paper)
   1. Human-computer interaction.   I. Palanque, Philippe, 1966-
II. Paternò, Fabio, 1960-   III. Series
QA76.9.H85F68   1997   97-27729
004'.01'9- -dc21   CIP

Typesetting: Camera ready by editors

34/3830-543210 Printed on acid-free paper

Preface

There is a growing interest in the application of formal methods to human-computer interaction (see for example (Paterno 95, Palanque & Bastide 95, Bodart & Vanderdonckt 96, Roast & Siddiqui 97, Harrison & Torres 97)) as user interface design and development is an area which is rapidly emerging, sometimes without well defined basic concepts and methods. This is a strong limitation as it means that sometimes designers provide solutions which only have a partial validity and which are difficult to understand and to reason about.

User interfaces represent a challenging application area for formal methods. Their internal structure is becoming increasingly complex as there is a continuous demand to have them supporting more and more devices, media, users, tasks, environments, with more and more dialogues active at the same time. Besides this the approaches in this area have to consider the most complex system in this world: the human user, whose behaviour cannot be described prescriptively.

The first relevant works in this area (Harrison & Thimbleby 90, Dix 91) aimed mainly to give precise definitions of important concepts and properties. Now there is a growing discussion about whether the application of formal methods to Interactive Systems can be useful in the design, analysis and evaluation of realistic case studies. This requires systematic methods able to consider multiple aspects and to address medium-large specifications.

We believe that in this type of application of formal methods one key aspect is not limited to the identification of a notation for developing formal specifications of user interfaces, as some believe: rather it is the identification of a systematic method indicating how the model underlying the formal approach selected can be used to express the relevant concepts of this application domain in order to represent design choices, to discuss them and to reason about their properties.

All the approaches considered in this book have taken into account some aspects of the web environment. The WWW environment is one of the most successful software products of recent years. Millions of people use it every day in order to search for, exchange, and modify information. The reason for this choice was that everybody knows this application so can immediately understand what problems we are discussing.

In the book some of the most well-known approaches developed in research laboratories and universities in many countries are presented. It thus gives a good updated review of the current state of the art in this field. We really hope that these works can be a useful basis for further research work and industrial applications able to solve the many problems still open.

Philippe Palanque, Fabio Paternò

Sydney, July 1997

References

Bodart F., Vanderdonckt J. (ed.) (1996), Proceedings Design, Specification, Verification of Interactive Systems'96, Namur, Springer Verlag.

Dix A. (1991), Formal Methods in Interactive Systems, Academic Press.

Harrison M., Thimblebly H. (1990), Formal Methods in Human-Computer Interaction, Canbridge University Press.

Harrison M. & Torres J.(ed.) (1997), Proceedings Design, Specification, Verification of Interactive Systems'97, Springer Verlag.

Palanque P., Bastide R. (ed.) (1995), Proceedings of Design Specification Verification of Interactive Systems'95, Tolouse, Springer Verlag.

Paterno' F. (ed.) (1995), Interactive Systems: Design, Specification and Verification Springer Verlag Heidelberg, Focus on Computer Graphics Series, ISBN 3-540-59480-9

Roast C., Siddiqui J. (ed.) (1997), Proceedings of the workshop on Formal Aspects of the Human-Computer Interface, Springer Verlag.

Contents

3 Software Architecture Modelling: Bridging Two Worlds
Using Ergonomics and Software Properties   49
L. Nigay and J. Coutaz

4 A Formal Approach to Consistency and Reuse of Links in
World Wide Web Applications   75
R. Pontin de Mattos Fortes, M. do Carmo Nicoletti and A. Neto

5 Using Declarative Descriptions to Model User Interfaces
with MASTERMIND   93
T. Browne, D. Davilla, S. Rugaber and K. Stirewalt

Part II Approaches to the Formal Specification

6 XTL: A Temporal Logic for the Formal Development of
Interactive Systems   **121**
P. Brun

Part III Approaches to the Formal Evaluation

List of Contributors

P. Alencar, P. Bumbulis, D. Cowan, C. Lucena
Department of Computer Science
University of Waterloo
200 University Avenue West,
Waterloo, Ontario
N2L 3G1, Canada
palencar@csgrs6k1.uwaterloo.ca

T. Browne, D. Davilla, S. Rugaber, K. Stirewalt
College of Computing,
Georgia Institute of Technology,
Atlanta, GA 30332-0280, USA,
kurt@cc.gatech.edu

P. Brun
LRI, Bâtiment 490,
University of Paris Sud,
91 405 ORSAY Cedex France
philippe@lri.fr

D. Carr
Institutionen for Systemteknik,
Lulea Tekniska Universitet,
S-97187 Lulea, Sweden
David.Carr@sm.luth.se

A. Dix, R. Mancini
School of Computing, Staffordshire,

PO Box 334,
Stafford ST18 0DG, UK
A.J.Dix@soc.staffs.ac.uk

D. J. Duke
Department of Computer Science,
The University of York,
Heslington, York, YO1 5DD, UK
duke@minster.cs.york.ac.uk

A. Hussey, D. Carrington
Software and Verification centre,
School of Information Technology,
The University of Queensland,
Brisbane, Qld, 4072, Australia
ahussey@it.uq.edu.au

C. Johnson
Department of Computing Science,
University of Glasgow,
Glasgow, G12 8QQ, Scotland
johnson@dcs.gla.ac.uk

L. Nigay, J. Coutaz
CLIPS-IMAG,
University of Grenoble,
BP 53,
38041 Grenoble Cedex 9, France
Laurence.Nigay@imag.fr

P. Palanque, R. Bastide
LIS-FROGIS,
University of Toulouse 1,
Place Anatole France,
31042 Toulouse Cedex, France
palanque@cict.fr

F. Paternò, S. Meniconi
CNUCE-CNR,
Via S. Maria, 36,
56126 Pisa, Italy
f.paterno@cnuce.cnr.it

R. Pontin de Mattos Fortes, M. do Carmo Nicoletti, A. Neto
Depto. Computacao - ICMSC,
University of San Paolo,
S.Carlos SP - CP 668 - CEP 13560-970, Brazil
renata@icmsc.sc.usp.br

E. Schlungbaum
University of Rostock,
Department of Computer Science,
D-18051 Rostock, Germany
schlung@informatik.uni-rostock.de

J.C. Torres
Dpt. de Lenguajes y Sistemas Informaticos,
ETS Ingenieria Informatica,
Av. Andalucia 38,
E-18071 Granada, Spain
jctorres@ugr.es

P. Wright, N. Merriam, B. Fields
Department of Computer Science,
The University of York,
Heslington, York, YO1 5DD, UK
pcw@minster.york.ac.uk

Chapter 1:
Specifying History and Backtracking Mechanisms[1]

1. Introduction

Whereas most of the chapters in this book are specifying the same Netscape-like WWW browser from different perspectives, this chapter takes a single element of a browser, the history mechanism, and compares the formal specification of this aspect of four different hypertext browsers: Netscape Navigator, HyperCard, Microsoft Windows Help system and Think Reference.

The World Wide Web is (amongst other things) a giant hypertext and, as with any hypertext system, users are likely to follow wrong or uninteresting links, to want to return to previously visited nodes and (if they do not have superhuman memory and accuracy) are all likely to get completely 'lost in hyperspace' (Conklin 87). History mechanisms are one of the ways users regain control back in such circumstances, allowing them either to get an overview of where they have been, or simply to go backwards step by step through previous nodes.

Finding useful information in large hypertext systems such as the WWW is difficult and time consuming. If there were no history mechanism users would have to leave bookmarks or write down the URL of any interesting Web page before navigating further, for fear that they might not be able to get back without having to repeat the whole complex search process. Having a history mechanism or even simply a 'back' button means that users can navigate links knowing that if the place they get to is uninteresting they can return. This enables users to engage in a variety of deep and exploratory search strategies and to perform a simple undo of erroneous or unfortunate navigation. Indeed, studies of Web browser's use have shown that 30–40% of all movements between pages are made using the 'back' button (Catledge & Pitkow 95; Tauscher & Greenberg 97).

Tauscher and Greenberg's studies have also shown that a large proportion of revisited pages have been recently visited and hence are likely to be in a history list. Thus a well-designed history mechanism can significantly reduce the effort of finding these pages. This can be seen in terms of Information Foraging Theory (Pirolli & Card 95), which suggests that the most efficient interface is one that

---

[1] **Related work**: http://www.soc.staffs/ac/uk/~cmtajd/topics/undo/

increases the rate of (useful) information gain per unit time. If recent pages are valuable, they need to be accessible with the minimum of physical (keystrokes) and mental (cognitive load) effort. If the page is in the history list it will certainly reduce the physical effort. However, it is clear that cognitive effort will not have been similarly reduced, as many users find history mechanisms quite confusing (Cockburn & Jones 96; Tauscher & Greenberg 97).

This difficulty even extends to attempts to formalise aspects of hypertext systems! One reason for the difficulty is that history mechanisms are reflexive: they involve the user and the designer in looking at the process of interaction. Whilst surfing the Web, users are deeply *engaged* in the activity; they are not thinking *about* what they are doing, they are simply *doing* it. However, when they use the 'back' button or invoke a history mechanism they must make this shift from acting to thinking about their actions. That is, the very use of any history mechanism is a breakdown in interaction (Dix et al. 97).

The reflexive nature of history mechanisms makes specification difficult too. During normal interaction the system can be regarded as being in some state (the current node or page) which the user's actions (navigating links) modify. However, the history mechanism needs to talk about the past states of the system. This means that the system must keep a record of where it has been – previous states. Of course, this record of previous states must be part of the current state of the system!

This reflexiveness is also evident in undo mechanisms for interactive applications such as word processors. In such applications, the system also has to keep some track of previous user actions in order to undo their effect (and possibly redo also). In fact, when formally modelling such systems history and undo mechanisms are virtually identical. The authors have been studying formalisation of undo and the same general formal techniques apply directly to hypertext history.

There is no single history model applied in all Web browsers and hypertext systems. Indeed, some browsers embody two simultaneous but different methods. In this chapter we will examine and specify several history mechanisms from four different hypertext systems. In all, we will see six different history mechanisms at work. This accords with previous observations of the wide variety of history mechanisms found in hypertext systems (Bieber et al. 97; Tauscher & Greenberg 97). In two cases our history mechanisms correspond almost exactly with undo mechanisms found in other applications. Perhaps the most surprising thing is not the variety of mechanisms, but the fact that some browsers embody two simultaneous different methods. Two of the four browsers studied had two different history lists, one for their 'back' command and one for their menu-based history. However, even sharing a common history list does not mean that 'back' and menu selection will have consistent effects on the list!

We will begin the next section by discussing some of the general issues for specifying history. In section 3 we will model each of the mechanisms using the same general framework. Because of the similarity of presentation we are able to compare (in section 4) the mechanisms with each other, ignoring other aspects of the different underlying hypertext systems. We are also able to compare them with similar undo mechanisms.

2. Reflexive Specification

We have already noted that history mechanisms are by their nature reflexive. The history mechanism needs to keep track of previous states, but the data structures used to keep this trace of previous states must themselves be part of the state. Happily this apparent infinite regress is not quite as bad as it seems. We can consider the system as having two levels of state. First, the state of the system if it had no history mechanisms: the current Web page or node being visited plus any additional information about the viewing of the node such as the portion currently being displayed for a large scrolled page. Second is the state of the system augmented with history information. Components of this second bigger state will correspond to instances of the original smaller state.

We will model both kinds of state using a variant of the PIE model (Dix & Runciman 85; Dix 91) originally developed as a general model of interactive systems.

2.1 Browser Commands and State

So, first we ignore the state and commands associated with history mechanisms. That is, we imagine a browser with no 'back' button, nor any history list. The set of states of the system we will denote S. In the case of Web browsing this state will include the URL of the current page, the position it is currently scrolled to, the contents of any fields if it is a form and even perhaps the state of any JAVA applets executing in the current page. User actions modify this state. The set of user actions we denote C (commands) and their effect is modelled by a state update function *doit*:

$$doit : S \times C \to S$$

Within any session browsing will start from some initial state (e.g. the user's home page); we write s_0 for this. Also, it is useful to consider the effect of whole sequence of user commands. We call this 'history' of commands H ($H=C^*$).[2] If necessary we will use the obvious extension of *doit* to whole histories of commands and also define the interpretation function I as follows:

$$I : H \to S$$
$$I(h) = doit(s_0, h)$$

That is, the interpretation gives the state reached if the history h is the complete trace of user commands since the browsing session began.

---

[2] The word 'history' is used in several linked, but different, senses. At this point we are looking at the command history, whereas up to now we have simply talked about 'history' mechanisms as those which allow the user some access to previously visited states or nodes; later we will formally model this 'history' using sequences of states.

2.2 Components of the Browser State and Command Classes

As noted above, the state will typically consist of two things: the name or location of the node being visited (say from a set N) and some viewing information (V). That is:

$$S = N \times V$$

Given such a state s we will refer to the two components as $s.loc$ and $s.view$.

This then is the state of the browser. In addition, there is the current state of the hypertext being browsed; that is, the content associated with any node:

$$Htxt = N \rightarrow Content$$

This mapping between location and content may be:

- fixed – as in the case of CD-ROM-based hypermedia and also Windows Help
- modified by the user – as is the case with editable HyperCard stacks
- modified or even constructed dynamically by other users or processes – as is the case with WWW pages, especially those generated by CGI scripts

However, for the purpose of this chapter we will concentrate on the state of the browser and effectively assume the hypertext itself is fixed.

Returning to the browser, we can use the two components of the state to distinguish two classes of commands:

- active – those which may change the location of the browser:
  $\exists s \in S$ **such that** $doit(s, c).loc \neq s.loc$
  For example, clicking on a link.
- passive – those which only ever change the view:
  $\exists \, s \in S$ **such that** $doit(s, c).loc = s.loc$
  For example, scrolling the text.

History mechanisms typically only record *locations* visited, not every intermediate state. So, for example if there is a 'back' button and we used it immediately after a passive command we would expect to return to the node before the last active command. There are two further complications. First, some browsers (including Netscape Navigator and most Web browsers) do keep track of some view information for previously visited nodes. Other hypertext browsers simply return you to a standard state for the node (e.g. scrolled to the top). Second, the behaviour when an active command actually stays on the same node may cause confusion. For example, what should happen when a normally active command doesn't cause a change to a different node, for example if an HTML anchor points to itself? In the case of both Netscape and HyperCard this does not add an entry to the history used for their respective 'back' functions. That is, they rely on the instance of the use of the command being active. However, note that in the WWW different URLs (locations) may refer to parts of the same document (using labels such as 'mypage.html#top'). These *are* regarded as different locations even though they are the same physical page!

Although this behaviour is interesting, and a major source of confusion for the user, we will ignore it for the rest of this chapter. Instead, we will simply assume that the state consists solely of the location of the current node or page and that all user commands are active. This is to prevent our formulations of different mechanisms becoming too bogged down with side conditions of the form 'if the command c is active'.

2.3 History Commands and State

The commands in C are simply those for navigating within and between pages. If we include an explicit history mechanism then the possible commands will be augmented by those for accessing this history: the 'back' button, history list or 'GO' menu. This augmented set of user commands we will call C^a and the corresponding traces of commands H^a.

Similarly the state will be augmented by additional components. We will call this augmented state S^a. As previously noted the components of this will typically contain instances of the 'original' state set S. For example, a simple one-step history mechanism where the 'back' button allowed one to view the previous state only might keep two copies of the state: $S^a = S \times S$. In fact all the examples we will look at keep much more extensive history mechanisms and store some sequence of states.

Looking at this augmented system, we see that it too has a state update function $doit^a$, initial state $s^{a,0}$, and derived interpretation function I^a:

$$doit^a : S^a \times C^a \to S^a$$
$$I^a : H^a \to S^a$$
$$I^a(h) = doit^a(s^{a,0}, h)$$

The exact form of the augmented commands, state and behaviour depends on the particular history mechanism and we will refer to these by superscripts: e.g. C^{net}, $doit^{net}$, etc. for Netscape.

Although the augmented system has additional state to manage history, the user is principally aware of the current page or node being visited. This can be represented by a mapping *proj* giving for any state of the full system the current node and view of that node:

$$proj : S^a \to S$$

2.4 Model and Implementation

In section 3 we will give explicit models of the augmented state of different browsers. For example, for Netscape we have:

$$S^{net} = Nat \times S^+$$

where *Nat* is the set of natural numbers $\{0,1,2,...\}$ and S^+ is the set of *non-empty* sequences of states. Note that this does not mean that Netscape Navigator *implements* its history mechanism in this way, just that this is a faithful model of its *behaviour*. This is even more important in modelling undo mechanisms where it would be ridiculously inefficient to store copies of the state and instead a record of *changes* is kept.

Another important difference between actual implementations and the abstract specifications given here is that in the real browser a large proportion of the state consists of information about the context of the browser and preferences of the user. The state we are referring to is only that directly associated with the nodes being visited. History is *not* undo – we do not expect the 'back' button to reverse the effect of resizing a window, so this information would be stored once, separate from the history of browsing states. Also a lot of development effort and storage in Web browsers is dedicated to efficiency, especially the caching of recently visited pages. Again this is ignored for the purposes of this chapter.

2.5 Conservativeness of State

If the user never used any history commands the augmented system should behave exactly like the original system:

$$\forall h \in H : proj(I^a(h)) = I(h)$$

In fact, we expect it to behave like the original system even between uses of history commands. That is, if the user issues a normal navigation command, we expect the effect on the augmented system to exactly parallel that of the original browser without undo.

$$proj(s^{a,0}) = s_0$$
$$\forall c \in C, s \in S^a : proj(doit^a(s, c)) = doit(proj(s), c)$$

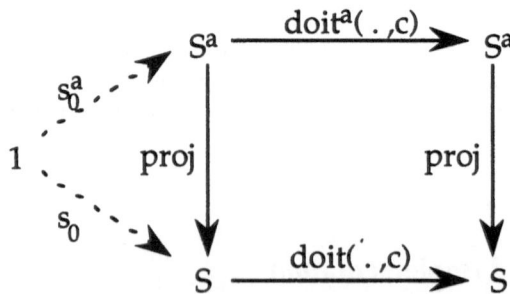

Figure 1: Conservativeness of state

We call this condition *conservativeness of state*. It is equivalent to the commutativity of the diagram in Figure 1. It is very important as it means that the user does not need to be aware of the history mechanism except when it is being explicitly invoked.

This is a fundamental property of any system enhancement which purports to extend the functionality of the original system. In particular, it is essential for any sensible history or undo mechanism. Happily, all the history mechanisms we examine in the next section satisfy this condition.

Conservativeness does not capture specific properties of the history mechanism itself, but instead simply states that the original system is preserved within the augmented system. In section 4, we will return to this issue.

3. Six History Mechanisms

In this section, we will look at the history mechanisms from four different hypertext browsers. In the case of two of these browsers, Windows Help and HyperCard, each has two simultaneous mechanisms at work giving rise to six history mechanisms in total. The fascinating thing is that they are *all* different. No wonder users get confused!

The systems we examine are:

- Microsoft Windows Help – used by most Windows applications to display hypertext help. This has two history mechanisms: a button labelled 'back' and a 'history' menu.
- Think Reference – a hypertext help/reference manual used by many Macintosh programmers. This has a single mechanism accessed by either selecting from a pull-down 'go back' menu or simply clicking the 'go back' button which acts as the menu's pull-down tab.
- Netscape Navigator – the WWW browser. This has a single mechanism, which can be accessed several ways: 'back' and 'forward' buttons, a 'go' menu and a 'history' window.
- HyperCard – the Macintosh hypertext/interface tool. This has two mechanisms: a 'back' button and a 'go recent' window.

3.1 Windows Help – a Stack and a Trace

As noted Windows Help has two mechanisms: a button labelled 'back' and a 'history' menu.

3.1.1 Windows 'back' – a stack

The 'back' button is simply stack based: each press of the button takes you one step back. The augmented state S^{wBk} can thus be modelled as a non-empty sequence of states (from S) – the stack of visited nodes, the last of which is the current state:

$$S^{wBk} = S^+$$
$$proj^{wBk}(bs) = last(bs)$$

When an ordinary navigation command (from C) is issued, the effect is to use the normal navigation *doit* function on the current state (location) to get the new current state and to add it to the history. The back command simply pops an element from the stack of past states if it is non-empty, otherwise it does nothing:

$$doit^{wBk}(bs, c) \quad\quad = \quad\quad bs\hat{\;}doit(last(bs), c) \quad\quad c \in C$$
$$doit^{wBk}(< s >, back) \quad = \quad\quad < s >$$
$$doit^{wBk}(bs, back) = \quad\quad chop(bs) \quad\quad\quad len(bs) > 1$$

N.B. these equations use *len* which gives the length of a sequence, *last* which gives the last element of a sequence, and *chop* which removes the last element from a sequence. The operation $x\hat{\;}y$ is the concatenation of y to the sequence x. The same notation will be used for the concatenation of two sequences.

3.1.2 Windows 'history' – a trace

The history mechanism keeps a trace of all states visited and adds the new state to the sequence every time a new node is visited. The state is thus similar to that for the back command:

$$S^{wHy} = S^+$$
$$proj^{wHy}(hs) = last(hs)$$

This is navigated by using a menu which shows all nodes in the history list and allows the user to choose one. We will call the command which chooses the nth element from the menu *choose(n)*. We can assume that n only takes on sensible values as it is impossible to select items not on the menu!

If we look at the behaviour on the history list, ordinary navigation commands simply add to the history list, whereas using *choose(n)* revisits the relevant node:

$$doit^{wHy}(hs, c) \quad\quad = \quad\quad hs\hat{\;}doit(last(hs), c) \quad\quad c \in C$$
$$doit^{wHy}(hs, choose(n)) \quad = \quad\quad hs \quad\quad\quad\quad\quad\quad\quad n = len(hs)$$
$$= \quad\quad hs\hat{\;}hs[n] \quad\quad\quad\quad\quad \text{otherwise}$$
$$\text{(N.B. } 1 \leq n < len(hs))$$

Compare this with the *back* mechanism: when using 'back' the last state is removed from the back-stack, whereas when choosing from the history list the new state is added to the history. Also note carefully the conditions on the behaviour of *choose(n)*. If the current item from the history list is chosen nothing happens. However, the condition is $n = len(hs)$ not $hs(n) = last(hs)$. That is, although selecting the top element does not cause a repetition in the history list it is possible to get repeats by selecting another entry further down in the history list which happens to be the same as the current state. For example, suppose you have navigated to nodes a, b, c and then back to b. The history menu would read *abcb* (actually the menu is vertical with a at the bottom). If you then selected the fourth entry nothing would happen, but if instead you selected the second entry (also *b*) the history list would then read *abcbb*!

Similar things can happen with the back-stack although this is not immediately visible. However, if you perform actions which visit the same node several times in a row, these are all recorded in the back-stack. Subsequent use of 'back' leads to stuttering at that node. This is very different from the behaviour of equivalent 'back' commands which we will encounter in Netscape and HyperCard (and to some extent Think Reference) which avoid repeats based on the semantics of actions (whether the same node is revisited) rather than the syntax (the last item from the history menu).

3.1.3 Combining 'back' and history

These two mechanisms do not share a single history, but in fact both are maintained. That is, the full state is really of the form:

$$S^{win} = S^+ \times S^+$$

Both the back-stack and the history should have the same current state:

$$\forall\ [bs,hs] \in S^{win} : last(bs) = last(hs)$$

The projection can then be constructed from either of these:

$$proj^{win}([bs,hs]) = last(bs) = last(hs)$$

The first component in the state is the back-stack and the second the history trace. We have already specified the effects of ordinary commands on all components of the state, but need to also specify the effects of the *back* command on the history trace and of the *choose(n)* command on the back-list:

$$
\begin{aligned}
doit^{win}([bs,hs], c) \quad &= \quad [bs\hat{\ }doit(last(bs), c),\ hs\hat{\ }doit(last(hs), c)] \quad c \in C \\[6pt]
doit^{win}([<s>, hs], back) &= \quad [<s>, hs] \\
doit^{win}([bs\hat{\ }s, hs], back) &= \quad [bs, hs\hat{\ }last(bs)] \quad len(bs) \geq 1 \\[6pt]
doit^{win}([bs, hs], choose(n)) &= \quad [bs,hs] \qquad\qquad\qquad\qquad n = len(hs) \\
doit^{win}([bs,hs], choose(n)) &= \quad [bs\hat{\ }hs[n],\ hs\hat{\ }hs[n]] \qquad\quad otherwise \\
&\qquad\ (1 \leq n < len(hs))
\end{aligned}
$$

It is unlikely that users will be aware of this complex interweaving between the two history mechanisms. At least if they get confused they can always use the history list which has the trace of everything.

3.2 Think Reference – a Recency Ordered Set

We look next at Think Reference. This is a programmer's on-line reference system supplied with the Symantec C++ compiler for the Macintosh. It also has a simple one-click mechanism which can be accessed by clicking a 'go back' button on its control panel (Figure 2).

Figure 2: Think Reference control panel

If only this method of access is used and *so long as no node is visited twice* it behaves exactly like the 'back' button in Windows Help.

In addition, if the 'go back' button is held down a menu appears showing the *previously* visited node (not including the current node). This functions in a similar fashion to the Windows history list: when the user navigates to a node *which has not been previously visited* the previous node is simply added to the end of the current history list. However, if a previously visited node is revisited or if the user selects a node from the 'go back' menu, the behaviour is different – the previous instance of the current node is removed from the history list. That is, if you visited nodes in the order *a*, *b*, *c* then again *b* and finally *d*, the history list would simply read *acb* rather than *abcb*.

In the case of Think Reference the two mechanisms, 'go back' menu and 'go back' button, share a common history list rather than having two. However, the 'go back' button is *not* simply a shorthand for selecting the last element in the list. Whereas simply clicking the 'go back' button always reduces the length of the history list (until it is empty), selecting the last element of the menu leaves it the same length. Although the top element is removed (to become the new current node) it is replaced with the previous current node, effectively toggling the current node and the previous node.

This behaviour is clear if we look at the history model of Think Reference:

$$S^{thk} = S \times S*$$

Note that in this case the second component of the state is $S*$, a possibly empty sequence of states. This is to reflect the fact that the Think Reference 'back' menu does not include the current state

$$proj^{thk}([s, hs]) = s$$
$$doit^{thk}([s, hs], c) \quad = \quad update(s, doit(s, c), hs) \quad c \in C$$
$$doit^{thk}([s, <>], back) \quad = \quad [s, <>]$$

$$doit^{thk}([s, hs\hat{\ }s_n], back) \quad = \quad [s_n \, hs \,]$$
$$doit^{thk}([s, hs], choose(n)) \quad = \quad update(s, hs[n], hs) \qquad (1 \leq n \leq len(hs))$$

Again we assume that the menu selection *choose(n)* can only select actual elements of the history list.

The effect on the history list has been defined using a subsidiary function *update*. This emphasises the fact that the effect on the history is identical whether a new state is visited due to navigation or the use of the 'go back' menu. It also emphasises that using 'go back' as a button, *back*, is different from selecting the top of the 'go back' menu, *choose(len(hs))*.

$$update: S \times S \times S* \rightarrow S^{thk}$$
$$update(old, new, hs) = [new, hs']$$
$$where \quad hs' \quad = \quad hs[1 \ldots m-1]\hat{\ }hs[m+1 \ldots len(hs)]\hat{\ }old$$
$$\qquad \qquad \qquad if \exists m \textbf{ such that } h[m] = new$$
$$\qquad \quad = \quad prune^{thk}(hs\hat{\ }old) \qquad otherwise$$

We can see now that in the model *back* is the only forgetful command; both navigation, $c \in C$, and 'go back' menu choice, *choose(n)*, simply add to or re-order the history list, the 'go back' button truncates it. (In fact, there is some forgetfulness in the others too as the history menu loses some of the oldest nodes if it gets too long. This behaviour is modelled by the *prune^{thk}* function.)

To see the effect the combined history has on *back* consider the following scenario. Imagine you have followed links in the order *a*, *b*, *c* then *b* as previously. The node *b* is current and you press 'go back'. The current node becomes *c*. You press 'go back' again and rather than *b* (as you would get with Windows Help) you get to *a*.

The history list is more 'economical' than Windows Help in that it doesn't repeat the same node name. This is especially noticeable if you move rapidly back and forth from a table of contents which would otherwise consume limited menu slots. The apparently good step of making the two mechanisms share a common history list means, however, that simple 'go back' has some occasional strange behaviour.

3.3 Netscape – a Stack with Pointer

We now come to Netscape Navigator and WWW browsing. Netscape has a 'go' menu which behaves somewhat similarly to the Windows Help history list in that it is a trace of previously visited nodes. Duplicates are allowed and may even arise from labelled links within a single Web page which are regarded as separate entities. The current node is always in this list, but is not necessarily the last element in the list and Netscape puts a tick against the current node. The state history recorded in this menu is also used for the 'back' and 'forward' buttons which move the tick backwards and forwards through the list.

Thus the state consists of a non-empty sequence of nodes and a pointer:

$$S^{net} = Nat \times S^{+}$$

$$proj^{net}([p, hs]) = hs[p]$$

The operation of the 'back' and 'forward' buttons and menu selection within the 'go' menu all simply manipulate the pointer, leaving the history list itself unchanged:

$doit^{net}([1, hs], back)$	$=$	$[1, hs]$	
$doit^{net}([p, hs], back)$	$=$	$[p - 1, hs]$	$p > 1$
$doit^{net}([p, hs], fwd)$	$=$	$[p, hs]$	$p = len(hs)$
$doit^{net}([p, hs], fwd)$	$=$	$[p + 1, hs]$	$p < len(hs)$
$doit^{net}([p, hs], choose(n)$	$=$	$[n, hs]$	$(1 \leq n \leq len(hs))$

The most complicated case is normal navigation (!), which prunes those states after the current state in the history list.

$$doit^{net}([p, hs], c) = \quad [p + 1, hs[1 \ldots p]^\frown doit(hs[p], c) \quad c \in C$$

So, Netscape manages to unify a simple 'back' button with menu-based history. In fact, regarding 'back' and 'forward' for navigation as parallel to 'undo' and 'redo' for update, the Netscape history is identical to undo in Microsoft Word 6.0. However, the price it pays is that, like Word 6.0, it is forgetful. One of the advantages of having a history mechanism is that it allows you to recover from mistakes. You click on a link, decide the page you have got to is not what you want to see and so press the 'back' button.

We have referred to the similar effect of undo as reducing the *risk* of interaction (Dix et al. 96). However, the fact that navigation may cause some of the history to be forgotten means that every navigation action itself becomes risky. Imagine you have spent some time navigating various Web pages and find a really useful site. With foresight you should of course leave a bookmark at once, but you are too busy seeking information ... You want to refer back to a previous page you have seen during your search so you use the 'go' menu (or the 'back' button) to go back a few steps to the page. By using 'back' and 'forward' or menu selection you flick back and forth comparing the information on the two pages. Then you notice an intriguing link on the *older* page and without thinking you click it. Instantly you have lost track of all the pages since that point – risk!

3.4 Hypercard – a First Use Ordered Set and a Navigable Trace

Finally we will look at HyperCard, a Macintosh program which is a cross between a hypertext authoring tool and interface prototyping tool. As it is programmable its default behaviour can be modified in various ways, but for the purpose of this chapter we will look at its default behaviour when used as a simple hypertext browser.

Like the other systems it has a 'back' button and a more extensive history in the form of a 'recent cards' window. All the other systems refer to nodes or pages by name. In contrast, the HyperCard 'recent cards' window has a miniature view of each card visited (Figure 3).

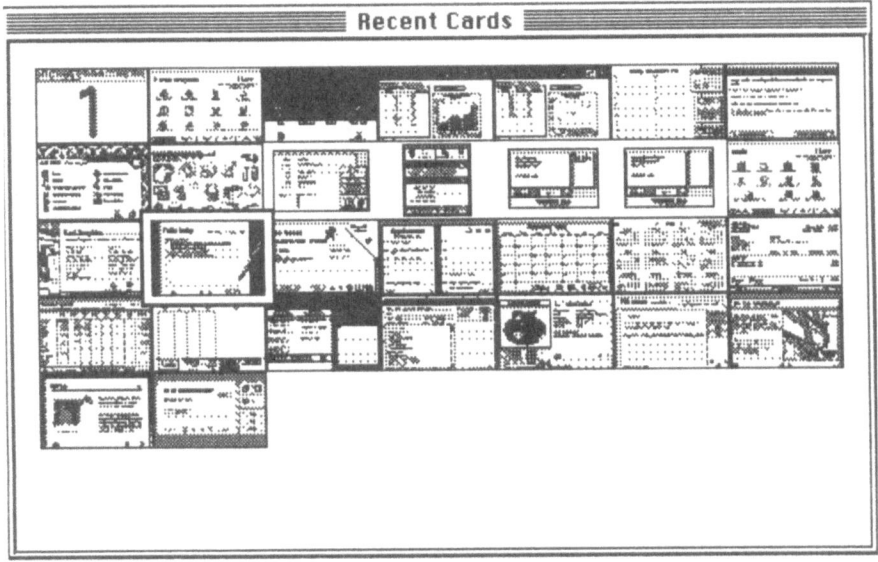

Figure 3: HyperCard 'recent cards' window

As was the case for Windows Help, these two mechanisms 'back' and 'recent' behave virtually independently. Although the 'back' button at first appears to behave similarly to the stack-based mechanisms of the other systems, it is actually significantly more complex. Hence we'll deal with the 'recent cards' window first.

3.4.1 HyperCard 'recent cards' – a first use ordered set

Rather like the Think Reference 'go back' menu, the HyperCard 'recent cards' window has no repeats. However, it achieves this by simply not adding a new node to the window if it is already there. Like Netscape it keeps track of which is the current node, in this case by adding a box around the relevant card image (second card on the third row in Figure 3).

The state of the system can thus be represented in a similar fashion as pointer and non-empty sequence:

$$S^{HCrt} = Nat \times S^+$$
$$proj^{HCrt}([rp, rw]) = rw[rp]$$

The update function for selection from the window is trivial (exactly like Netscape):

$$doit^{HCrt}([rp, rw], choose(n)) \qquad = \qquad [n, rw]$$

The update when a navigation command is used is slightly more complex. If the card is already in the recent window it is not added, otherwise it is added to the end. However, adding a card to the recent window may mean that there are too many cards to fit in the window in which case the first row of cards is scrolled off the top and disappears for ever.

$$doit^{HCrt}([rp, rw],c) = \quad addRecent(doit(rw[rp], c), rw) \quad c \in C$$
$$addRecent(s, hs) \quad = \quad [n, hs] \qquad \exists n \text{ such that } hs[n] = s$$
$$= \quad [len(hs'), hs'] \quad \text{otherwise}$$
$$\text{where } hs' = prune^{HCrt}(hs\,\hat{}\,s)$$

The function $prune^{HCrt}$ represents the scrolling off of excess cards. Note that the current card is always in the 'recent cards' window (either it is already there when there is no pruning, or it is at the end). However, the previous card can easily be pruned. Imagine you visit card a, then visit lots of other cards so that the 'recent cards' window becomes full, with a on the top line. You then visit a again. As a is already on it, the window does not change. Then you go to another card b which you haven't visited before. This new card b is added to the end of the 'recent cards' window and the top line including a is scrolled away!

3.4.2 HyperCard 'back' – a navigable trace

Happily you can get to the previous card using the 'back' option in the HyperCard 'Go' menu (there is no corresponding 'forward'). However, this is probably the only simple thing about it. In fact its specification is simpler to understand than its behaviour so we'll start with that. Like the Netscape history it can be thought of as a trace of past states with a pointer:

$$S^{HCbk} = Nat \times S^+$$
$$proj^{HCbk}([bp, bs]) = bs[bp]$$

Ordinary navigation commands add the new state to the end of the history and set the pointer to that location:

$$doit^{HCbk}([bp, bs], c) \quad = \quad addBack(doit(bs[bp], c), bs) \qquad c \in C$$
$$addBack(s, hs) \qquad = \quad [len(hs), hs] \qquad\qquad\quad last(hs) = s$$
$$= \quad [len(hs) + 1, hs\,\hat{}\,s] \qquad \text{otherwise}$$

The 'back' command moves the pointer backwards, but it also adds the new current state to the end of the history:

$$doit^{HCbk}([bp, bs], back) = doBack(bp, bs)$$
$$doBack(0, hs) \qquad = \quad [0, hs]$$
$$doBack(p, hs) \qquad = \quad [p-1, hs\,\hat{}\,hs[p-1]] \qquad p > 0$$

The effect of this is to store a backwards history at the end whilst using 'back'. Suppose you visit the cards a, b, c and d and then use *back* three times. The card being shown will be a. Now you navigate to e. If you then use back again repeatedly, you would see the nodes in the order e, a, b, c, d, c, b, a. This is because the stored history was *abcdcbae*. That is, HyperCard did not just record the end point of your going back, but every step along the way. As the history used by 'back' is not visible this behaviour can be very confusing. Note also that 'back' steps further and further back until any other command is used at which point the pointer jumps again to the end of the list. At this point further use of 'back' will undo the last command, but then start acting a bit like a forward command, reversing the effect of previous undos!

In some ways the behaviour is quite reasonable, it records every state you are in – a true history. However, the sheer number of intermediate states with no visible list or menu to orientate oneself makes this very confusing. In fact, this behaviour is identical to that of Emacs undo, which appears to be equally confusing. Indeed, when experimenting with Emacs the authors were only able to make sense of its behaviour when they found explicit documentation on its undo mechanism.

Some experimental systems have largely similar history systems, but their history of visited nodes is explicitly displayed as a branching tree (Cockburn & Jones 96; Ayers & Stasko 95). An alternative would be simply not to record the 'backwards' states while undoing and to use simple video-recorder-like buttons to wind back and forward through recent history. However, given the variety of history mechanisms on offer, each presumably selected as the best candidate by its respective designer, it would be foolish to declare which is best without strong empirical evidence.

3.4.3 Combining 'recent cards' and 'back'

The overall state of HyperCard requires both history and pointers:

$$S^{HC} = Nat \times S^+ \times Nat \times S^+$$

As with Windows Help these two must share a common current state:

$$proj^{HC}([rp, rw, bp, bs]) = rw[rp] = bs[bp]$$

The recent window is updated by cards visited by 'back' in the same way as ordinary navigation. Also use of recent is treated as normal navigation by the

$$
\begin{aligned}
&doit^{HC}([rp, rw, bp, bs], c) = [rp', rw', bp', bs'] \qquad c \in C \\
&\text{where } [rp', rw'] \quad = \quad addRecent(s', rp, rw) \\
&\qquad\quad [bp', bs'] \quad = \quad addBack(s', bp, bs) \\
&\qquad\quad\quad s' \qquad\quad = \quad doit(rw[rp], c) = doit(bs[bp], c) \\
&doit^{HC}([rp, rw , bp, bs], choose(n)) = [n, r, bp', bs'] \\
&\text{where} \quad [bp', bs'] \quad = \quad addBack(rw[n], bp, bs) \\
&doit^{HC}([rp, rw, bp, bs], back) = [rp', rw', bp', bs'] \\
&\text{where} \quad [bp', bs'] \quad = \quad doBack(bp, bs) \\
&\qquad\quad [rp', rw'] \quad = \quad addRecent(bs'[bp'], rp, rw)
\end{aligned}
$$

One thing to note here is the effect of ineffective commands, that is commands which do not change the current card. In the case of the recent window the new (unchanged) card is the same as one of the existing cards in the window, hence there is no change in the recent window. Similarly, the *addBack* function does not add superfluous copies to the end of its history list. However, as a side effect of such an ineffective command the 'back' pointer gets reset to point again to the end of the list. For example, suppose you have used 'back' to move back several cards and then open the 'recent cards' window. You change your mind and simply reselect the current card thinking this will have no effect (which is correct normally), however, this has reset the back pointer and so 'back' starts to behave like 'forward'!

4. Comparing the Methods

4.1 Back or Not Back?

All the browsers implement a single button press (in some cases also available as a function key or menu option) labelled 'back' or 'go back'. At first sight these appear to behave equivalently. You navigate to a new node, you press 'back' and you are back to the previous node. In fact, so long as you only use 'back' once and haven't just revisited a node, they do indeed all behave the same. This is OK, but what about when you use it repeatedly?

Actually, the equivalence is a little stronger than that. Even when you use 'back' several times (with no intervening commands) *all* the systems behave equivalently *so long as* (i) it has been a long time since you used 'back' last (more commands than the number of 'back's you are about to use) *and* (ii) there haven't been any recent revisited states. The first condition (i) is there because of HyperCard's rather odd backwards/forwards history of states.

If condition (i) is dropped then Windows Help, Think Reference and Netscape all behave identically. When no other history command is used and no state is visited more than once these mechanisms all behave identically – a simple stack. However, when the same state is revisited more differences emerge. Windows Help can have multiple instances of the same node one after another in the stack, Think Reference removes the older instance of a node from the history list when it is revisited and Netscape's stack does not have successive multiple instances unless they are to different labels in the same page!

So even for something as simple as going back there are four different interpretations for four different hypertext browsers.

4.2 Visible History

Each browser also had its own visible method of selecting from past states. This took the form of a textual menu or window in most cases and the graphical 'recent cards' window for HyperCard. The differences here are more marked between the browsers: a stack with pointer for Netscape, complete trace for Windows Help and different 'without repetition' versions of the history for Think Reference and HyperCard 'recent cards'.

In both the latter cases only a limited number of past states are recorded, so not having repetitions is important to avoid losing too many past states when the history is pruned. Think Reference retains the most recent entries, so that the list is always guaranteed to hold the most recent $n-1$ states where n is the length of the menu (it always keeps the very first state hence $n-1$). In contrast HyperCard prefers to keep the images of cards in the same position; that is, it exhibits a kind of display inertia or visual consistency. This same principle is continued when a whole row of images is scrolled off the top of the card. This 'wastes' screen space compared with simply deleting the first entry, but means that a card always occupies the same position in the row.

4.3 One Mechanism or Two

In two of the systems we considered, button press 'back' and visible history shared a common mechanism. In the other two they had separate mechanisms.

Those with separate mechanisms had *no* means of making the history use by 'back' visible. As we have seen, there are many different interpretations of the ideal behaviour of 'back', and the lack of visibility makes it difficult for users to learn the behaviour and to predict the effect of their actions. However, if the 'back' mechanism were made visible then the user would surely expect to be able to navigate using this as well as the alternative visible history, which leads naturally to a questioning of the need for two such mechanisms!

Netscape and the Think Reference get round this difficulty by having a single unified mechanism. However, in so doing they sacrifice one aspect or other. Netscape has a bias towards the idea of the stack and so does not keep track of all visited nodes, only those on the 'path' from the initial home page. On the other hand Think Reference keeps a complete track of all visited states (up to a maximum), but in so doing compromises the simple behaviour of 'back'.

4.4 Completeness of Histories

The history mechanisms have different levels of completeness; that is, in how much information they retain.

- backtracking – Some 'back' commands remove the nodes through which they backtrack, either straightaway (Windows Help) or at the end of the 'history' subdialogue (Netscape – when ordinary navigation is used).
- resource limitations – Some systems have a maximum number of elements that can be in the history list: in HyperCard the number of card icons that can fit in the window, in Think Reference ten items, in Windows Help about forty, in Netscape apparently unlimited, but not all available from the menu (only fifteen under Windows 3.1 and thirty two on the Macintosh).
- repeated elements – Partly because of resource limitations some systems try to suppress repeated items. Many try to stop subsequent elements in the history being identical, others look at the whole history: Think Reference removing the

previous occurrence and HyperCard recent not adding duplicates. This whole area is complicated by the different rules used to determine what is the 'same'!

- granularity – As well as issues of what constitutes the 'same' state, systems also differ on what constitutes a change of state. For example, in Windows Help we saw that selecting the current node in the history window did not get recorded as a new (repeated) state, but selecting the same node from further down the list did. In HyperCard, typing or scrolling text on a card does not constitute an action as far as 'back' is concerned (in the sense that the pointer keeps moving backwards), but any navigation action even when it does not change the current card (even using recent and reselecting the current card) breaks the chain of backward movement. There is also a similar sort of granularity effect in Netscape whereby a sequence of 'back' and 'forward' commands acts as a unit broken by the first 'normal' navigation command.

An obvious question to ask about a history mechanism is: if you have once visited a node in a hypertext can you guarantee to be able to find it again using the history mechanism? Because of either resource limitations or explicit 'forgetting' the answer is NO for all the mechanisms we have seen, with the exception of the HyperCard 'back' command (although even that may have some large internal limit we have not discovered). However, in the case of HyperCard although getting to any past state is *possible* it is hardly trivial!

It is strange that completeness is the property that you would expect of a visual 'history' window, but in fact the only example that is really complete (albeit complex) is a stepwise 'back'!

4.5 Searching

Whereas visual history suggests a record of past states, the obvious application of stepwise 'back' is to facilitate depth first searching. In fact, so long as the depth is not so great that resource limitations take effect and so long as there are no repeated nodes in the search tree, this is *possible* with all the 'back' mechanisms. In the cases of Netscape, Windows Help and Think Reference the obvious algorithm can be used:

1. Start with some initial node to search from
2. if you have investigated all interesting links from the current node:
   2.1. if this is the initial node: FINISH
   2.2. if not, use the 'back' command
   2.3. continue from the beginning of step 2
3. choose an interesting link from the current node
4. navigate to the chosen node
5. continue from step 2.

HyperCard is obviously rather different (!); however, strangely enough the same algorithm works. It works, but in a very different fashion. You will visit all the nodes *eventually*, but with an large number of repeats. Indeed, using the above algorithm, to search a tree with n nodes will typically (for a balanced tree) take around $O(n^2)$ commands, compared with about $2n$ for the other mechanisms.

5. History and Undo

We have already noted that history and undo have many similarities.

5.1 State and Conservativeness

In Section 2 we discussed the multi-level nature of browser state and the *conservative extension* relationship between the levels. In each example we have seen how a given browser navigation behaviour (without history), modelled by the simple *doit* function, is extended by history mechanisms to give the overall system behaviour *doit^a*. Further, in each case we have seen how the overall system state space S^a is composed of several instances of the simple state (S) and sequences thereof.

Note that in each case the underlying browser navigation is different, but in fact any of the history mechanisms could have been applied to any underlying browser. For example, we could imagine using HyperCard's 'back' button and recent window in a Web browser. The abstraction of the formalism can help us see the similarities and differences.

In addition, at this level descriptions of history and undo are virtually identical. In the case of undo, we also use a two-level model of the underlying system and the overall system augmented with undo (and possibly redo) commands.

The state conservativeness condition is also clearly necessary for any sensible undo system. In addition, for undo systems we have also used a similar condition for the command history. In addition to the *proj* function relating the augmented state S^a to the underlying state S, we also have a function *eff*, the effective history, linking the augmented command history H^a and the underlying command history H. This should agree with *proj* in the sense that Figure 4 should commute. We call this relationship *encapsulation*.

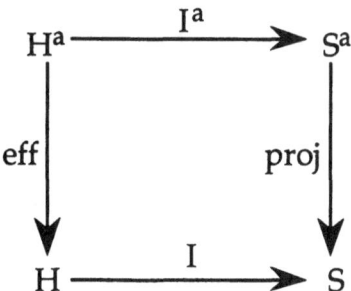

Figure 4: Encapsulation

The effective history is thus a sequence of commands on the underlying system which would have given rise to the same underlying state as obtained by the full system (with history/undo). On its own it merely captures the fact that the augmented system cannot reach underlying states that are not reachable by the original commands. This is surely a property that should also hold for any history mechanism (and indeed does for all those considered here).

In addition, we can state a conservativeness condition on the command history:

$eff(<>) = <>$

$\forall\, c \in C, h \in H^a : eff(h\hat{\ }c) = eff(h)\hat{\ }c$

It can also be expressed as a commuting diagram (Figure 5).[3]} This basically says that ordinary commands simply add to the effective history – again, a property of any sensible history mechanism.

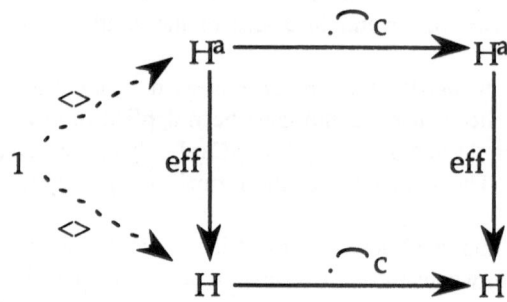

Figure 5: Conservativeness of effective history

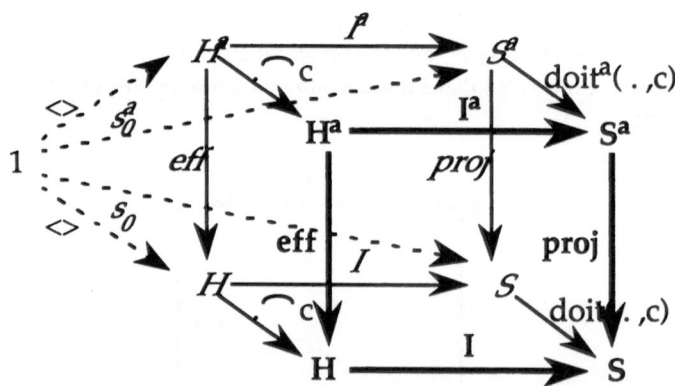

Figure 6: The cube

---

[3]Note that '1' in the diagram is the set with only one element. It is used as a categorical 'trick' to capture an initial state within a commuting diagram.

In fact, if an augmented system both is an encapsulation and has a conservative effective history, then it follows that the state is also conservative. These properties together we call a *conservative encapsulation* and this is the fundamental property that must hold true of any augmented system whether for undo or history. The three commuting diagrams can be put together into a single elegant (albeit somewhat full) commuting diagram we call *'the cube'* (Figure 6).

Note that *conservative encapsulation* only tells us what happens when the additional facilities are *not* being used – it is about the preservation of the original system within the augmented system. The individual behaviour of the additional commands (for history or undo) need to be considered separately.

5.2 Names, States, Icons and Actions

The cube links together the user actions and state in a system. These to some extent form complementary views of the behaviour of a system. One of the biggest differences between history and undo systems is not their behaviour, but the presentation of history to the user.

In the case of a single 'back' or 'undo' action they both behave similarly; the focus is on the currently displayed state. The reflexive aspect is weak – although users have to think sufficiently *about* the interaction to decide to use back or undo, they do not see any representation of the history itself.

When we look at visible history lists and undo menus the situation is quite different. We noted that the history mechanism in Netscape is identical, in terms of its formal description, to that of Microsoft Word 6. In each case there is a list of states with a pointer to the current location within the list. The back (or undo) command moves the pointer back through the list, the forward (redo) command moves the pointer forward. In the Netscape menu one is shown exactly this, a list of *names* of the pages one has visited with a tick on the current one (where the pointer is). In contrast, Word 6 has two menus, the undo menu listing the *commands* that got you to the current state and the redo list showing the *commands* that lead on from the current state.

This reveals a fundamentally different orientation in the way we look at and talk about the system. Hypertext systems talk about *where* you have been; undo systems about *how* you got there.

In a word processor there is no convenient name for the states. They are simply the same document with more or fewer changes and edits. Even if the system has some name for them, it is unlikely that it will be meaningful for the user (with the possible exception of timestamps). The natural thing for the user is to think "I'd like the document as it was before I deleted the big paragraph".

In contrast many hypertexts have convenient titles for the pages or nodes; for example, Web pages have a <title> tag to give the page a name, and also a URL. This forms an easy reference point for the user (so long as the titles are sufficiently informative!). It is also more natural for the user to think "I'd like to get back to that page about history mechanisms".

HyperCard faces problems here as it has some database-like aspects and it is quite common to have many anonymous cards. A menu with items such as 'card id

7392' would not be generally accepted as user friendly! This is why it opts for the alternative iconic approach, relying on our ability to match visual features. This would obviously not be very useful on the heavily text-based pages of a Help system, and would be totally useless for an undo facility of a word-processor, but might work for the WWW. In fact, on the Macintosh, many graphics programs set the icon of files to be a thumbnail of the file contents, on the principle that this will be more readily recognisable than the file name. Unfortunately, HyperCard still has problems with database-style applications as all the records are simply copies of the same card with different details: not very easy to distinguish from a thumbnail!

This state vs. command emphasis is also evident if you try to construct the effective history functions for the different history mechanisms. It is possible to construct them, but difficult to do so without explicit reference to the state. This is because the rules for adding to the history are more semantic based than those for undo, which simply add commands of a particular class whether or not they were effective in the particular context. Because undo is more command oriented it tends to have simpler (syntactic) algebraic properties. For example, with a pure backtrack undo and any normal command c in *any* context we have:

$$c \quad undo \quad \sim \quad null$$

An equivalent history property for most of the systems we have looked at would need a side condition to say "except in contexts where the command c is passive".

6. Summary

Given the number of different solutions to the design of a history mechanism, it is not surprising that users find it difficult to comprehend! By modelling these different solutions within a generic formal framework, we have been able to examine the history mechanisms in isolation from other features and also to see the similarities and differences between systems. In addition it has allowed us to see clearly the connection between history and undo mechanisms. However, it has also highlighted important differences between history in hypertext systems and undo in manipulative systems in terms of the emphasis on state vs. commands, and in the notion of state itself.

We have seen that even the simplest history mechanism, the 'back' button, has had a different interpretation in each system studied. This suggests that users need a clear indication of what 'back' is doing. However, we also saw that attempts to unify the expected behaviour of a 'back' button with a visual history posed problems as well.

Although many people report confusion with Netscape's history mechanism it is clearly one of the more straightforward offerings! Its main fault in terms of its underlying model is that it is not a full history. However, the source of confusion does not lie in this but in the comprehension of what constitutes going to a new page. This confusion is not helped by the fact that there is nothing in the 'go' menu to indicate visually which entries are to labelled positions within pages, and which to the page as a whole.

In this chapter we have not sought to give an overall judgement on the best history mechanism but to specify clearly those mechanisms that are in use and some of the trade-offs between different desirable properties. The range of different mechanisms shows that there is no current consensus on what constitutes the best form of hypertext history. Indeed, the authors have also analysed Internet Explorer and found that it embodies three different history mechanisms. An additional complication that we have not considered in the paper is the behaviour of 'back' in Web browsers that support frames. When users are allowed to go 'back' on a frame-by-frame basis it is possible to reach states (in terms of combinations of frame contents) that are *unreachable* via ordinary browsing. Such a state of affairs would *not* constitute an encapsulation.

Developers of history mechanisms are faced with a hard task. Modern interfaces emphasise action – doing things, whereas history is reflexive – talking about doing. Formal specification can help comparisons between different models for this, and the reflexive nature is clearly captured in the models we have presented. However, the challenge for the developer is finding appropriate ways to portray and interact with this reflexive information at the user interface.

Acknowledgements

Many thanks to Fiona for proofreading this chapter and converting it, including all the mathematics, into Word.

Chapter 2:
How to Model a Web (Without Getting Tangled in Nets)

1. Introduction

This is not a chapter about assessing the "design" of the World Wide Web, or human issues in the interface of a browser. And it certainly does not put forward a case that the design of Web browsers could somehow be improved through the use of formal specification techniques. Rather, the aim of this chapter is simply to demonstrate how, in the early stages of designing an interactive system, it is possible to use an existing state-based specification language to capture some of the issues concerned with what the system might do. In this context, a WWW browser serves as a convenient example.

In one sense, a case study like this represents a modest contribution to the literature on formal methods and interactive systems. However, much of the work that has been reported has focused on the use of:

(a) process-oriented notations (algebras (Hoarre 85) and nets (Jensen 90)),
(b) novel notations (MAL and interactors (Duke & Harrison 95)), or
(c) hybrid methods combining several formalisms (for example, action systems and CSP (Bramwell et al. 95)).

Interactive systems encapsulate a number of issues that are driving the development of formal methods in general, and so exploration of a range of techniques in this area should contribute to improvements in the power and tractability of these methods in the wider context of rigorous software development. However, with the possible exception of the process and net oriented work such as (Paternò & Faconti 92) and (Palanque et al. 96), it is unlikely that these techniques will enter industrial use, at least in the short term. Issues of utility aside, there are two factors that mitigate against the use of novel methods: training and support. Although the number of companies with access to formal methods experience is growing, by far the best known languages are Z (Spivey 92), VDM (Jones 90), and CSP (Hoare 85), CCS (Milner 89) and LOTOS (ISO 88, Paternò & Faconti 92). These are also the languages for which tool support - in the form of well engineered, robust, industrial quality tools - is available. Given that the difficulty of assessing the benefit of formal methods in general software development, let alone for user interface issues, it seems reasonable to conclude that, if formal methods are to be employed for user interface design issues, then they will need to be methods that are known, well documented, and supported by effective and robust tools. This, and the highly operational nature of interaction, is one factor that may motivate user interface designers to focus on process oriented notations and Petri Nets as modelling formalisms. The premise of this chapter is that these notations may be employed most effectively in the detailed design stage of software development. At the specification level a state oriented approach can provide a useful description of *what* the system should do, without requiring the designer to become enmeshed in the kind of detail best captured by other formalisms (hence the title).

The main contribution of this chapter is to demonstrate how a "standard" state-based specification language could be used to specify aspects of an interactive system such as a Web browser. The Z notation was chosen as:

- it was known to the author,
- it is supported by industrial quality tool for checking and reasoning with the language,
- it is well documented with introductory texts, and
- it is going through a process of standardisation.

By looking at how well Z can be used in this context, this chapter also helps to identify specification issues that more novel work is seeking to address. A secondary aim of the chapter is to explore an approach to structuring the specification based on levels of concern. Much of the work on interactive systems promotes organising specifications or design models around user tasks (Palanque et al. 96), or into object-like structures (Duke & Harrison 93). Again, these may be all be useful in particular contexts, but it is argued that at an early stage of a system's development it may be more helpful to use a generic framework, one that does not confuse concerns over how the software is organised with issues about the tasks that the software might support. The approach taken here is derived from work on modelling interaction using StateCharts (Degani & Kirlik 95). In this approach a system is decomposed into five components:

- **Environment**: the context which the system is affecting or is affected by;
- **Plant**: the components that the operator controls, and views via the display;
- **Display**: what is shown to the operator;
- **Controls**: what the operator can do to change the plant;
- **Tasks**: the tasks that the operator is carrying out.

This is the framework used to organise the Z specification. Section 2 of the chapter describes the environment and plant of a Web browser, and demonstrates how parts of a specification can be developed through a process of embellishing a simple model to introduce further details. This process also helps to identify why and where some of the key engineering compromises within the Web might have been introduced. Section 3 considers the interface of a browser, in terms of the display it provides and the controls that it offers over the plant. A first "integrated" model of the system is developed in Section 4, but does not address the behaviour in case of error, which is the focus in Section 5. Interaction with the system (representing the "task" level in the hierarchy above) is described in Section 6. Throughout these sections certain key points are highlighted in the discussion, and are revisited in a general discussion on issues in using model based techniques for interactive systems which concludes the chapter. A glossary of notation is provided.

2.   The Plant and Environment

2.1   A Simple Model of Hypertext

The idea of the World Wide Web may have began with a simple conceptual model of a distributed hypertext system. Basically, a hypertext consists of a collection of nodes, which in the WWW are called *pages*, and *links* that connect pages (nodes) on a user-defined basis, for example chaining together semantically related parts of documents, or ideas, or whatever is being recorded on a page. At this stage, we can think of a page just as a "thing" that is of interest within the model being developed. All we want to represent is that things called pages exist, and for this we can use Z's "given type" mechanism to introduce a type (set) representing all possible Web pages.

>   [*page*]

The environment in which any Web browser operates consists of the collection of all Web pages, and the links that exist between them. These two structures are represented within a schema, drawn as a named box divided into two parts. In the top half, the names *pages* and *links* are introduced to represent the set of pages that exists on the Web at some point in time, and the links that exist between pages. Below the dividing line we write predicates - statements or assertions - that are true about the Web over all time.

$$
\begin{array}{|l}
\hline
Env_{page} \\
\hline
pages : \mathbb{P}\,page \\
links : page \leftrightarrow page \\
\hline
\mathrm{dom}\,links \subseteq pages \\
\hline
\end{array}
$$

The subscript "*page*" has been appended to the schema name, as this is the first of a number of environment models that will be developed; this particular level is concerned with pages. Successive steps will add further detail to the evolving model. The predicate of the schema asserts that the domain of the "links" relationship is contained within the set of pages that exist. In other words, a link can only exist on the Web if the page that is linked *from* exists. The operator "dom" is part of the standard Z toolkit (Spivey 92); Z gains its expressive power by using simple mathematical concepts such as sets and relations. In order to support concise specification, the standard "toolkit" includes a number of functions and operators on these structures, some of which are written using symbols that are not part of the standard set theory taught in schools and colleges. This can make specifications in Z appear daunting, and where possible in this chapter simpler, if perhaps more verbose, representations have been employed. In the author's experience, the difficulty of learning Z is not so much in acquiring the lexemes or syntax (no more difficult than, say, learning a new programming language), but in knowing how to make effective use of the structures provided by the language to build simple yet tractable models of systems.

If we were using Z to document conceptual ideas about the design of a new interactive system, then the mathematical text given above would only be one part of the document. Specifications, like any other formal document (program text, design document, etc.) should be supported by explanatory text, diagrams or other representations that help the reader to understand the context, rationale, and implications of what is being specified. There is nothing new in this.

The "conceptual model" of the Web requires that all links be from a page that exists, but do not require the following, that there are no dangling links, that is, a link from a page to one that does not exist in the system.

$$NoDanglingLinks \mathrel{\widehat=} [Env_{page} \mid ran\ links \subseteq pages]$$

The absence of this property from the Web has an impact on the design of interfaces for accessing the Web. Unlike self-contained hypertext systems that may have inspired the Web designers, the creation, deletion and modification of Web pages are completely independent from the infrastructure and mechanisms used to access those pages. The environment model describes the context in which the system(s) controlled by the user will operate. This controlled system is called the *plant*, and in the case of the Web, corresponds to the internal states of the browsers that are used for viewing pages. A given type is defined to represent browsers,

$$[browser]$$

and the state of the plant then extends that of the environment model with the set of browsers that exist at some point in time, and the page *(loctn)* which a browser is being used to view. The *system* consists of the environment plus the plant.

$$
\begin{array}{l}
\underline{\ Plant_{page}\ \underline{\hspace{3cm}}} \\
browsers : \mathbb{P}\ browser \\
loctn : browser \nrightarrow page \\
\hline
dom\ loctn \subseteq browsers
\end{array}
\qquad
\begin{array}{l}
\underline{\ System_{page}\ \underline{\hspace{3cm}}} \\
Env_{page} \\
Plant_{page} \\
\hline
\end{array}
$$

The predicate on the structure of the plant indicates that if a browser is viewing a location, then it must exist within the system. However a similar constraint linking viewed pages to those that exist in the environment,

$$PageExists \mathrel{\widehat=} [System_{page} \mid ran\ loctn \subseteq pages]$$

is problematic. In principle, there is nothing to say that a page might not be removed from the Web at some point after it has been loaded into a browser, and although operations on the environment have not been included in this model (for space reasons), the fact that the environment can change is reflected by our inability to assert invariants such as *PageExists*.

> **Key point:** Even a very simple abstract model of a system can help generate reflection and insight into the structure and intended behaviour of that system.

So far, the specification has concerned models of the state of the system. It is now possible to begin describing the operations that are supported on the plant. These will leave the environment unchanged, and this observation can be used to simplify their description. We define a page system operation *PageOp* as one that changes the state of $Plant_{page}$ (expressed as $\Delta Plant_{page}$), but leaves the state of the environment unchanged (written ΞEnv_{page}). By convention, schemas named $\Delta State$ and $\Xi State$ are used in Z to describe operations over a state space modelled using a schema called *State*. This convention is described in books such as (Hayes 92), (Potter et al. 91), and (Spivey 92).

$$PageOp \triangleq \Delta Plant_{page} \wedge \Xi Env_{page}$$

At this level of detail, four operations are relevant to the model. Two of these allow the creation and deletion of a browser:

```
┌─ Createpage ──────────────        ┌─ Deletepage ──────────────
│ PageOp                            │ PageOp
│ n! : browser                      │ n? : browser
├──────────────────────            ├──────────────────────
│ n! ∉ browsers                     │ n? ∈ browsers
│ n! ∈ browsers'                    │ browsers' = {n?} ◁ browsers
│ {n!} ◁ loctn' = {n!} ◁ loctn
```

In $Create_{page}$, we indicate that the identity of the new browser, represented by the output $n!$, is one that does not occur in the initial set of browsers, but does exist after the operation. We further require that the location of all browsers, other than $n!$, is unchanged, but say nothing about the location of the new browser. Use of "under-determined" operations in state based models is a powerful means of controlling the level of detail. Subsequent parts of a specification can strengthen the requirements on this operation, perhaps by indicating that a browser initially is associated with a specific location.

The remaining two operations are to load the page from a given address, and to follow a link. As following a link amounts to loading a page identified by the link, we can model the load operation first, and then use it to define the "follow" operation. $Load_{page}$ has two inputs - a browser, and a page - and provided that the page and browser exist, sets the location of that browser to the given page.

$\_Load_{page}$ _____
$PageOp$
$b?$: $browser$
$p?$: $page$

$p? \in pages \ \wedge \ b? \in browsers$
$loctn' = loctn \oplus \{b? \mapsto p?\}$
$browsers' = browsers$

The operation of following a link can be described here by composing the load operation with an initial condition in which a page $p!$, linked to the page currently being viewed by the browser, is selected and output.

$\_SelectLink$ _____
$System_{page}$
$b?$: $browser$
$p!$: $page$

$(loctn(b?), p!) \in links$

At this level of abstraction, $Follow_{page}$ is defined as an operation in which $SelectLink$ is used to find a new page, and then $Load_{page}$ is used to load this selected page. This can then be described in Z using the schema piping operator, which identifies output variables in the first schema with similarly named input variables of the second schema; here the identified variables are $p!$ and $p?$. There are similarities here to the notion of interface refinement (Hayes & Sanders 95).

$$Follow_{page} \ \widehat{=} \ SelectLink \gg Load_{page}$$

We will not be reusing this definition of $Follow_{page}$ in the remainder of the specification. In subsequent steps it will be necessary to extend the $Load_{page}$ operation to larger and more detailed states, and this means that the definition of a compound operation like $Follow_{page}$ must be put off until all of its components are available. Also, the operations defined thus far are partial. That is, they have non-trivial preconditions. In the case of $Load_{page}$ for example, the page $p?$ must exist, and the specification does not say what will happen if the user attempts to load a non-existent page. These concerns will be addressed separately, in Section 5.

| Key point: | Specification is an interactive process, and in a real development the final specification document will have been arrived after several intermediate attempts, and will probably be structured to best convey the overall structure of the system, and to set out what it does and the rationale and requirements for the system. |

2.2 The Effect of Distribution

The ideal view of the Web presented in the previous section makes no reference to the technology needed to support such a system. Technological considerations do impact and shape the design of an artefact, and so it is useful to consider how they can be accommodated in the evolving specification. Two issues are of concern here. The first is that browsers do not access Web pages directly.They rely on the existing communication infrastructure, and in particular the existence of a Web server that has access to the required page. Secondly, once access has been obtained, the transfer of a page from one site to another is *not* an atomic operation, and in particular is not atomic from the viewpoint of the user (otherwise there would be no point in providing users with the ability to interrupt loading). The approach taken to introducing the concept of server into the model mirrors that used in Section 2.1 to define pages and browsers.

A given type,

[*server*]

is defined to represent servers, and then a schema is used which identifies the servers that exist at any point in time, and their relationship to other concepts in the model. A word should be said though about what is meant by "server", and on the problem of validating a specification in general. In the real Web, requests for page accesses are sent to communication ports on computers that typically provide a gateway between an oganisation's local network, and the wider system. A process on the gateway accepts requests via this port, and may then generate a "child" process to deal with it. This level of detail could be included in the specification. However, it is not detail that users need to be aware of, or even detail that is reflected in the interface. And if a formal model was being used to derive the design of a Web browser from an initial conceptual model, it is not something that we would introduce at this point.

In this model, a server is taken to represent the resources that a gateway provides in order for a client to access the Web page. The specification abstracts away from the nature and organisation of those resources, and instead the model simply represents which resources are able to provide access (manage) to a given Web page. Servers form part of the environment in which a Web browser exists, and are introduced into the state model by extending the initial environment specification. This is done in two steps, with the "new" parts of the specification introduced first into a self-contained schema, and then combined with the existing environment model. The rationale for this will be explained shortly.

$$
\begin{array}{l}
\_Env_{server} \underline{\qquad\qquad\qquad\qquad} \\
servers : \mathbb{P}\ server \\
manages : server \leftrightarrow page \\
\underline{\qquad\qquad\qquad\qquad} \\
\mathrm{dom}\ manages = servers
\end{array}
$$

Again, the decentralised nature of the Web means that the invariant is weaker than one might wish; in particular, we cannot impose the following requirement,

Accessible $\widehat{=}$ [*Env*$_{server}$ | ran *manages* $\subseteq$ *pages*]

that any page managed by a server actually exists; nor in fact can we insist that every page must be managed by some server, since the computers on which servers run may fail. Such failure could again be modelled explicitly, as an operation within a comprehensive description of the environment, but serves no purpose in this chapter.

Key point: Careful choice of abstractions, for example using a single concept of server in place of hosts and processes, allows a specification to be written concisely.

Our next concern is to describe the functional state of servers that is relevant to understanding user interaction with the Web. At any point in time, some servers are free, while others will be busy managing requests for pages received from browsers. The $Plant_{server}$ specification defines sets to represent the free and busy servers, and for each busy server, the identity of the client (browser) and task (page) that is being handled.

$$
\begin{array}{l}
\underline{\quad Plant_{server} \rule{5cm}{0.4pt}} \\
\textit{free} : \mathbb{P}\ \textit{server} \\
\textit{busy} : \mathbb{P}\ \textit{server} \\
\textit{client} : \textit{server} \nrightarrow \textit{browser} \\
\textit{task} : \textit{server} \nrightarrow \textit{page} \\
\rule{5cm}{0.4pt} \\
\mathrm{dom}\ \textit{client} = \textit{busy} \\
\mathrm{dom}\ \textit{task} = \textit{busy}
\end{array}
$$

$$
\begin{array}{l}
\underline{\quad System_{server} \rule{5cm}{0.4pt}} \\
\textit{Env}_{server} \\
\textit{Plant}_{server} \\
\rule{5cm}{0.4pt} \\
\langle \textit{free}, \textit{busy} \rangle\ \text{partitions}\ \textit{servers} \\
\forall\, s : \textit{busy} \bullet (s, \textit{task}(s)) \in \textit{manages}
\end{array}
$$

The predicates in the plant schema indicate that additional data is known about busy servers. For the combination of plant and environment, we further require that every server is either free or busy, but not both, and that if a busy server is handling a request for a page, that page must be one that the server manages.

The operation of loading a page must now be represented in terms of a lower level protocol which consists of three elements: requesting a connection, transferring data, and closing a connection. In other words, the previously atomic model of loading a page must be realised as a transaction involving a number of more primitive operations. As before, operations on the plant will not affect the environment, and so we can define an generic operation on $Plant_1$ by:

$$ ServerOp \mathrel{\widehat{=}} \Delta Plant_{server} \wedge \Xi Env_{server} $$

However, we can go further, as operations on this level of the model will concern a single server. We can produce a general operation *frame* that identifies the server that will be manipulated, and requires that all other servers within the Web are unchanged.

$$
\begin{array}{l}
\underline{\quad \Phi OneServerOp \rule{5cm}{0.4pt}} \\
ServerOp \\
s? : server \\
\rule{5cm}{0.4pt} \\
\{s?\} \mathbin{\lhd} client = \{s?\} \mathbin{\lhd} client' \\
\{s?\} \mathbin{\lhd} task = \{s?\} \mathbin{\lhd} task'
\end{array}
$$

The first two operations represent a browser requesting a page from a server, and disconnecting from a server. For the *Connect* operation, the input variable *s?* of the framing schema is renamed to be an output, to reflect better the operational view that the server that responds to a request is a result of a *Connect* request.

$$
\begin{array}{|l}
\hline
\_Connect_{server} \underline{\hspace{3cm}} \\
\Phi OneServerOp~[s!/s?] \\
Load_{page} \\
\hline
s! \in servers \\
p? \in pages \\
s! \in free \\
(s!, p?) \in manages \\
busy' = busy \cup \{s!\} \\
client'(s!) = b? \\
task'(s!) = p? \\
\hline
\end{array}
\qquad
\begin{array}{|l}
\hline
\_Disconnect_{server} \underline{\hspace{3cm}} \\
\Phi OneServerOp \\
\Xi System_{page} \\
\hline
s? \in servers \\
s? \in busy \\
free' = free \cup \{s?\} \\
\hline
\end{array}
$$

In addition, we also need to promote the operations for creating and deleting a browser, defined in the previous section. These do not alter the new parts of the plant or environment, and so can be defined using schema operations.

$$Create_{server} \mathrel{\hat{=}} Create_{page} \wedge \Xi System_{server}$$

$$Delete_{server} \mathrel{\hat{=}} Delete_{page} \wedge \Xi System_{server}$$

We are not however going to promote the $Load_{page}$ and $Follow_{page}$ operations, as these do not exist (at least as explicit operations) at this level. Loading now consists of connection, followed by disconnection, while following a link could again be defined by composing load operation with the selection of a link.

Key point:	The ability to compose a specification from a collection of smaller components is critical to managing the complexity of complex system models. Finding how the model of the system can best be organised within the structures and compositional mechanisms provided by a given language is one of the challenges of specification, and is often best resolved by a process of trial and iteration.

2.3 Integrating Pages and Servers with HTML

So far, Web pages have been viewed as atomic entities; the model has only been concerned with their existence. Once however we begin to view the process of loading a page as a non-atomic operation, it becomes useful to extend the model to capture some of the internal structure of pages. Web pages are (usually) written using HyperText Markup Language (HTML), and we can view a page as a sequence of HTML statements. To do this, we "push back" the curtain of abstraction, and now introduce these commands as given types. Some HTML commands will be of particular interest; these are the commands that identify and define links from one page to another, and are represented by a subset of the HTML type called *link*. A document is modelled as a sequence of HTML commands.

[*HTML*]

link : ℙ *HTML*

doc == seq *HTML*

Further details concerning the structure of links can be obtained by defining functions that map elements from the set *link* to another HTML command that defines the "anchor" that should appear on the page, and the name of the page that is the target of the link. Here we assume that no anchor can itself be a link.

> *anchor* : *link* → *html*
> *target* : *link* → *page*
> ──────────────────────────
> ran *anchor* ∩ *link* = ∅

Introduction of HTML allows the evolving structure of the environment to be extended by a mapping that associates each page with a HTML document. Rather than do this as a self contained step in the style of pages and servers, we use this step to integrate the page and server models into completed environment and plant descriptions. The WWW environment consists of the page and server environments, plus mapping that takes each page to the HTML document that it represents. For a link to exist from page *src* to page *dst*, there must be a HTML command in the content of page *src* that has *dst* as its target.

> ┌─ *Env_www* ──────────────────────────
> │ *Env_page*
> │ *Env_server*
> │ *content* : *page* ⇸ *doc*
> ├──────────────────────────────────────
> │ dom *content* = *pages*
> │ ∀ *src* : *pages*; *dst* : *page* •
> │   (*src*, *dst*) ∈ *links* ⇔
> │   ∃ *h* : *link* • *h* ∈ ran *content*(*p*) ∧ *target*(*h*) = *dst*

With the introduction of the concept of a document content, the model of the plant can be extended to account for the document that is actually loaded at any point in time. To support modelling of the non-atomic load operation, it is also useful to represent the part of a document to be processed by each busy server. Recall that there is nothing to prevent a page from being deleted or updated after it has been loaded, and this could also occur while the page is being transmitted. There is thus no requirement that in any given state the document being processed by a server is related to the content of that page in that state.

$$
\begin{array}{|l}
\_Plant_{www} \rule{4cm}{0.4pt} \\
\hline
Plant_{page} \\
Plant_{server} \\
process : server \nrightarrow doc \\
loaded : browser \nrightarrow doc \\
\hline
\mathrm{dom}\,process = busy \\
\mathrm{dom}\,loaded = browsers \\
\end{array}
\qquad
\begin{array}{|l}
\_System_{www} \rule{3cm}{0.4pt} \\
\hline
Env_{www} \\
Plant_{www} \\
\end{array}
$$

An operation on this extended plant leaves the environment unchanged.

$$WWWOp \,\widehat{=}\, \Delta Plant_{www} \wedge \Xi Env_{www}$$

Transfer of HTML from a server $s?$ to its client is modelled by the following operation, in which a non-empty prefix of the document being transmitted is appended to the documented loaded at the client browser. All other browsers and servers are unaffected by this transfer. In the operation, an output $k!$ represents the "packet" of HTML transferred from server to browser.

$$
\begin{array}{|l}
\_transfer \rule{7cm}{0.4pt} \\
WWWOp \\
s? : server \\
b? : browser \\
k! : doc \\
\hline
s? \in busy \wedge b? \in \mathrm{dom}\,loctn \\
k! \neq \langle\rangle \\
\exists\, remainder : doc \mid b? = client(s?)\ \bullet \\
\quad process(s?) = k! \,^\frown remainder \\
\quad process'(s?) = remainder \\
\quad loaded'(b?) = loaded(b?) \,^\frown k! \\
\{s?\} \vartriangleleft process = \{s?\} \vartriangleleft process' \\
\{s?\} \vartriangleleft loaded = \{s?\} \vartriangleleft loaded' \\
\end{array}
$$

The $Connect_{server}$ and $Disconnect_{server}$ operations are promoted to the WWW level. Connecting to a server has the effect that the server must be ready to process the content of the requested page, while the browser is made ready to receive the document. Disconnection means that the server is no longer processing a document, but does not affect the document at the browser end.

$$
\begin{array}{|l}
\_Connect_{www} \rule{3.5cm}{0.4pt} \\
WWWOp \\
Connect_{server} \\
\hline
content' = content \\
process' = process \oplus \{s? \mapsto content(p?)\} \\
loaded' = loaded \oplus \{b? \mapsto \langle\rangle\} \\
\end{array}
\qquad
\begin{array}{|l}
\_Disconnect_2 \rule{3cm}{0.4pt} \\
WWWOp \\
Disconnect_{server} \\
\hline
content' = content \\
process' = \{s?\} \vartriangleleft process \\
loaded' = loaded \\
\end{array}
$$

Creating and deleting a browser also affects the HTML level of the system. Nothing is said about the content of a new browser, but the content of all other browsers is unchanged. A browser that has been deleted has no associated content.

┌─ *Create$_{www}$* ──────────────
| *WWWOp*
| *Create$_{server}$*
├─────────────────────────────
| *content′ = content*
| *process′ = process*
| *{b?} ◁ loaded′ = {b?} ◁ loaded*
└─────────────────────────────

┌─ *Delete$_{www}$* ──────────────
| *WWWOp*
| *Create$_{server}$*
├─────────────────────────────
| *content′ = content*
| *process′ = process*
| *loaded′ = {b?} ◁ loaded*
└─────────────────────────────

┌─────────────┐
│ **Key point:** │   Incremental specification allows detail to be added just when required,
└─────────────┘   allowing attention to be focused on one issue at a time.

3. The Interface: Display and Controls

The interface of a Web browser provides the user with two facilities: a display showing the overall state of the plant, and controls that allow the user to effect and affect operations on the plant. Both of these components involve rather more detail about individual browsers than has been considered thus far, and it is useful to adopt a different strategy for modelling this. Rather than extend the "global" model of the system with a number of attributes, each expressed as a mapping from browsers to some type, we will first generate a series of "local" models concerned with the display and controls of individual browsers, and then as the final step of this section lift these to the level of the whole system.

3.1 Display

Abstraction allows the contents of a Web browser display to be modelled concisely, in terms of four components: the location being viewed, the contents of the page (if any) that is loaded or being loaded, a message line, and a progress indicator for showing the status of transfers. A number of messages can be displayed for the user. These are introduced formally as values of a free type; the comments hint at the role of each message.

message ::= okay   — no specific information to present
      | *pageNotFound*   — a particular page could not be found
      | *serverNotFound*   — a particular server could not be found
      | *unableToConnect*   — a connection could not be made to a server

We have previously introduced the type "page" to represent the names (locations) of Web pages. Before a connection is made, a browser has no such location, and to represent the difference between displaying some page location and no location we introduce the following type.

OptPage ::= nolocation | at⟨⟨page⟩⟩

The state model of the display is defined below. Its components represent the location being viewed (if any), the message on the display, the document on the display, and a progress indicator for conveying information during transfer. This is actually modelled by two variables; *progSpan* is a number representing the total size of the data to be downloaded, while *progDone* represents the amount of data actually transferred at some point in time.

```
┌─ Display ──────────────────────────────────────
│  location : OptPage
│  message : message
│  document : doc
│  progSpan, progDone : ℕ
└────────────────────────────────────────────────
```

No operations are defined explicitly on the display; changes to the display state will be considered once the whole interface is defined. Note that the specification says nothing about *how* this information is shown to the user, or whether for example there are multiple renderings of certain components.

| Key point: | No special notation is *necessary* for producing a model of a display. If it were important for example to capture spatial properties of display components, then these should be introduced as observables, the same way as for any other structure in the system. Some initial ideas towards a general framework for modelling the structure of displays and other presentations can be found in (Duke & Harrison 94). |

3.2 Control

The control part of the specification describes the means by which the user can invoke operations. There is an overlap between the display and controls, in that for a direct manipulation interface, many of the controls are an intrinsic part of the display. The pragmatic approach taken here is to limit the display to structures that carry information to the user, and the control component to structures that are used to invoke operations, even if this also involves an element of display.

Commands come in two categories, those that are a fixed part of the interface (though may be disabled), and those that exist because of the content of the page currently being viewed. That is, we can think of the links within the HTML document as commands (to load a specific page) that are invoked whenever the user selects that link.

$$command ::= load \mid stop \mid exit \mid goto《link》$$

Three "fixed" commands, load, stop and exit are modelled, and are always available as "buttons" on the display. At any time, at most one button from those available may be selected. In a direct manipulation interface where buttons are rendered as distinct regions on a display that can be selected using a pointing device, this variable would represent the button, if any, that is pointed to by the mouse.

```
┌─ Controls ─────────────────┐      ┌─ Push_controls ──────────────┐
│ buttons : ℙ command        │      │ ΞControls                    │
│ enabled : ℙ command        │      │ c! : command                 │
│ selected : ℙ command       │      ├──────────────────────────────┤
├────────────────────────────┤      │ selected = {c!}              │
│ {load, stop, exit} ⊆ buttons│      │ c! ∈ enabled                 │
│ #selected ≤ 1              │      └──────────────────────────────┘
│ selected ⊆ buttons         │
└────────────────────────────┘
```

The effect of "pushing" a button can be modelled as an operation that has a command as its output. A command is only defined when an enabled button is pushed, and so this operation is partial. The interface of a browser consists of the display, plus the controls, and the "goto" controls are exactly those links contained in the document on the display.

```
┌─ Interface ────────────────┐      ┌─ Push_interface ─────────────┐
│ Display                    │      │ ΞDisplay                     │
│ Controls                   │      │ Push_controls                │
├────────────────────────────┤      └──────────────────────────────┘
│ ∀ l : link • goto(l) ∈ buttons│
│       ⇔ l ∈ ran document   │
└────────────────────────────┘
```

The operations of creating and deleting a browser, making and breaking a connection, and transferring a packet of data each involve the interface of a browser. Their effect on the interface is captured in the next section, in which the local model of the control and displays are integrated with the global model of the Web and the browsers that utilise it.

4. The System

Each browser in the system has its own interface. To represent this, we define a new model, *System*, that extends the final "Web system" model containing the global environment and plant states with a mapping, *local*, that takes each browser to its *Interface* state. The invariant part of this schema explains how part of the state is reflected in the display, corresponding to the idea of a "rendering relation" described in (Duke & Harrison 93).

```
┌─ System ───────────────────────────┐
│ System_www                         │
│ local : browser ⇸ Interface        │
├────────────────────────────────────┤
│ dom local = browsers               │
│ ∀ b : browser | b ∈ dom loctn •    │
│     local(b).location = loctn(b)   │
│     local(b).document ⊆ loaded(b)  │
└────────────────────────────────────┘
```

The location shown on the display of each browser is the location being visited by that browser, while the document on the display is a subset of whatever has been loaded into the browser. By requiring only that the displayed document be a subset of, rather than strictly equal to, we give a specifier (and implementor) freedom to extend the model to incorporate issues such as browsing through a large document.

It is usual in Z for operations involving a "local" state, such as *Interface* in this example, to be "promoted" to an operation that acts on the complete state (here *System*). This is done by identifying one or more instances of the local state within the global model, whose values in the states before and after the global operation are to be related according to the local operation. There is a standard way of doing this in Z. It involves creating a framing schema that contains both the variables of the global state ($System_{www}$) and local state (*Interface*), and a predicate that links a binding formed from the local state variables to a specific instance of that state. If S is the name of a schema, which may be part of some larger context as a result of inclusion, then a binding for S can be defined in that context by the expression θS. This binding is simply a mapping from each variables in S to its value, much like an instance of a record in a programming language such as Ada.

In the case of this specification, the situation is reversed. We have a collection of operations on the global state, for example $Connect_{www}$ and $Delete_{www}$, that we want to extend to the local states. Nevertheless, the same mechanism can be employed, and we begin by setting up the framing schema, $\Phi System$. In this schema, the instance of the *Interface* state involved in the operation is identified by the variable $b?$, and a binding for this state before and after a local operation is generated using the expressions $\theta Interface$ and $\theta Interface'$.

$\Phi System$

$\Delta System_{www}$
$\Delta Interface$
$b? : browser$

$local(b?) = \theta Interface$
$local'(b?) = \theta Interface'$
$\{b?\} \lhd local = \{b?\} \lhd local'$

To illustrate promotion and some of the issues that it generates, we consider first the operations of creating a browser and making a connection.

$Create_0$

$\Phi System$
$Create_{www}$

$message' = okay$
$location' = nolocation$
$enabled' = load, exit$
$progSpan' = 0$
$progDone' = 0$

$Connect_0$

$\Phi System$
$Connect_{www}$

$message' = okay$
$location' = p?$
$enabled' = stop$
$progSpan' = \#process'(s?)$
$progDone' = 0$

The two promoted operations, given below, combine the local operation (e.g. $Create_{www}$) and the model of global state change ($\Phi System$) with predicates that describe the specific effect of the promoted operation over the combined state. These schemas have a "0" subscript after their names because, for reasons we will discuss, these are not the final specification of the operations.

Although these schemas now model the effect of the operations over the full state, they are not in a final form, since the before and after states still include the state variables of the local states. We can obtain a cleaner model by indicating that these local variables are internal to the operations. Z provides several operators that effectively "hide" part of the state, and the one that is most suitable here is the existential quantifier for schemas. Given the following two schemas,

$$
\begin{array}{|l}
\hline S \\\hline
x : \mathbb{N} \\
y : \mathbb{N} \\\hline
x < y \\\hline
\end{array}
\qquad
\begin{array}{|l}
\hline T \\\hline
S \\
p : \mathbb{N} \times \mathbb{N} \\\hline
p = (x, y) \\\hline
\end{array}
$$

the schema $\exists S \bullet T$ is like T, but with all of the variables from S removed from the signature and instead existentially quantified within the predicate, as shown below.

$$
\begin{array}{|l}
\hline \exists S \bullet T \\\hline
p : \mathbb{N} \times \mathbb{N} \\\hline
\exists x : \mathbb{N}; \; y : \mathbb{N} \bullet x < y \; \wedge \; p = (x, y) \\\hline
\end{array}
$$

The same technique could now be applied to the *Create* and *Connect* operations, by hiding the schema that describes the local state change, in this case $\Delta System_{www}$.

$$Connect_1 \mathrel{\widehat{=}} \exists \, \Delta System_{www} \bullet Connect_0$$

$$Create_1 \mathrel{\widehat{=}} \exists \, \Delta System_{www} \bullet Create_0$$

However, as variables that become hidden through quantification cannot be accessed or referenced by extensions to the enclosing schema, hiding must be the last step of the specification process. And although our specification now describes the intended behaviour of operations over the Web state, it only describes *normative* behaviour, and it useful at this point to take a brief detour to the problem of error.

5. To Err is Human...

Consider the operation of opening a connection to a Web server. On examining the text of $Connect_{server}$ we can see that this operation is *partial*. It has a number of preconditions, such as:

- the server must exist;
- the server must be free;
- the requested page must be managed by that server.

The effect of an operation when invoked outside of its precondition is not defined, and one step that can usefully be carried out in the specification process is to document how the system should behave in the case that the precondition guarding the normative behaviour of the system is violated. Like many specification languages, Z allows error situations and recovery to be described. In the case of Z, error conditions are modelled using the same schema framework as is used for the description of normative operation behaviour. Other notations, for example VDM-SL (Jones 90) provide explicit error clauses in operations as "syntactic sugar". Here, we introduce a schema to model the definition of specific errors, and the response that should result, as well as a schema that describes what the response should be in normative cases.

The approch taken to handling errors on the Web is for the interface to display a suitable message and the system to be left in some well defined state. We can model errors by using the $\Phi System$ frame as a starting point, and then including any input and output variables needed to describe the situation. In the case of making a connection, two such situations are when a given server could not be found in the system, and when the server exists but is busy. In both cases, the message (on the display) is updated, but the rest of the state - including the remainder of the display, the controls, and the global Web context - is left unchanged.

$$
\begin{array}{l}
\hline
\text{\_ServerNotFound} \underline{\hspace{3cm}} \\
\Phi System \\
\Xi Controls \\
\Xi System_{www} \\
s! : server \\
\hline
s! \notin servers \\
message' = serverNotFound \\
location' = location \\
document' = document \\
\hline
\end{array}
\qquad
\begin{array}{l}
\hline
\text{\_UnableToConnect} \underline{\hspace{2.5cm}} \\
\Phi System \\
\Xi Controls \\
\Xi System_{www} \\
s! : server \\
\hline
s! \in servers \wedge s! \notin free \\
message' = unableToConnect \\
location' = location \\
document' = document \\
\hline
\end{array}
$$

If a server can be found, and is available, the next problem that can be encountered is that the requested page does not exist within the collection managed by that server.

$$
\begin{array}{l}
\hline
\text{\_PageNotFound} \underline{\hspace{2.5cm}} \\
\Phi System \\
\Xi Controls \\
\Xi System_{www} \\
s! : server \\
p? : page \\
\hline
s! \in free \\
(s!, p?) \notin manages \\
message' = pageNotFound \\
location' = location \\
document' = document \\
\hline
\end{array}
\qquad
\begin{array}{l}
\hline
\text{\_PageError} \underline{\hspace{3cm}} \\
\Phi System \\
\Xi Controls \\
\Xi System_{www} \\
p? : page \\
\hline
p? \notin pages \\
message' = pageError \\
location' = location \\
document' = document \\
\hline
\end{array}
$$

Of course logically speaking, this error is not contingent upon the server being free, but the precondition reflects the fact that a browser can only determine that a page does not exist by *first* being able to contact a given server. So, although it is technically an error for a browser to request a page that does not exist anywhere in the Web, this error (given by *PageError*) cannot be detected unless a browser can contact every server in the system.

A robust version of the *Create* operation can now be defined by taking the *dis*junction of the normative description (*Create*$_0$) with the schemas that describe the error situations that an implementation should address (and for this reason we do not include *PageError*).

$$Create_1 \mathrel{\widehat{=}} Create_0 \lor ServerNotFound \lor UnableToConnect \lor PageNotFound$$

Potential errors arising from other operations such as *Transfer* and *Disconnect* could similarly be modelled, but space precludes us presenting the complete description of these operations.

> **Key point:** The separating of error situations from the description of normative processing is an important separation of concerns, and can help to make a specification comprehensible by allowing the reader to focus initially on the intended behaviour of the system. Specification languages typically support this separation either through compositional mechanisms like the schema operators of Z, or through specific clauses in descriptions.

6. Finishing Touches

There is one more key issue to be raised in this chapter, and as a prelude to discussing it we give the promoted forms of the remaining operations considered so far. *Transfer* and *Disconnect* are given below. They are mostly straightforward, except that as a page is loaded, any links on the page become available as commands, and the only fixed command available is to stop.

$$
\begin{array}{|l}
\hline
\_Transfer_0 _____ \\
\Phi System \\
Transfer_{www} \\
\hline
message' = message \\
location' = location \\
enabled' \setminus links = \{stop\} \\
progSpan' = progSpan \\
progDone' = \#loaded' \\
\hline
\end{array}
\qquad
\begin{array}{|l}
\hline
\_Disconnect_0 _____ \\
\Phi System \\
Disconnect_{www} \\
\hline
message' = okay \\
location' = location \\
enabled' \setminus links = load, exit \\
progSpan' = 0 \\
progDone' = 0 \\
\hline
\end{array}
$$

There are two remaining operations. The first is that of deleting a browser. As the interface of the browser does not exist after the operation, there are effectively no constraints on the final local state.

$$Delete_0 \mathrel{\widehat{=}} \Phi System \land Delete_{www}$$

The second operation is that of pushing a control, partially specified by *Push*$_{interface}$.

$$Push_0 \,\hat{=}\, \Phi System \land Push_{interface}$$

What has yet to be described is how the user actually invokes operations on the final system. To include this in the model, we make use of the $Push_0$ operation. A connection will be opened from a browser $b?$ if the push operation occurs when the *load* command is selected on that browser. The required specification is given below.

$$Connect_2 \,\hat{=}\, [Push_0 \mid c! = load] \,{}^{\circ}_{\circ}\, Connect_1 \setminus (c!)$$

Informally, the specification uses the sequential composition operator $\binom{0}{9}$ to describe a 2-step operation on the system. First, push occurs on some browser to select the *load* operation and achieve an intermediate state, and then the $Connect_1$ operation takes the system from the intermediate state to the final state.

The variable $b?$, identifying the browser that is involved, is an input to both parts of the operation and is thus common to the full operation. We have chosen to hide the command ($c!$) in the final operation, since for our purposes it is now purely internal to the description. It is important to note however that we have not specified how the name of the page for which the connection is being provided. At this level, it remains as an input to the compound operation. A more detailed description of the system might attempt for example to describe a data entry device, and to compose this as part of the full operation description. As it is, the specification of the *Connect* operation can be completed by carrying out the hiding step suggested in Section 4:

$$Connect \,\hat{=}\, \exists \, \Delta System_{www} \bullet Connect_2$$

Key point:	A model based language can provide the means needed to model dialogue, though the number of layers and amount of detail in the model becomes larger. A key question to ask about any specification is: at what point is the description starting to impinge on design issues? The aim of a formal specification is to set out the requirement about *what* a system is to do, leaving the designer and implementor free to find the most appropriate means of realising those requirements. For interactive systems, this borderline can be difficult to identify.

A similar approach can be taken to modelling the remaining operations.

$$Disconnect \,\hat{=}\, \exists \, \Delta System_{www} \bullet ([Push_0 \mid c! = stop] \,{}^{\circ}_{\circ}\, Disconnect_0 \setminus (c!))$$

$$Exit \,\hat{=}\, \exists \, \Delta System_{www} \bullet ([Push_0 \mid c! = exit] \,{}^{\circ}_{\circ}\, Delete_0 \setminus (c!))$$

Following a link can be modelled as an operation invoked by pushing a *"goto"* control, corresponding to a *link* command in the HTML text of a document. The one complexity here is that, if a transfer is in progress, the existing connection must be broken. To simplify presentation, the description is done in steps. The first step defines a schema *FollowReq* representing the invocation of a "follow link" command. The existence of an open connect is determined by whether there is a non-zero span in the progress space. This property could have been made more explicit by use of a mode variable. If a transfer is in progress, then *Disconnect* must take place before the *Connect* operation, and hiding is used to ensure that the server parameter to the first operation is not confused with that to the second. A final operation is then defined by hiding the intermediate state components.

$$FollowReq \mathrel{\hat{=}} [Push_0;\ p? : page \mid c! = goto(p?)] \setminus (c!)$$

$$Follow_0 \mathrel{\hat{=}} [FollowReq \mid progSpan = 0] \mathbin{\substack{o\\o}} Connect$$
$$\lor$$
$$[FollowReq \mid progSpan \neq 0] \mathbin{\substack{o\\o}} (Disconnect \setminus (s?)) \mathbin{\substack{o\\o}} Connect$$

$$Follow \mathrel{\hat{=}} \exists \Delta System_{www} \bullet Follow_0$$

The operation of creating a browser does not use the interface of a browser, but relies on the external environment in which the browser is located. That is, we are not modelling the "new window" operation provided by some browsers.

$$Create \mathrel{\hat{=}} \exists \Delta System_{www} \bullet Create_0$$

The definition of *Create* concludes the specification.

Key point:	The specification developed in this chapter describes (to the extent possible in the space available) *what* a Web browser should do, deliberately avoiding operational details of *how* the functionality should be achieved. That is for an implementor to decide, based on factors in the design context and on general software engineering principles and practices (see for example (Sommerville 92)).

7. Discussion and Conclusions

It is sometimes thought that interactive systems pose new or difficult challenges that require the development of novel specification techniques. The preceding sections have demonstrated one approach by which an existing and (comparatively) well-known specification language can be used to develop a state oriented model of a Web browser. Although the model is far from complete when compared with the functionality offered by current implementations, it does demonstrate that the approach is feasible. In this concluding section, some of the issues raised by the specification are considered.

The specification addresses only a limited number of operations, but it should be evident from the case study that the approach can readily accommodate features such as a history mechanism as a simple extension to the existing state. Organising the specification around the model of (Degani & Kirlik 95) helped to separate concerns about the global structure of the Web from issues such as the behaviour of the interface, at a cost of requiring multiple promotion steps and a large number of schemas. In practice, some of the small schemas introduced here for pedagogical reasons would be combined or extended into larger fragments, and the specification document would be supported by an index and the cross-referencing of definitions. The limitations of presenting a case study of this scale in a small amount of space and to a wide audience should not be overlooked in assessing the material presented here.

Arguably the main value of a state based approach like this is that it allows the specifier to capture the invariants that exist within the system, and to use the expressive power of first order logic to describe operations on this state at a high level of abstraction. Operations are defined over pre and post states, and one thing that a model like this leaves implicit is the "overall" behaviour of the main entities of interest. For example, one can argue that a browser must first be created, and then can engage in a history formed from *connect, transfer, follow* and *disconnect* events before being deleted. This lifecycle is implicit in the way that changes to the state enable and disable the precondition for these operations. However, having defined the semantics of these operations in Z, there is no reason that additional, possibly formal, representations of the system behaviour should not also be generated. State transition diagrams, StateCharts, and Petri Nets can all help to convey the dynamics of system components to the reader in a diagrammatic form, while a process algebra such as CSP could provide an alternative abstraction over the evolution of the system. There are some aspects of interaction between Web browsers and users that simply were not considered in the model.

These include issues ranging from the layout of the display, through time delays - for example in making connections and transferring data, to the knowledge and resources needed by users when interacting. There are well known techniques for including temporal issues in state-oriented specification, for example (Abadi & Lamport 92) and (Fidge 94). If timing issues were considered to be the central concern of the model, a different formalism might be suggested. Although this can add considerable clutter and detail to a specification, it is important to appreciate that there are no easy solutions to modelling the behaviour of complex systems. While it may be tempting to try and produce a "neat" specification by using a language with complex operators for modelling temporal or other specialised aspects of behaviour, this only hides the complexity within the semantics of the language. The price of complexity is then paid when attempting to reason, formally or informally, about specifications in such languages.

In this chapter there has been no attempt to reason formally about properties of the specification, or to argue about usability issues in the design of Web browsers. In a sense, the specification presented here was not produced with either purpose in mind. On the one hand, it contains a certain amount of operational detail (for example, how commands are invoked), to the extent that a non-trivial amount of time with a theorem proving assistant might be required to discharge all but the simplest obligations.

The counterpart is that the specification (deliberately) says little about how a user might interact with a browser. What is does do is to indicate how the information manipulated by a browser is related to and constrained by the data and resources available on the Web.

Appendix: Glossary of Notation

The notation used in this chapter is called Z. This appendix gives a brief account of some of the notation. There is a range of introductory and advanced texts and case studies such as (Hayes 92), (Potter et al 91) and (Spivey 92) that can be consulted for further information.

$\mathbb{N}$ Natural numbers: $\{0, 1, 2, \ldots\}$
$\mathbb{Z}$ Integers: $\{\ldots, -1, 0, 1, \ldots\}$

Logic

Let P and Q be predicates, and x a variable.

$P \wedge Q$ Both P AND Q hold
$P \vee Q$ Either P OR Q (or both) hold
$P \Rightarrow Q$ P IMPLIES Q: If P holds, so must Q
$P \Leftrightarrow Q$ P IF AND ONLY IF Q
$\forall x : S \bullet P$ For all values of x in S, P holds
$\exists x : S \bullet P$ There exists a value of x in S for which P holds

Sets

Let S and T be sets, P a predicate, E an expression, and t_i terms. Let x_i be variables, and let D be a declaration, e.g. $x_1{:}S, x_2{:}T$

$\varnothing$ Empty set
$\{t_1, \ldots, t_n\}$.   Set enumeration: the set of t_1 through to t_n
$\mathbb{P}\,S$ Power set: the set of all subsets of S
$E \in S$ Membership: the value E is a member of the set S
$\{D \mid P \bullet E\}$ Comprehension: the set of all values of E, such that P holds given D
$\{D \mid P\}$ The set of values for D such that P holds
$S \cap T$ Set intersection: the set of values in both S and T
$S \cup T$ Set union: the set of values in either S or T
$S \subseteq T$ Containment: S is a subset of T
$S \times T$ Cartesian product: the set of pairs (x, y) s.t. $x \in S$ and $y \in T$

Functions

Functions and relations are viewed as sets of pairs; a function is then a relation where every element in the domain of the relation is paired with exactly one element in the range of the relation. Let S and T be sets, and F and G be relations or functions:

$\{\}$	Empty function
$S \to T$	The set of functions from S to T
$\{x \mapsto y\}$	The function that maps x to y
$S \leftrightarrow T$	The set of relations between S and T
dom F	Domain: the set $\{x \mid \exists y \bullet (x,y) \in F\}$
ran F	Range: the set $\{y \mid \exists x \bullet (x,y) \in F\}$
$F \oplus G$	Overriding: $(F \oplus G)(x) = G(x)$, if $x \in$ dom G, (x) otherwise

Sequences

A sequence is a function whose domain is either empty (the null sequence) or is a set of contiguous natural numbers, e.g. $\{1,2,...,n\}$ for some $n \in \mathbb{N}$. This means that operators like "ran" can also be applied to sequences. Let X be a set, and S and T sequences:

$\langle\rangle$	Empty (null) sequence
seq X	The set of sequences whose range is a subset of X
$\langle x, y, \ldots, z \rangle$	Sequence enumeration: the sequence containing $x, y, \ldots, z$ in that order
$S \frown T$	Concatenation: $\langle s_1, \ldots, s_n \rangle \frown \langle t_1, \ldots t_m \rangle = \langle s_1, \ldots, s_n, t_1, \ldots t_m \rangle$

Chapter 3:
Software Architecture Modelling:
Bridging Two Worlds Using Ergonomics and Software Properties

1. Introduction

The process of designing and constructing user interfaces is critical for building systems that satisfy the customer's needs, both current and future. This process includes the original design of the interface, the implementation of the system, and the modifications to the operational system. These modifications are endemic in interactive systems. Since the user interface can account for approximately 50 per cent of total life cycle costs (Myers 89), the software engineer has a vested interest in constructing a user interface that both satisfies the customer and is constructed using the best available tools and techniques. In addition, the increasing complexity and size of software systems require sound engineering principles and frameworks to formally structure the design process into multiple but consistent perspectives.

Tools that support the development of user interfaces vary widely in complexity and power ranging from user interface toolkits to user interface generators. Although powerful, user interface generators cannot produce everything. Therefore, the user interface must be tuned to the specific case at hand. In turn, customisation requires programming, and good programming practice necessitates an architectural framework such as PAC-Amodeus. PAC-Amodeus is an hybrid multi-agent software architecture model that represents the organisation of the components of an interactive software. As any architectural framework, it consists of the description of an organisation of computational elements and their interactions (Shaw & Garlan 95).

Software tools for the construction of user interfaces will not eliminate architectural issues as long as the construction of user interfaces requires programming. Developers and maintainers of interactive systems need to rely on models:

- for identifying software components,
- for organising their interconnections,

- for reasoning about components and interconnections,
- for verifying ergonomic and software properties,
- for modifying and maintaining them in a productive way.

Software architecture may also be used to communicate a design solution to another development team such as the programmers. In this case, the description must be unambiguous. A model may reduce misinterpretation risks.

In this chapter, we present an agent-based architectural model PAC-Amodeus, for the purpose of assessing software designs. In order to clarify the role of a software architecture model, we first identify its use in a design and development process. In Section 3 we present our PAC-Amodeus model: the principles of the PAC-Amodeus model and guidelines for applying it. In Section 4, we show how PAC-Amodeus can be used in practice: we present a PAC-Amodeus software design solution of a WWW browser and its assessment in terms of ergonomic and software properties.

2. Software Architecture and Life-Cycle: Point of Contact of Two Worlds

As shown in Figure 1, software engineering structures design and implementation into 6 phases: requirements definition, specification, implementation, testing, installation and maintenance (ANSI 83). A more complete description of each phase can be found in (Bass & Coutaz 91, chapter 1). Basically,

1. Requirements definition is a formal or semi-formal statement of the problem to be solved. It specifies the properties and services that the system must satisfy for a specific environment under a set of particular constraints. Ideally requirements are defined in cooperation with the end-users.
2. Specification consists of high level design (i.e., external specifications) and internal design (i.e., internal specifications). High level design is concerned with the external behaviour of the computer system. This behaviour is described in terms of functionalities as perceived by the user of the future system. For each function, valid inputs and outputs are specified as well as error conditions. Internal design determines a software organisation that satisfies the specification resulting from high level design. Internal design covers the definition of data structures, algorithms, modules, programming interfaces, etc.
3. Implementation is the expression of the internal specification in terms of a set of programming languages and tools.
4. Testing involves debugging individual modules as well as performing their integration.
5. Installation consists of placing the software system into production.
6. Maintenance deals essentially with changes along with their side-effects in the software life cycle.

Software architecture is concerned with the Specification phase of the software engineering life cycle. As mentioned in the introduction, its role is to help the designer to identify the software components that implement the user interface portion of an interactive system. Thus, within the specification phase, a software architecture model deals with internal design.

Software architecture modelling starts with the design solutions selected in the design space and leads to the implementation of these solutions. Like the other modelling approaches, it enriches the design space with specific properties. At this level, salient properties might include software properties such as efficiency and reusability as well as ergonomic properties such as multithread dialogue and observability. As shown in Figure 2, software architecture modelling is a design activity at the turning point between two worlds: the user interface design field and the programming field. Because of its interlinking location, software architecture must take into account properties of the two worlds: ergonomic properties of the designed user interface and properties of the future implemented software. Consequently, it requires that the software designer establishes sound trade-offs between conflicting properties from multiple requirements: user-centered design requirements, software engineering requirements and ease of implementation (implementation cost and time constraints).

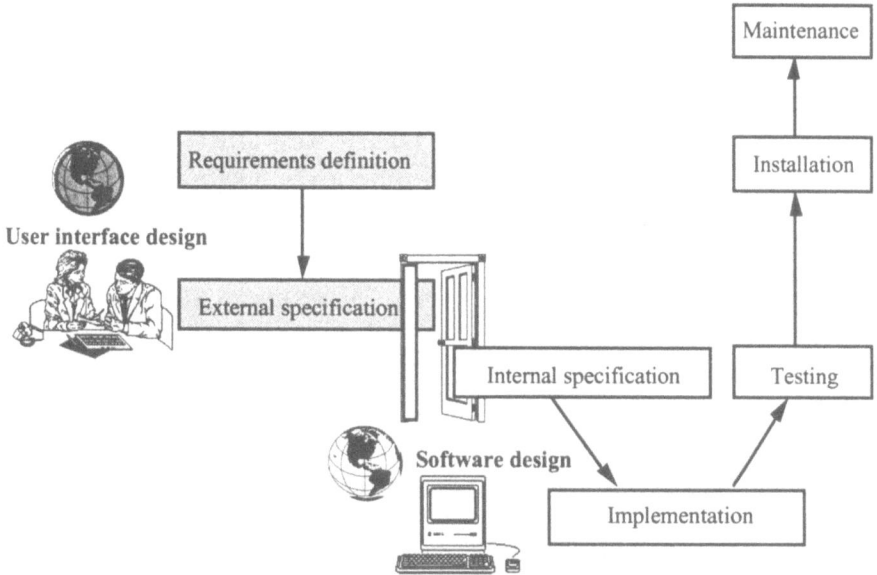

Figure 1: Software engineering life-cycle.

In (Gram & Cockton 96), we denote the properties derived from the user and the system perspectives as external and internal properties respectively:

- External properties: "The usability of an interactive system is linked to the quality of the dialogue, and quality shall here be expressed through the number of measurable properties of the dialogue." (Gram & Cockton 96, Chapter 2) "...user-centered properties of interactive systems ... promote a high quality from the perspective of the users." (Gram & Cockton 96, Chapter 2).

- Internal properties: "Internal properties are quality attributes of a system as seen from the developer's perspective, just as the external properties are system quality attributes as seen from the user's point of view." "Internal properties require a complete life cycle view. It is important to recognise that these properties are relevant from the conception of a system, beyond construction to modification and maintenance until its final demise." (Gram & Cockton 96, Chapter 3).

A given software architecture model does not verify all of the external and internal properties. Each software architecture model is suitable for a sub-set of properties. By "suitable" we mean that the model helps to either verify or assess a property. In the following section, we present PAC-Amodeus using the notion of internal and external properties as an analytic tool.

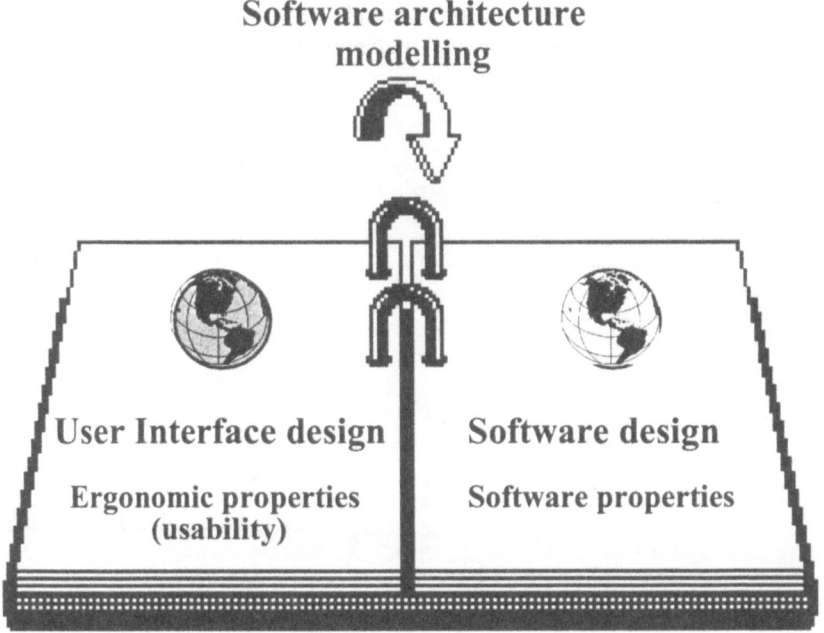

Figure 2: Software architecture at the turning point of two worlds.

3. Model and Method with PAC-Amodeus

PAC-Amodeus is a model applicable to the design of interactive software architectures. Designing a software architecture consists of defining the software units of the interactive system that support the external specifications of that system. An instance of a PAC-Amodeus architecture is a representation of the software architecture of a particular interactive system; this instance results from the application of a design method associated with the PAC-Amodeus model. A method is a set of directions (or procedures) for using a particular model that represents the artefact being designed and built.

In this section, we first describe the model in terms of its the software components and their interactions. We then discuss the external and internal properties that the model can support. By doing, so we emphasise the links between the external and internal properties. We finally conclude the section by providing guidelines for applying the model.

3.1 PAC-Amodeus, a Software Architecture Model for Interactive Systems

As shown in Figure 3, the PAC-Amodeus model is a refinement of the Arch/Slinky Model (Bass et al. 91).

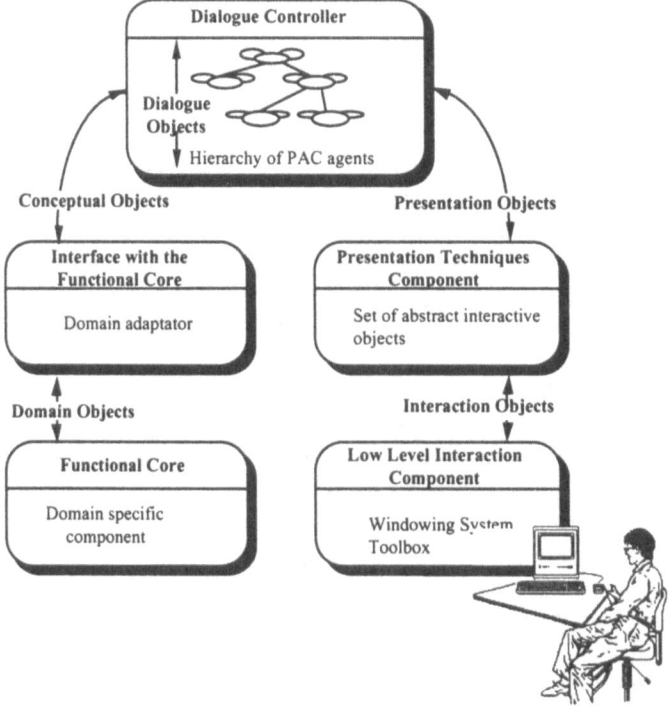

Figure 3: The PAC-Amodeus software components.

In turn, the Arch/Slinky model defines itself as a "Seeheim revisited" model. PAC-Amodeus reuses the main components advocated by Arch/Slinky: an interactive system is comprised of the functional core, the interface with the functional core, the dialogue controller, the presentation technique component, and the low level interaction component. In contrast to Arch/Slinky which does not provide any hint about how to organise the dialogue controller, PAC-Amodeus refines this component in terms of PAC agents (Coutaz 87). A more detailed description of PAC-Amodeus can be found in (Nigay & Coutaz 91, Nigay 94). The following paragraphs provide a synthesised definition of the various components illustrated in Figure 3.

The Functional Core (FC) implements the domain specific concepts. Ideally, the representation used to model domain concepts in the functional core is independent from the rendering of these concepts to the user. In general, this representation is driven by computational considerations.

The Interface with the Functional Core (IFC) serves as a domain adaptor between the functional core and the dialogue controller. Data exchanged with the functional core are the domain objects that the functional core exports towards the user (Coutaz & Balbo 91). Data exchanged with the dialogue controller are conceptual objects. These define perspectives on domain objects intended to match the user's mental representation of domain concepts. In other words, they transform computational objects into abstractions driven by considerations for the user's conceptual model.

At the other end of the spectrum, the Low Level Interaction Component (LLIC) denotes the underlying platform, both software and hardware. The LLIC includes basic interaction facilities such as a windowing system, a spoken language shell, and toolkits such as Motif™ and OpenLook™. It manages the physical interaction with the user: physical actions from the user are modelled as typed events which are time-stamped, queued, and analysed. Those events that are part of lexical tasks, such as window moving and window resizing, are processed locally by the LLIC. In the case of spoken-utterances, the LLIC may include mechanisms for confirmation allowing the user to intercept wrong recognitions or alleviate ambiguities. From the developer's perspective, the LLIC is an unavoidable component. It exists just like a constraint exists.

The Presentation Techniques Component (PTC) serves as an adaptor between the Dialogue Controller and the Low Level Interaction Techniques. Whereas the Interface with the Functional Core performs transformations at the conceptual level, the PTC performs adaptation at the rendering level. The communication with the Dialogue Controller is expressed in terms of Presentation objects. Presentation Objects convey data to be rendered to the user.

Presentation objects are translated in terms of interaction objects. The distinction between presentation objects and interaction objects is subtle. A presentation object may be modelled as an abstract interaction object or may be a new interaction technique built from LLIC components. Thus, the PTC defines a layer for portability between LLIC's components as well as a layer for extending LLIC services. For example, when the user interface of a system is expressed in terms of ready for use interaction objects, then the mapping between presentation objects and interaction objects is 1-to-1: presentation objects exist to ensure portability with regard to the LLIC component. On the other hand, if the user interface of the system has very specific requirements, then new classes of interaction techniques must be defined: presentation objects are used as extensions of interaction objects. As an example of extension performed inside the PTC, let us consider the Presentation Object that renders the concept of temperature in the form of a thermometer. The LLIC component includes graphic primitives, buttons and menus but does not provide thermometers. Thus, a new class (thermometer) will be defined in the PTC layer. This presentation object class will be expressed in terms of the basic interaction objects such as Draw-Line, Draw-Rectangle. It may as well be mapped into a voice message such as: "Current temperature is x° degrees Celsius".

The Dialogue Controller (DC) is the keystone of the model. It has the responsibility for task-level sequencing. Each task or goal of the user corresponds to a thread of dialogue. This observation suggests the choice of a multi-agent architecture. An agent or a collection of cooperating agents can be associated to each thread of the user's activity. Since each agent is able to maintain its own state, it is possible for the user (or the functional core) to suspend and resume any thread at will. PAC-Amodeus decomposes the Dialogue Controller into a set of cooperative PAC agents (Coutaz 87).

The dialogue controller receives events both from the functional core via the Interface with the Functional Core (IFC), and from the user via the Presentation Technique Component (PTC). In addition to task sequencing, bridging the gap between an IFC and a PTC requires data transformation and data mapping:

- An IFC and a PTC use different formalisms. One is driven by the computational considerations of the functional core, the other is toolkit/media dependent. In order to match the two formalisms, data must be transformed inside the dialogue controller.
- State changes in the IFC must be reflected in the PTC (and vice versa). Therefore links must be maintained between IFC conceptual objects and PTC presentation objects. A conceptual object may be rendered with multiple presentation techniques. Therefore, consistency must be maintained between the multiple views of the conceptual object. Such management is yet another task of the dialogue controller.

Experimental results suggest that task sequencing, formalism transformation, and data mapping must be performed at multiple levels of abstraction and distributed among multiple agents. Levels of abstraction reflect the successive operations of abstracting and concretising. Abstracting combines and transforms events coming from the presentation objects into higher level events until the IFC is reached. Conversely, concretising decomposes and transforms high level data from the IFC into low level information. The lowest level of the dialogue controller is in contact with presentation objects. Since agents should carry task sequencing, formalism transformation, and data mapping at multiple levels of abstraction, it is tempting to describe the dialogue controller at multiple grains of resolution combined with multiple facets.

At one level of resolution, the dialogue controller appears as a "fuzzy potato". At the next level of description, the main agents of the interaction can be identified. In turn, these agents are recursively refined into simpler agents as shown in Figure 4. This description applies the usual abstraction/refinement paradigm used in software engineering.

In addition to the refinement/abstraction axis, we introduce the "facet" axis. Facets are used to express the different but complementary and strongly coupled computational perspectives of an agent. These perspectives are similar to those identified for the whole interactive system:

- the functional core or Abstract facet (i.e., the A facet) defines the competence of the agent in the chain of abstracting and concretising. It may be related to some conceptual objects in the IFC;
- the dialogue controller facet (i.e., the C facet) controls event sequencing inside the agent, maintains a mapping between the A facet and the presentation facet of the agent;
- the presentation facet (i.e., P facet) is involved in the implementation of the perceivable behaviour of the agent. It is related to some presentation object in the PTC component.

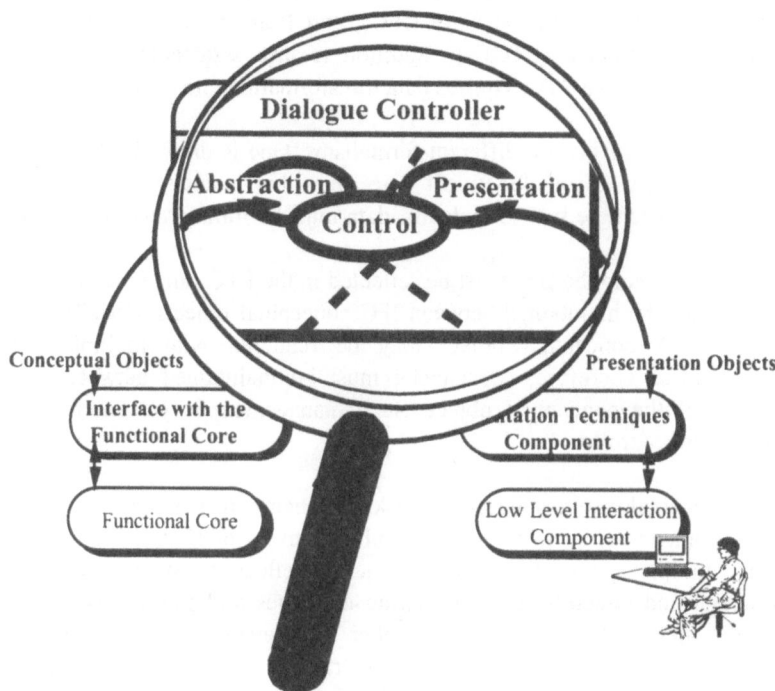

Figure 4: Zoom within the PAC-Amodeus Dialogue Controller, a PAC agent. Dashed lines represent possible relationships with other agents. Plain lines show the possible links with the surrounding components of the Dialogue Controller.

In summary, in PAC-Amodeus, the overall functional partitioning of an interactive system should be defined according to the following rule: the Low Level Interaction Component should be both device and interaction language dependent; the Presentation Techniques Component is device independent but still language dependent; the other components of the interactive system, including the Dialogue Controller, should be both device and language independent. The Dialogue Controller should be refined in terms of PAC agents. The hierarchical organisation of the Dialogue Controller in terms of PAC agents is motivated by the necessity of modelling computation at various levels of abstraction, the necessity of expressing the fusion and fission phenomena as well as parallelism at various levels of granularity. In addition to the vertical information flow within the PAC hierarchy, communication can also occur horizontally with the IFC and the PTC at various levels of abstraction through the Abstraction and Presentation facets of the PAC agents.

Having presented the main features of the PAC-Amodeus model, we are now able to discuss its relationships with internal and external properties.

3.2 User-Centered Design and Software Design: a Point of Contact Using Properties

In this section, we present the benefits of the PAC-Amodeus model in terms of external and internal properties. A list of external and internal properties can be found in (Gram & Cockton 96, Chapters 2 & 3). Here we present those that PAC-Amodeus deals with and that are useful for describing the case study. For each property, we point out whether the model carries the property or whether it supports its assessment.

3.2.1 External properties and PAC-Amodeus

In (Abowd et al. 92) external properties are classified in two categories: properties that support interaction flexibility and properties that characterise interaction robustness. This initial set has been extended in (Gram & Cockton 96, chapter 2). In this article, we examine the properties that relate to our case study only: device and representation multiplicity, multithreading, non-premptiveness, reachability, observability, and predictability.

"Device and Representation multiplicity" is defined as the capacity of the system to offer multiple input/output devices and interaction representations for communication. In PAC-Amodeus, the multiplicity of devices can be locally assessed in the Low Level Interaction Component (LLIC). The multiplicity of representations is implemented in terms of multiple presentation objects that are either managed in the Presentation facet of PAC agents in the Dialogue Controller (DC) or in the Presentation Techniques Component (PTC). PAC-Amodeus does not deliver "Device and Representation multiplicity" but supports its assessment by identifying the software components where the property should be implemented.

"Multi-threading" of the user/system dialogue allows for support of more than one task at a time. "Multi-threading" is delivered by PAC-Amodeus because of the agent decomposition of the Dialogue Controller (DC). Indeed an agent can be associated with one thread of the user's activity. Since a state is locally maintained by the agent, the interaction between the user and the agent can be suspended and resumed at the user's will. When a thread of activity is too complex or too rich to be represented by a single agent, it is then possible to use a collection of cooperating agents.

"Non-preemptiveness" refers to the degree of freedom the user has in deciding the next action to be performed. "Non-preemptiveness" has direct impact on the Dialogue Controller (DC). As explained above, the DC has the responsibility for task-level sequencing. Because PAC-Amodeus refines the DC in terms of small computational cooperative agents, it is easy to implement "non-preemptiveness". Conversely, it may be difficult to assess the property since dialogue control is distributed over a multiplicity of Control facets.

"Reachability" is concerned with navigation through the system states. We make a distinction between "backward" and "forward" reachability. "Backward reachability", such as undo, is useful for returning to some previous state. "Forward reachability" allows the user to reach any desired state from any current state. Each agent in the Dialogue Controller (DC) maintains a local state. The designer must therefore examine each agent to assess the property. Implementation of "reachability" may nevertheless be simpler because of its distributed implementation within every agent.

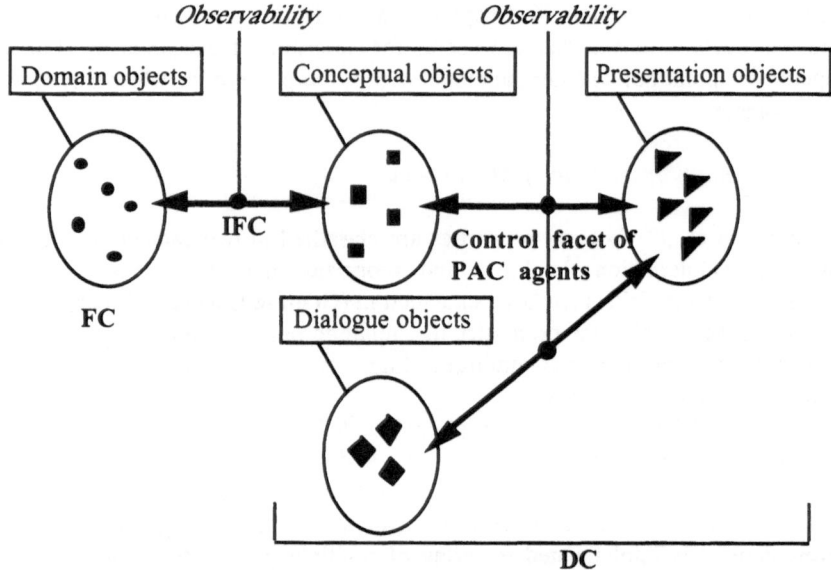

Figure 5: Observability property in the PAC-Amodeus model.

"Observability" allows the user to evaluate the internal state of the system from the perceivable representation of that state. It implies that the system makes relevant information available to the user. "Observability" is implemented in the Interface with the Functional Core (IFC), the Dialogue Controller (DC), and the Presentation Technique Component (PTC). Domain objects that are relevant for a given task must have a set of corresponding conceptual objects defined in the IFC. In turn, conceptual objects must be linked to presentation objects by the DC. In addition, each relevant piece of information (i.e.; dialogue object) maintained in the Abstraction facet of an agent that does not correspond to a conceptual object must also be related to a presentation object. Figure 5 summarises our analysis of observability for PAC-Amodeus.

"Predictability" of an interactive system means that the user's knowledge of the interaction history is sufficient to determine the result of future interaction. The knowledge can be reduced to the current observable state of the system so that the user needs not remember anything that is not currently observable. "Predictability" is also closely related to the "consistency" property. It implies that the behaviour of each agent in the Dialogue Controller must be consistent.

3.2.2 Internal properties and PAC-Amodeus

PAC-Amodeus is geared towards satisfying two internal properties: "modifiability" which is closely related to "maintainability" and "portability".
"Modifiability" is the effort required to modify a program. We identify three steps in modifying a program:

- identify the component to be modified,
- modify the component,
- test the new component and its integration into the program.

Modifiability of the code level is a crucial property for supporting a user-centered iterative design. PAC-Amodeus incorporates the two adapter components of Arch, the Interface with the Functional Core (IFC) and the Presentation Techniques Component (PTC), in order to insulate the keystone component (i.e., the Dialogue Controller (DC)) from modifications in its unavoidable neighbours: the Functional Core (FC) and the Low Level Interaction Component (LLIC). For example, it is example possible to modify the input and output interaction techniques in the LLIC and PTC (devices and languages) without endangering the code of the Dialogue Controller.

"Portability" is the effort required to transfer a program from one hardware configuration and/or software system environment to another. The Presentation Techniques Component (PTC) acts as a mediator between the Dialogue Controller and the Low Level Interaction Component (LLIC) which is system environment dependent. It is therefore possible to change the underlying physical and software platform by only modifying the PTC.

The agent decomposition of the Dialogue Controller (DC) is a useful mechanism for satisfying additional internal properties: agent models in the DC stress a highly parallel modular organisation and distribute the state of the interaction among a collection of co-operating units. Modularity, parallelism and distribution are convenient mechanisms for supporting the iterative design of user interfaces and for implementing physically distributed applications:

- An agent defines the unit for functional modularity. It is thus possible to modify its internal behaviour without endangering the rest of the system.
- An agent defines the unit for processing. It is thus possible to execute it on a processor different from the processor where it was created. It is also possible to use instances of a class of agents to present a concept on distinct workstations. This property is essential for implementing groupware.

3.3 From Model to Reality: How to Apply PAC-Amodeus

Our own experience with PAC-Amodeus reveals two interesting but dual observations:

- Software designers have few difficulties in understanding the role of the five software components of the arch. Therefore, they have few problems in describing the functions and objects implemented in each component.
- Conversely, software designers have trouble identifying the appropriate agents which, at run time, will support the behaviour described by the external specifications of the interactive system.

Although PAC-Amodeus demonstrates interesting properties with regard to interaction principles, it is too general to guide the software architecture design process. In particular, the refinement of the Dialogue Control component in terms of PAC agents needs to be made more precise. The heuristic rules presented next provide an operational apparatus for this refinement. These rules have been implemented in the form of an expert system, PAC-Expert (Nigay 94). As mentioned in Section 2, they imply a bottom-up analysis starting from the external specifications of the system. They are organised along three issues: object and group content, group links and hierarchy revision. The concept of group can be mapped onto the "Objects group" defined in (May et al 96): it corresponds to a presentation objects group as perceived (hopefully) by the user. For instance, a window on the screen forms a group. If the user interface is well designed, presentation objects in a group maintain a semantic relationship: they are related to the same task or to the same domain or dialogue object.

3.3.1 Object and group existence

Rule 1: Use an agent to implement an elementary presentation object.
We have observed that users of PAC-Amodeus have difficulty in bounding the recursive decomposition of the agent hierarchy. We recommend the following bottom-up approach: refine the decomposition down to the elementary presentation objects as specified in the external specifications (e.g., a push button, etc.).

Rule 2: Use an intermediate agent to implement a group object.
We then recursively build upon the elementary agents by identifying group agents as shown in Figure 6. For example a tool palette is a group of push buttons, each of them being implemented as an agent.

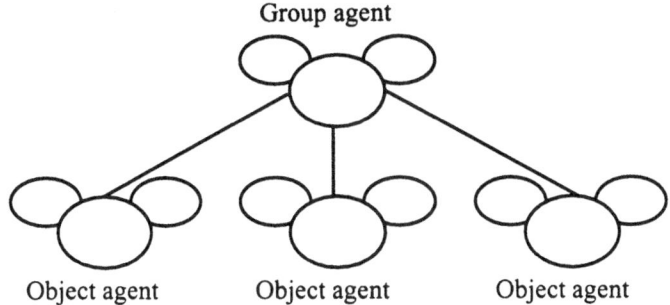

Figure 6: Object and group agents.

3.3.2 *Group links*

We identify two types of links: semantic and syntactic. Such links are not translated in terms of groups at the user interface level, otherwise Rules 1 and 2 can be applied. Rules 3 and 4 deal with semantic links while Rule 5 correspond to syntactic links.

Rule 3: Use isomophic agents to reflect the composition of conceptual objects.
It is often the case that conceptual objects are composed of conceptual objects. For example, a program is composed of modules which in turn is composed of procedures, etc. If the relation of composition must be conveyed to the user, then one can define a similar composition in terms of agents in the dialogue controller. A hierarchy of agents isomorphic to the hierarchy of conceptual objects is thus defined.

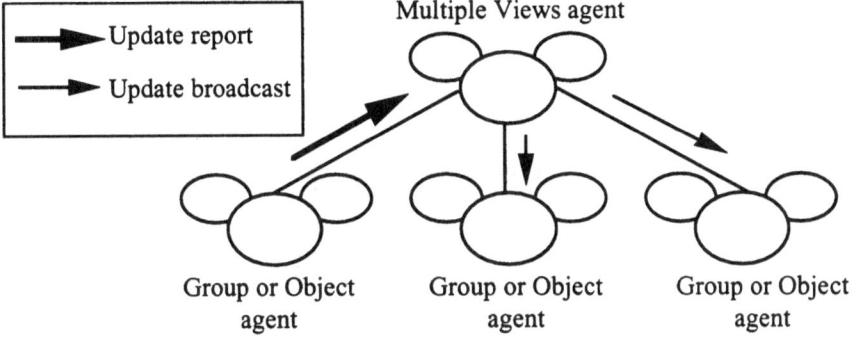

Figure 7: Multiple Views agent.

Rule 4: Use an agent to maintain visual consistency between multiple views.
According to the software principle which stresses "mutual ignorance" to enhance reusability, agents which implement the views of a semantic concept should not know each other. As shown in Figure 7, a "Multiple view" agent is introduced to express the dependency. Any action with visual side effect on a view is reported to the Multiple view which broadcasts the update to the other siblings.
Rule 5: Use an agent to synthesise actions distributed over multiple agents.

Group agents are related by a "syntactic link" when a set of user actions distributed over these agents can be synthesised into a higher abstraction (i.e., the fusion phenomenon). For example, to draw a circle, the user selects the "circle" icon in the tool palette agent, then draws the shape in the workspace agent. These distributed actions are synthesised by a cement agent into a higher abstraction (i.e., the command "create circle"). This agent, which maintains a syntactic link between its sub-agents, is called a "cement agent". Again, if the tool palette and the drawing area are contained in the same window (a group) Rule 2 applies. Rule 5 would be applied if the tool palette were independent of the drawing area.

3.3.3   Hierarchy revision

Once the hierarchy of agents has been devised using rules 1 to 5, we recommend the hierarchy should be analysed using the following rules:

Rule 6: An interaction object is not an agent.
If the Presentation Techniques Presentation (PTC) levels can implement an agent in a straightforward way, then turn the agent into an interaction (or presentation) object and make it part of the Presentation facet of the parent agent (i.e., the facet gets connected to the interaction/presentation object). For example using a toolkit such as Motif™, a push button is not an agent because a push button is implemented by Motif™.

Rule 7: An agent and its single sibling can be combined into one agent.
If a parent agent has one single sibling and future evolution of the system does not lead to additional siblings and information transfer between agents is not for free, then it may be useful to combine the two agents into a single one.

We now illustrate the application of our heuristic rules with the description of a case study.

4.   A Case Study: a WWW Browser

Our case study is based on the Netscape (Netscape) user interface whose screen dump of Figure 8 shows an example. We show how to design the software architecture for this exemplar applying the model and the rules presented in Section 3. We then assess the resulting architectural design based on the internal and external properties presented in Section 3.2. In so doing, we show which external properties are satisfied in the Netscape user interface and which internal properties are supported by our PAC-Amodeus architectural design.

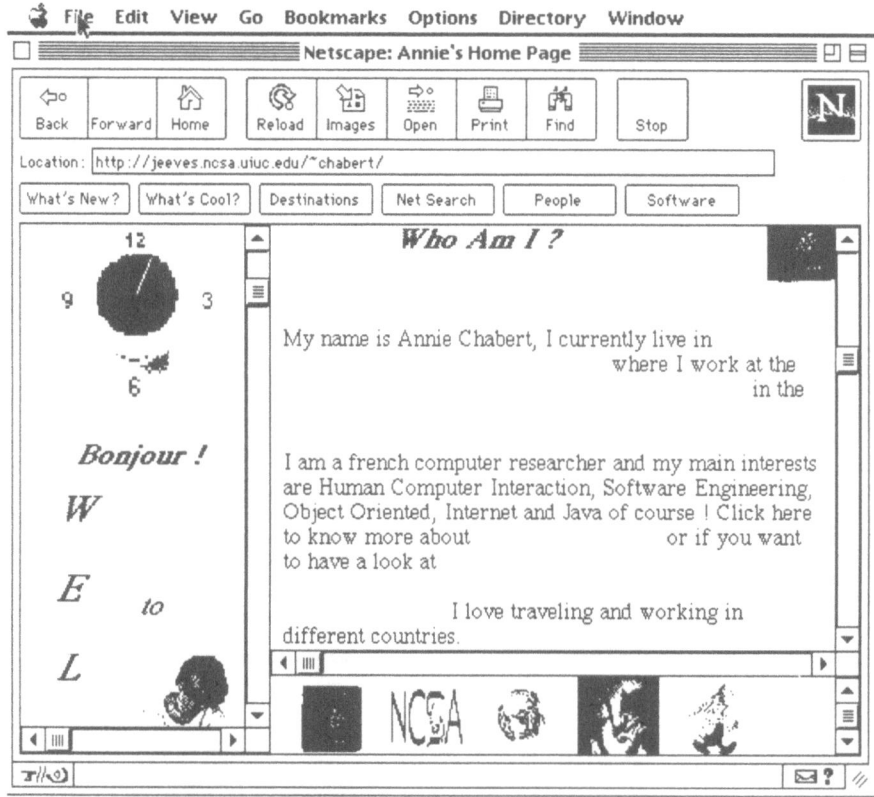

Figure 8: The Netscape user interface. The current page contains three frames (Netscape). A frame is a mechanism that allows the page designer to display several HTML (HTML) pages within a single page.

4.1 Software Design

In this section we explain how to generate the software design of the user interface of Figure 8 by applying the model. The first design step consists of identifying the functions and objects in the five software components advocated by PAC-Amodeus. Section 4.1.1. describes the results of this design step. Having identified the content of the five components, we then recommend the refinement of the Dialogue Controller in terms of agents: Section 4.1.2. shows how we applied the rules in order to build the hierarchy of agents.

4.1.1 Overall architecture of the Netscape browser

As shown in Figure 9, the Functional Core (FC) hosts the functions that are dependent on the internet network connection (http protocol):

- connection to the distant web server,

- receipt of the HTML (HTML) pages.

In addition, the FC manages access to local files that can be directly loaded by the browser including user's preferences such as bookmarks, and possibly the cache memory. Cache memory is used to keep local copies of frequently accessed pages in order to reduce network load.

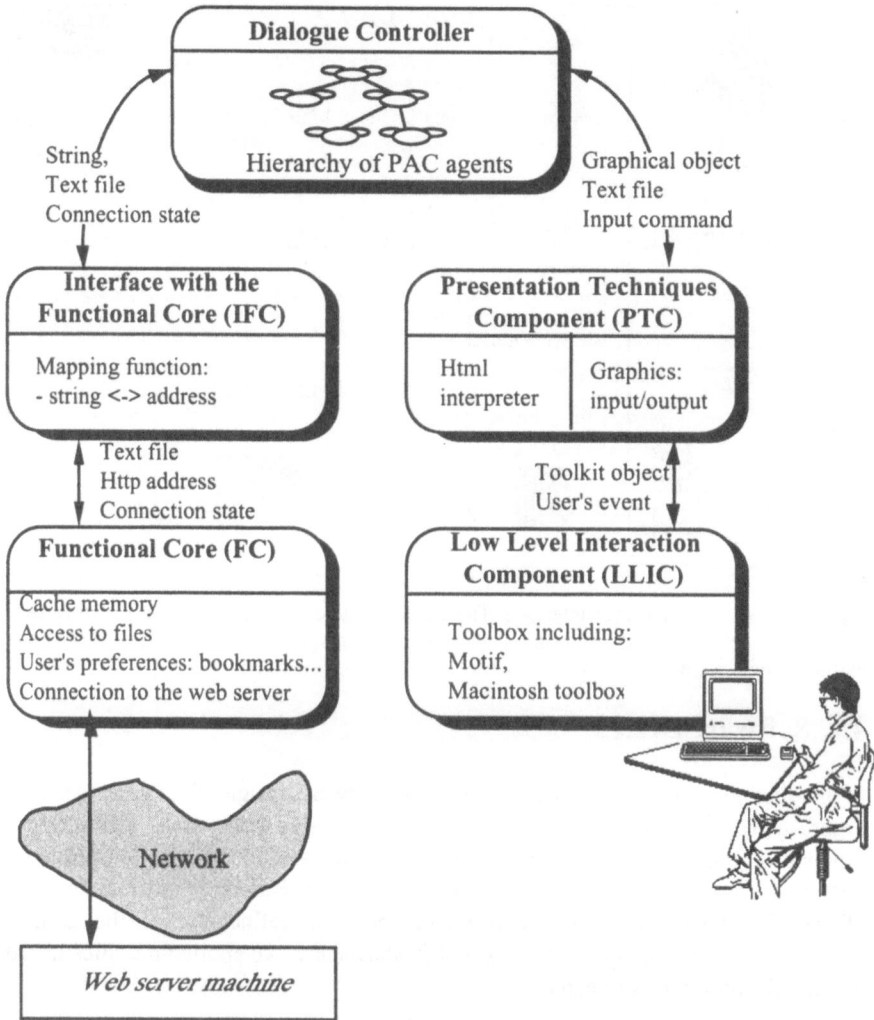

Figure 9: Overall architecture of the exemplar of Figure 8 developed using PAC-Amodeus.

The Interface with the Functional Core (IFC) serves as a buffer between the Dialogue Controller (DC) and the Functional Core (FC). It maintains a mapping between the concepts of the FC (e.g., http addresses and text files) and the concepts that belong to the DC (e.g., strings and pages). For example, the IFC receives a string from the DC that it translates into an http address understandable by the FC. The IFC allows communication between its two surrounding components by implementing a communication protocol. It is therefore possible to receive information through the network via the FC and to handle user events through the DC.

At the other end of the spectrum, the Low Level Interaction Component (LLIC) denotes the underlying software and hardware platform. It manages the graphical output and mouse-key events. As a result, this component is dependent on the underlying platform. For example, on the Macintosh™, this component embeds the Macintosh toolbox. On UNIX workstations, it includes the Motif™ toolbox.

The Presentation Techniques Component (PTC) is split into two main parts: the graphical definition (input and output) and the HTML interpreter. The PTC receives presentation objects from the Dialogue Controller (DC) that are mapped onto interaction objects. Interaction objects are toolbox dependent. The PTC serves as a buffer between the underlying platform (LLIC) and the Dialogue Controller. It thus makes the DC platform independent.

Finally the Dialogue Controller is responsible for task sequencing. It is not dependent on the network protocol nor on the software and hardware platform. In particular, the DC is toolbox independent and HTML independent. We refine it in terms of PAC agents in the following section.

4.1.2 Refining the dialogue controller in terms of PAC agents

The hierarchy of PAC agents is derived using the rules presented in Section 3.3. We start with Rules 1 and 2: each presentation object, such as a button, is a PAC agent and each presentation group including palettes, menus and windows are agents. For example, the "Palette1" agent models the part of the window where the command buttons including "Back" and "Forward" are displayed. Its Abstraction facet maintains the list of corresponding commands. When the user selects one of the buttons, the corresponding event is received by the Presentation facet. The "Palette1" agent sends a message to the "Browser" agent which will in turn translate the command in terms understandable by the IFC: an http address. The Abstraction facet of the "Browser" agent will send this address to the IFC.

We then apply Rule 6 to minimise the number of levels in the hierarchy. Since toolboxes provide menus and buttons, we do not need agents to manage them. Using the user interface shown in Figure 8, we obtain the two hierarchies of agents presented in Figure 10.

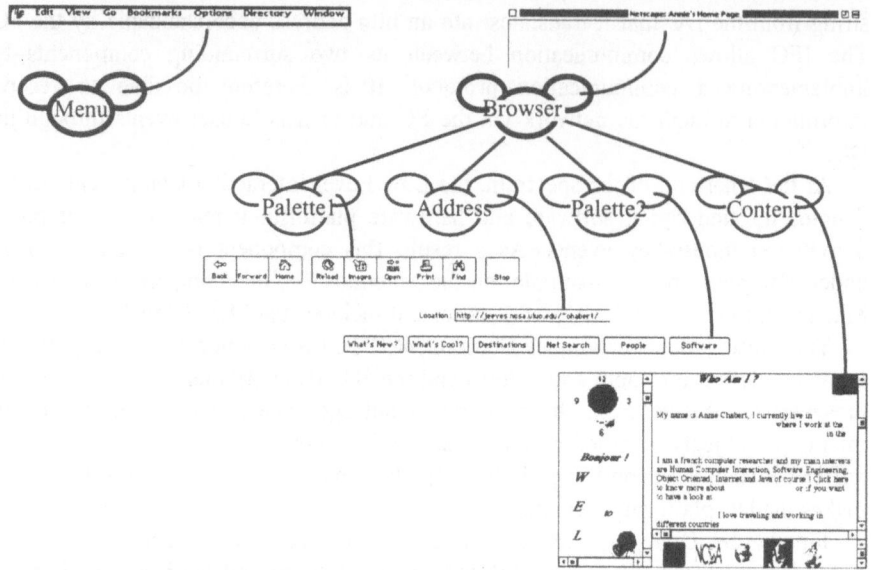

Figure 10: First refinement step: result from the application of Rules 1, 2 and 6.

Because several browsers may be opened simultaneously, Rule 5 applies to maintain syntactic links between the multiple browsers. For example, images can be dragged and dropped between browsers. We apply Rule 5 to maintain those user's actions distributed over multiple browsers: Figure 11 presents the corresponding hierarchy.

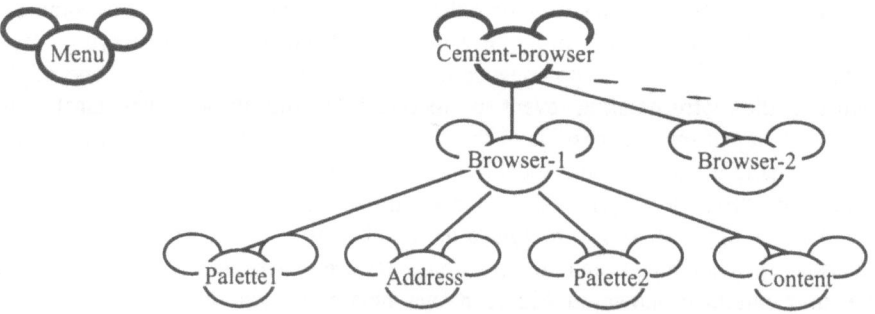

Figure 11: Second refinement step: result from the application of Rule 5.

The Control facet of the "Cement-browser" agent maintains a mapping between the current opened browsers and corresponding PAC-agents. This correspondence can be implemented as a table: when a new browser is created, the "Cement-browser" agent dynamically creates a new "Browser" agent and adds a new line in the table.

Finally, we identify syntactic links between the main menu (the "Menu" agent) and the opened browsers (the "Cement-browser" agent). For example the user can select an http address in the "Go" menu to load an already accessed HTML page. The selection will be received by the Presentation facet of the "Menu" agent and must thus be sent to the current active browser. A new "Cement-root" agent must then be designed to maintain such communication between the "Menu" agent and the "Cement-browser" agent. In order to do so, Rule 5 is again applied. Figure 12 presents the final hierarchy of agents that refines the Dialogue Controller.

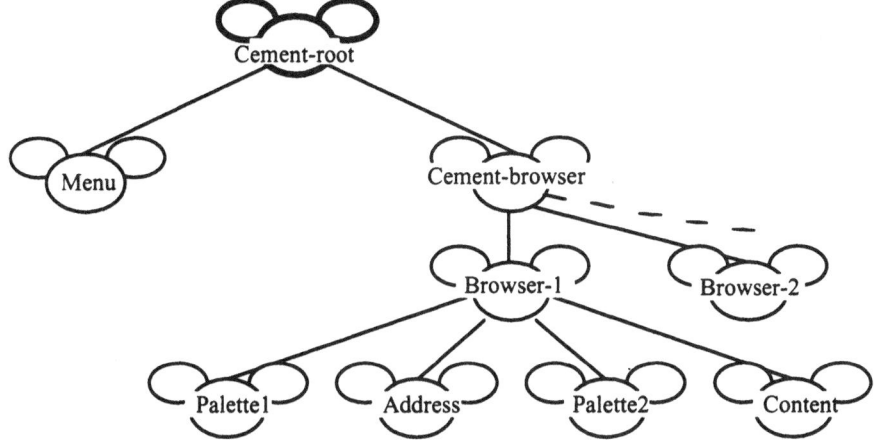

Figure 12: In the final refinement step; Rule 5 is applied.

4.2 Scenario: Messages Passing

To better understand the roles of each agent, we explain the information flow through the hierarchy of agents in the context of two scenarios.

4.2.1 First scenario: dynamic instantiation of a browser

Figure 13 shows message passing through the hierarchy of agents in the context of the following scenario: the user has already opened two browsers. The user then selects the option "New Web Browser" in the "File" menu (1). The command is received by the Presentation facet of the "Menu" agent. It is important to note that the Dialogue Controller (DC) does not know how the user has specified the command: the DC is interaction technique independent. It receives semantic description of commands, not user's physical actions. For instance, the user can select the option in the menu by using the mouse or by typing the short cut "⌘N" using the keyboard. Therefore a speech interface can be envisioned without modifying the DC. Spoken utterances, however, such as "Create a new browser", requires the modification of both the Low Level Interaction Component (LLIC) and the Presentation Techniques Component (PTC). The DC is left unchanged provided that the introduction of speech does not generate extra tasks such as negotiations.

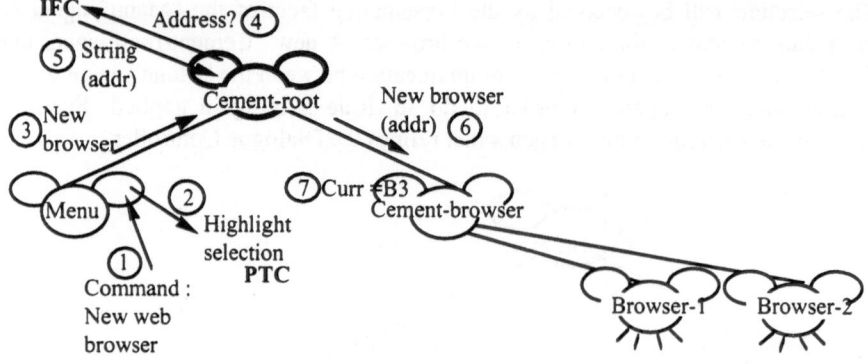

(a) Before the creation of new agents

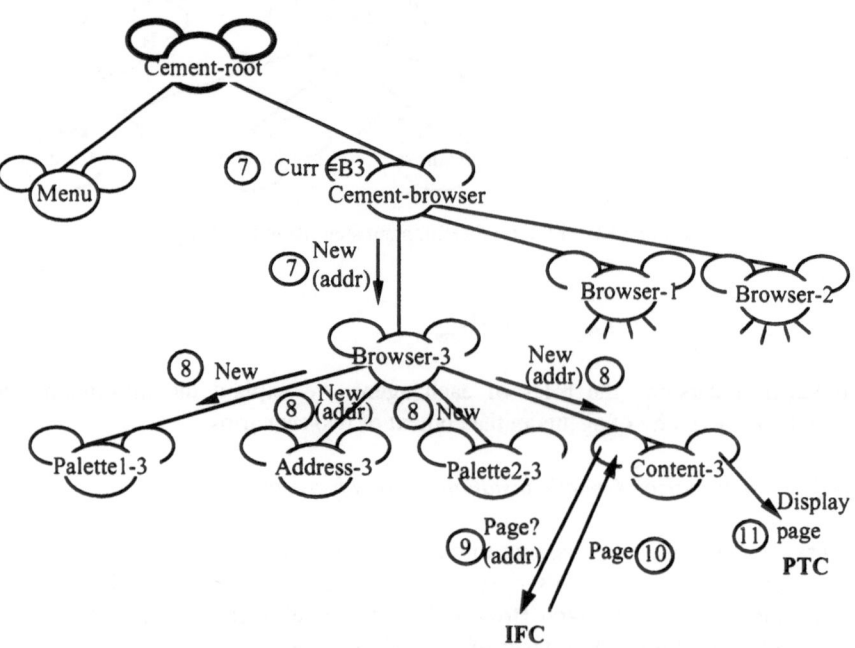

(a) After the creation of new agents.

Figure 13: Opening a new browser: messages passing through the hierarchy of agents.

The Presentation facet of the "Menu" agent, which processes the user's mouse selection (1), produces a partial immediate feedback: it highlights the selection. The "Menu" agent, which cannot perform any more processing, sends the command to its parent agent, the "Cement-root" (3).

The Abstraction facet of the "Cement-root" agent sends a message to the Interface with the Functional Core (IFC) asking for a first page (4). If a "Home" page has been specified by the user, the Functional Core (FC), via the IFC, will provide the corresponding http address to the DC (5). If there is no home page specified in the FC, the Abstraction facet of the "Cement-root" agent will receive the Netscape http address. Having received an address, the Control facet of the "Cement-root" agent sends a message to the "Cement-browser" agent in order to create a new browser. This message contains the address (6).

The "Cement-browser" agent dynamically creates a new "Browser-3" agent (Figure 13-b) and adds a new line in the mapping table that contains the identification of the newly created PAC agent (7). Meanwhile, the Abstraction facet updates the local variable that contains the identification of the current active browser (7).

In turn, the newly created "Browser-3" agent initialises its local history in its Abstraction facet and dynamically creates its sub-hierarchy (8). Initially, the new "Palette1-3" agent contains the two buttons "Back" and "Forward" set to inactive state. The state of the buttons is maintained by the Abstraction facet of "Palette1-3" while the presentation of the buttons is defined by the Presentation facet. The new "Address-3" agent displays the address provided by its parent agent. Finally, the Abstraction facet of the new "Content-3" agent sends a request to the IFC asking for the page that corresponds to the address (9). The Abstraction facet of "Content-3" will first receive messages from the IFC that describe the current internal state of the FC (e.g., "Connect: Contacting host..."). These states are displayed by the Presentation facet of "Content-3". When the Abstraction facet receives the text file (10), it is reflected back to the PTC via the Presentation facet of "Content-3" (11). The PTC is then able to interpret the new page and displays it. Because the address is now validated, the "Content-3" agent sends the address back to its parent. Through the hierarchy ("Cement-browser" -> "Cement-root" -> "Menu"), the address is sent back to the "Menu" agent that updates its "Go" and "Window" menus.

4.2.2 Second scenario: browsability using hypertext links

In this scenario, we consider browsability using hypertext links. Two browsers are opened. The user drags a link from a browser to the second one. The corresponding page is loaded in the second browser. The first browser remains unchanged and is still active.

As shown in Figure 14, the selection of the link is received by the Presentation facet of "Content-1" (1). Its Presentation facet performs a partial immediate feedback by changing the colour of the selection (2) while its Control facet sends the corresponding address to its parent(3), the "Browser-1" agent. In turn, "Browser-1" sends the address to its parent "Cement-browser" (4). "Cement-browser" maintains the selected address in its Abstraction facet (5).

Drag events are processed locally by the PTC. When the user releases the mouse button, the corresponding event is received by the Presentation facet of the "Content-2" agent (6) which performs a lexical highlight feedback. The Control facet of "Content-2" sends the event to the "Cement-browser" agent via the Control facet of the "Browser-2" agent (7 and 8).

Now, the "Cement-browser" agent is able to combine the two user's actions, action1 and actions 2 into a meaningful command. It asks "Browser-2" to open the new address that has been selected (10). As in the previous scenario, the "Browser-2" agent modifies its local history in its Abstraction facet and broadcasts the new address to the "Palette1-2" agent, to the "Address-2" agent and to the "Content-2" agent. The "Palette1-2" agent may have to modify the state of its "Back" button. The "Address-2" agent displays the new address and the "Content-2" agent sends a request to the IFC in order to obtain the new page to be displayed. When the page is received, it is displayed by the PTC. Because the address is correct, the "Content-2" agent sends it back to its parent as a confirmation message. As opposed to the previous scenario, the validated address is not sent to the "Menu" agent because the "Browser-2" agent is not active. But if the user selects the window of the second browser in order to make it active, the whole history of accessed pages maintained by the "Browser-2" agent will be sent back to the "Menu" agent.

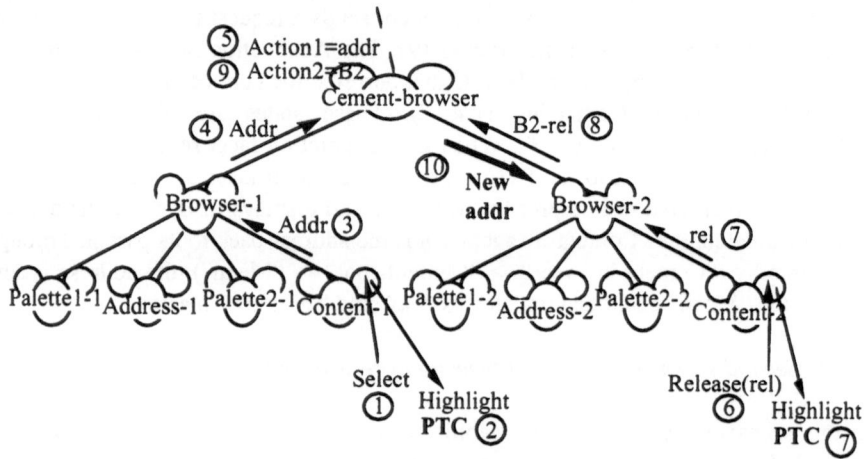

Figure 14: Browsing using links: messages passing through the hierarchy of agents.

4.3 Properties

Having designed the software architecture of the case study, we now consider our solution in the light of the external and internal properties selected in Section 3.2.

4.3.1 External properties

"Device and Representation multiplicity" is supported in the Low Level Interaction Component (LLIC) and the Presentation Techniques Component (PTC). For instance, in the first scenario (Section 4.2.2.) we present two ways of specifying the command "New Web Browser": the selection of a menu option using the mouse or by using a keyboard short-cut. This is one simple example of "device and representation multiplicity". If we add new interaction techniques such as speech input, the designer will have to modify the LLIC and the PTC. The Dialogue Controller will remain unchanged.

"Multi-threading" is carried out by agent decomposition of the Dialogue Controller. In the case study, the user can freely switch between browsers. Because we have designed a sub-hierarchy of agents per browser and a "Cement-browser" agent, the property is clearly satisfied.

"Non-preemptiveness" is visible at the Dialogue Controller (DC) level; the DC has the responsibility of task-level sequencing. At any time, every agent is ready to receive events from the Presentation Techniques Component (PTC) and from the Interface with the Functional Core (IFC). For example, the user can stop the process of loading a page at any time: because the IFC implements a communication protocol between the Functional Core (FC) and the DC, it is possible to receive information through the network via the FC and to handle user events (i.e., the "Stop" command) via the PTC: this is managed within the DC organised as a hierarchy of PAC agents.

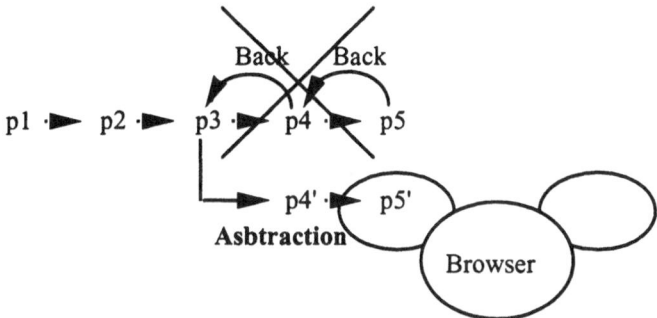

Figure 15: Interaction trajectory managed by the Abstraction facet of the "Browser" agent.

In order to assess the "reachability" property, the designer must examine the Abstraction facet of every agent: the implementation of the interaction state is distributed in the Abstraction facet of multiple agents. For example, let us consider the Abstraction facet of the "Browser" agent. It maintains the history of the accessed pages. It describes an interaction trajectory as shown in Figure 15: each state is an accessed page. By closely looking at the management of this history, we conclude that the "reachability" property is not satisfied because when the user comes back to a previous state and starts from there a new interaction trajectory, the previous trajectory is lost. It is no longer possible to come back to a previous state. To satisfy "reachability", the designer must modify the Abstraction facet of the "Browser" agent.

As shown in Figure 5, "observability" can be easily checked in the Interface with the Functional Core (IFC) and in the Control facet of the agents that populate the Dialogue Controller (DC). For example, one can check that the internal states of the Functional Core (FC) are sent to the DC in order to be made perceivable to the user: to examine data passing, the designer must look into the IFC. In addition, within the DC, one can check that the internal state in the Abstraction facet of an agent is made perceivable to the user. In order to do so, we must look into the Control facet responsible for data passing between the Abstraction facet and the Presentation facet. Using the "Browser" agent as an example, one can easily conclude that the history is not completely observable by the user. Only one part of the history is made perceivable to the user in the "Go" menu. For example, when the user selects links in frames (Netscape), the accessed pages are not presented in the "Go" menu. Instead, this information is maintained in the Abstraction facet of the "Browser" agent in order to return to a previous page within a frame. Such information displayed on screen would be very useful. Figure 16 schematically presents the problem related to the observability property in the "Browser" agent.

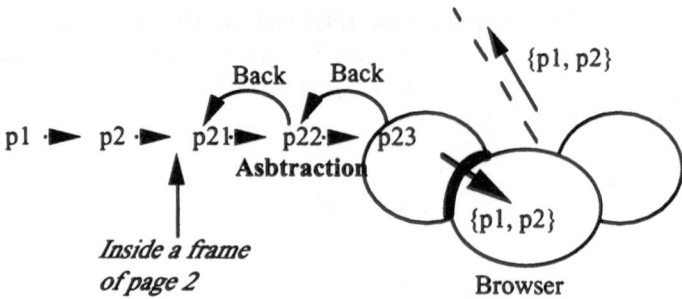

Figure 16: Observability and the "Browser" agent.

As explained in Section 3.2, the "predictability" property is closely related to the "consistency" property. To assess this property the designer must check that the behaviour of the agents in the Dialogue Controller (DC) is consistent. For example we consider the management of frames within a page as shown in Figure 8. Each frame will be managed by an agent namely the "Frame" agent that is a sibling of the "Content" agent. From the user's perspective, such a frame will be perceived as small browser within a browser. But the behaviour of the "Frame" agent is not consistent with the behaviour of the "Content" agent. For example it is possible to drag a picture or a link from one browser to another one (scenario 2) but it is not possible to do so between two frames. This is a case of non-consistent behaviour: when the user drags a link between two frames he cannot predict the correct result.

4.3.2 Internal properties

Modifiability of the software is clearly satisfied because of a high modularity of our software design and of the clearly identified links between modules. For example in the context of a user-centered iterative design we can modify the presentation of an agent without endangering the rest of the code. In the previous section we gave several examples of local modifications within a facet of an agent.

Portability of the software is satisfied because the Presentation Technique Component (PTC) makes the rest of the code independent of the underlying platform. The Dialogue Controller which is the more complex code is independent of the toolkit and the windowing system. This property is crucial for a WWW browser such as Netscape which runs on several platforms.

5. Conclusion

With the advent of new technologies such as WWW, the user interface portion of interactive systems is becoming increasingly large and complex. Architectural modelling is therefore becoming a central problem for large, complex systems. In addition, software architecture modelling is a design activity at the turning point between two worlds: the user interface design field and the programming field. Because of its interlinking location, software architecture must take into account properties of the two worlds: ergonomic properties of the designed user interface and properties of the future implemented software.

In this chapter we have focused on one software architecture model, PAC-Amodeus and a method to apply it. We have also explained how PAC-Amodeus can help the designer to satisfy and assess the ergonomic and software properties. The model, the method and the properties have been illustrated by a case study, a WWW browser.

Acknowledgements

This work has been supported by project ESPRIT BR 7040 Amodeus II. It was influenced by stimulating discussions with the IFIP WG2.7 "User Interface Engineering" members, and our Amodeus partners. Many thanks to G. Serghiou for reviewing the chapter.

Chapter 4:
A Formal Approach to Consistency and Reuse of Links in World Wide Web Applications

1. Introduction

It is widely known that hypermedia systems, which are strongly based on human computer interaction, have been accepted as an innovative framework which plays an important role in current computing environments.

Hypermedia design is a human activity that is complex mainly due to the large amount of information to be processed. The lack of guidelines on what factors should be considered when creating a hyperdocument makes the task even harder. Since there is no consensus on what methodology to use in order to produce a "good" hyperdocument, it is very common to find a poorly written hyperdocument lacking a well organised structure. It is interesting to note, however, that it is difficult to define exactly what "good" means and, consequently, it is very hard to measure "how good" a document is. Due to the fact that hypermedia engineering is currently emerging and therefore still lacks formalisation, hyperdocument authorship is yet to be well defined and is generally not approached in a very systematic way.

In literature there are a large number of different metrics, many of them subjective, that are used as criteria for evaluating a hyperdocument (Brown 90, Hatzimanikatis et al. 95). An adequate design-oriented subset of them proposed in (Garzotto et al. 95) consists of: richness, ease, consistency, self-evidence, predictability, readability and reuse.

This chapter focuses on the formal aspects of two of these metrics, namely, consistency and reuse. The notions of reuse and consistency as stated in (Garzotto et al. 95) are: "reuse considers the use of objects and operations in different contexts and for different purposes" and "consistency measures application regularity". It is well known, from the field of software reuse in Software Engineering, that appropriate software reuse leads to improvements during the software development phase. In the context of hyperdocuments authoring, according to (Garzotto et al. 95), an appropriate reuse of objects promotes consistency, predictability and richness.

This chapter offers a tool for the automated evaluation of a Web site based on an analysis of the links of the site, and formalises the various cases of consistency and reuse of links that are detected. It is organised as follows: Section 2 highlights the importance of analysing a hyperdocument taking into account its structural and content levels. In Section 3 we propose a systematic approach for examining a hyperdocument by analysing its link structure, and in Section 4 this approach is formalised. The functional structure of a tool named LiOS (**Link-Oriented System**) is briefly presented in Section 5, which describes its three main modules. The results from some experiments with LiOS are discussed in Section 6 and our conclusions are presented in Section 7.

2. Perusing the Anchoring Layer

In order to define which measurements are important in the evaluation of a hyperdocument, it is necessary first to define, among its main characteristics, those that can be measured and, among them, those which are relevant to be measured, and then establish an appropriate range of values for them.

Following the Dexter reference model for hypertext systems proposed in (Halasz & Schwartz 90), hyperdocuments will be considered in this work at two distinct levels of granularity: at the content level and at the structural level. The Dexter model also defines a third level (*presentation layer* in hypertext systems), which is orientated to the resulting forms of display at runtime. Although this chapter is mainly concerned with the analysis of the hyperdocument structure, we believe that by providing ways of improving its structure, we are indirectly contributing to the improvement of the presentation layer, which is the ultimate issue of this book. At the content level (*within the component layer*), the informational contents of the nodes and the existing interrelations within each single node, such as paragraphs and titles, are focused. At the structural level (*the storage layer*) the focus is directed at the interrelations between nodes and links.

A hyperdocument can be independently approached at any of these levels of granularity. In (Salton et al. 94) the writers focus on the content level of a hyperdocument in order to propose a strategy which automatically defines its links. The work described in (Botafogo & Shneiderman 92) and in (Rivlin et al. 94) deals with its structural level, analysing the connectivity of the graph which describes the hyperdocument and proposing algorithms for the identification of possible aggregations, hierarchies and metrics.

In order to approach structural consistency and reuse in a systematic way, we had to take into account both levels of granularity of a hyperdocument. This was due to the fact that the identification of link reuse is strongly supported by anchors, which can be considered part of an interface layer (named *"Anchoring"* in the Dexter model), that exists between the structural level and the content level. By using the Anchoring mechanism, the user interacts with the hyperdocument by means of the hypertext system. It should be pointed out that Anchoring is a mechanism specific to the hypertext system and should also be evaluated with relation to its contribution to hyperdocument quality. The analysis of the Anchoring layer can subsidise a subsequent improvement of the human-computer interaction by means of the improvement of the hyperdocument itself.

3. The Link Oriented Approach for Checking Consistency and Reuse

It is well known in literature that a hyperdocument structure can be seen as a graph (Botafogo & Shneiderman 92, Stotts et al. 92). It is common to find research work using this formal view of a hyperdocument structure in order to facilitate the analysis of some of its major characteristics. We have adopted the formal graph view when developing the LiOS tool, since LES[4], which is used for describing the hyperdocument structure, can be seen as a graph description language.

It should be noted, however, that in order to be able to check for consistency and reuse, we had to approach the hyperdocument structure under a *relational view*, as well. Only by adopting a relational view could the *virtual structures* we identified, namely *aggregation* and *degeneration*, be detected. It is worth noting that, while trying to identify the possible virtual structures, three issues were considered:

1. existing techniques for node naming - the Universal Resource Locator (URL) of a document used in WWW is already an established and accepted technique for this;

2. the fact that there is no established technique for naming links. This gives rise to a certain degree of freedom to the author of the hyperdocument that might possibly make the hyperdocument more difficult to manage;

3. the fact that the larger the volume of information in a hyperdocument is, the higher the probability for reuse of nodes and links to occur.

In order to make a systematic and exhaustive search for all possible virtual structures, a tree representing the possible reuse cases was created, as shown in Figure 1. The reuse cases were defined based on unidirectional links. The definitions were supported by the results obtained by analysing the reuse of the components of unidirectional links, namely: **source-node, destination-node** and **source-anchors**[5]. Each of these components was approached through reuse, with respect to other links, in the context of a hyperdocument. By associating a binary valued reuse attribute (0:no and 1:yes) to each of the three components, the possible reuse cases of link components added up to 8 (2^3), ranging from what was identified as case 0 up to case 7.

---

[4] LES (Statechart Language Specification) is a language which allows the textual description of the structural components of a hyperdocument, according to the Statechart syntax and semantics (Harel 87).

[5] It is a common practice that anchors in source-nodes and anchors in destination-nodes are treated differently. An anchor is necessary in the source-node since it is the starting point of a link to another node (generally). At the arrival node, in general, an anchor is an entry point to that node and it does not need to be presented to the reader.

The tree structure in Figure 1 represents the eight possible cases which resulted from combining the components of the links, starting with links which have a different source-node, different source-anchor and different destination-node (case 000_2, labelled 0) up to those which have the same source-node, same source-anchor and same destination-node (case 111_2, labelled 7).

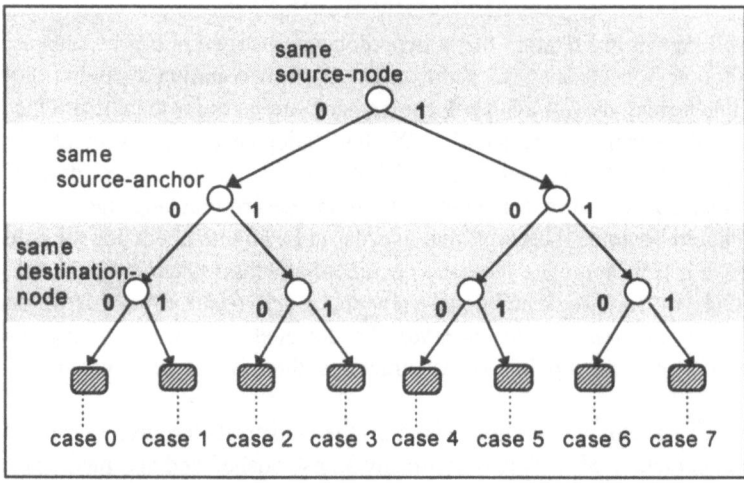

Figure 1: Tree representing the reuse cases of link components

Using the formal graph structure of a generic hyperdocument, as defined in (Parunak 91), as well as the semantic attached to link reuse, a classification of the possible reuse cases of link components was carried out. Three main reuse situations were identified and the corresponding links classified either as **general**, **unusual** or **contextual**. The empirical results presented in Section 6 reinforce the fact that the proposed taxonomy of links can be adopted as a sound metric for evaluating hyperdocuments.

A semantic view of the eight identified cases, grouped by their classification, is presented in Figure 2 (a), (b) and (c), where the rounded rectangles represent nodes named A, B, C and D, the arrows represent the links and labels "x" and "y" correspond to the value of two different source-anchors.

Cases 3 and 4 are considered **general links**; case 3 can be interpreted as an abstraction of index pages (more than one link with the same source-anchor arriving at the same destination-node) and case 4 as an abstraction of table-of-contents page (more than one different link leaving the same source-node).

Case 0 and case 7 are categorised as **unusual links** in the context of link reuse since they represent the unusual situations of no reuse and of total reuse, respectively. The identification of a link reuse belonging to case 0 or case 7 suggests the need for a deeper analysis, since each case corresponds to an "extreme" case.

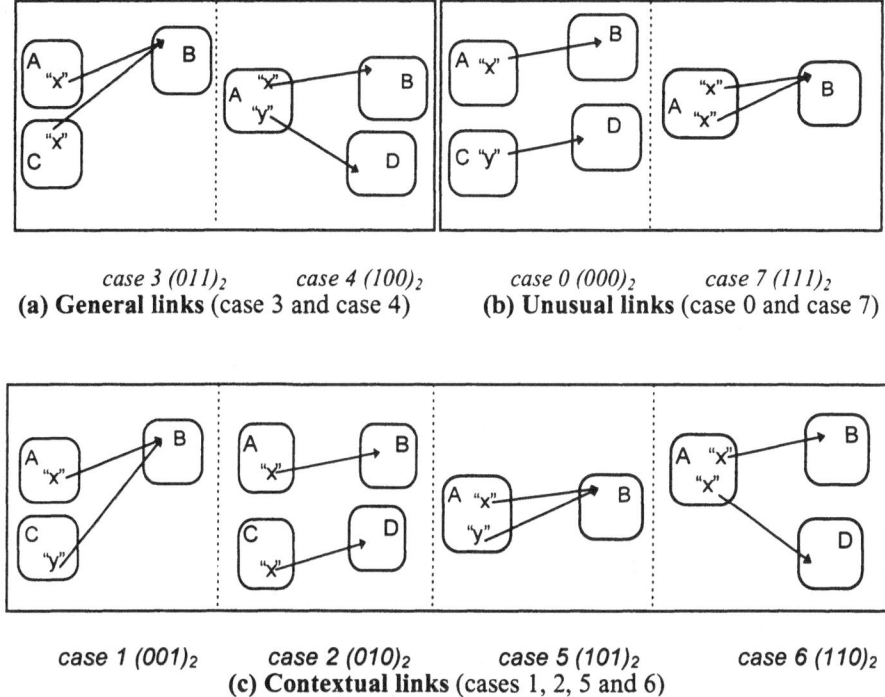

case 3 (011)₂   *case 4 (100)₂*   *case 0 (000)₂*   *case 7 (111)₂*
(a) General links (case 3 and case 4)   **(b) Unusual links** (case 0 and case 7)

case 1 (001)₂   *case 2 (010)₂*   *case 5 (101)₂*   *case 6 (110)₂*
(c) Contextual links (cases 1, 2, 5 and 6)

Figure 2: Classification of link cases based on their component reuse

Finally, cases 1, 2, 5 and 6 are classified as **contextual links**. Apparently, the situations described by these cases could be considered abnormal, but before doing so, a closer examination of the node itself (its contents and the region which surrounds the anchor) should be carried out in order to ascertain its abnormality.
Note that, in odd-numbered cases, we are considering links which, besides having the same destination-nodes, arrive at the same entry-point.

To get a more generic view of the proposed taxonomy, a study of the possible abstractions that exist or could be created in each of the eight identified cases was conducted, aimed at:

- generalising the link classification procedure, and
- providing alternative ways of detecting virtual structures that can be implicitly defined during the authoring process.

Based on a careful and systematic study of all possible abstractions, two generic procedures for creating an abstraction were identified:

1. **aggregation** (identified by "**g**"): when the derived cases are created by grouping destination-nodes;

2. *degeneration* (identified by "*d*"): when a link which leaves and arrives at the same node is created.

It must be noted, however, that aggregation only deals with destination-nodes; this is due to the fact that grouping of source-nodes has already been considered previously (cases 4, 5, 6 and 7). Both procedures are illustrated in Figure 3, where case 5 is derived from case 1 by aggregation of source-nodes and case 5d derives from case 5 by degeneration.

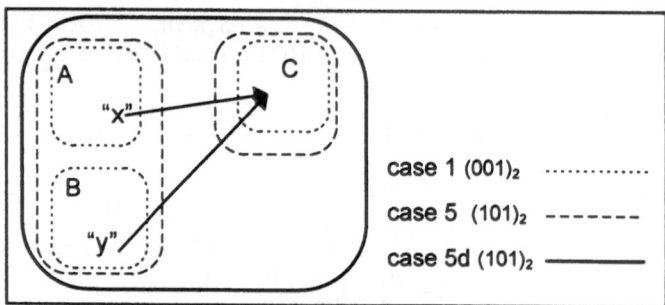

Figure 3: Case 1 leads to case 5 by aggregation and case 5 leads to case 5d by degeneration

To exemplify our systematic approach let us take as an example case 0, which identifies situations where links have different source-nodes, different destination-nodes and different source-anchors. A complete view of the whole derivation process is presented in Figure 4.

As stated earlier, case 0 has no reuse of any link component. By exhaustively deriving all possible cases (using aggregation, degeneration or a combination of both), case 4 has been identified as one among many possible derivations from case 0. The links described in case 0 and case 4 are characterised by having different source-anchors and different destination-nodes. What distinguishes case 0 from case 4 is the fact that the source-anchors are placed in different nodes (case 0) and in the same node (case 4). Case 4 represents grouping of the source-nodes displayed in case 0, namely, A and C, in just one node, A.

Two other aggregations were carried out from case 0 and case 4 by grouping the destination-nodes: one identified as case 0g and the other as case 4g, respectively. The degeneration procedure applied to case 0, case 4 and case 0g gave rise to case 0d, case 4d and case 0gd respectively. One of the two other cases not yet mentioned, which is in the last level of the tree pictured in Figure 4, can be obtained by applying degeneration to case 4d or equivalently, by applying degeneration to case 4g. That is why it can be identified as both: case 4gd or case 4dd. The last one, case 0gd is derived by applying aggregation to case 0d.

Finally, after going through the abstraction process for each of the eight cases, cases 0, 1, 2 and 3 were chosen as **primitive cases**, because they give rise to others by aggregation or degeneration and they are not derived from any other case by means of the same operations.

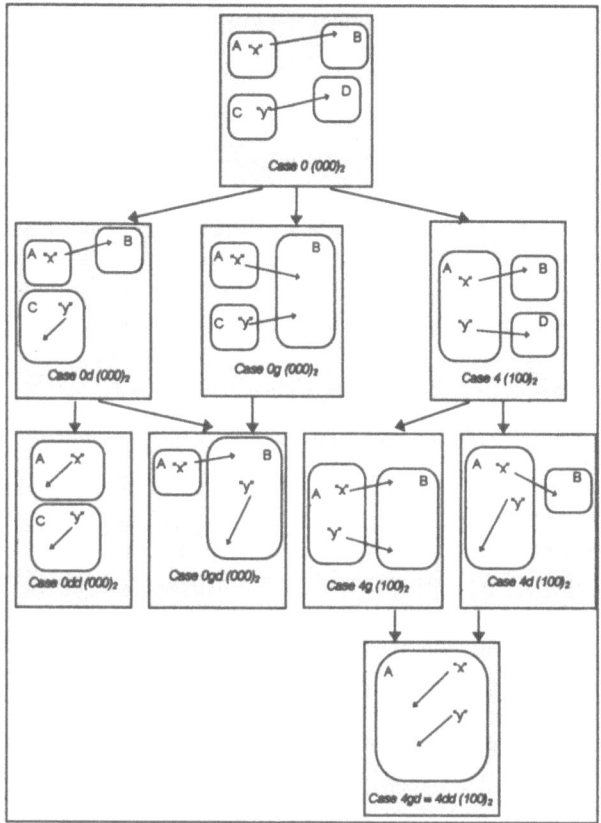

Figure 4: Cases derived from case 0

Based on the primitive cases, following the systematic approach exemplified earlier, all the possible abstractions of those cases were derived by means of degeneration, aggregation or a combination of both, as shown in Table 1. It can be noted that, by allowing virtual structures (aggregation, degeneration or both), 20 new cases can occur.

primitive cases	derived cases by *aggregation*	derived cases by *degeneration*	derived cases by both
case 0	0g, 4, 4g	0d, 4d, 0dd	0gd, 4gd
case 1	5	5d	—
case 2	2g, 6, 6g	2d, 6d, 2dd	2gd, 6gd
case 3	7	7d	—

Table 1: Primitive cases and their possible derivations through aggregation, degeneration or both

The next section presents a normalisation of the systematic approach for link analysis just presented, where each of the eight identified cases of link component reuse is formally described.

4. Recovering Links: a Formal Approach

In this section we begin by introducing the formal definition of a hyperdocument used as a basis for establishing the formalisation of link reuse cases. According to (Parunak 91), a graph-based hyperbase is an ordered triplet $H = <N, A, L>$ of nodes, anchors and links respectively, where:

- $N = \{N_1, ...N_m\}$ is a set of information nodes
- $A = \{A_{11}, ...A_{mp}\}$ is a set of anchors, where each node N_i has one or more anchors $\{A_{i1}, ..., A_{iq}\}$
- $L = \{<A_{ij}, A_{kl}>\}$ is a set of links, i.e., a set of ordered pairs of anchors
- In order to use this definition for the purpose of link reuse formalisation, the following observations should be taken into account:
- N can be unitary. This happens when the hyperdocument has only one node. Obviously the set $N = \{N_1, ...N_m\}$ should be finite, where m represents the number of nodes belonging to N.
- A link also can be defined between two anchors in one same node, i.e., some $<A_{ij}, A_{il}>$, where A_{ij} and A_{il} are anchors placed on node N_i.
- The set of anchors of node N_i will be noticed by A_i. If node N_i has p anchors, i.e., the set of its anchors is $\{A_{i1},..., A_{ip}\}$, the number of elements of A_i is p, i.e., $|A_i| = p$
- $L \subseteq A \times A$ and does not exist $<A_{ij}, A_{ij}>$, for $1 \le i \le m$ and $|L| \ge 1$
- Let $<A_{ij}, A_{kl}> \in L$. The anchor A_{ij} is named source-anchor and A_{kl} destination-anchor

To identify the links belonging to each link reuse case, we extended Parunak's definition by introducing two new functions:

1. *source-anchor*: $L \rightarrow A$ such that *source-anchor*$(<A_{ij}, \_>) = A_{ij}$, a function which extracts the source-anchor from a link

2. *name*: $A \rightarrow$ *<string>* | *<icon>*, which maps an anchor to its value (or its icon) presented to the user during navigation

Next, set-based descriptions of each of the eight identified cases (depicted in Figure 1 and in Figure 2), are presented. We have chosen to introduce some redundancy in the notation, aiming to make it clearer and more uniform. That is why, for example, we write $<N_r, N_t>$, $r = t$, instead of $<N_r, N_r>$.

Thus, for $1 \le i, j, r, t \le m$, and $1 \le k \le |A_i|$, $1 \le l \le |A_j|$, $1 \le s \le |A_r|$, $1 \le x \le |A_t|$, the set-based descriptions are:

Case 0 $(000)_2$ -

(0a) $\{< <N_i, N_j>, <A_{ik}, A_{jl}>, <N_r, N_t> > \mid$
$name(source\text{-}anchor(<A_{ik}, A_{rs}>)) \neq name(source\text{-}anchor(<A_{jl}, A_{tx}>)),$
$i \neq j, r \neq t \}$

(0b) $\{< <N_i, N_j>, <A_{ik}, A_{jl}>, <N_r, N_t> > \mid$
$name(source\text{-}anchor(<A_{ik}, A_{rs}>)) \neq name(source\text{-}anchor(<A_{jl}, A_{tx}>)),$
$i \neq j, r = t, s \neq x \}$

Case 1 $(001)_2$ -

(1) $\{ < <N_i, N_j>, <A_{ik}, A_{jl}>, <N_r, N_t> > \mid$
$name(source\text{-}anchor(<A_{ik}, A_{rs}>)) \neq name(source\text{-}anchor(<A_{jl}, A_{tx}>)),$
$i \neq j, r = t, s = x\}$

Case 2 $(010)_2$ -

(2a) $\{ < <N_i, N_j>, <A_{ik}, A_{jl}>, <N_r, N_t> > \mid$
$name(source\text{-}anchor(<A_{ik}, A_{rs}>)) = name(source\text{-}anchor(<A_{jl}, A_{tx}>)),$
$i \neq j, r \neq t \}$

(2b) $\{< <N_i, N_j>, <A_{ik}, A_{jl}>, <N_r, N_t> > \mid$
$name(source\text{-}anchor(<A_{ik}, A_{rs}>)) = name(source\text{-}anchor(<A_{jl}, A_{tx}>)),$
$i \neq j, r = t, s \neq x \}$

Case 3 $(011)_2$ -

(3) $\{ < < <N_i, N_j>, <A_{ik}, A_{jl}>, <N_r, N_t> > \mid$
$name(source\text{-}anchor(<A_{ik}, A_{rs}>)) = name(source\text{-}anchor(<A_{jl}, A_{tx}>)),$
$i \neq j, r = t, s = x\}$

Case 4 $(100)_2$ -

(4a) $\{< <N_i, N_j>, <A_{ik}, A_{jl}>, <N_r, N_t> > \mid$
$name(source\text{-}anchor(<A_{ik}, A_{rs}>)) \neq name(source\text{-}anchor(<A_{jl}, A_{tx}>)),$
$i = j, k \neq l, r \neq t \}$

(4b) $\{< <N_i, N_j>, <A_{ik}, A_{jl}>, <N_r, N_t> > \mid$
$name(source\text{-}anchor(<A_{ik}, A_{rs}>)) \neq name(source\text{-}anchor(<A_{jl}, A_{tx}>)),$
$i = j, k \neq l, r = t, s \neq x \}$

Case 5 $(101)_2$ -

(5) $\{ < <N_i, N_j>, <A_{ik}, A_{jl}>, <N_r, N_t> > \mid$
$name(source\text{-}anchor(<A_{ik}, A_{rs}>)) \neq name(source\text{-}anchor(<A_{jl}, A_{tx}>)),$
$i = j, k \neq l, r = t, s = x\}$

Case 6 $(110)_2$ -

(6a) $\{ < <N_i, N_j>, <A_{ik}, A_{jl}>, <N_r, N_t> > \mid$
$name(source\text{-}anchor(<A_{ik}, A_{rs}>)) = name(source\text{-}anchor(<A_{jl}, A_{tx}>)),$
$i = j, k \neq l, r \neq t \}$

(6b) $\{< <N_i, N_j>, <A_{ik}, A_{jl}>, <N_r, N_t> > \mid$
$name(source\text{-}anchor(<A_{ik}, A_{rs}>)) = name(source\text{-}anchor(<A_{jl}, A_{tx}>)),$
$i = j, k \neq l, r = t, s \neq x \}$

Case 7 $(111)_2$ -

(7) $\{ < <N_i, N_j>, <A_{ik}, A_{jl}>, <N_r, N_t> > \mid$

$$name(source\text{-}anchor(<A_{ik}, A_{rs}>)) = name(source\text{-}anchor(<A_{jl}, A_{tx}>)),$$
$$i = j, k \neq l, r = t, s = x\}$$

It can be observed that the existence of sets a) and b) for the even-numbered cases (which do not have the same destination) represent the occurrence of destination-anchors placed in a) different destination-nodes, and b) in the same destination-node, but arriving at different entry-points.

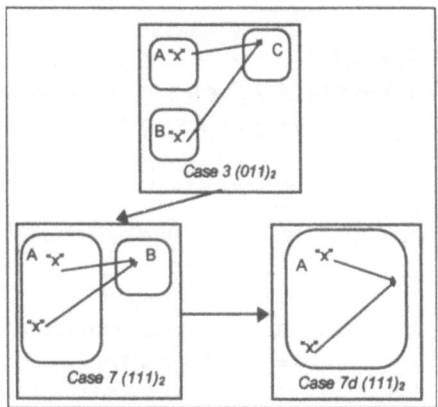

Figure 5: Case 7 and case 7d derived from case 3

The formal approach for describing each of the eight identified cases also covers the formal description of any of the 16 possible derivations obtained from case 0 up to case 7. For example, case 7d illustrated in Figure 5, is a degeneration of case 7, because the source-node and the destination-node of case 7 have become a single node which is both the source-node and the destination-node of case 7d. It is important to note that case 7d can also be described using the same set-based description that describes case 7; of course, the restriction of having the same node for source and destination-node is offset by requesting that $i = r$. This can be seen as a specialisation of the formal description given for case 7.

Table 2, below, gives the link reuse cases covered by it for each set-based description presented.

description	covers	description	covers
(0a)	0, 0d, 0dd	(4a)	4, 4d, 4dd
(0b)	0g, 0gd	(4b)	4g, 4gd
(1)	1	(5)	5, 5d
(2a)	2, 2d, 2dd	(6a)	6, 6d, 6dd
(2b)	2g, 2gd	(6b)	6g, 6gd
(3)	3	(7)	7, 7d

Table 2: Set-based descriptions and the corresponding link reuse cases they cover

5. Analysing Link Reuse Cases: The LiOS Tool

To implement the consistency and reuse criteria for analysing and evaluating hyperdocuments, we have chosen a *link-oriented approach*, which is based on the structure of the hyperdocument.

To peruse both consistency and reuse of link components, an automatic tool named LiOS (Fortes 96) was developed, based on the identification and recovery of the following objects: link, source-node, source-anchor and destination-node. These objects are diagrammatically shown in Figure 6, using the notation proposed in (Coleman et al. 94).

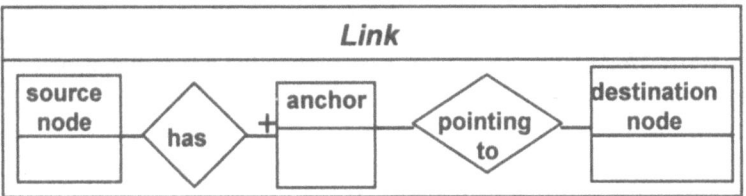

Figure 6 - The components of an object "link"

The modular functional structure of the tool was defined, based on this object model, as shown in Figure 7. The structure is basically composed of three main modules: the *HD Representation Module*, the *Converter Module* and the *Presentation Module*. A brief description of each of these modules is shown below.

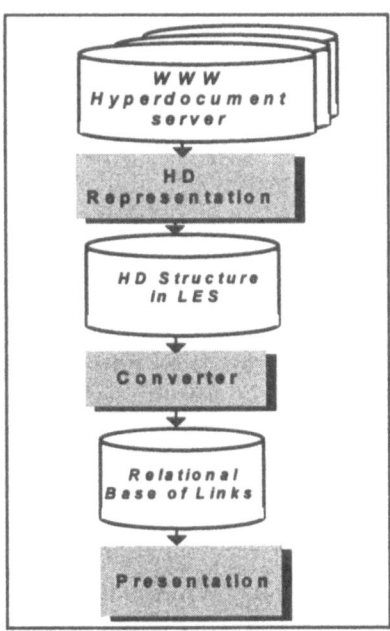

Figure 7 - Functional structure of LiOS, a link-oriented tool

The *HD Representation Module* scans the hyperdocument following its local links and generates an ASCII file, containing the structure of the hyperdocument described in LES (Fortes & Masiero 91). The structure itself can be seen as a set of links, each of them described as a Statechart transition. To describe the links in LES, we used the convention that an anchor, presented to the reader in the source node, corresponds to an event that might possibly be triggered by him/her, i.e., it corresponds to a link.

Since the scanning process does not follow links through the HTTP protocol, it produces a local hyperdocument structure representation containing only the links belonging to the author's production. An important characteristic of the functionality of the *HD Representation Module* is related to the URL address decoding process, aiming at standardisation, in order to identify the real reuse of link components.

The *Converter Module* is responsible for converting the ASCII file, generated by the *HD Representation Module*, into a relational data base, where links are represented as t-uple having the form:

(id-link, source-anchor, source-node, destination-node, destination-anchor)
where:

> id-link = link-identifier (primary-key);
> source-anchor = event;
> source-node = source;
> destination-node.destination-anchor = destination.

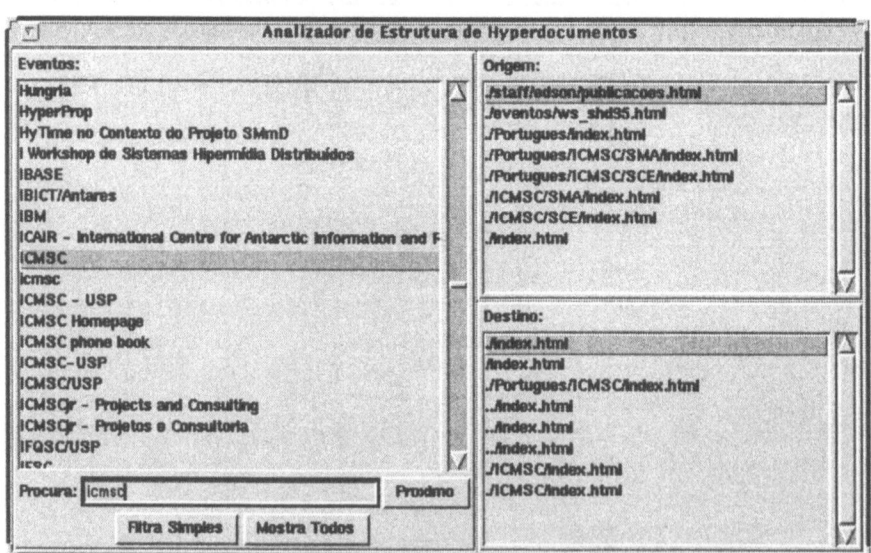

Figure 8 - Window presenting the links of a WWW hyperdocument, showing the source and destination nodes which are connected by them

The *Presentation Module* is responsible for presenting the user with a list of all the existing links in the hyperdocument, so that they can be selected for further examination. The module focuses on the links and then on the nodes they connect. This module's main window shows a list of all the source-anchor names used in the hyperdocument and makes them available for selection. Selecting any of these anchor names gives the user access to two new lists: the first, containing all the source-nodes which have, as their starting point, the selected anchor and the second, containing all the destination-nodes which can be reached from that same anchor. Figure 8 shows a screen dump of the *Presentation Module*, where "Eventos", "Origem" and "Destino" are the Portuguese words for events (meaning source-anchors), source (source-node) and destination (destination-node).

To understand how the *Presentation Module* works let us imagine the situation pictured in Figure 9, where the link named "here" links document Doc1 to Doc11 and Doc12 and another link, also named "here", links document Doc2 to Doc21. Clicking on link "here" would result in documents Doc1, Doc1 and Doc2 being shown as source-nodes and Doc11, Doc12 and Doc21 being shown as destination-nodes.

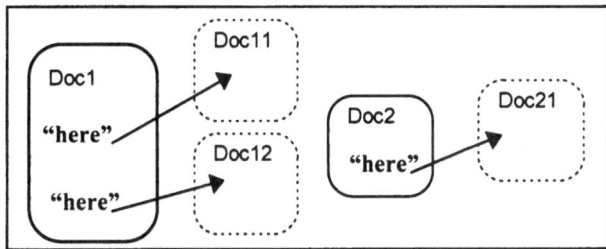

Figure 9 - An example of a possible situation dealt with by the *Presentation Module*

6. Experimenting with LiOS — Empirical Results

It is worth reminding the reader again that this chapter focuses mainly on a formal model of hypermedia structure, and addresses link reuse cases rather than formal methods for the design of interactive systems, which is the main issue of this book. Nevertheless, we believe that, since both fields are closely interrelated, this chapter offers a useful contribution toward evaluating a hyperdocument insofar as link reuse is concerned, and it can therefore help improve the quality of a hyperdocument, with obvious benefits to computer-human interaction. Indeed, the exercise of blending these two fields has been gaining increased interest on the part of the HCI community as can be seen, for instance, in (Yamada 95).

The systematic link reuse approach to hyperdocument analysis, its formalisation and its implementation were carried out already with WWW applications in mind. The project this chapter describes was proposed and designed for the analysis of WWW hyperdocument applications. It was assumed, right from the inception of this study, that a hyperdocument in its HTML description would be the main focus of the project, considering we were mainly concerned with the improvement of its structure. Thus, as far as the Web Browser Case Study is concerned, we do not have much to add to what we have pointed out earlier, that is: by improving the hyperdocument structure, we indirectly improve its visualisation and other features that a Browser can make available.

In order to evaluate its contribution, the LiOS tool was experimentally used in two different sites. The hyperdocument of one site (Instituto de Ciências Matemáticas de São Carlos - Universidade de São Paulo, site *http://www.icmsc.sc.usp.br*) is identified in this work as ICMSC-site and the hyperdocument of the other site (Instituto de Física de São Carlos - Universidade de São Paulo, site *http://www.ifsc.sc.usp.br*) as IFSC-site. We would like to point out that LiOS is currently operating with a specified set of hyperdocuments, i.e., it uses only "local" links of a certain site. In order to deal with links from more than one site, the tool must be adjusted to accept the other site's address as a parameter.

Both Websites used in our experiment can be considered "good" hyperdocuments for checking the link reuse approach, mainly due to the fact that:

- they have several webmasters; pages can be created and maintained by the administrative staff, lecturers, researchers and students. Since some of the webmasters are students, responsibility for the management of the whole hyperdocument frequently changes over from one person to another;
- the volume of nodes and links in these webs are considerable, reaching the thousands;
- the ICMSC-site and the IFSC-site were created in mid-1994 and are among the first produced in Brazil;
- the information available in both hyperdocuments is quite heterogeneous and, despite the fact that some of the basic information is kept permanently, they have been constantly altered by the inclusion/removal of nodes and links (temporary lectures, exercises, manuals, etc.).

The main goal in conducting a few empirical experiments was to gather data to support the research and analysis of reuse cases in order to get feedback concerning the applicability and usefulness of the approach implemented by LiOS. The whole experiment intended, as well, to compare the evolution of reuse cases over a period of time, in an attempt to discover a possible bias in hyperdocument maintenance procedures.

Data was collected on three different occasions (September-95, November-95 and July-96) from the ICMSC-site, and are referred to in this work as ICMSC/Sep-95, ICMSC/Nov-95 and ICMSC/July-96 respectively, and on just one occasion (July-96) from the IFSC-site, which is referred to in this work as IFSC/July-96.

Table 3 shows the counts obtained from queries about the incidence of links in each of the reuse cases identified previously. The results reveal important information about how links have been used in both hyperdocuments. For a better understanding of the data presented in Table 3, some conventions must be explained:

- the value of R represents the total of distinct occurrences of links in each relation resulting from a query in SQL. It corresponds to the value returned by the function COUNT( ), which counts the number of registers in a table. More specifically, the value of R corresponds to the number of types of links which have a certain reuse (the type of reuse is defined by the grouping operator (*group by*) specified in the query);

- the number of effective links given by the value of L corresponds to the value returned by the function SUM( ), which adds up the number of incidences for each type of grouped link;
- to count the incidence of links belonging to each case we took into consideration the "subset" relation. By using this relation, one particular link can be seen as belonging to more than one case.

It should be noted that the percentages of all cases added up will not amount to 100%; this is because links are not considered exclusively as belonging to just one case. A certain node can play the role of source node in different types of links. Only the set of incidences of links classified as case 7 does not contain any of the other sets of links (associated with other cases). All the other cases, from 0 to 6, can either contain or be contained in another case.

Observing the results in Figure 10, obtained from the data ICMSC/Sep-95, ICMSC/Nov-95 and ICMSC/July-96, we can see that the volume of links increased over time. Although it is rather premature to state that this tendency will always occur, informally it can be justified by noting that, after a while, authors gradually feel more confident and begin improving their documents by creating new links. A closer look at Figure 10 allows us to state that:

- The links classified as general links are the most common kind found in a hyperdocument structure;
- The links classified as unusual links (case 0 and case 7) are those which would rarely be found in a hyperdocument structure. Nevertheless, the number of such links was greater than expected; this may be due to the fact that many nodes, mainly in the ICMSC-USP-WWW, resemble very long textual documents full of cross references;
- The contextual links (case 1, 2, 5 and 6) are the least common cases expected to be found among the links. Despite this fact, however, two opposing tendencies can be observed in regard to their use:
  - ⇒ Where "modularity" is concerned, the reuse of objects (nodes or pages) is a very important and emphasised practice. In the context of modularity, therefore, an increase of contextual links suggests a "possibly good" hyperdocument when used in an appropriate way.
  - ⇒ Since contextual links somehow promote ambiguity and/or inconsistency, there is a tendency for this kind of link to be avoided and consequently, for its frequency to decrease. Thus, the decrease in the number of contextual links may be evidence that the team of authors has been concerned with the quality of the hyperdocument.

case	ICMSC-site September/95	ICMSC-site November/95	ICMSC-site July/96	IFSC-site July/96
	2,334 links 1,406 nodes	2,433 links 1,419 nodes	8,066 links 1,201 nodes	3,255 links 546 nodes
0	R=19 L=19 (0.81%)	R=18 L=18 (0.74%)	R=26 L=26 (0.32%)	R=46 L=46 (1.41%)
1	R=127 L=413 (17.69%)	R=118 L=361 (14.77%)	R=426 L=1,583 (19.62%)	R=135 L=503 (15.45%)
2	R=89 L=281 (12.03%)	R=83 L=196 (8.02%)	R=356 L=1,198 (14.85%)	R=101 L=362 (11.12%)
3	R=227 L=649 (27.80%)	R=261 L=712 (29.14%)	R=1,076 L=3,541 (43.9%)	R=348 L=1,200 (36.86%)
4	R=155 L=1,674 (71,72%)	R=169 L=1,735 (71.01%)	R=801 L=7,117 (88.23%)	R=339 L=2,678 (82.27%)
5	R=86 L=216 (9.25%)	R=82 L=209 (8.55%)	R=165 L=358 (4.43%)	R=93 L=217 (6.67%)
6	R=29 L=182 (7.79%)	R=16 L=150 (6.13%)	R=55 L=257 (3.18%)	R=36 L=76 (2.33%)
7	R=34 L=140 (5.99%)	R=36 L=145 (5.93%)	R=83 L=244 (3.02%)	R=26 L=54 (1.66%)

Table 3: Counts from queries about the incidence of links of each one of the reuse cases of link components — experiments with ICMSC-USP and IFSC-USP WWW servers

What can be stated from those two opposing views is that an increase or decrease in the number of contextual links is inconclusive and that additional information must be provided in order to be able to make a conclusive statement about the quality of the hyperdocument, as far as link analysis is concerned.

It is worth mentioning that the empirical results obtained, i.e., the percentage of link cases, were presented to the webmasters in order to get some feedback about the relevance of those numbers. Their comments lead us to conclude that some problems at a website can be detected with the tool. According to them, for example:

- "— Many **case 0** links were detected due to the fact that a hypertext in HTML has only unidirectional links. As pages are presented by systems which have backtrack buttons, like Mosaic and Netscape, many of them do not have any backtrack link and therefore they have no reuse. Generally speaking, however, those occurrences are avoided."

- "— Many **case 1** links could be redefined for the sake of uniformity and could, consequently, be "transformed" into case 3 links. Nevertheless, few of those links were created deliberately to reuse the contents of destination pages."

- "— The reuse of link names (source-anchors) as seen in **case 2** is very practical to indicate a sequential direction; this is typical when the author wants the reader to follow a certain pre-defined "path" (e.g. classroom notes). On the other hand, when the hyperdocument is read looking for a specific piece of information, this kind of reuse can cause disorientation."

- "— The more **case 3** links there are the better, because this implies uniformity of terms."

- "— The high occurrence of **case 4** links is due to index-pages. It would be very interesting to perform a study concerning the rate of distribuition of links in relation to the number of distinct records."

- "— The use of different links on the same pages should be avoided. Many of the existing occurrences of cases such as **case 5** links come from newcomers who use the WWW to exchange information."

- "— It seems that **case 6** links are a consequence of the direct transcription of texts into hyperdocuments; the hyperdocument often inherits the reuse of words from the original text (which employs reuse in order to prevent word overload)."

- "— **Case 7** links are generally avoided when identical links are close together on the page in order to prevent a "polluted" document. Case 7 links usually happen in hyperdocuments which originate from printed manuals; the long pages in the hyperdocument reflect the pages of the manual printed on paper."

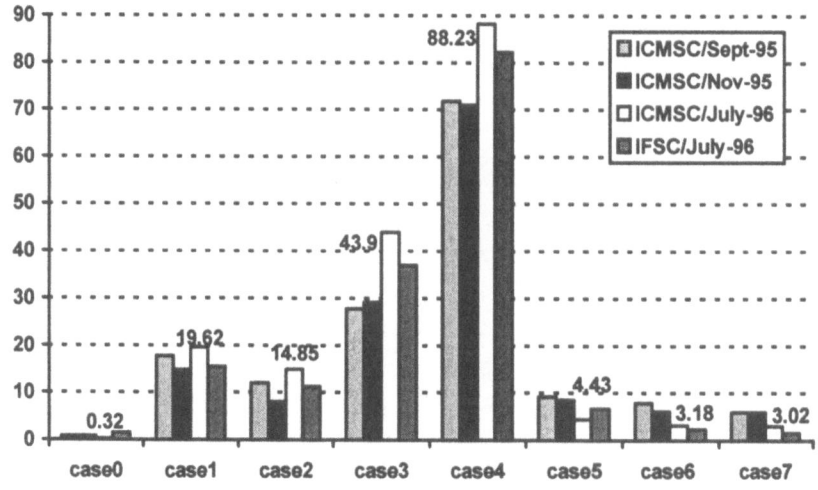

Figure 10: Percentage of links per case

7. Conclusions

This paper describes a link-oriented approach which has been used for webmasters to peruse the consistency of components in links. The formalisation of this approach is also presented. We have also shown how a classification of reuse of link components was systematically created. The main conclusion we have reached so far is that the identification of virtual structures and their formalisation has provided the authorship process with several alternatives for reorganising a hyperdocument.

The main goal of the work described in this paper was to provide means to help a hyperdocument writer to produce and maintain a consistent document. We believe that, by identifying the virtual structures, the author will have alternative views for reorganising the hyperdocument so as to avoid ambiguity and improve navigation. This would contribute to the improved use of the available hypermedia application structures. Use of the framework enables the author to evaluate the organisation, style and uniformity of the hyperdocument he/she is creating.

Also presented herein is the LiOS tool used for analysing the structure of link connections among documents on a Web server. LiOS aims to provide help to authors in correcting possible structural problems detected among Web pages.

As for future work, we intend to provide mechanisms for identifying the semantic network associated with the hyperdocument structure by expressing its underlying organisation, using virtual structures.

Acknowledgements

This research was partially supported by FAPESP and CNPq (ProTeM III-CC).

Chapter 5:
Using Declarative Descriptions to Model User Interfaces with MASTERMIND

1. Model-Based User Interfaces

1.1 Motivation

MASTERMIND (MM) (Szekely et al. 95) is a research project in the area of model-based user interfaces. It is a joint effort of the Graphics, Visualization, and Usability Center (GVU) of the Georgia Institute of Technology (GT) and the Information Sciences Institute (ISI) of the University of Southern California. This chapter describes the model-based user-interface technology developed at GT and how it can be applied to designing a web browser.

Graphical user interfaces (GUIs) are difficult to construct and, consequently, suffer from high costs. The research question that MASTERMIND seeks to address is the extent to which automatic generation of GUIs from declarative descriptions can reduce costs and enforce design principles. If, in addition, the declarative descriptions are broken into separate components, called models, modularity of the specification is improved, and advanced features such as design critics, context sensitive help, and dynamic reconfiguration are enabled.

MASTERMIND supports designers. Their job is to design user interfaces for software systems. They may or may not participate in the design of the software systems themselves. There may be more than one designer, and the designers may be broken into teams. Furthermore, the teams may be divided along functional lines, with, for example, one team responsible for screen layout, one for dialogue, and one for application software. Multiple designers require modularization and integration. Given a declarative specification mechanism, this implies strong support for consistency checking among the parts of a design.

designer: someone who specifies or constructs user interfaces using MASTERMIND

Our customers produce user interfaces. MASTERMIND is designed to support the rapid production of high quality and powerful user interfaces. It can accomplish these goals because it is model-based.

model: a declarative specification of the structure and behaviour of a software component

Models are declarative because they do not contain procedural code (e.g., strands of C++ code). Instead, models contain descriptive statements at a high level of abstraction. An added benefit is that the declarative style enables inferencing about an interface, both at design time and when the interface is eventually used by its end users.

end user: the ultimate users of the interfaces constructed by MASTERMIND

MASTERMIND declarations can be both abstract, thereby supporting rapid development, and detailed, providing precise control of the behaviour of the interface being designed. That the models are declarative and modular enables inferencing at either UI generation time or at run-time. The inferencing mechanism supports design critics, thereby improving quality, and powerful run-time features such as context-sensitive help, thereby extending the capability of the interface being designed. Hence, MASTERMIND addresses its customer's requirements of productivity, power, and quality.

1.2 State of the Art

Schlungbaum and Elwert provide an examination of other model-based approaches to user-interface generation, the different models they use, and the interfaces generated from the models (Schlungbaum & Elwert 96) . In their examination, they distinguish the approaches with three main criteria:

- the notation used to express the models
- the run-time environment they provide
- the explicit use of dialogue modelling

The notations that these systems use are often developed for the individual system. A number of groups have developed systems to use well-known software engineering notations. Sometimes these systems provide their own run-time support to control and execute the interface, while other systems only produce a description of an interface to then be used by other user interface management systems (UIMS).

UIDE (Foley & Sukaviriya 95) uses its own notation to declare a model of the application tasks to control the interface and an interface model to describe operations and constraints on application-independent tasks. These models are also used to generate run-time context-sensitive help automatically in the UIDE run-time environment. UIDE does not use explicit dialogue but rather relies on the use of preconditions and postconditions to sequence activity.

HUMANOID (Szekely et al. 93) uses a declarative language to express application semantics, presentation, input gestures and results, constraints on the ordering of commands and inputs, and side-effects of user actions. Presentation and gestures are defined using templates, whereas the dialogue constraints are derived from the application semantics. HUMANOID also provides a run-time system to control the designed interface.

MECANO (Puerta 96) also provides its own language (MIMIC) to define models of the type of users, the tasks and goals of the user, the domain that the user can affect by means of the interface, the presentation of the interface, and the dialogue between user and interface. These models are used by their own run-time system to generate and control the interface.

TRIDENT (Bodart et al. 95) , GENIUS (Janssen et al. 93) and JANUS (Balzert et al. 96) all take a different approach in that they use software engineering notation for their models. Specifically, TRIDENT uses Activity Chaining Graphs and Entity-Relationship diagrams to express user tasks and sequencing information. GENIUS uses an existing data model to define views that are used by Dialogue Nets and for layout generation, whereas JANUS interfaces are generated by the application of knowledge-base information to the results of object-oriented analysis. All three of these systems also generate a text description of the interface to be used by an existing UIMS.

TADEUS (Schlungbaum & Elwert 96) uses models of the task, problem domain, and user to specify the requirements for a user interface. A dialogue model is then developed from those three domain models, describing both the static layout and dynamic behaviour of the system. These four models are then used to automatically generate an interface along with some additional information supplied by the designer.

While these systems are almost evenly split on whether they develop their own notation and their own run-time environment, only MECANO and TADEUS use an explicit dialogue model. MASTERMIND also includes an explicit Dialogue Model believing that such information will help generate better and easier-to-use interfaces.

2. The MASTERMIND Conceptual Architecture

2.1 MASTERMIND Models

MASTERMIND supports the automatic construction of user interfaces from declarative models. Three types of models are currently supported: the Presentation Model, the Dialogue Model, and the Interaction Model. (See Figure 1.) In addition, a user-interface state model (the Context Model) is now being designed. Furthermore, the interface between the user interface and the application must be specified by the designer. Because this application interface specification (the Application Wrapper) does not specify any semantics, it is not a full-blown model. Nevertheless, it serves an essential role in the overall design of the user interface.

2.1.1 The presentation model

The Presentation Model (PM) describes the constructs that can appear on an end user's display and the dependencies among them. It is being developed by our colleagues at ISI. A brief summary is presented in the Sidebar: The ISI Presentation Model.

2.1.2 The dialogue model

The Dialogue Model (DM) describes the various low-level input activities that may be performed by the end user during the course of using a MASTERMIND-generated UI. The model also includes the relative orderings of the activities and the resulting effects they have on the presentation and the application.

2.1.3 The interaction model

The Interaction Model (IM) specifies the set of possible low-level interactions between the end user and the MM run-time environment. The set is determined by the underlying toolkit technology with which MM code is generated. Moreover, an interaction's primary value is in specifying communication from the end user to the other components of MM. We think of this communication as being *tight* in the sense that efficiency concerns are paramount. Specifically, we want to take advantage of underlying toolkit interactors to implement the interaction. And the interaction is atomic in the sense that no MM dialogue reasoning is used to affect the interaction.

interactor: one of a fixed set of toolkit software devices for communicating end-user actions to MM

2.1.4 The application wrapper

The fourth component that we use is called the Application Wrapper (AW). It specifies the interface between MM and the application functionality. The Wrapper is specified using IDL, the interface definition language for the CORBA distributed computing environment (Corba 91). The Application Wrapper specification includes method signatures and data item declarations for features that the application makes accessible to the UI. Because names and types are specified but semantics are not, the AW does not qualify as a MM model. Nevertheless, it provides an essential piece of the declarative description from which a MM UI is generated.

2.1.5 The context model

An important, but not yet developed, part of the MM conceptual architecture is the Context Model (CM). This model describes designer-specified state information of which the UI must be aware. For example, if it is possible for an end user to select a particular visible item and if it is important for the selected item to be visually highlighted, then it may be useful to define a Context item corresponding to *currently selected item*.

2.1.6   Other models

The MM run-time architecture supports any number of cooperating models. Among those we think promising to eventually explore are a user model (e.g. novice or expert), a toolkit model (the underlying UI software for managing the screen and capturing end-user actions), a display-device model (enabling intelligent screen real-estate management), and the evolution of the Application Wrapper into a first- class model.

2.2   The Ontology of MASTERMIND Models

The MASTERMIND model ontology is influenced by two ideas. The first is programming language design, which provides foundations for any modelling process. The second is object-oriented user-interface toolkit technology, which provides abstractions and control mechanisms.

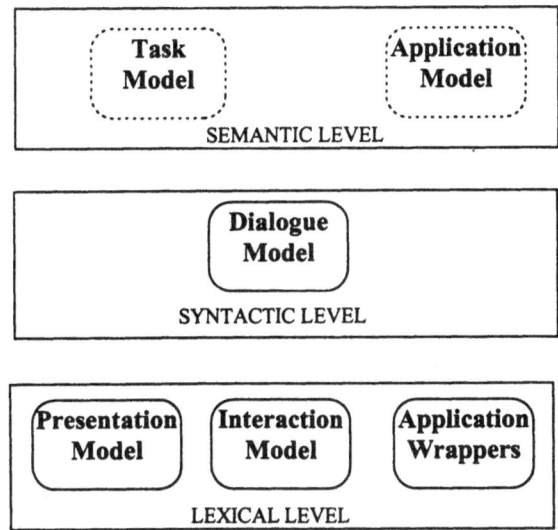

Figure 1: Models in MASTERMIND

ontology: a description (like a formal specification of a program) of the concepts and relationships that can exist for an agent or a community of agents (Gruber 96)

Interface design is analogous to programming language design (Foley & van Dam 95). Interfaces can be thought of as being composed of two languages: one in which the end user communicates to the computer, and one in which the computer communicates to the end user. The act of engineering interfaces can be therefore thought of as the simultaneous design of these two languages. Independent of this is the emergence of new abstractions in the object-oriented user-interface toolkit community (Myers 90, Myers et al. 90, Myers et al. 92). Two constructs, constraints and interactors, permit sufficiently declarative models to instantiate the design ontology and compile into executable code.

constraint: a declarative software device for enforcing dependencies among components of a UI

The language analogy suggests applying the phases of programming language design to the simultaneous design of the input and output languages. There are three phases in this process: semantic, syntactic, and lexical design.

2.2.1 Semantic design

Semantics refers to the meaning or intentions of the end user. Users of interactive systems form mental models that help them organise activity and navigate through the system. User task analysis (Diaper 89) is applied to codify a system at this level. The MASTERMIND task model represents mental models as a collection of hierarchical user tasks. This conceptual model is refined into a detailed semantic model of the system by incorporating the functional requirements of the application, as shown in Figure 1.

A detailed semantic model relates user intentions to application actions and results. Unfortunately, this information does not completely specify a user interface. In HTA (Diaper 89), for example, user tasks are recorded in natural language, as opposed to a language with a machine interpretation. Furthermore, task models tend to be optimistic, assuming that users will always complete the tasks that they begin. For these reasons, we may not use task and application models as programs to be compiled by a code generator. Rather, designers will complete the interface specification by refining these models into more concrete models, which we classify *syntactic* and *lexical*. Code generators then synthesise the concrete models into a running application.

2.2.2 Syntactic design

Forms in the syntactic model represent procedures that, when executed, cause some semantically prescribed effect to occur. The primary difference between syntactic and semantic models is that syntactic models are specified procedurally (as an ordered series of steps); whereas semantic models are non-procedural (declarative). Dialogue techniques are syntactic; whereas the user tasks that these dialogue techniques are employed to accomplish are semantic.

2.2.3 Lexical design

A lexical model, describing low-level tokens, is defined alongside the syntactic model. For the input language, these tokens include keystrokes, mouse clicks, or mouse motion. For the output language, these tokens include output characters, beeps, or graphical widgets. Sometimes lexical tokens are organized into *gestures*.

gesture: a stereotypical sequence of end-user input actions such as clicking on an object and then moving the mouse

MASTERMIND models address the syntactic and lexical levels. The language analogy, while conceptually elegant, is not feasible if the lexical level embodies keystroke level input events and atomic output events like beeps, or flashes. This is analogous to a compiler whose lexical analyser feeds single characters to its parser. Lessons learned from compiler theory show that single characters are inappropriate tokens because they inject too much complexity into the corresponding parsers. To see how this problem manifests itself in UI design, consider a drag-and-drop interface. A burst of activity begins with an end user clicking down on an icon. Immediately a shadow icon appears, and as the end user moves the mouse, the shadow icon changes its position on the screen. The burst of activity ends when the end user releases the mouse button signifying a drop over some other icon. If we consider each mouse move event and icon redraw to be tokens, then the syntactic description of drag-and-drop is extremely complex. Compiler theory suggests that we simplify this problem by making tokens more abstract than just mere input and output events. In compilers, tokens embody patterns of input characters. Lexical UI design should, therefore, identify patterns of input-output events and treat these patterns as tokens. User-computer interfaces are characterised by bursts of tight, high-volume, feedback-intensive, input-output event sequences, and these sequences can be described by patterns. To represent lexical patterns, we pull ideas from object-oriented UI toolkits.

Object-oriented toolkits like Garnet (Myers et al. 90) and Amulet (Myers et al. 95) provide interactors that encapsulate these tight input-output protocols into implemented units that may be selected from a library and specialised to a particular use. In both toolkits, the number of interactors is fixed and relatively small. The MASTERMIND Interaction Model is an abstraction of interactors, and we consider it a lexical model. As another example, consider how window sizes might need to change dynamically to accommodate the insertion or deletion of graphical objects. Object-oriented toolkits use constraints to declare that an object's attributes should be dynamically recomputed when another object's attributes change. This mechanism abstracts away a great deal of sequencing that would otherwise have to be implemented in the two languages. The MASTERMIND Presentation Model allows designers to use constraints when specifying presentation layout, and we consider it a lexical model. The final lexical specification is the MASTERMIND Application Wrapper. The AW is currently nothing more than an application program interface (API) for invoking behaviour in a (possibly distributed) application. Treating it at the lexical level allows us to consider method invocations as tokens.

The syntactic component of design is captured by one MASTERMIND model, the Dialogue Model. Syntactic models abstract a meaningful ordering structure over tokens described in the lexical models. In programming languages, syntactic models are usually specified by context-free grammars whose terminal symbols correspond to tokens in a lexical model. Unfortunately, there are ordering mechanisms in dialogue models that are not expressible using context free grammars. The essence of grammars, however, is hierarchical ordering constraints over tokens. The MASTERMIND Dialogue Model declares hierarchical ordering constraints over Interaction tokens.

In MASTERMIND, task organisation and application functionality are semantic concepts. Interaction, presentation, and application invocation are lexical concepts, and dialogue is a syntactic concept. These models must precisely define the input and output languages and express their interleaving.

3. The UI Generation Process

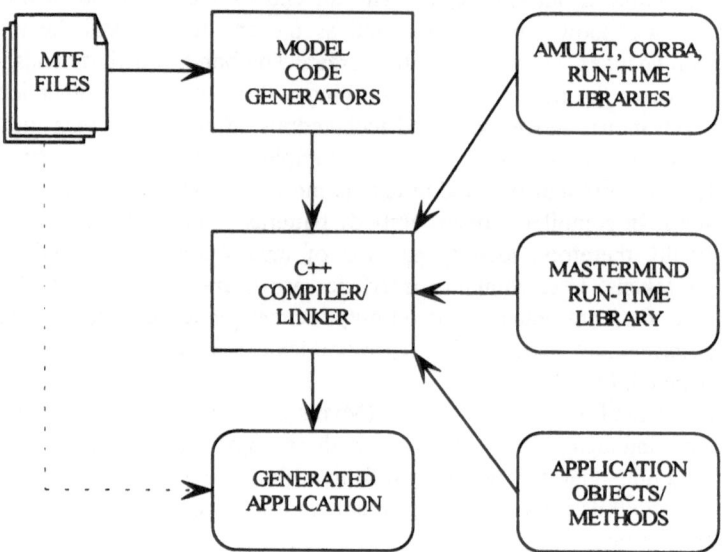

Figure 2: The MASTERMIND UI generation process

MASTERMIND tools synthesise user interfaces from three distinct models of UI behaviour. To go from models to executable code, MM employs model-specific code generators. Each code generator outputs C++ source files which are then compiled and linked with a number of run-time libraries. Because there are necessarily dependencies among models, model instances must refer to elements of other model instances. We use the MASTERMIND textual format (MTF), a frame-based notation, for expressing instances of models in the ontologies (Presentation, Dialogue, and Interaction). This process is depicted in Figure 2. Note that the only files a user must edit are the MTF files. The dashed line connecting the MTF files to the generated application indicates that the MTF models are used at run-time (e.g., to support context-sensitive help).

The MASTERMIND architects have defined the ontology for each model, in a second notation called the MASTERMIND representation language (MRL), to be a set of classes with attributes. Each class has a fixed number of attributes, and each attribute has a fixed type (class). In an ontology, classes are related by subclass inheritance, meaning that if class *A* contains two attributes *foo* and *bar*, a class *B* subclassed from *A* contains two attributes named *foo* and *bar* of the same type in *A* and any additional attributes declared specific to *B*. Subclass inheritance governs relative names and types of attributes, not their values.

MASTERMIND architect: one who defines model ontologies

Designers who build models in the ontologies specify instances of these classes. These instances are called *objects*, and MTF provides a mechanism called prototype-instantiation that creates a new object (called an instance) from a prototype by copying all of the attributes of the prototype into the instance. When attributes of a prototype object change, the corresponding attributes of instances of the prototype object change accordingly. For this reason, we call prototype-instantiation another form of inheritance. Whereas subclass inheritance relates name and type of attributes; prototype inheritance relates values of attributes in different objects.

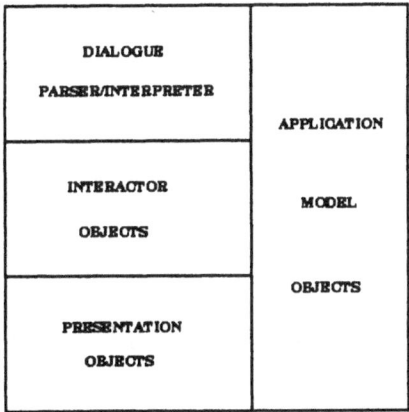

Figure 3: The MASTERMIND run-time architecture

Occasionally, designers will want to subvert the prototype-instance relation. This is done by explicitly overriding an inherited attribute with a new value or expression. Overriding is particularly useful for specialising behaviour. As designers gain experience in defining and using models, we expect them to build new interfaces by instantiating objects from old interfaces and overriding a few attributes to fit these objects into the new context.

In addition to prototype-instance inheritance, MTF allows attribute values to be specified as *formulas,* computing one attribute value from the values of other attributes. Our code generators translate formulas into code that maintains the run-time consistency of the attribute values under dependent attribute modification. The Presentation Model code generator, for example, translates formulas into constraints which are kept consistent by a run-time object system. The Interaction code generator, on the other hand, translates formulas into methods and adds calls to these methods at appropriate points in the code generated from other models.

Generated applications are cast onto the run-time architecture depicted in Figure 3. The architecture has features reminiscent of the Seeheim (Pfaff & ten Hagen 85, Bass et al. 91) model, and object-oriented models like PAC (Coutaz 87). Like both PAC and Seeheim, dialogue control is separated from presentation and application functionality. Dialogue, presentation and interactors may directly observe the application state, but only the dialogue component may effect a change in the application. In contrast with Seeheim, the MASTERMIND architecture rejects a rigid boundary between dialogue and presentation in favour of a more fluid boundary, constituted by interactor objects. Interactor objects encapsulate tight protocols of dialogue state, application state, user input, and presentation feedback.

4. The MASTERMIND Dialogue Notation

The MASTERMIND Dialogue Notation allows designers to specify the permissible ordering of the end-user interactions that carry out some task. The notation described below is textual. In Section 2 a graphical design tool is described that provides an alternative notation. A dialogue model is an expression in this notation, and a dialogue parser is a computational mechanism generated from a dialogue model. This relationship between model and parser is similar to that between a context-free grammar and its associated parser. Elements of dialogue models are called *symbols* and may be either tokens or variables.

A dialogue entity that the designer distinguishes in the Dialogue Model is called a *dialogue symbol*. Dialogue symbols are given names and other attributes and are either tokens or variables. A *dialogue token* is a terminal symbol that represents either an application invocation or a user interaction. A *dialogue variable* is a non-terminal symbol that represents an ordered aggregate of other symbols. Variables are related to these other symbols by production rules.

4.1 Dialogue Tokens: Interaction-Application Invocation

End-user interactions and application invocations are the tokens accepted by the dialogue parser. Think of them as being leaves in a parse tree. Application invocation tokens are specialised with the information that MASTERMIND needs to invoke a computational service when this token is expected to occur during execution. Interaction tokens represent notification by an interaction technique specified in the Interaction Model.

interaction technique: a construct that "implements the hardware binding portion of a user-computer interface design" (Foley & van Dam 95)

When an interaction token is expected, the associated interactor is enabled. When an interactor is enabled, it may accept device input and notify a dialogue token. If, on the other hand, this token is no longer expected by the dialogue (perhaps because an alternative was selected) then the interactor associated with this input is disabled. When an interactor is disabled, it may not accept device input. When an interactor notifies a dialogue token, the dialogue parser considers this token to be accepted.

4.2 Dialogue Variables: Composite Ordering

The Dialogue Model allows designers to organise tokens using a declarative mechanism similar to production rules in context-free grammars. The most common form of ordering in this language is achieved by declaring an ordering (i.e., temporal) invariant over a sequence of subdialogue symbols. MASTERMIND supports five such invariants, each denoted by an operator: **alt** (alternative), **seq** (sequential), **par** (parallel), **excl** (exclusive execution), and **until** (execute until).

We chose this particular set of orderings over others because they represent distinct points in a two-dimensional design space of control regimens. The first dimension captures ordering policy; whereas the second captures preemption. MASTERMIND supports three ordering policies: sequential, alternative, and unconstrained. The sequential policy imposes a linear ordering, the alternative policy imposes an exclusive (choose-one) ordering, and the unconstrained policy imposes a "do all" ordering but does not specify a relative ordering among the constituent sub-dialogues. Our first interpretation of the alternative ordering policy, for example, deduced the user's choice of subtask from the first recognised interaction with any subtask. That is, if the user is faced with choosing from among three subtasks T1, T2, and T3, and he or she performs an interaction within T2, we deduce that T2 was the choice and disable tasks T1 and T3. The **alt** operator implements this behaviour.

The second dimension in our design space specifies operators which simplify the declaration of preemptive behaviour. Preemptive operators allow user actions to signify the premature interruption of a sub-dialogue. Internet browser interfaces must provide support for preemption, because some operations, like loading a distant URL, may consume more time than a user will allow. The STOP button and the ability to click on a new link before a page has completed loading, both demonstrate preemptive behaviour. The MASTERMIND operators **until**, and **excl** are preemptive variants of **seq** and **alt**, respectively. The declaration **until (T1, T2)** is the same as the declaration **seq (T1, T2)** with one important difference. In the latter declaration, the dialogue T2 is not enabled until T1 has completed. In the former declaration, however, T2 is enabled for the duration of T1, and if the system detects activity in T2 before T1 completes, T1 is terminated. Similarly, the declaration of **excl (T1, T2)** is the same as the declaration **alt (T1, T2)** with one important difference. In the latter case, activity within T1 disables T2. In the former case, however, both T1 and T2 remain enabled until one or the other completes. If activity is observed in T1 and activity is later observed in T2 before T1 is completed, T1 is terminated and reenabled from the beginning.

	Sequential	Alternative	Unconstrained
Non-preemptive	seq	alt	par
Preemptive	until	excl	par

Figure 4: Dialogue Model design space

Designers may specify tasks to be either optional or repeatable. In either case there are two possible agents who may choose whether to execute the optional task or repeat the repeatable task. These agents are the end user and the environment. We see the agent of choice as being independent of the nature of the ordering and so define four possible combinations, as shown in Figure 5.

	User Choice	Environment Choice
Optional	opt	cond
Repeatable	loop	while

Figure 5: Dialogue Model choice operators

The vertical dimension specifies optional behaviour. The designer could allow an end user to optionally execute a task, that is, to skip the task or execute it only once. Alternatively, the designer could allow the end user to skip the task, or execute the task once and then repeat the whole process. These alternatives correspond to the distinction between conditional statements and loops in programming languages. The horizontal dimension specifies the agent that enacts the optional behaviour. The agent could be the end user or it could be the application. When the end user is the agent, the optional tasks have behaviour that is non-essential to the accomplishment of the goal. For example, a mail tool allows you to enter a subject for a message, but does not require it. When the machine is the agent, however, the method of achieving the goal changes in response to the condition of the external environment.

4.3 Data Parameters

Because dialogue has the responsibility of sequencing interactions and application invocations, dialogue productions are a natural place for the transfer of data from the user into the application methods. Furthermore, the hierarchical nature of dialogue models gives rise to a convenient lexical scoping for temporary data variables. For the sake of consistency in model naming, we call these local variables data parameters. The designer may introduce zero or more data parameters with any dialogue symbol. Data parameters may be initialised, and sub-dialogue symbols may see and modify the parameters of their ancestors in the hierarchy. Data parameters may be modified either by an interaction technique binding (discussed in Section 5.2) or by an *effect*, which is a declarative specification of the state of the dialogue after the activity associated with a dialogue symbol completes. Likewise, data parameters may be used by interaction techniques, supplied as parameters to application methods, or occur in dialogue-symbol-enabling preconditions. We do not use preconditions or effects in the web browser example, and so do not expand upon these topics here.

4.4 Dialogue Validation

Dialogue models specify the legal orderings of user and system interactions. We implement Dialogue Models by generating a component called a dialogue parser. The parser maintains a running representation of the current dialogue state, dynamically computing the set of interactions legal in this state, and enabling only the interactors associated with this set. Generating a parser automatically from a hierarchical dialogue specification is complicated by the fact that the language associated with hierarchical dialogue specifications is not context free. We solved this problem by identifying a set of hierarchical temporal operators and building canonical state machines that, when connected according to a dialogue hierarchy, enforce the intent of each operator. The state machines are complex, and we employed a technique called symbolic model checking (McMillan 92) to validate them against a set of desired behaviours. This degree of confidence is a direct benefit of the model-based approach. The technology allowed us to confidently create a dialogue parser generator, and we expect it will also be useful for driving dialogue debugging tools.

Sidebar: The ISI Presentation Model

The MASTERMIND Presentation Model (Szekely et al. 95) was developed at ISI. Though thorough coverage is not provided in this chapter, the following summary is intended to provide sufficient background to understand the web browser case study described below.

Presentation Models are declared as a hierarchical collection of method-less objects whose attributes are related by formulas. These model objects are translated into run-time objects with special attributes called *slots*. Run-time slots store values that may be set in one of two different ways. An external agent may physically place a value into a slot, or a slot value may change automatically in response to changes in other slot values. The mechanism that enforces the latter behaviour is a constraint. Presentation Models have a declarative mechanism called an *expression* that establishes inter-attribute dependencies. These expressions are translated into run-time constraints. In addition to establishing dependencies among Presentation-Model object attributes, expressions may also establish dependencies upon application-object attributes. Expressions, therefore, are the mechanism for Presentation–Application binding. They represent an adequate communication mechanism for the Presentation Model and the Application Wrapper because the flow of information is always one-way, from the Application Wrapper to the Presentation Model.

5. Binding in MASTERMIND Models

The example in the sidebar describes communication between the Application Wrapper and the Presentation Model. This straightforward communication mechanism is not sufficient for the general case of inter-model communication. The communication between the Presentation and Interaction Models, for example, involves a two way communication that is an example of inter-model *binding*.

binding: the process by which a designer specifies the occurrence of a specific inter-model dependency

Binding relates elements and behaviours of one model to elements and behaviours of another. The binding problem occurs in any multi-model system, and it occurs between any pair of related models. Binding is generally difficult because models might have different mechanisms for composing model elements, and a binding must respect each mechanism in order to be used correctly. This unfortunate property can lead to inelegant and technically esoteric binding strategies, and it precludes any hope of a universal binding notation. The MASTERMIND approach fits a custom binding strategy to each configuration of interdependent MASTERMIND models. Currently there are only four such configurations: Presentation-Interaction, Presentation-Application, Dialogue-Application, and Dialogue-Interaction.

Presentation-Interaction cooperation comprises a high volume of tightly synchronised input and output activities. Interactors field user input events, decide what purpose they represent and set Presentation slots as appropriate. Interactor objects are the run-time images of design-time abstractions called interaction techniques. The manifestation of a binding between interaction techniques and Presentation Models is an attachment of interactor objects to run-time Presentation-object slots. Details of these bindings are declared in the Interaction Model. Designers, when specialising interaction techniques to a particular application, give the name of objects or attributes that instantiate the technique. The Interaction Model translator then uses this information to build an interactor object and attaches it to the appropriate run-time Presentation objects.

The binding of Presentation and Application models is one-way only; information flows from Application-Wrapper objects into the presentation. Method invocation is declared in the Dialogue Model and represents a binding of Dialogue Model and Application Wrapper. This binding is accomplished at design time by associating a token with the methods that need to be called. As suggested by the programming language analogy of Section 2, as parse state (dialogue state) changes at run time, tokens may become expected. When this occurs, corresponding methods are invoked, and the symbols are considered matched. The binding of data flowing into and returning from a method call is accomplished using a data parameter.

The Dialogue Model distinguishes two classes of tokens. One represents application invocation and the other user interaction. Associating dialogue terminals with user interactions is a binding of the Dialogue Model to the Interaction Model. As with Presentation-Interaction bindings, the specification of Dialogue-Interaction binding is a specification of dialogue terminal obligations.

5.1 The MASTERMIND Interaction Model

Presentation and Dialogue Models do not directly model end-user input. MASTERMIND defines input in a separate Interaction Model. The Interaction Model ontology appeals to the influence of input on model binding and the mutually exclusive nature of interactions.

Interaction techniques implement the hardware binding portion of interface design. MM interactions abstract this definition to the binding of input-event sequences with Presentation, Dialogue, and Application Model behaviour. The ternary nature of these bindings makes them difficult to delegate to either the Dialogue or Presentation Model. The X Windows Xt toolkit, for example, employs widgets that invoke application callbacks when user events occur. For interactions like drag-and-drop, this approach necessarily scatters the implementation of the binding among all possible widgets that might participate. This is not only difficult to implement but also difficult for designers to reason about.

The Interaction Model ontology is organised into classes whose names mimic those of familiar interaction techniques. Attributes of these classes capture information needed to bring the design time binding to run-time fruition.

Interaction techniques represent natural dialogue tokens because they are logical end-user computer exchanges, and, due to mutual demands upon shared resources, because they tend not to be interleaveable. A shared resource in this context is an input device like a mouse, the keyboard focus, or voice input. For example, consider dragging and dropping one presentation object over another. MASTERMIND considers this one logical interaction. It cannot be interleaved with, say, clicking a button because during one or the other interaction the mouse is being used and cannot be relinquished temporarily to complete the other. Interactions encapsulate access to shared resources into atomic tokens that can be ordered according to the Dialogue Model. These interactions are complicated by the tight web of resource interdependencies that govern an interaction. A specific interaction might involve feedback to the end user, a commitment to a specific dialogue token, and communication with an Application Wrapper. The designer must understand how the pieces of these three components interact in order to specify the behaviour he or she has in mind.

Because interaction techniques naturally capture logical end-user interactions, and because they also localise complex multi-model dependencies, MASTERMIND allows designers to choose an interaction technique and then supply information that completes the binding of the three models according to the interaction protocol. For the direct manipulation example, the designer would choose a DragAndDrop interaction technique, supply the names of presentations to which it should apply, and supply the names of the dialogue tokens to notify when the interaction completes. Some interaction techniques may require a large number of designer-supplied parameters to complete the binding. This, unfortunately, gives the Interaction Model a synthetic feel, but we envision a tool that will allow designers to graphically attach interaction techniques to Dialogue and Presentation models so that many of these parameters may be inferred rather than explicitly supplied.

The Web Browser Case Study (presented in Section 7) uses two interaction techniques, Selection and FormBasedEntry, which we introduce here. Common to all techniques is the notion that they are enabled and disabled according to the state of dialogue objects. We define the super-class of all interaction techniques to capture this behaviour:

InteractionTechnique
   enable when [dialogue-symbol] **is** [dialogue-state].
   disable when [dialogue-symbol] **is** [dialogue-state].

The **enable:when:is:** statement identifies a dialogue symbol whose transition into dialogue-state enables this interaction technique. The **disable:when:is:** statement performs a similar function for disabling the technique. Though interaction techniques always activate dialogue tokens, the techniques themselves may be enabled and disabled by dialogue variables.

5.2 Selection Interaction Techniques

Myers (Myers et al. 96) distinguishes two kinds of selection. In one the user can mouse over the possible selections and observe interim feedback from the interface. This feedback identifies the selection that will be chosen should action be taken. In the other form, no such feedback is given. These two forms have different interaction protocols and different binding obligations. We therefore represent them in two separate interaction techniques: **OneShotSelection** and **InterimFeedbackSelection**. The binding obligation of selection techniques typically must associate Presentation entities with dialogue entities and possibly transfer some application-specific data in the process. We have observed that this association has two natural cardinalities. Either many presentations may be associated with a single dialogue token as in a drawing tool that allows the user to choose one of many presentations to delete, or presentations can be in one-to-one correspondence with dialogue tokens, as in an Email tool whose buttons denote different functions to perform. To capture this association, the Interaction Model provides designers with a template called a **PresentationDialogueAssociation** (PDAssoc). Selection interaction techniques are parameterized by this association. The two cardinalities have different features, and so we define two subclasses of **PDAssoc**: **OneToOnePDAssoc** and **ManyToOnePDAssoc**. The template for each appears below:

ManyToOnePDAssoc : PDAssoc
  choose [part-name] from [pres-group].
  within [dialogue-token] assign [dialogue-parameter] to [pres-datum].

This template assumes that many-to-one associations occur when the end user must select one from among many parts of a presentation group. The **choose:from:** statement identifies a group (**pres-group**) from which the end user will choose a part and gives this chosen part a name (**part-name**) which can be used in the **within:assign:to:** statement that follows. The latter statement identifies a dialogue token to be activated when the selection is made and allows the designer to bind some data from the presentation object (**pres-datum**) to a data parameter (**dialogue-parameter**) of the dialogue token. The **pres-datum** object is usually defined by means of a formula over the designated **part-name**. The code generator checks to make sure that the types of these entities are compatible.

OneToOnePDAssoc : PDAssoc
  assign [presentation-object] to [dialogue-token].
  within [dialogue-token] assign [dialogue-parameter] to [pres-datum].

The **OneToOne** association is similar to the **ManyToOne** except that the **choose:from:** statement is replaced by one or more **assign:to:** statements. The

assign:to: statement simply identifies dialogue tokens to notify when certain presentation objects are selected.

With this in place, the two selection techniques are simple to use:

OneShotSelectionInteraction : InteractionTechnique
    bind [PDAssoc].

InterimFeedbackSelectionInteraction : InteractionTechnique
    bind [PDAssoc].

Because each inherits from **InteractionTechnique**, they inherit the enable-disable syntax.

5.3 Form Entry Interaction Technique

Text entry interactions are abstracted into the more general interaction technique **FormBasedEntry**, which controls text entry with and without the support of application completion queries. The relevant attributes of this technique are listed below:

FormBasedEntry : InteractionTechnique
    notify [dialogue_token] upon [input_events]
    attach to [presentation]

    enable input when [dialogue_symbol] is [dialogue_state]
    disable input when [dialogue_symbol] is [dialogue_state]

Unlike the **Selection** technique, text entry has two logical interpretations for being enabled. Enabling could mean that it is legal for users to enter text into the field, or it might mean that it is legal for users to communicate a commitment of edited text to the system. In text entry, the user often communicates the commitment by hitting the return key. We allow designers to apply this distinction by providing two separate enable-disable specialisations, one for input and one for dialogue activation. Of course, the enabling for text entry and the enabling for commitment entry are often synonymous.

6. The MASTERMIND Design Method

Building a UI in MASTERMIND means constructing models. From the examples that we have tried, we are beginning to understand how best to go about this. Our current understanding forms the basis for a model-based user-interface design method. There are five components to an application system built using MASTERMIND. These components are distinguishable by what they are designed from and their corresponding position in the MASTERMIND design method.

- components designed from artifacts (AW, DM, PM)

- a component that binds other MASTERMIND components (IM)
- a component for shared data communication between all components (CM)

In MASTERMIND, there are three components which are relatively independent of each other, because they are designed not from other MASTERMIND models and bindings but rather from design artifacts. These components should be the first ones built in MASTERMIND, because of their close relationship to the design method, and because they can be designed independently of each other with little modification required for integration. This provides a design team with the ability to work on several components at the same time, with specialists devoted to each component.

These components are the Presentation Model (which is developed through prototyping or storyboarding), the Application Wrapper (developed from the application code), and the Dialogue Model (designed based on a formalised task analysis and specification). While some coordination in developing these components is required, such as common naming for application methods listed in the AW and invoked by the Dialogue Model, it is at a high level. A small amount of time spent during design to agree on the application and interface components and to application method and parameter names should be enough to allow the completion of these models independently so that little if any modification is required.

Once the Presentation, Application, and Dialogue components have all been designed, the next step is to build the components that are responsible for the binding and communication among them. The first step is the binding of the presentation to the behaviour of the system (its dialogue). That is the purpose of the interaction component. Because there is already an implied binding between the Dialogue Model and the Application Wrapper (through the use of a common naming convention for application methods), binding the Dialogue Model to the Presentation unites all of the components into a single system.

The final component that needs to be constructed is the Context Model. It is only after all of the other components are designed and integrated, that a designer can be certain of which additional information needs to be shared between components, what application data are reflected in the presentation or affects which action the user is capable of performing next. By waiting until all of the other components are designed to build this model, the amount of modification to any of the earlier components is minimised.

7. Case Study

7.1 Context: Web Browsers

While the relationship between MASTERMIND components can be examined in the abstract, it is more difficult to explain the actual method for designing the individual components in such a manner. For this reason, the development of individual components will be examined in the context of designing the user interface for a web browser.

First, a simple browser will be designed, capable of web navigation, saving pages to files, and printing a hardcopy of the page. This will not only demonstrate the process for designing MASTERMIND components, but will also show how the Application Wrapper, Dialogue Model and Presentation Model can be developed independently and how that provides flexibility for prototyping. In addition, it will demonstrate how MASTERMIND allows multiple interactions to accomplish the same task, and how different interactions can use the same application code to accomplish different goals.

Once the simple browser has been developed, a history mechanism will be added to the system to maintain a list of which web pages the user has visited and to offer operations such as traversing forwards and backwards through the list or jumping to any point in the list. This demonstrates how a MASTERMIND application can easily be modified and evolved over time.

7.2 Dialogue Model Example

For this example, assume that the following design specifications for the browser have been given. That is, the browser is to allow the end user to do the following:

- visit a new page by giving the URL
- go to a specified home page
- request a reload of the current page
- print a copy of the current page on a specified printer
- save a copy of the page to a specified filename
- stop any one of the previous actions at any time they are in progress
- quit the web browser at any time

The first step in the design method is to identify all of the operations that the end user can perform according to the specification, not how the user performs them or specifies them, but the actual functions they can perform. In this specification there are seven: open a new page, go to a home page, reload the current page, print a page, save a page, stop an action, and quit the application. Note that there is no differentiation between opening a page by name, or by following a link—that is a distinction of how the URL is provided, not whether one is specified, and so it is not a distinction made in the User-Task Model.

The next step is to determine how these operations are related to one another. (See Figure 6.) Because **Stop** can affect **Open, Home, Reload, Print** or **Save**, it suggests that those five actions should be related. Because we want the browser to be able to perform only one of these actions at a given time, and that once one of them is started, the other actions are no longer available, we use an **alt** ordering to organise these five operations together.

  Stop should be available whenever one of these five operations is being performed, and executing a **Stop** action should abort the current activity. This fits the idea of an **excl** ordering. **Stop** will be available until one of the other actions completes, but if **Stop** is activated, it will abort the current action. These pairings complete the basic navigation available to the browser.

The **Navigate** grouping, though, only allows one action to be completed. Because the browser allows any number of actions until the user decides to quit,

Navigate should be in an infinite **while** loop. This still allows **Stop** to abort any current action, but will then allow the user to choose a new action. **Quit** is then related to the ability to **Navigate** by another **excl** ordering. Because **Navigate** is an infinite loop, the only way the dialogue can terminate is through the **Quit** action. This analysis provides us with exactly the desired behaviour for the browser.

Finally, the implementation and behaviour of each of these actions needs to be defined. It would be easy to design **Quit, Stop, Home** and **Reload** all to be single application methods which get invoked; they need no other information from the system other than what the application would already have, therefore they are leaf nodes in the model.

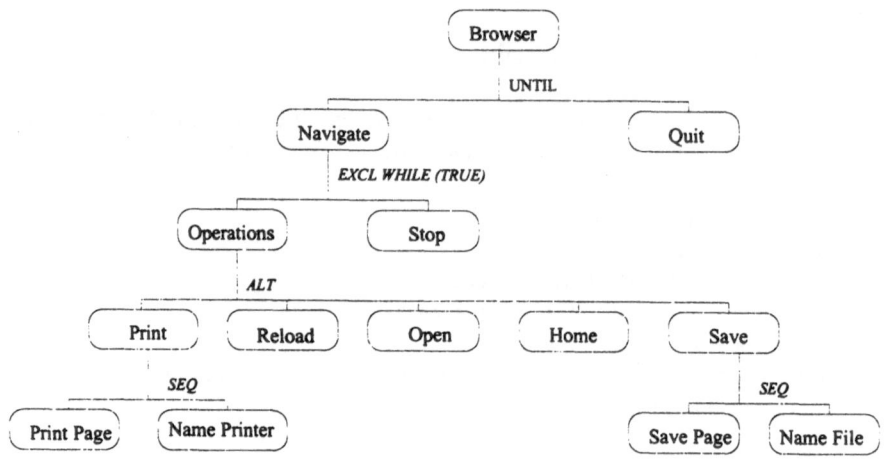

Figure 6: Dialogue Model for simple browsing

Open can also be defined as a single application method which takes a parameter indicating the URL of the page. This parameter needs to be determined in some manner (by user interaction), but no matter how the URL is determined, the behaviour is the same. For this reason, **Open** is also just a single node in the model.

There are two steps to either saving or printing the page. The first step is to express the intention to **Save** or **Print** the web page. The second step is to then determine the parameters required for the application. When saving a page, the parameters required for the application are the filename desired, and for printing a page, the name of the printer. Only after that information is obtained can the application method be invoked to accomplish this action. **Save** and **Print** therefore have a structure of having two children in a **seq** ordering. The first child is used to capture the intent to perform the action, while the second child obtains the parameter information from the end user and invokes the application method.

Of course **Save** and **Print** could be implemented as single actions depending on the style of the interface. For instance, if a list of printers was always displayed to the user, then choosing the printer might be a single action like **Open**. Providing such lists, though, clutters up the screen. It is more common that these features be provided only when the user expresses an interest in them, and this is the behaviour assumed in this model.

7.3 Presentation Model Example

Because presentation has been the focus of the work done by ISI, it is treated here only in the details that are necessary for the understanding of the other components of the system. For the presentation of a web browser, only a few presentation primitives are required: window, button, text field, and label. These are common forms of presentation, and so other details regarding them are ignored in this discussion.

A text field is used to represent the current URL of the browser, as well as being used to let the user enter a new URL. It only needs to be one line and to be editable by the user. Ignoring such considerations as the actual layout, it can be described by the following:

URL_field : Text_Field
visual_parameters
  editable = TRUE
layout_parameters
  width = 80
  lines = 1
  label = "URL:"

All of the remaining functions of the browser are to then be available either in the form of a button or by a choice from a menu. Menus are not yet one of the primitives supported. Menus are just a window which contains a collection of buttons. Recall that there is no behaviour or interaction attached to buttons, because they are purely a display notation.

The menu can be defined as follows:

Browser_Menu : Window
parts
  Home_item : Button
  Print_item : Button
  Reload_item : Button
  Save_item : Button
  Quit_item : Button

The browser itself is simple a window with a number of parts in it: the menu, the buttons, the URL text field, and a sub-window for the display of the page. So the entire presentation for the browser (other than layout and some other detailed parameters) is given by the following:

Browser : Window
parts

URL_field : Text_Field
File_Menu : Browser_Menu
Display : Window
Home_button : Button
Print_button : Button
Reload_button : Button
Save_button : Button
Stop_button : Button
Quit_button : Button

The only other objects required is the pop-up windows for saving pages or selecting a printer. These are simply defined as windows that either contain a Menu (for selecting which printer to use), or a Text Field (to name the file you wish to save).

7.4 Interaction Techniques for a Web Browser

The presentation object browser has three parts which react to input through interaction techniques. The **File_Menu** is controlled by a selection interaction technique that displays interim feedback, the various buttons are controlled by a selection interaction technique without interim feedback, and the URL_field is a text field that is controlled by a **FormBasedEntry** technique.

The menu of choices binds menu items to dialogue symbols in a one-to-one correspondence. These correspondences are expressed as instances of **OneToOnePDAssoc** classes:

MenuChoices : OneToOnePDAssoc
  assign Browser.parts|Browser_Menu|.parts|printItem| to
        Dialogue.PrintPage.
  assign Browser.parts|Browser_Menu|.parts|reloadItem| to
        Dialogue.Reload.
  assign Browser.parts|Browser_Menu|.parts|homeItem| to Dialogue.Home.
  assign Browser.parts|Browser_Menu|.parts|saveItem| to
        Dialogue.SavePage.
  assign Browser.parts|Browser_Menu|.parts|exitItem| to Dialogue.Quit.

In each line of the association, a button in the browser menu is connected to a token in the Dialogue Model. At run time, if any of these dialogue tokens are not enabled, the labels in the corresponding buttons will be grayed out. The interaction technique that employs this binding is called **FileMenu** in analogy to the Netscape browser **File** menu that contains similar options:

FileMenu : InterimFeedbackSelectionInteraction
  enable when Dialogue.Browser is enabled.
  disable when Dialogue.Browser is disabled.
  bind MenuChoices.

This interaction technique is enabled whenever the **Browser** dialogue symbol is enabled (which is the lifetime of the session), and disabled only when this symbol is disabled. Note that by capturing all of the Presentation-Dialogue binding in **MenuChoices**, only one entity need be updated to add functionality to the menu. The binding of operation buttons to dialogue tokens is also a one-to-one correspondence:

ButtonChoices : OneToOnePDAssoc
  assign Browser.parts|printButton| to Dialogue.PrintPage.
  assign Browser.parts|reloadButton| to Dialogue.Reload.
  assign Browser.parts|homeButton| to Dialogue.Home.
  assign Browser.parts|saveButton| to Dialogue.SavePage.

OpButtons : OneShotSelectionInteraction
  enable when Dialogue.Browser is enabled.
  disable when Dialogue.Browser is disabled.
  bind ButtonChoices.

Note that the dialogue tokens activated by **ButtonChoices** overlap with those of **MenuChoices**. MASTERMIND allows designers to express bindings without concern for overlapping functionality in the knowledge that the code generators will work out the details.

Finally, the interaction technique attaching input to the text field **URL_field** is given below:

URLInput : FormBasedEntry
  enable input when Dialogue.Operations is enabled.
  disable input when Dialogue.Operations is active.

  enable activation when Dialogue.Open is enabled.
  enable activation when Dialogue.Open is disabled.

  attach to Browser.parts|URL_field|.

In this technique, input is enabled at any time that the symbol **Operations** is enabled but inactive. Users may only commit selections, however, when the dialogue symbol **Open** is enabled.

7.5 Dialogue Model Evolution: Web Browser History Mechanism

Once the browser has been created, adding new functionality to the system is a simple job in MASTERMIND . In this case, a history mechanism is added to the browser. The first job is to decide what functionality the history mechanism must provide. The end user is allowed to traverse the history list in a linear fashion (**Back** and **Forward** functions) or to jump directly to any web site already in the history list. Each of these choices is a navigation operation of the same type as **Home** or **Open** and therefore will simply be additional choices available to the user at the same time. That is, they will be children of the **alt** ordering of **Operations**.

The next step is to decide how they will be implemented. **Back** and **Forward** are simple uses of the history list which need no information other than the history list itself. For this reason, it is decided that they will be developed as application methods that can just be invoked by the Dialogue Model, making them single nodes. In addition to the application method they invoke, the model also needs to know the conditions under which they may be invoked. That is, **Back** should only work if there is a previous page to return to, and **Forward** should only work if the current page is not the last page in the history list. This requires information to be added to the Context Model described below.

It looks as though going to any place in the history list can be implemented by yet another Interaction binding to the **Open** process. This will not work however. Where following a link or typing in a URL directly already provide the URL parameter that is required by the application method, the history mechanism can not provide such a value unless the history list is constantly displayed to the user. This is undesirable due to the amount of screen space the list uses. Hence, an approach similar to **Print** will be used. That is, there is a step to view the history list and then another step to choose a page from that list. The history task needs two children defined, one for each of these steps. It can then invoke the same application method as **Open**, with its own parameter.

These are the only changes required to the Dialogue Model for the addition of the history mechanism. The only changes required to other models are the creation of two new application routines (**Back** and **Forward**) and their specification in the AW, two new CM variables (to maintain information on the current history list), and appropriate presentation and interaction techniques for the new dialogue symbols to represent. The evolved Dialogue Model is shown in Figure 7.

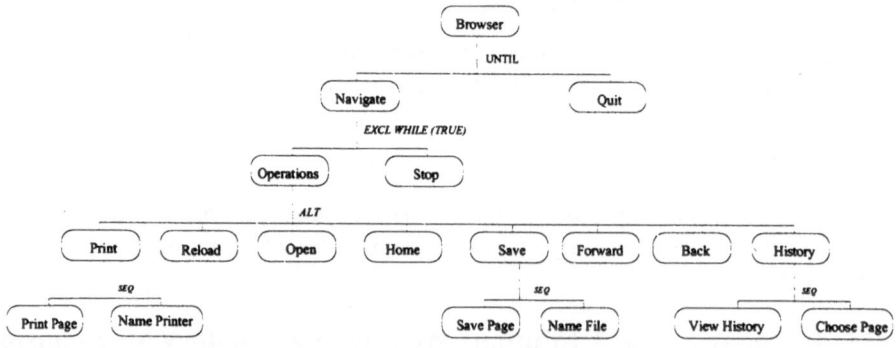

Figure 7: Dialogue Model for the browser with history mechanism

7.6 Presentation Model Evolution: Web Browser History Mechanism

The presentation features for the history mechanism are merely additional instances of the objects already defined. Three new instances of **Buttons** are declared for **Back, Forward** and **History**. In addition, each of these three items is included in the initial menu of the system. This can be easily handled by the inclusion of **Back, Forward** and **History** in the application operation list.

The only additional presentation that is needed is the presentation of the history list. This is defined as a simple window which contains a Menu, is initially set to be non-visible, and only becomes visible when the user attempts to choose from the list. This structure has the following form:

History_Window : Window
data_parameters
   history_list : sequence < URL >
parts
   history : Button
   replicate [history] for history_list

This new window is the only additional coding necessary for the Presentation Model other than the addition of the new operations in the application operation list. The replication system of the Presentation Model automatically handles the new menu item and buttons for the new operations.

7.7 Interaction Model Evolution: Web Browser History Mechanism

The new input behaviour is easily added to the existing interaction techniques. The behaviour of the new buttons and menu option need only be added to the Presentation-Dialogue associations. The **ButtonChoices** association should be extended with three new assignments:
assign Browser.parts|forwardButton| to Dialogue.Forward.
  assign Browser.parts|backButton| to Dialogue.Back.
  assign Browser.parts|historyButton| to Dialogue.History.

Likewise, the **MenuChoices** association should be extended with:
assign Browser.parts|Browser_Menu|.parts|forwardItem| to
       Dialogue.Forward.
  assign Browser.parts|Browser_Menu|.parts|backItem| to Dialogue.Back.
  assign Browser.parts|Browser_Menu|.parts|historyItem| to
       Dialogue.History.

The history selection pane represents a more complicated interaction and showcases a typical **ManyToOnePDAssoc:**

GoToURLAssociation : ManyToOnePDAssoc
choose hist_url from History_Window.parts|history_menu|.
within Dialogue.History assign hist_url.data_parameters|url|
    to data_parameters|the_url|.

With these changes and a regeneration of the code, the extension is complete.

8. Status

8.1 Code Generators

Each of the MASTERMIND models has a corresponding code generator. The implementation of the code generators requires three steps. Each code generator takes as input a textual MTF files and produces one or more C++ source files. Because MTF is a syntactic format as opposed to a compilable language, the code generators are distinguished by the model-specific domain knowledge they apply in synthesising code from models. The maturity of the code generators is a function of the depth or precision of the model ontologies. The Presentation code generator is the most mature as evidenced by the depth of the Presentation ontology. Next is the Dialogue code generator which generates state machines implementing the ordering constraints. The newest and least mature technology is the Interaction Model code generator. This generator currently resembles a macro processor more than a compiler, but, as the Interaction ontology becomes more well-defined, we expect this to change.

We have tried several validations of our modelling and code generation approach. One of the most interesting occurred prior to when we were able to integrate our technology with ISI's Presentation engine. In this exercise we used HTML as our Presentation notation. That is, we wanted to generate forms-based web applications where screen updates consist of automatically generated HTML pages. While bandwidth limitations make this approach prohibitively slow for practical situations, the simplicity of the HTML presentation language was such that we could readily drive the page construction process from our Dialogue Model.

8.2 Dukas[6]

Dukas is MASTERMIND's graphical dialogue-modelling tool. With this tool, dialogue designers can create hierarchical trees, identifying both types of leaf nodes and also relationships among dialogue symbols (e.g., ordering, parent-child). All of the properties of Dialogue Models important for their connection to the other MASTERMIND models are also editable from within Dukas. The screen shot in Figure 8 shows the basic layout of Dukas and the Dialogue Model for a browser's history mechanism.

---

[6] Paul Dukas is the composer of the *Sorcerer's Apprentice*.

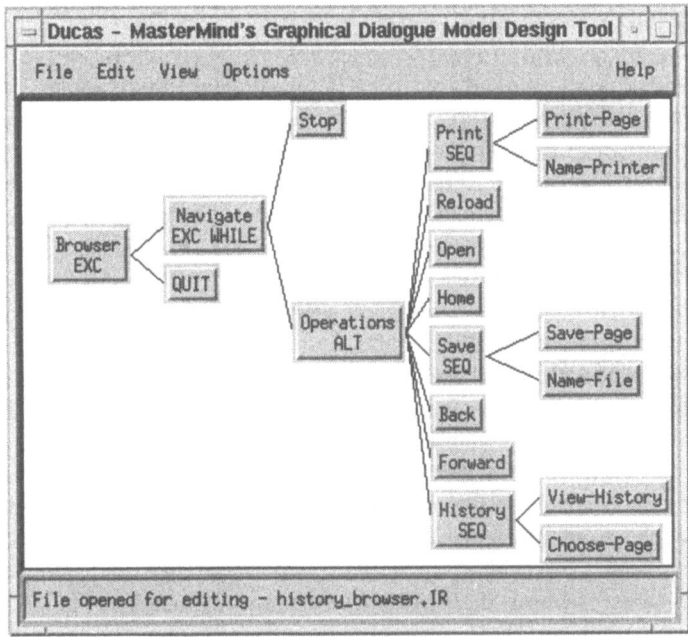

Figure 8: The Dukas model of the browser history mechanism

Dukas currently allows basic Dialogue-Model editing, but there are several additions planned for future implementation. Some of these additions are enhancements to the look-and-feel of the tool. For example, in the future, the ordering of a group of nodes will be indicated by their shape on the display. A tool palette will be added to allow for easier editing of Dialogue Models. Currently the different editing commands are accessible with various combinations of mouse and keyboard input. Also, indication of which node is currently selected, and the ability to select a group of nodes will be added to Dukas. Because Dialogue Models can become larger than the display, making it difficult to see the entire model at once, the ability to expand and contract the tree will be included. A separate overview window which shows a smaller view of the entire tree is another enhancement planned for future versions of Dukas.

In addition to enhancements to the look of Dukas, several features are planned which will extend the modelling capabilities of this tool as well. For example, the creation of Dialogue Models often requires the use of prototypical subtrees of tasks. In future implementations, Dukas will allow a designer to reuse subtrees that are part of a library (e.g., the dialogue representing a file dialogue box). The designer will also be able to create and save his or her own subtrees into a library. One of the important features enabled by the MASTERMIND approach is the use of on-line *advisors* that will be able to make suggestions to the dialogue designer by detecting various design patterns (i.e., groups of nodes and orderings) during the design process. In the future, Dukas will be able to make such intelligent suggestions to the designer.

8.3 Contributions and Future Directions

MASTERMIND is a model-based user-interface generation system. Its specific contributions include a user-task-oriented design method, a dialogue-specification notation from which provably correct implementations are automatically generated, and an ontology for binding Presentation, Application, and Dialogue components. We are developing code generators for our models and integrating them with the Presentation Model code generator developed at ISI. We are also enhancing our Dialogue Modelling tool, Dukas.

Our immediate concern is to complete works on the MM code generators and to explore the other models described above, particularly the Context Model. Once this is done, we will be able to claim that we can generate complete user interfaces. At this point we can begin exploring some of the possibilities raised by having models available. For example, having models available at design time enables the use of design critics which can suggest improvements to a design or enforce style rules. Run-time models enable truly powerful context-sensitive help mechanisms that can have some hope of understanding what it is that the end user was trying to accomplish with a user interface. Finally, we would like to explore interesting application areas such as the MASTERMIND web applications. In particular, we would like to replace HTML with Java as a presentation engine in the Internet application demonstration we described in Section 8.1.

Acknowledgements

The MASTERMIND project effort is sponsored by the Defense Advanced Research Projects Agency, under contract number N66001-94-0-603D. The U.S. Government is authorised to reproduce and distribute reprints for Governmental purposes notwithstanding any copyright annotation thereon.

The views and conclusions contained herein are those of the authors and should not be interpreted as necessarily representing the official policies or endorsements, either expressed or implied, of the Defense Advanced Research Projects Agency, or the U.S. Government.

Chapter 6:
XTL: A Temporal Logic for the Formal Development of Interactive Systems

1. Introduction

1.1 Temporal Logic and HCI

Temporal logics have been widely used for the specification of reactive systems and there exist important works which prove its utility for the modelling of such systems (Manna & Pnueli 92). Temporal logic is more rarely used in the development cycle of interactive systems. In spite of this, Chris Johnson has proved its interest for the HCI domain using temporal logic at different stages of the life cycle: requirements, task analysis (Johnson 94), specifications of the system (Johnson 93), and of course proof of properties (Johnson 95). He has essentially used a classical temporal logic - CTL (Emerson &Srinivasan 89) - and more recently Lamport's TLA (Lamport 94) for the analysis of accidents (Telford & Johnson 96).

Classical temporal logics like CTL (Emerson & Srinivasan 89), TL (Pnueli 86) or TLA (Lamport 94) are well adapted to reactive systems but they are lacking of expressiveness to specify interactive systems. For example you can't possibly express loops directly because the semantics of loops is not defined. In other words you are generally limited to a linear description of the system. ITL (Moskowski 86) is an executable temporal logic which solves most of the expressiveness problems, being also a programming language which integrates temporal logics operators as well as flow of control constructs.

1.2 The XTL Formalism

We have developed XTL (eXtended Temporal Logic) to avoid most of the limitations of classical temporal logics and integrate more than flow of control constructs into it.

XTL is a temporal logic based formalism with a precise semantics. Compared to more classical temporal logics and to formalisms dedicated to the specification of interactive systems (finite states machine (Harel & Naamad 96), ICOs (Palanque 92)), XTL has been built to formally cope with rarely supported problems. In particular, XTL is adapted to the specification of temporal problems in a qualitative and a quantitative point of view. It can cope with the specification of concurrency (i.e. interleaving *and* parallelism) and singular behaviours like interruptions, interruptions followed by interleaving... In fact, the treatment of singularities is one of the strong points of the formalism.

1.3 The Other Way of Reading this Chapter

We have divided this chapter in two parts. While part 1 is dedicated to the XTL formalism and the presentation of its semantics, part 2 deals with the modelling of a Web browser using XTL. We could have used an alternative solution and gradually presented the solution. Nevertheless, dividing the chapter in two parts allows two ways of reading it. If you are already familiar with temporal logic, you can linearly read this chapter, compare its semantics with other temporal logics and then compare its use with the use of other formalisms. If you are not, you can switch to part 2 which is easy to read and understand because the syntax of XTL is close to the syntax of programming language, and then go back to part 1 to understand the formal underpinnings.

This chapter is divided in eight sections. Sections 2 to 6 form part 1 and present the different aspects of the XTL formalism. The very bases of the formalism and the qualitative operators are presented first in sections 2 and 3. Then, we introduce the flow of control constructs (section 4), the operators related to interruptions and concurrency (section 5), and finally the operators related to modularity (section 6). Section 7 forms part 2 and deals with the case study. In this section, we also present some material related to real-time constraints.

2. The Very Bases of XTL

In this section we define a temporal logic formalism adapted to the specification of interactive systems. We first define simple bases of the formalism and we then gradually introduce new operators and new concepts.

We consider the specification of interactive systems from a behavioural point of view, that is to say the evolution of a system during its execution. For each program P, this execution can be classically described as a linear sequence of states associated with events. There are numerous formal representations specifying the specific behaviour of a system and thus considered as its semantics.

We first adopt the Manna and Pnueli's approach (Pnueli 86): we consider that the behaviour of a program P is represented by the set of its possible executions E(P). We then focus on the execution predicates of a program P. A predicate π is valid on P, if π is satisfied on E(P), i.e. for any execution of P.

Compared to classical definitions (Ben Ari 93, Manna & Pnueli89, Emerson & Srinivasan 89), we consider that a program can be executed in a concurrent way along several activity paths for the user. We first introduce the notion of execution paths in order to deal directly with concurrent situations.

2.1 Basic Definitions

2.1.1 Definition 1: execution path

An execution path is an infinite (eventually finite) sequence of states characterising, by its associated predicates, the evolution of a program P from the beginning to the end of an execution.

A program P can be composed with several execution paths in order to describe concurrent behaviours, eventually synchronised.

2.1.2 Definition 2: sequence of states

A sequence of states σ: $s_0, s_1, \ldots, s_k$ is a linear sub-sequence of states of an execution path.

Remark : An execution path is a particular sequence of states.

2.1.3 Definition 3: length of a sequence of states

Let σ: $s_0, s_1, \ldots$ a sequence of states characterising the execution of a program P on an execution path S_p .

If σ is a finite sequence of states σ: $s_0, s_1, \ldots, s_k$ we define the length of σ, denoted $|\sigma|$ as $|\sigma| = k+1$.

If σ is an infinite sequence of states, $|\sigma| = \infty$

2.1.4 Definition4: concatenation of two sequences of states

Let two sequences of states σ_1 : $s_0, s_1, \ldots, s_k$ finite and σ_2 : $r_0, r_1, \ldots$ eventually infinite. We define the concatenation of σ_1 and σ_2 denoted $\sigma_1 + \sigma_2$ as

$$\sigma_1 + \sigma_2 = s_0, s_1, \ldots, s_k, r_0, r_1, \ldots$$

2.1.5 Remarks

$|\sigma_1 + \sigma_2| = |\sigma_1| + |\sigma_2|$

If $|\sigma| < \infty$, we denote Pref(σ) the set of σ finite prefixes, and Suff(σ) the set of σ finite suffixes.

The concatenation of two execution paths is not defined and has no meaning in XTL.

2.1.6 Temporal logics and execution paths

The concept of execution path is not really new in temporal logic formalisms (Enjalbert 84). But, it has never been really exploited. Nevertheless, we believe that this concept makes the logic easier to use and to understand for designers or developers, and it's all the more important as the logic is expressive and can deal with a large number of concrete situations (especially in concurrent situations).

3. The XTL Formalism

In this section we define the vocabulary we use, the language formation rules, the interpretation rules for the expressions, formulas and assertions, the basic temporal operators. The language we describe and the syntactic formation rules are slightly different from those of languages of the same kind (TL (Pnueli 86), ITL (Moskowsky 86), TLA (Lamport 94)...). The main difference comes from the language semantics which permit parallelism problems and related ones to be treated easily. In the next sections we introduce new concepts which make the logic far different from the usual ones. Temporal logics usually have a limited number of operators to be able to analyse particular properties. XTL has been developed with expressiveness in mind to be able to cope with a large number of concrete problems and has a large number of operators and constructs.

3.1 Vocabulary and Symbols

3.1.1 Variables

The set of variables $V=\{p,q,r,..\}$ over the logic is formed over the alphabet $A=\{A,B,...,Z,a,b,...,z,0,1,...9,-,\_\}$.

Every variable has a type and ranges over a validity domain.

We use five data types: Boolean, integer, string, list and set.

We also call Boolean variables, propositional variables or propositions.

Here are four examples of variables: A, b, user_recovery_on_error_no , __A-123, signal, ...

3.1.2 Functions, symbols and constants

We use n-ary functions ($n \geq 0$) and constants, considered as no argument functions ($n=0$).

We use constants true and false over the Boolean; 0,1,2... over the integers.

We use as functions over propositional variables, logical connectors: $\neg$, $\vee$, $\wedge$, $\rightarrow$, $\leftrightarrow$ and the basic functions +,-,*,/,mod... over the integers.

We also have the functions symbols: add (adding an element to the front of a list), concat (concatenating two lists), head (returns the head of a nonempty list), tail (returns the tail of a nonempty list) over lists, and , $\cup$, $\cap$ over sets.

3.1.3 Predicates symbols

We have predicates symbols ($<$, $>$,...) over the integers, the predicate symbol 'null' over the lists (testing if a list is empty), and $\subset$, $\subseteq$, $\in$, $\notin$ over sets.

We also use the predicate symbol '=' between two elements of the same type.

3.1.4 Other symbols

Universal and existential quantifiers: $\forall$, $\exists$

3.2 Syntax of Expressions

(i) Every variable is an expression
(ii)N-ary functions $f(e_1, e_2, ..., e_n)$, where $(n \geq 0)$ and $e_1, e_2, ..., e_n$ are expressions, are also expressions. Every constant is considered as a 0-ary function.
   Every expression is built by applying a finite number of times the rules (i) and (ii).
   Here are examples of syntactically correct expressions:
   $A + (3b * c)$, head(l) +b - (c mod4)

3.3 Syntax of Formulas

(i)Every Boolean variable is a formula
(ii)The n-ary predicates $p(e_1, e_2, ..., e_n)$, where $(n \geq 0)$ and $e_1, e_2, ..., e_n$ are expressions, are formulas.
(iii)The equality of two expressions denoted: $e_1 = e_2$ where e_1 and e_2 are two expressions of the same type is an expression.
(iv)If p and q are formulas, then $\neg p$, $p \wedge q$, $p \vee q$, $p \leftrightarrow q$, $p \rightarrow q$ are formulas
(v)Every formula is built by applying a finite number of times the rules (i) to (iv)

   Here are examples of syntactically correct formulas:
   $x \geq 3y + 5$, $\neg(x > 3) \vee (y = 4)$, $(null(s) \vee \neg p) \rightarrow (q \wedge r)$

3.4 Syntax of Assertions

(i) Every formula is an assertion.
(ii) If p is an assertion and 'u' a variable, then: $\exists u$: p and $\forall u$: p and are assertions.
(iii) If p and q are assertions, then: $\neg p$, $p \wedge q$, $p \vee q$, $p \leftrightarrow q$, $p \rightarrow q$ are assertions.
(iv) Every assertion is built by applying a finite number of times the rules (i) to (iii)

   Here is an example of a syntactically correct assertion:
   $\exists t$: $\forall x \in A$: $((x \bmod t) > c) \rightarrow (\neg p \vee q)$

3.5 Model of the Logic

A model for the logic denoted $M = < S, F, L >$ is defined as follows :
- $S = S_0, S_1, ... S_K$ where every Si $(1 \leq i \leq k)$ is an execution path.
- F is a partial binary relation over S such that:
(i) F: $S_p \rightarrow S_p \times S_q$
(ii) $F = \{(s_i, s_j) / s_i \in S_p \text{ and } s_j \in S_q\}$

- F is a partial binary relation over S that gives the set of synchronisations between processes running on different execution paths.
- L is an assignment of true atomic propositions in each state.(L is a truth function over S into the powerset of V_p .)

Remark : L allows the context of the current process to be managed. After an interruption, this allows the context preceding the interruption to be recovered.

3.6 Interpretation

The model $M = <S, F, L>$ satisfies the formula q on $s_i \in (S_p \subset S)$ denoted $M, S_p, s_i \models q$ is defined by the following rules:

$M, S_p, s_i \models q$ iff $(q \in L(s_i))$ for every propositionnal variable q.

$M, S_p, s_i \models$ true and not $M, S_p, s_i \models$ false

3.6.1 Classical operators

$M, S_p, s_i \models p \vee q$ iff $M, S_p, s_i \models p$ or $M, S_p, s_i \models q$

$M, S_p, s_i \models p \wedge q$ iff $M, S_p, s_i \models p$ and $M, S_p, s_i \models q$

$M, S_p, s_i \models \neg p$ iff it is false that $M, S_p, s_i \models p$

$M, S_p, s_i \models p \rightarrow q \equiv M, S_p, s_i \models \neg p \vee q$

$M, S_p, s_i \models p \leftrightarrow q \equiv M, S_p, s_i \models (p \rightarrow q) \wedge (q \rightarrow p)$

3.6.2 Future operators

(i) The operator next denoted 'N'
The formula Nq holds at state s_i if and only if the formula q holds at the next state s_{i+1} .

$M, S_p, s_i \models Nq$ iff $|S_p| \geq i+1 \wedge M, S_p, s_{i+1} \models q$

(ii) The operator eventually denoted 'E'
The formula Eq holds at state s_i if and only if the formula q holds at a future state following s_i.

$M, S_p, s_i \models Eq$ iff there exists $(j \geq i)$ such that $M, S_p, s_j \models q$

(iii) The operator always denoted 'A'
The formula Aq holds at s_i if and only if q is always true from s_i.

$M, S_p, s_i \models Aq$ iff for all $(j \geq i)$ $M, S_p, s_j \models q$

(iv) The operator Until denoted 'U'
The formula pUq holds at s_i if and only if p holds continuously until q holds.

$M, S_p, s_i \models p U q$ iff there exists $(j \geq i)$ such that $M, S_p, s_j \models q$ and for all k such that $(j < k \leq i)$, $M, S_p, s_k \models p$

3.6.3 Past operators

(i) The operator Previous denoted 'Ps' :
The formula Ps q holds at s_i if and only if q has held in the previous state s_{i-1}.

$M, S_p, s_i \models$ Ps q iff i>0 $\wedge$ $M, S_p, s_{i-1} \models$ q

(ii) The operator since denoted 'S'
$M, S_p, s_i \models$ p S q iff there exists (0≤j≤i) such that $M, S_p, s_j \models$ q and for all k

(j<k≤i) $M, S_p, s_k \models$ p

The formula p S q holds if and only if q held at state s_j in the past and p has held continuously from s_j to the present state s_i.

3.6.4 Convention

We'll use the notation S $\models$ q standing for $M, S_o, s_o \models$ q each time there will be no ambiguity . If there is no ambiguity on the model M we'll denote $s_i \models$ q instead of $S_o, s_o \models$ q. We'll also use these notations to express that several processes can run on different execution paths i.e. in a concurrent way.

4. Other Operators: Flow of Control Constructs

In this section we introduce new operators, derived from classical ones, which allow us to modify the scope of a temporal formula to zero, one or several states. We also introduce the independent order operator and some various constructs like while-loops or the conditional expression if-then-else.

4.1 Definition 5 : Power

We recursively define the raise of an operator 'O' to a certain power as follows:

For (n = 0) we have: $O^0 p =$ true

For (n = 1) we have: $O^1 p = p$

For (n > 1) we have: $O^n p = O^{n-1} Op$

4.2 The Operator 'Empty'

$M, S_p, s_k \models$ empty iff $\left| s_k, s_{k+1} \right|_{S_p} = 0$

4.3　p Holds One or Several Times

We express a temporal formula p holds one or several times from a starting state as follows:

$$S_j, s_k \models \text{p+} \text{ iff } \exists \text{ n>0 such that } |S_j| \geq k+1 \text{ and } S_j, s_k \models p \land Np \land \ldots \land N^{n-1}p$$

4.4　p Holds Zero or Several Times

We express a temporal formula p holds zero or several times from a starting state as follows:

$$S_j, s_k \models \text{p*} \equiv \text{empty} \lor \text{p+}$$

4.5　p Holds Zero or One Time

We express a temporal formula p holds zero or one time from a starting state as follows:

$$S_j, s_k \models \{p\} \equiv \text{empty} \lor p$$

4.6　p Holds Exactly n Times

We express a temporal formula p holds exactly n times from a starting state as follows:

$$S_j, s_k \models p^n \text{ iff } n \geq 1 \text{ such that } |S_j| \geq k+n \text{ and } S_j, s_k \models p \land Np \land \ldots \land N^{n-1}p$$

We can remark this definition is slightly different from the one of the operator '+'. The difference is the number of repetitions known in advance and at least equal to one. Otherwise, a number of repetitions equal to zero would mean p never holds, which can be expressed differently.

4.7　Independent Order of Two Tasks p and q

We sometimes need to specify that two tasks can be executed independently, that is their order of execution is not important. In terms of temporal logic, we say the execution order of two formula p and q is independent if and only if p holds at a given state before q or conversely.

$$S_j, s_k \models p \& q \equiv (S_j, s_k \models p \land Nq) \lor (S_j, s_k \models q \land Np)$$

4.8 The If-Then-Else Construct

We can easily define the if-then-else construct in temporal logic as follows:

$S_j, S_k \models$ if p then w else x $\equiv (p \rightarrow w) \wedge (\neg p \rightarrow x)$

4.9 The While Construct

We define the while construct in XTL as it is defined in ITL (Moszkowsky 86):

while p do q $\equiv (p \wedge N[\text{while p do q}])$ else empty

5. Operators Related to Interruptions and Concurrency

In this section we introduce operators related to tasks or processes interruptions. Our aim is not to make a classification of interruptions, but to give tools to be able to describe them in most cases. In fact, we consider interruptions in a large sense. We are here more interested in the semantics of interruptions than in constructing a catalogue of operators with each operator associated with one kind of interruption. In the following sub-sections we introduce eight different operators which, when used alone or with other operators, allow most types of interruptions to be described. It is then the work of the designer to determine if what we call an interruption is in fact an exception, an error, a failure... For a discussion about singularities -i.e. exceptions, errors, failures...- (Jambon 96) can be a good guide.

5.1 <] Interruption without Resumption

If p and q are valid states formulas, we define p interrupted by q as follows:
$S_j, S_k \models p <] q$ if and only if there exists a decomposition of p in 'n' sub-formulas such that:

$p \equiv p_1 \wedge N p_2 \wedge ... \wedge N^{n-1} p_n$ and

$i \geq 1$ and $|S_j| \geq k + i + 1$ and $S_j, S_k \models p_1 \wedge S_j, S_{k+1} \models p_2 \wedge ... \wedge S_j, S_{k+i} \models p_i$

$\wedge S_j, S_{k+i+1} \models q$

$p<]q$ holds at state s_k if and only if p can be split up in 'n' sub-tasks such that the first i sub-tasks (i>0) are executed first, then q.

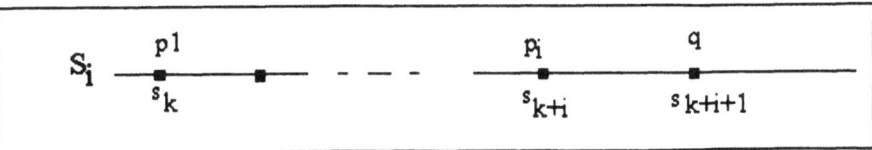

Figure 1: Interruption without resumption 'p<]q' : a part of p is executed first, then q

5.2 <r] Interruption with Resumption

If p and q are valid states formulas, we define p interrupted by q with resumption as follows: $S_j, s_k \models p <r] q$ if and only if there exists a decomposition of p in 'n' sub-formulas such that:

$$p \equiv p_1 \wedge N p_2 \wedge \ldots \wedge N^{n-1} p_n \wedge (q \neq \text{empty}) \wedge$$

$$i \geq 1 \text{ and } |S_j| \geq k+i+1 \text{ and } S_j, s_k \models p_1 \wedge S_j, s_{k+1} \models p_2 \wedge \ldots \wedge S_j, s_{k+i-1} \models p_i \wedge$$

$$S_j, s_{k+i} \models q \wedge S_j, s_{k+i+1} \models p \wedge (L(S_{k+i+1}) = L(S_{k+i-1}) \cup q)$$

p <r] q holds at state s_k if and only if p can be split up in 'n' sub-tasks such that the first i ones (i>0) are executed first, then q, and finally p is executed in its entirety after the previous environment was recovered.

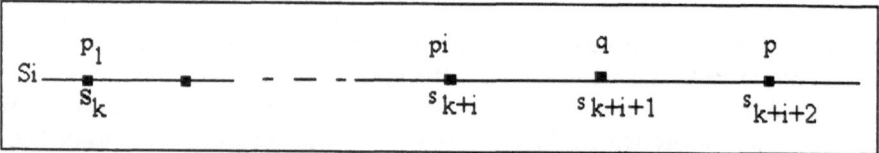

Figure 2: Interruption with resumption at the beginning of the interrupted task

In the previous definition, we have imposed (q≠empty) which means the interruption of p by q is certain. It can be a better idea to introduce a weak version of this operator in order to treat the cases where p can possibly be interrupted by q. It brings us a way to manage possible users' errors, and also to treat the cases where p will not be interrupted.

We define the weak version of this operator '<w]' as follows:

$$S_j, s_k \models p <w] q \equiv (p <r] q \wedge (q \neq \text{empty})) \vee ((q = \text{empty}) \wedge S_j, s_k \models p)$$

5.3 <-] Interruption with Resumption at the Point of Interruption

If p and q are valid states formulas, we define p interrupted by q with resumption at the point of interruption as follows:

$S_j, s_k \models p <-] q$ if and only if there exists a decomposition of p in 'n' sub-formulas such that:

$$p \equiv p_1 \wedge N p_2 \wedge \ldots \wedge N^{n-1} p_n \wedge$$

$$i \geq 1 \text{ and } |S_j| \geq k+i+1 \text{ and } S_j, s_k \models p_1 \wedge S_j, s_{k+1} \models p_2 \wedge \ldots \wedge S_j, s_{k+i-1} \models p_i \wedge$$

$$S_j, s_{k+i} \models q \wedge S_j, s_{k+i+1} \models p_{i+1} \wedge \ldots \wedge S_j, s_{k+n} \models p_n$$

p <-]q holds at state s_k if and only if p can be split up in at least two sub-formulas p1 and p2 such that p1 is executed first, then q, and finally p2.

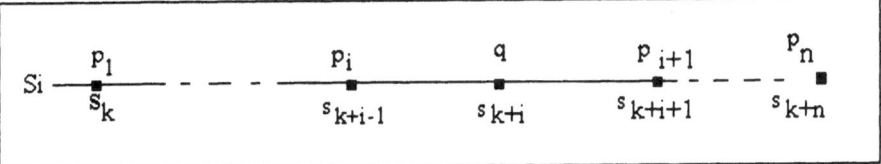

Figure 3: Interruption with resumption at the point of interruption

5.4 <(Pt) Interruption with Resumption at a Particular Point

If p and q are valid states formulas, we define p interrupted by q with resumption at a particular point 'Pt' as follows:

$S_j, S_k \models p <(i_0)q$ if and only if there exists a decomposition of p in 'n' sub-formulas such that:

$$p \equiv p_1 \wedge Np_2 \wedge \ldots \wedge N^{n-1}p_n \wedge$$

$1 \leq i \leq n$ and $|S_j| \geq k + i + 2$ and $S_j, s_k \models p_1 \wedge S_j, s_{k+1} \models p_2 \wedge \ldots \wedge S_j, s_{k+i} \models p_i \wedge$

$S_j, s_{k+i+1} \models q \wedge S_j, s_{k+i+2} \models p_{i_0} \wedge (L(S_{k+i+2}) = L(S_{k+i}) \cup q) \wedge (1 \leq i_0 \leq n) \wedge \ldots \wedge$

$S_j, s_{k+i+2+n-i_0} \models p_n$

p <-(Pt) q holds at state s_k if and only if p can be split up in 'n' sub-formulas such that the first 'i' ones are executed first, then q. Afterwards, we resume the execution of p at a particular point, in other words from a particular sub-formula before the sub-formula number 'i', and we recover the previous context.

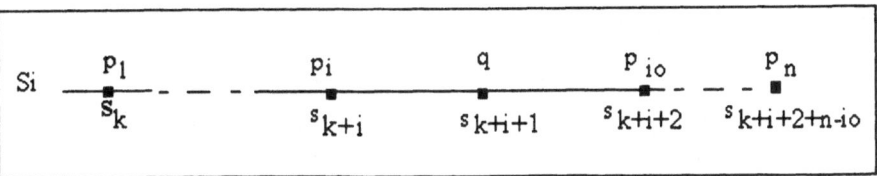

Figure 4: Interruption with resumption at a particular point of the interrupted process

5.5 || : Parallelism of Two Synchronised Processes

If p and q are valid states formulas, we define p and q hold synchronised in parallel at state s_k as follows:

$S_j, s_k \models p \parallel q$ if and only if:

$S_j, s_k \models p \wedge S_{j+1}, s'_{k'} \models q$ with $(s_k, s'_{k'}) \in F_j$ and $|s_0 s_k|_{S_j} = |s'_0 s'_{k'}|_{S_{j+1}}$

p and q, two synchronised processes, run in parallel if and only if they run on different execution paths and have started at the same time.

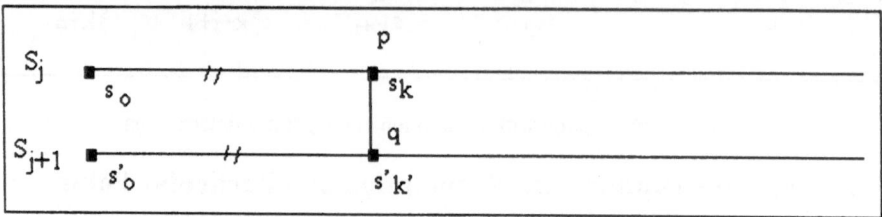

Figure 5: Parallelism of two synchronised processes

Remark: parallelism of two processes from a particular point

We can also specify that two processes run in parallel only during a certain amount of time if we use a construct based on the operators $\|$ and N (next).

Suppose two processes p and q such that p and q run in parallel after the execution of a sub-operation of p. In other words p can be split up in two sub-processes p1 and p2 such that we have: $\models p1 \wedge N(p2 \| q)$.

Till now, we have described a qualitative model of time. But most of the time we need a quantitative model to specify real time problems. In section 7, we describe how to include a real time model into the logic so that we can also describe synchronisation independently of the eventual decomposition of processes into sub-processes.

5.6 Parallelism without Synchronisation

If p and q are valid states formulas, we define p and q hold in parallel at state s_k as follows:

$S_j, s_k \models p \parallel\!\!\parallel q$ if and only if

$S_j, s_k \models p \wedge S_{j+1}, s'_{k'} \models q$ with $(s_k, s'_{k'}) \in F_j$ and $\left|s_0 s_k\right|_{S_j} \leq \left|s'_0 s'_{k'}\right|_{S_{j+1}}$

p $\parallel\!\!\parallel$ q if and only if p and q run on different execution paths. p can begin its execution before q, so both don't have to run in parallel during their whole execution.

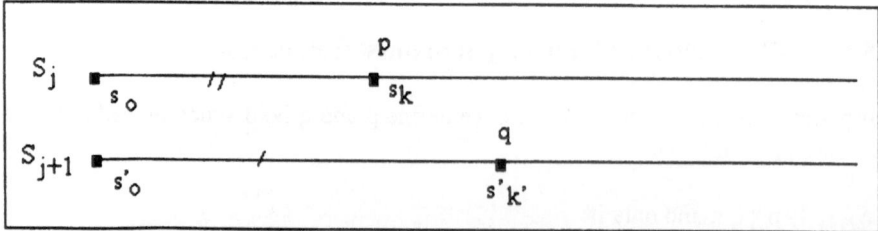

Figure 6: parallelism without synchronisation of two processes

5.7 <|| Interruption Followed by Parallelism

In this sub-section we describe a variant of the parallelism without synchronisation. In this variant we don't specify when the process p is being interrupted by the process q which forces both to run in parallel.

If p and q are valid states formulas, we define p is interrupted by q and then run in parallel at state s_k as follows:

$S_j, s_k \models p <\|\ q$ if and only if there exists a decomposition of p in 'n' sub-formulas such that:

$p \equiv p_1 \wedge Np_2 \wedge \ldots \wedge N^{n-1}p_n \wedge \exists\ i, (0 < i < 1)$ such that:

$S_j, s_k \models p \wedge \ldots \wedge\ \ S_j, s_{k+i-1} \models p_{i-1} \wedge S_j, s_{k+i} \models \ \text{true} \ \wedge\ S_j, s_{k+i+1} \models p_i \wedge \ldots \wedge$

$S_j, s_n \models p_n$ and $S_{j+1}, s'_{k'} \models q$ with $(s_{k+i}, s'_{k'}) \in F_j$ and $\left|s_0 s_{k+i}\right|_{S_j} = \left|s'_0 s'_{k'}\right|_{S_{j+1}}$

p <|| q holds at state s_k if and only if p1 -a first part of p- is executed, then q interrupts p for a short while (eventually empty), and finally p2 (the second part of p) is executed while q continues to run on another execution path.

It follows that p <|| q $\cong$ p1 $\wedge$ N(q || p2). Nevertheless, compared to the definition of the parallelism of two processes, we don't need to precise when both processes run in parallel after the interruption of one of them.

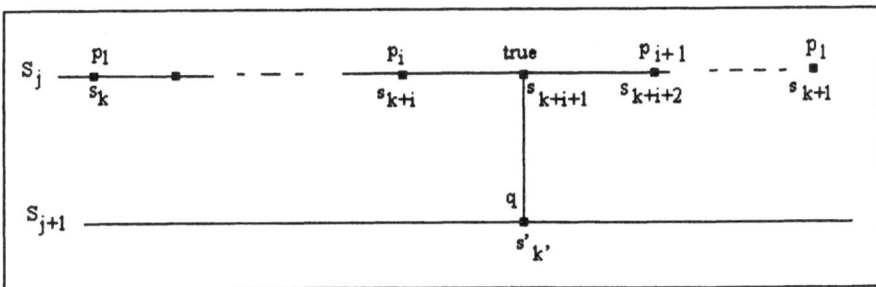

Figure 7: Interruption followed by the parallelism of two processes

5.8 <> Interleaving

Two processes or tasks may be interleaved if and only if they can perform actions one after the other on the same execution path. In practice, a user can begin a task, switch to another, then switch back to the first one and so on in a sort of multi-threaded dialogue. In a certain sense, interleaving is similar to multiple interruptions between two processes with resumption at the points of interruption.

5.8.1 Definition 6: ordered intermixed sequence and interleaving

Let p et q, two formulas such that there exists a decomposition of p in 'm' sub-formulas and a decomposition of q in 'n' sub-formulas such that:

$p \equiv p_1 \wedge Np_2 \wedge ... \wedge N^{m-1}p_m$ and

$q \equiv q_1 \wedge Nq_2 \wedge ... \wedge N^{n-1}q_n$

Let σ a sequence of states of length n+m such that: $\sigma = s_0, s_1, ... s_i, ... s_{m+n-1}$ and σ strictly encloses the two ordered sets $\{p_1, p_2, ... p_m\}$ and. $\{q_1, q_2, ... q_n\}$.

In σ, p_{i+1} ($1 \leq i \leq m$) can only happen after p_i and q_{i+1} ($1 \leq j \leq n$) can only happen after q_i. p_i ($1 \leq i \leq m$) and q_i ($1 \leq j \leq n$) happen independently in σ.

If σ exists, we say that σ is an ordered intermixed sequence and p et q can be interleaved which we denote p <> q.

5.8.2 Example

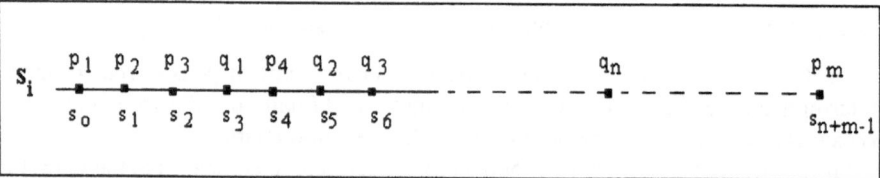

Figure 8: Example of interleaving between two tasks p and q (p<>q)

5.9 <<> Interruption Followed by Interleaving

We define the interruption followed by the interleaving of two tasks as follows: p begins its execution, then is interrupted by q, and finally p and q are interleaved.

In a formal way:

Let p and q two formulas such that there exists a decomposition of p in 'm' sub-formulas such that:

$p \equiv p_1 \wedge Np_2 \wedge ... \wedge N^{m-1}p_m$,

$p_\alpha \equiv p_1 \wedge Np_2 \wedge ... \wedge N^{i-1}p_i$ with $(1 \leq i < m-1)$,

$p_\beta = p_{i+1} \wedge Np_{i+2} \wedge ... \wedge N^{m-i+1}p_m$ with $(1 < m-i+1 < m-2)$

and there exists a decomposition of q in 'n' sub-formulas such that:

$q \equiv q_1 \wedge Nq_2 \wedge ... \wedge N^{n-1}q_n$ and $q_\beta \equiv q_2 \wedge Nq_3 \wedge ... \wedge N^{n-2}q_n$

it follows that: $p <<> q \equiv p_\alpha \wedge Nq_1 \wedge N^{\cdot}(p_\beta <> q_\beta)$.

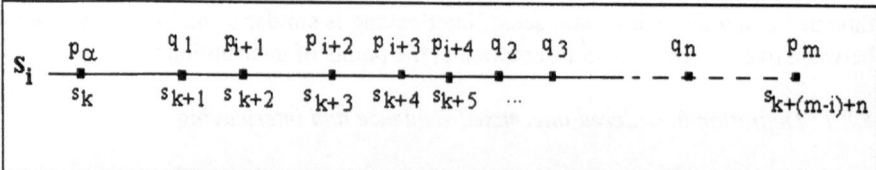

Figure 9: Example of interruption followed by interleaving for two tasks p and q

We can remark that the interruption followed by interleaving is in fact a particular case of interleaving as we introduced it in the previous subsection. Moreover, we can give an approximation of the new operator in the following way:

p<<>q $\cong$ p1 $\wedge$ N(p2 <> q).

6. Operators Related to Modularity

6.1 The Operator Chop Denoted ';'

The operator chop in XTL has a different semantics of the operator chop -also denoted ';'- in the ITL formalism. In XTL the operator chop is only a mean to improve readability. We define the operator chop as follows:

$S_j, s_k \models$ p;q $\equiv$ $S_j, s_k \models$ p $\wedge$ Nq

6.2 The Operator 'Module'

The operator module is another way to improve the readability of specifications. 'Module' gives us a way to write specifications in a syntax close to a programming language. We define the operator 'module' as follows:

$S_j, s_k \models$ module p q $\equiv$ $S_j, s_k \models$ p $\leftarrow$ q

7. Part 2: The Case Study

7.1 Description

The case study consists in the description of a Netscape-like Web browser. We use XTL for the specification of different important parts of the browser, and especially the parts which requires a precise model of time. Our specification is divided into several modules, each of them describing a user's task connected with the system's actions.

The case study contains the specification of different specific features such as:

- History within a session (back, forward, goto, ...)
- Non-preemptiveness of the server (i.e. Stop and Exit are always active)
- Systematic system's feedback (information about the interaction state)
- Nevertheless, the case study doesn't include two specific features for space reasons:
- Bookmarks management
- Browsing within a html page (use of scroll bars, keys, ...)

In the following subsections, we prefix all formulas with 'u_' when the formulas concern a user's action and we consider that the other formulas concern the system's behaviour. To improve the readability of the specifications we use parentheses and brackets to group together formulas. We also use 'and', 'or', and 'not' instead of their symbolic representation.

7.2 The Web Client

In this section we describe the use of the Web client. We will gradually improve our specifications in order to analyse problems due to non predictability or retrieval failure in the following sub-sections.

We first describe a simple general scheme of interaction between the user and the browser. In the initial state the user starts from his home page. Then the interaction takes place: the user enters a URL and «request_page» makes a request to the server. In favourable cases the server finally gets the page (get_page) and concurrently stores the URL to be reuse later (the two actions could also happen sequentially). Otherwise the system prevents the user by a failure_warning. If no problem occurs during the page retrieval then the system displays the page and concurrently stores it in a cache. The process can then be reproduced infinitely.

```
module u_request1
home_page;
 while(true)
[
 u_enters_URL;
 request_page;
 (get_page ||| store_URL) OR failure_warning;
 if not failure_warning then
    display_page ||| store_page_in_cache_directory
]
```

This first approach of the problem can easily be refined. For example we can specify precisely how the user enters the URL of the page he wants to retrieve (u_enters_URL), or what are the interaction details with the server when the browser makes a request (request_page). We will now look closely at the different points of this specification in order to make it more precise

7.3 Server and Client Side of a Request

We now describe the dialogue between the client, i.e. the browser, and the server during the retrieval of a page:

```
module request_page1
 client_displays('connect: looking up host');
 (client_contacts_host |||
   client_displays('connect: host contacted waiting for reply') U
   (host_replies_to_client OR retrieval_failure);
 if host_replies_to_client then
 [
```

```
    client_displays('transferring data');
    ( host_sends_data|||client_displays('transferring_data'))U host_closes_connection;
    client_displays('document done')
  ]
  else
    client_displays('unable to contact host: server may be down or unreachable');
```

The retrieval of a page begins with an information feedback: 'connect: looking up host'. Then the client tries to contact the server and concurrently informs the user that it is waiting for a reply (client_displays('connect: host contacted waiting for reply')). The two actions last until the server replies, unless there is a retrieval failure. If the server replies the transfer begins and lasts until the page is retrieved and the server closes the connection.

7.4 The Web Client Revisited

In the previous specification we have not precisely shown that the user can eventually stop the transaction at any time. We can also add that a retrieval failure can happen at any time during the retrieval process due to an overloaded net or a server's problem for example. We can then refine our first specification of the Web client to take these remarks into account:

```
module u_request2
home_page;
  while(true)
[
  u_enters_URL;
  request_page <] {u_selects_stop OR retrieval_failure};
  if not u_select_stop then
    (get_page ||| store_URL) OR failure_warning;
  else
    client_displays('tranfert interrupted');
  if not failure_warning then
    display_page ||| store_page_in_cache_directory
]
```

In this new specification we have made clear that the process request_page can eventually be interrupted by the user or by a retrieval failure. We have use the operator '<]' to specify that if there was an interruption it would be without resumption, and the operator '{}' to specify that the interruption is not certain anyway.

7.5 Real-Time Constraints

In the specification of the dialogue between the browser and the server (sub-section 8.3) we used the operator until 'U' to express that we were waiting for an answer from the server or a notification of a retrieval failure. We could be more precise if we had a clock to express real-time constraints and used a timer instead of a qualitative operator.

7.5.1 Definition 6: clock

We define a clock as an infinite sequence of states such that the rate of the clock is fast enough for the sequence of states to appear continuous. Formally we have:

$$clock = S_c \in S \,/\, Card\{s_i \in S_h\} = \infty \wedge \forall i, j \in N, |s_i, s_{i+1}| = |s_j, s_{j+1}|$$

7.5.2 The function S

We can then define a function S which takes a sequence of states as parameters and returns a number in seconds:

$$S: \quad N \quad \to N$$
$$|s_i, s_j|_{S_c} \to ns$$

7.5.3 The operator _inf_

Then the operator _inf_ fixes a maximum amount of time between two states p and q such that:

$$S_j, S_k \models p \;(t \text{ inf } ns)\; q \text{ if and only if}$$

$$S_j, s_{k+1} \models q \;\Leftarrow\; S\left(|s_k, s_{k+1}|_{S_j}\right) \le ns \wedge S_j, s_k \models p \text{ and}$$

$$\neg\, S_j, s_{k+1} \models q \;\Leftarrow\; S\left(|s_k, s_{k+1}|_{S_j}\right) > ns \wedge S_j, s_k \models p$$

To put it a different way, p (t inf 6) q is true if q comes at most 6 seconds after p.

7.6 Server and Client Side of a Request (bis)

We can then improve our specification and replace the operator 'until' by a timer such that the server has, say 90 seconds, to reply to the client unless we consider there is a retrieval failure:

```
module request_page2
  client_displays('connect: looking up host');
  (client_contacts_host |||
    client_displays('connect: host contacted waiting for reply') (t inf 90)
    host_replies_to_client;
    if host_replies_to_client then
```

```
[
  client_displays('transferring data');
  ( host_sends_data|||client_displays('transferring_data'))U host_closes_connection;
  client_displays('document done')
]
else
[
  retrieval_failure;
  client_displays('unable to contact host: server may be down or unreachable');
]
```

8. Conclusion

The great expressiveness of XTL (compared to other formalisms and especially compared to other temporal logics) is one of the strong points of the formalism. Thanks to the introduction of a qualitative model as well as a quantitative one and a large number of operators, XTL allows us to specify a large number of systems very precisely. In particular the treatment of concurrency and interruptions, which is often neglected, allows to take these problems in account almost exhaustively. In the case study we did not show how to use XTL to prove system's properties. Nevertheless we have to make clear that XTL allows this kind of demonstration (like every temporal logic) thanks to its precise semantics. For example, Chris Johnson used CTL to deal with presentation delays in the Web browsers (Johnson 95). One can argue that as XTL has a great expressiveness, demonstrations made with the help of XTL must be more precise than with another temporal logic. Last but not least, XTL has a syntax close to that of a programming language which makes the specifications easy to read and understand even tough one is not familiar with the formal underpinnings of the formalism.

Chapter 7:
Interaction Object Graphs: An Executable Graphical Notation for Specifying User Interfaces

1. Introduction

Interaction Object Graphs(IOGs) are a graphical specification method based on an extended state machine. Their goal is to provide an understandable representation of man-machine dialogues. (Wasserman 85) used finite state machines to specify dialogues. However, state diagrams have severe problems when used to specify more complex dialogues. The number of states and transitions required grows uncontrollably as common interaction techniques such as modal dialogue boxes are introduced. Direct manipulation interfaces also introduce the possibility that the user will interleave tasks. While easily modelled by parallel processes, task interleaving is very difficult to describe with a finite state machine. Some form of extended state machine is required to handle direct manipulation interfaces. A number of methods have been tried. (Jacob 86) used an extended state machine which grouped states into meta-states and allowed transitions from a meta-state. Parallelism was handled implicitly by the execution environment. (Wellner 89) adapted Harel's statecharts (Harel 88) for use in dialogue specification. Statecharts include explicit parallelism and a history-based meta-state restart. (Palanque & Bastide 94) used Petri nets as their extended state machine.

All of the above notations use an abstract representation of the display which makes it difficult to envision the appearance of the dialogue on the computer. Except for Palanque and Bastide's Interactive Cooperative Objects, interface data is represented as annotations and not explicitly in the diagram. IOGs (Carr 94, 95) add both a pictorial component to help the reader visualise how the interaction will appear on the screen and explicit representation of data changes.

This chapter begins with a brief description of IOGs. It then applies them in an extended example, the specification of a WWW browser. This is followed by a brief discussion of some dialogue analyses that are possible with IOGs.

2. Interaction Object Graphs

2.1 Interaction Object Graph State Diagrams

IOGs were designed to add widget specification to Interface Representation Graphs (Rouff & Horowitz 91). However, they can be used to specify the entire interface. They combine the data flow and constraint specifications of IRGs with the statechart execution model (Harel 88). This expands the statechart to show data relationships as well as control flow. IOGs add a display state and a representation for widget attribute data in order to permit specification of low-level interaction objects which cannot be specified by Interface Representation Graphs. Below is a brief description of the IOG state diagram, and a transition description language used to specify transition conditions.

In addition to IRGs, the IOG state diagram traces its lineage from UAN (Hartson & Hix, 93, Siochi & Hartson 89) and statecharts. Statecharts added four new state types to the traditional state diagram. These states are used in IOGs. They are: the XOR meta-state, the AND meta-state, and two types of history state.

The meta-states can contain both normal states and other meta-states. Transitions from meta-states are inherited by all contained states. This helps reduce the problem of arc explosion. The XOR meta-state contains a sequential transition network. Exactly one state inside of an XOR meta-state is active when the XOR state is active. On the other hand, an AND meta-state contains more than one transition network. Each of these networks executes in parallel.

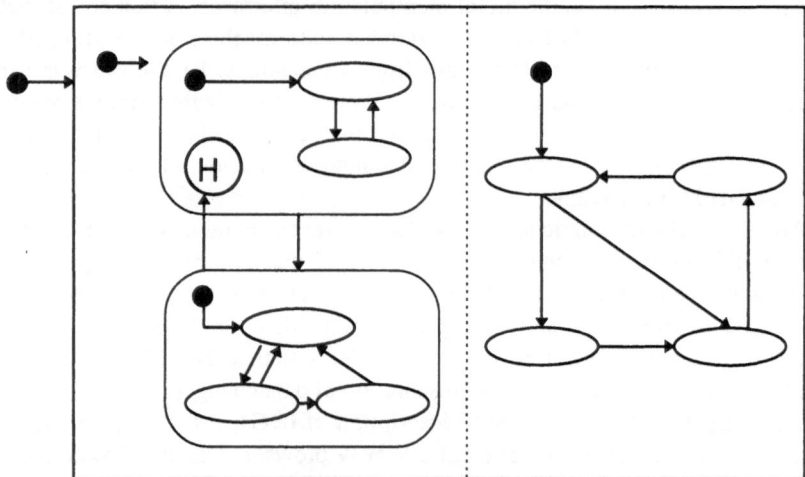

Figure 1: Example statechart

Figure 1 shows an example statechart. The large rectangle is an AND meta-state. It is divided into XOR meta-states by a dashed line. In this case there are two XOR meta-states. When the AND meta-state is active both the left and right XOR meta-states will be active. The black dots with arrows pointing from them indicate starting states. So, the AND meta-state is a starting state. Note, that all XOR meta-states also have starting states. The right XOR meta-state contains four standard states and the arcs between them. The left XOR meta-state itself contains two meta-states. The upper one is its start state and it will be active first. If the condition (unseen) on the transition to the lower XOR meta-state becomes true, then the lower XOR meta-state will be come active. This will happen no matter which of the standard states in the upper meta-state are active. They both inherit this transition from the meta-state which contains them. Similarly, the three standard states in the lower meta-state inherit the transition to the state with a circle and an H. This state is a history state.

A history state can only be contained in an XOR meta-state. Whenever a transition transfers control from a meta-state, the history state remembers which state was active immediately before the transition. If a later transition returns control to the history state, the meta-state is returned to the remembered state. History states help control state explosion. To see this, consider a specification of a help system which is independent of the user interface. An ordinary transition network would require replicating the help-system specification once for every state in the user interface. Otherwise, there would be no way to return to the user interface state that was active before help was requested. A statechart history state could receive the return transition from the help system, and only one copy would be required. There are two types of history states. They differ in how they treat a return when the last active state was a meta-state. The *H* state restarts meta-states at their start state and provides one level of history. On the other hand, the *H** state restarts meta-states at their history state, when they have one, thereby allowing multilevel history.

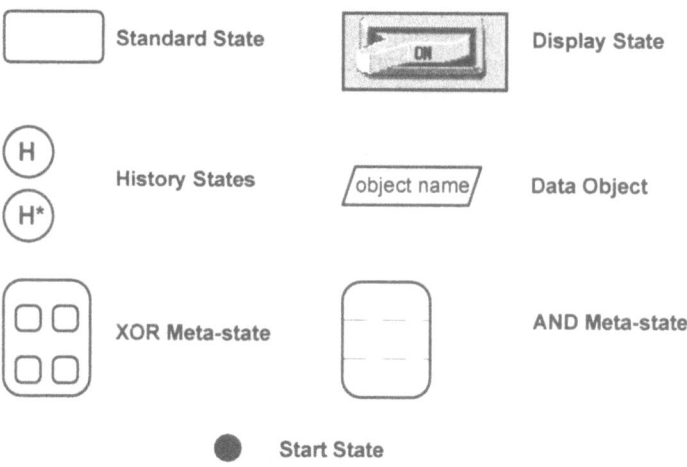

Figure 2: IOG node symbols

IOGs add two additional node types to the statechart, data objects and display states. Data objects represent the storage of a data item, and control is never passed to them. They can only be destinations for the data arcs discussed below. Display states are control states that have a change in the display associated with them. In IOG diagrams a picture of the display change is used whenever possible instead of a program-like statement such as *draw(ActiveON)*. Data objects are represented as parallelograms (Figure 2).

IOGs also add two special arc types, the event arc and the data arc. Events allow the designer to define messages which may be lacking in the underlying specification model. For example when specifying the trash can in the Macintosh interface, one needs to know when a file is being dragged over it as opposed to when the pointer is being dragged over it. One way to do this would be for the file icon to generate a *dragging-started* event and a *dropped* event. The trash can would then be highlighted whenever the pointer was over it between a *dragging-started* event and a *dropped* event. An event is represented by a special transition passing through an *E* in a diamond (Figure 3).

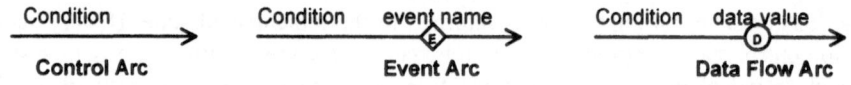

Figure 3: IOG arc symbols

Data flow is represented in a manner similar to events – an arc passing through a *D* in a circle (Figure 3). A data flow arc may have any node as a source and can only terminate at a data object or have an unspecified termination. In addition, at least one end must be attached to a data object. Data flow arcs with data objects as a source, whose destination arrow is unspecified, and whose destination is outside of the containing interaction object, indicate externally-readable data (Figure 4). This data may be used by the application or attached to other user interface components as a more complete specification is constructed. Data flow arcs with data objects as destinations represent updating the data object. If the arc's source is a control state, it represents a change in the value when the arc conditional is satisfied. In this case, the data flow arc is labelled with the new object value. An arc without a source represents externally-writable data.

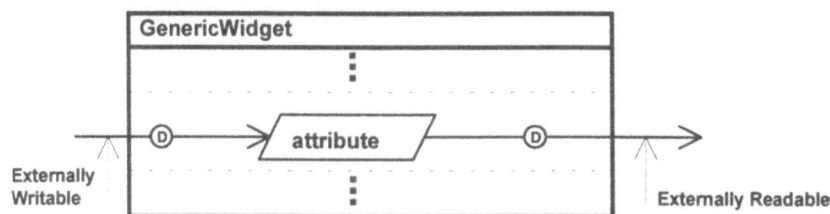

Figure 4: A readable and writable widget attribute in an IOG

Constraints are useful in specifying one attribute of the user interface in terms of others. With constraints it is simple to restrict an icon to be contained within a window or to map the values of a slider to a specific range. IOG data arcs support a form of one-way constraints by expressing the data value as an equation in terms of other attributes. Together with the condition on the data arc, these equations provide a means to constrain one attribute in terms of another with a Boolean guard. For example, specifying that in a given state (call it *S*), the image of a widget will follow the mouse cursor can be done with a constraint. This is accomplished by drawing a data arc from *S* to the data object representing the widget's location. Now, specify that the new value for the location is: the old location + the change in the mouse position. The condition for the arc would be: the mouse position changes. This results in the widget following the mouse while the widget control is in state *S*.

2.2 Interface Data Model

In order to describe the transitions between states, an abstract model of the user interface and a description language for that model are required. IOGs abstract the interface into the following objects: Booleans, numbers, strings, points, regions, icons, view ports, windows, and user inputs. A brief description of these objects follows.

Booleans, numbers, and strings (BNS) are the usual abstractions with the usual operations. It should be noted that numbers contain both the real and integer data types. In addition, any of these may be converted into an icon representation by the operator *icon(BNS, point, font, fontsize)* or *icon(BNS, region, font)*. Both operators convert the Boolean, number, or string *BNS* to a text representation, and then convert the text representation into a picture. If specified with a point, the resulting icon is as big as it needs to be to hold the picture of the text representation. If a region is specified, the icon is the size of the region. Fonts and font sizes may be omitted. In that case defaults will be used.

Points are an ordered pair of numbers (x,y). Points have the algebraic operators which are normally associated with them. A point may be assigned a value by writing *p=(x,y)*. In addition, *p.x* and *p.y* represent the x and y coordinates from the point *p*.

A region is a set of display points defined relative to an origin called the *location*. The location of the region is always the point (minx,miny) where minx and miny are the smallest x and y coordinates in the region. Regions have a *size* operator which returns the height and width of the smallest rectangle which covers the region. Regions also have an *in* operator which tests if a point is in the region. This is written *Region.in(pt)* and returns a Boolean value. Although regions are not restricted to be rectangular, rectangles are most commonly used. Note, a region cannot be visible on the display. There is no drawing operation associated with a region.

Icons are regions with pictures. That is, some points in the region have a colour number attached to them and are shown on the display. Icons add the operations *draw* and *erase*. In addition, if the origin of the icon is changed, there is an implicit *erase-draw* operation sequence. Unless otherwise specified, the region associated with an icon is a rectangle. So, *icon("text", pt, default, default)* would produce an icon with the upper-left corner at *pt*. The picture would be the word *text* in the default font and size. There would be a region associated with the icon. This region would be a rectangle with its upper-left corner at *pt* and of sufficient area to cover the text.

A view port is a region with an associated mapping function for some underlying application data. The mapping would be in two parts, conversion to a world-coordinate-system graphics representation and projection onto the display. For example, text would first be converted from ASCII to a font representation and a location on a page. The page would then be projected onto the display. The mapping is controlled by a projection function (*proj*), a translation point (*translate*), and a scale-change point (*scale*). If *convert* is the conversion function for some object in some view port, then the function *translate + proj(scale, (convert(object)))* would be the view port mapping. Parts of objects projected to points not in the region are not displayed, and objects in view ports are addressed relative to the view port location. Windows group the above objects together. They add a level attribute which determines window stacking relative to other windows. They can be viewed as view ports containing only objects already mapped to display coordinates. A window assigned a lower-level value obscures an overlapping window assigned a higher-level value.

Objects are addressed in the specification using a dot notation. For example, *win.icon1.location.x* would be the x coordinate of the location of icon, *icon1*, in window, *win*.

2.3 Event Description Language

User inputs are mapped to IOG events, numbers, points, and Boolean variables. Keyboard input is represented by quoted strings when the text is important ("quit⏎" when the word *quit* is typed and followed by a carriage return) or key events, similar to those in UAN, when the event is important (*LShiftv* for left shift key pressed). The mouse is mapped into a point for location (*M@*), a point for relative change (*M∆*), a Boolean indicating it moved (*∆M*), button change events (*Mv, M^, M2v, ...*), and button status variables (*Mdn, Mup, M2dn, ...*). Since the value of the mouse location is tested frequently, *in[Region]* is written as a shorthand for *Region.in(M@)*. The special notations *~[Region]* and *[Region]~* describe the events of the mouse entering and leaving the *Region*. These symbols can be combined in expressions. The operators from the 'C' language are used for these expressions. (Most commonly, && for logical AND, || for logical OR, and ! for logical NOT.) A more complete description can be found in (Carr 95).

3. Specification of a WWW Browser

Let's consider the specification of a simplified WWW browser using IOGs. The browser is a window which contains a menu system, a row of buttons, a type-in field for the current URL, and a viewing area for the current web page. In addition, the browser includes a list of URLs which represent the browsing history. Finally because the buttons duplicate menu selections, there is a need to specify a translation of menu selection events and button selection events into a set of common application events.

Figure 5 shows the top-level specification of the browser. At this point the specification is just six AND meta-states collected into a single AND meta-state which represents the window. This illustrates the basic grouping mechanism for IOGs, containment. The details of substates are hidden in order to make the diagram readable.

wwwBrowser::Window		
menus	buttonBlock	history::URLVector
currentURL	cmdGenerator	page::WebPage

Figure 5: Web browser specification major components

3.1 Button Panel Specification

The buttons which provide shortcuts for some frequently used menu selections are probably the simplest to specify, so let's consider them first. Figure 7 shows the *buttonBlock* meta-state. It is just a placeholder containing five buttons: *back, forward, home, reload,* and *stop*. The events generated by clicking these buttons will be used in the *cmdGenerator* to generate browser control events. Figure 6 shows a generic button. The button can be disabled by the *disable* event and enabled by the *enable* event. It also generates a *click* event which signals that it has been selected and a *press* event which signals that the user has pressed in the button area. These events are named using the dot notation so the *click* event from the *back* button becomes *back.click*.

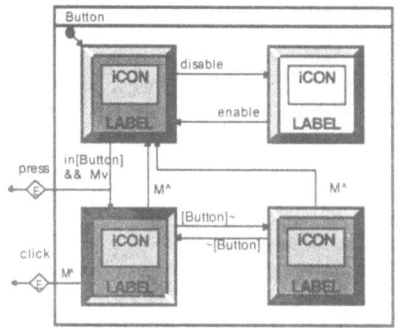

Figure 6: Generic button

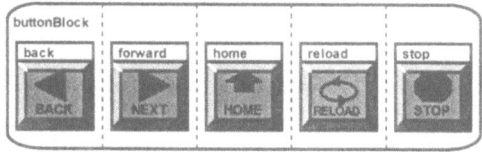

Figure 7: Browser buttons

3.2 Menu System Specification

The menus are also straightforward to build. One begins with a menu bar (Figure 8). The bar holds all of the top-level menu items and generates an event, *active*, that activates the entire menu system. Menu entries are either a menu item or a menu item combined with controls for an associated drop-down menu.

Figure 9 shows the specification of a menu item in the Macintosh style. It has two modes, enabled and disabled, with the *enable* and *disable* events moving between them when the menus are not active. The *menus.active* event causes the menu item to go into a state where it shifts between being active and inactive depending on the position of the mouse pointer. Moving the mouse pointer into a menu item (or having pressed the mouse button while inside of it) causes the item to become active. This causes an *active* event which can be used in controlling the visibility of the pop-up menu associated with the item.

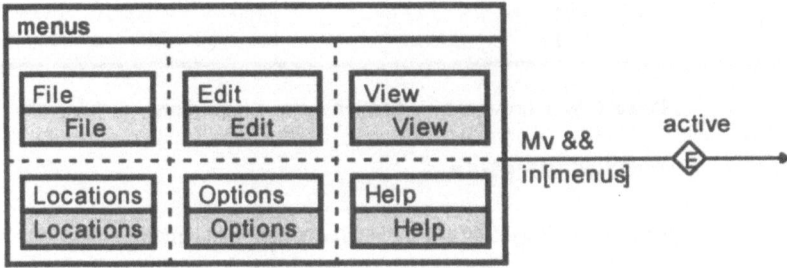

Figure 8: Menu bar

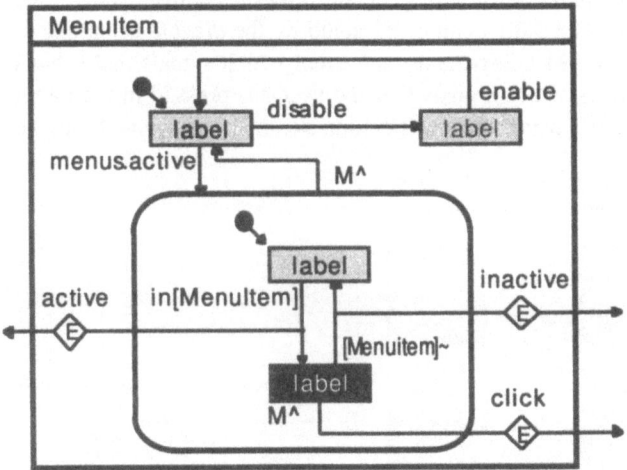

Figure 9: Menu item

The only piece of the menu system that remains to be specified is the behaviour of a menu item that has a pop-up menu associated with it. This is shown in Figure 10. The lower meta-state shows the control of the pop-up menu. It starts out invisible. When the associated menu item is selected its *active* event triggers a state change that causes the pop-up menu to become visible. Moving outside of the associated menu item causes the pop-up menu to become invisible again unless the pop-up menu itself has been entered. At this point the menu stays until all pop-up menus descended from this item are exited. This is signified by the *[∪?PopUp]* region and this would have to be specified exactly for each pop-up menu item. This is not a trivial task.

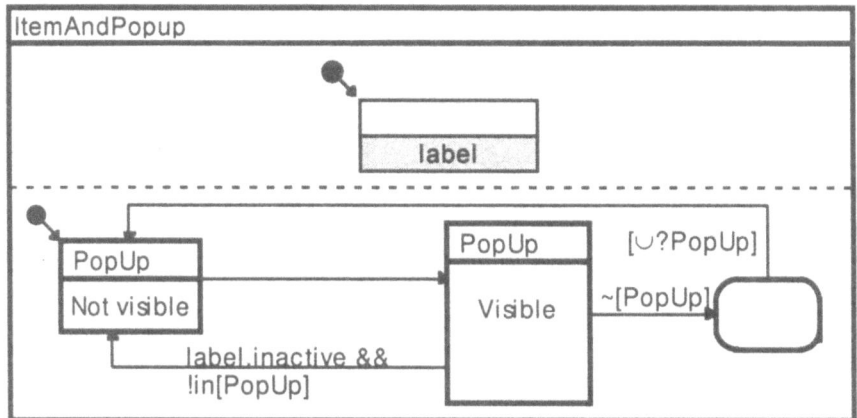

Figure 10: Pop-up menu control

3.3 Specification of URL Loading with History

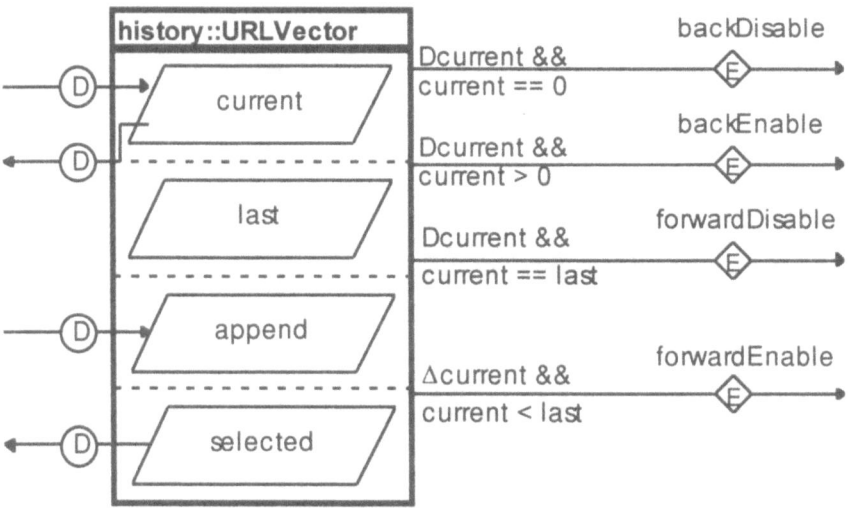

Figure 11: URL history with associated button control events

The specification of the URL loading mechanism will use three viewports. The first is a type-in text field that contains the current URL (Figure 12). The external behaviour of this viewport is described by the transitions on the *text* data item. The second viewport is the web-page display area (Figure 12). It is assumed that this viewport formats HTML appropriately and that clicking on a link will eventually result in the associated URL being placed in the *selected* data item. The final viewport is the URL history (Figure 11). This last viewport is more complex. It is assumed to have a vector of elements. This vector expands and contracts according to the number of elements in it. Associated with the vector are four additional data items: *current, last, append,* and *selected.* The *current* data item is the index of either the last element appended to the list or of the last element selected from the list. This depends on the last operation. In addition, changing *current* causes *element[current]* to be placed in *selected.* The *last* data item is the index of the last element in the list. Changing the *append* data item results in the new URL being inserted at *current+1* and the new element becoming the *last.* Finally, the vector of elements is displayed as part of the menu system, and when the user chooses an element from the list it is place in *selected.* These data relationships can be specified with IOG data arcs, but they are not shown in Figure 11.

The interaction between the current URL, selection of an item from the history list, and selection of a new URL on the WWW page is shown in Figure 12. This is expressed as a series of data arcs. Selecting a new item on the WWW page causes *page.selected* to change. This in turn is propagated to *currentURL.text* and from there to *history.append.* Similarly, selecting a URL from the history list causes this to appear at *history.selected*, and this is propagated to *currentURL.text.* The propagation of this back to *history.append* is prevented by the condition (*currentURL.text != history.selected*) on the return arc.

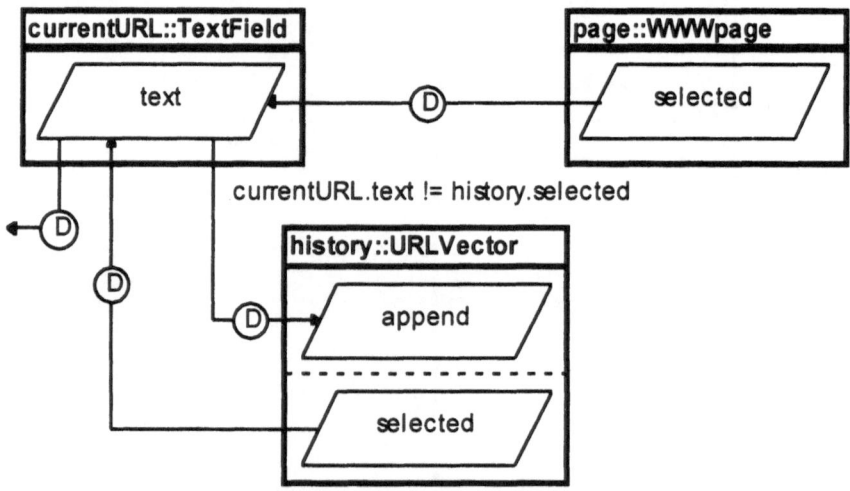

Figure 12: Interaction between, *currentURL, history,* and *page*

The actual retrieval of the new URL is not a function of the user interface and is not specified here. However, the IOG model allows attachment of data arcs to application code in a callback mechanism. Here the unattached arc from *currentURL.text* would be used as a callback into some network code.

Browser history is also affected by buttons and menu items. Figure 13 shows how the forward, back, and home functions are implemented. A command corresponding to the function is generated as an event, and this becomes the precondition to a data arc which acts on a *history* data item. Since the data arcs from Figure 12 still apply even though they are not shown, history and the current URL are correctly maintained.

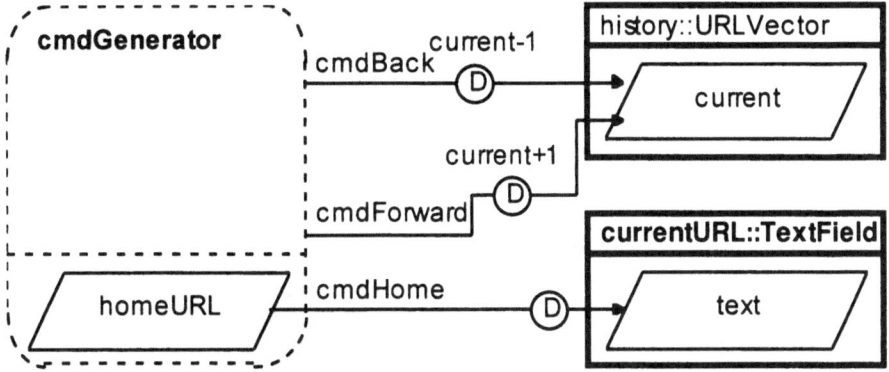

Figure 13: Action of menus and buttons on the browser history

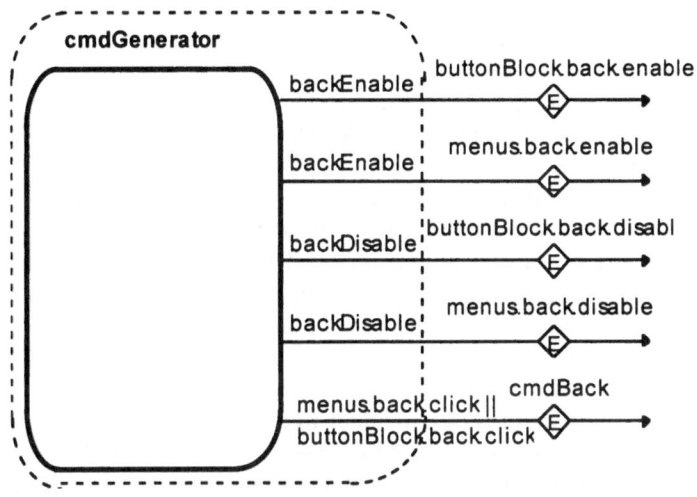

Figure 14: Event translation for the back button

3.4 Specification of Browser Commands

The user shortcuts implemented by the buttons duplicate menu functions. In order to treat both the menu items and the buttons in a uniform manner, events from the menu items and the corresponding buttons need to be joined into a common event. This enables the rest of the specification to be in terms of the common event and helps isolate it from changes in the menu or button block. Similarly, enable and disable events need to be split so that both the button and the menu item are properly handled. Figure 14 shows an example of this mapping for the back button. Other buttons are handled similarly.

4. Analysing Interaction Object Graphs

Once one has a formal description of a user interface, there is the possibility of analysing it to locate errors. Besides errors in the specification with respect to the notation, it is desirable to relate the notation to user interface properties and test correctness against the properties as well. If one can test against user interface properties, there is some assurance that the interface is better than one which cannot be so verified.

(Dix 91) defined an algebraic model of the user interface and then related the user interface properties of "predictability", "observability", and "reachability" to the model. Predictability requires that we ask the question, "Given a configuration of the user interface and a user input, can the user predict the result?" This question must be answered in terms of what the user can see on the screen. The IOG concept of a view port makes it impossible to answer this question entirely from the IOG. (An assumption about the predictability of the view port must be made.) Observability can be considered a super-set of predictability. In order to be observable, a user must be able to infer the state of user-interface attributes from the state of the screen. Again, an assumption about view port observability would be necessary to answer questions about observability with IOGs. Finally, for reachability we simply ask, "Is it possible to get to all configurations?" (Monk 90) defined a semiformal notation, action-effect rules, in order to analyse an interface for the properties of predictability, reachability, completeness, consistency, and reversibility. Predictability and reachability are defined as in Dix. Completeness is defined in relation to user actions. Thus, a system is considered complete if there is a response to all user actions. Consistency involves a comparison of responses for an action in different modes. Finally, reversibility was a measure of the number of actions required to reverse a given action.

Violations of the above properties are frequently caused by some type of programming or specification error. While it would be impossible to prove a widget error free, some common errors should be detectable. For example, many widgets have a direct mapping between a display state (display node in IOGs) and the value of a widget attribute of some enumerated type. At least for those states which represent the widget when the user is not manipulating it, it would be desirable to verify that the attribute value could be guaranteed. This property is a form of the state invariant described in (Atlee & Gannon 93). If "idle" states represent the widget when the user is not manipulating it, state invariance for idle states is closely related to the usability concept of observability of underlying system state. Forgetting a data arc is one common cause of this error. Other properties to check could include freedom from "sink states" and "dialogue completion". A sink state is one which once entered cannot be left and is a violation of the reversibility principle of direct manipulation interfaces. Dialogue completion would insure that the widget returned to an idle state when the user stopped manipulating it. While related to reachability, dialogue completion imposes additional constraints on the system.

4.1 State Invariance

Limited analysis IOGs for correctness with respect to two user-interface properties is possible. The first is state invariance. A widget such as a switch or radio button displays visual feedback that is dependent upon the value of an underlying data attribute value. It is important that the state of the widget on the display correctly indicates the value of that attribute. So, the designer writes an invariant for some subset of the states in the IOG specification and demonstrates two things. First, all paths into the state satisfy the invariant. Second, if the value of the attribute is changed by a parallel operation, then the display state of the widget changes.

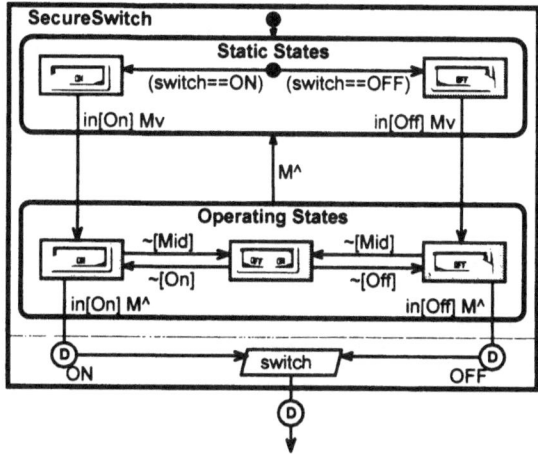

Figure 15: IOG specification of a switch

To illustrate the state invariance and dialogue completion properties an example widget not used in the browser will be used. This example is a type of light switch that is common in the United States. The switch widget in Figure 15 should display the "off" image of a switch when the user is not manipulating the switch, and the switch attribute value is *OFF*. So, the invariant for the "off" state in the *Static States* meta-state would be *Switch = OFF*. It is rather easy to show that this is satisfied. There is only one path into this state and it has a precondition of *Switch == Off*. So, the "off" picture will only be displayed if the value of the switch attribute is *OFF*. Since the switch attribute is read-only, one doesn't need to worry about changes to that attribute. Similarly, one can show that the "on" state in *Static States* preserves a *Switch = ON* invariant.

4.2 Dialogue Completion

The second property is dialogue completion. To demonstrate this property the designer marks a subset of states in the specification as representing the widget in a steady state. Next, the designer chooses a user-dialogue completion event. Now, it must be shown that for every state in the specification when the dialogue-completion event occurs, the specification will enter one of the previously chosen states and remain there until the next external event. If the chosen states also have state invariance, then one can be assured that the widget will return to a steady state when the user isn't operating the widget, and that it will correctly display the attribute value.

In Figure 15 the states contained in the *Static States* meta-state represent the widget in the steady state. The states contained in the *Operating States* meta-state represent those that are active in the dialogue. The dialogue-completion event is releasing the mouse button. One can see that there is exactly one control arc that can be active from a dynamic state - the arc from the *Operating States* meta-state back to the *Static States* meta-state. So, this widget satisfies both the state invariant and the dialogue completion event.

If the reader believes that these properties are without meaning, look at Figure 16. This is a switch similar to that in Figure 15, but the dialogue is specified differently. Trying to show the dialogue-completion property on the "on" state contained in *Operating States* requires that one show $M^\wedge \Rightarrow ((M^\wedge \ \&\& \ in[On]) \ || \ (M^\wedge \ \&\& \ !in[On] \ \&\& \ !in[Off]))$. This cannot be done and in fact under the right circumstances the widget can be left in the "on" state while the switch is off.

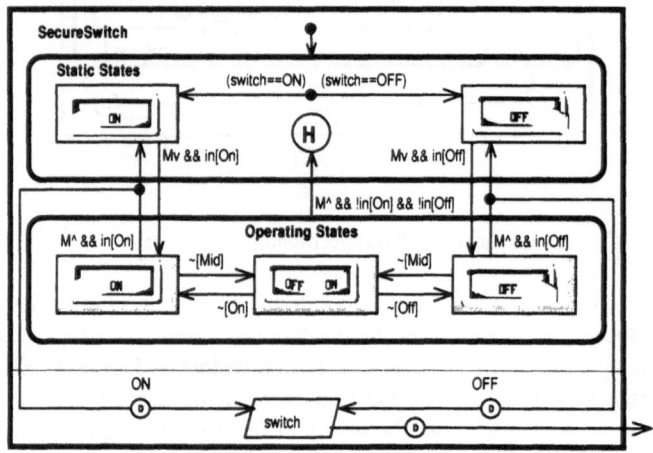

Figure 16: Erroneous IOG specification of a switch

5. Conclusion

Interaction Object Graphs represent an improvement in user-interface specification languages. They add a representation for the visual aspects of the user interface and a representation for data. Neither of these are found in existing specification techniques. While they seem to be more understandable, experiments with actual users show that error rates when manually interpreting them are high (Carr 96). This is not a problem isolated to IOGs, but seems to apply to all specification methods.

This suggests that the specification community must spend more effort on creating usable notations.

A partial solution to the problem is to have an executable notation. IOGs are executable, and a C++ class library to build and interpret them exists. However, tools that go directly from the diagram to executable code are needed.

Also useful would be automatic tools to analyse state invariance and dialogue completion. In addition, further research is needed to map other user-interface properties into a form that can be checked on an IOG. One problem with automatic analysis is that view ports are not specified within the IOG system and a notation to specify them should be developed.

In spite of their shortcomings, IOGs represent a scaleable method for graphically specifying user interfaces. They can be used for small dialogues or entire interfaces. They give a clear visualisation of how the user interface will look for dialogues with discrete steps. IOGs avoid the scalability problems of transition diagrams. They improve on statecharts by providing both an interface visualisation and a representation for data.

The representation of data and visualisation of the interface is an advantage that IOGs have over other state-based representations (Jacob 86, Wasserman 85, Wellner 89). Interactive Cooperative Objects (Palanque & Bastide 94) and Interface Representation Graphs (Rouff & Horowitz 91) represent data explicitly, but do not provide any interface dynamics visualisation. User Action Notation also lacks data representation and visualisation capabilities. Also, to date no interpreter exists for UAN. Grammar-based solutions such as task-action grammars (Payne & Green 89) while theoretically executable have difficulty expressing the concurrency required to specify direct-manipulation interfaces. Other methods of executable specification are rule-based systems such as UIDE (Gieskens & Foley 92) and by demonstration as in Druid (Singh, Kok & Ngan 90). Rule-based systems divide the interactions between components into separate rules. This makes it very difficult to understand system behaviour for non-trivial systems. Systems that create interfaces by demonstration generally do not have a visual representation of the interface behaviour, although one could be developed. In fact, a state-based representation that was initially developed by demonstration and then further refined by an editor might be very useful.

Acknowledgements

I wish to thank Carl Rollo for his work in implementing the Microsoft Windows' interface and implementing the animated specifications. I would also like to thank him for proof-reading drafts of this chapter. Special thanks also go to Sylvia Sheppard and Christopher Rouff of NASA Goddard Space Flight Center for their encouragement and support. Much of this work was carried out while I was at the Human-Computer Interaction Laboratory of the University of Maryland, and I would like to thank my colleagues there for their suggestions for improvements in the development of IOGs.

Chapter 8:
Specifying a Web Browser Interface Using Object-Z

1. Introduction

A specification describes the functions that a system provides to its users without explanation of how those functions are implemented. A user interface specification is a description of a system from the perspective of its users (i.e., a description of the view of the system that is provided to users); such a specification is useful for developing user interface designs. A specification of a user interface indicates those functional aspects of the interactive system (data and operations) that are perceivable by the user and the logical organisation of information provided by the interface.

In this chapter, we consider a formal method for specifying and designing user interfaces using the Object-Z language (Duke, Rose & Smith 94). This chapter is an extension and revision of our work reported in (Hussey & Carrington 96b). Our approach structures the specification and design of the user interface using interactors (user interface components). Such components define part of the behaviour and appearance of the user interface. Composing the interactors for a user interface produces the behaviour and appearance of the user interface as a whole.

Formal notations, such as Object-Z, are increasingly accepted for specifying functional aspects of software systems; however their use in user interface development is less common. This is despite widespread support for the view that formal methods ease system development. Formal notations provide a mechanism for accurate communication of specifications and designs (Aslett 91, p.2). The precision required to write a formal specification assists in detecting "inconsistencies and ambiguities" in a system (Duke & Harrison 94). The effort invested in producing a formal user interface specification and design is repaid through the resulting documentation of the user interface. In addition, a formal development process allows demonstration of the consistency of a user interface design with the abstract system specification. Of course, using formal methods does not guarantee correct software; "on the contrary, ... they are merely a means of achieving higher integrity systems when applied appropriately" (Bowen & Hinchey 95). Formalisms do not guarantee that a design will be aesthetically pleasing or even that it will conform to established guidelines (Dix 91, p.14).

Section 2 describes the language model that provides a framework for explaining the scope of interactive system specification. Section 3 describes the interactor model, which is an object oriented model for structuring specifications of interactive systems. We apply the language model in the context of an interactor-based approach to specification. Section 4 justifies our choice of Object-Z as our notation for interactor-based specification. The specification techniques described in Section 3 are applied to a case study in Section 5. Section 6 provides an analysis of this work.

2. The Language Model

We use the Seeheim model to characterise the boundary between user interface specification and user interface design (Green 83). User interaction can be decomposed into three elements:

1. semantic — abstract meaning associated with syntactic constructs;
2. syntactic — valid sequences of events;
3. lexical — lexemes comprising events (e.g., keystrokes, mouse actions, visual presentation of system output).

For example, to draw a line in a graphics package, the user selects start and finish points using the mouse (see Figure 1).

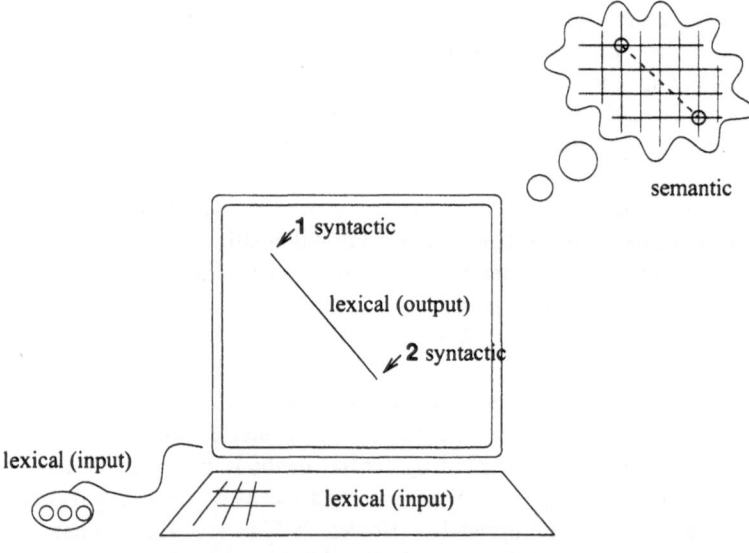

Figure 1: Semantics, syntax and lexemes

The mouse manipulations and subsequent output are lexemes, whereas the required sequence of point selections defines syntax. The abstract semantics of a line are that it is the most direct path between two points.

The specification of a user interface defines the semantic and syntactic aspects of the user interface. Determining lexemes is a design activity rather than a specification activity because it involves the description of how the system presents its functions to the user. A specification of a system should not constrain the modality (visual, audio etc.) of the interaction (Duke & Harrison 94). Specification is restricted to description of semantics and syntax.

The language model implies that we should be able to produce separate syntactic and semantic specifications. However splitting syntax and semantics is difficult, to the extent that attempting to separate the two may impair the clarity of a specification. There is usually a close relationship between syntactic and semantic descriptions because both are dependent on the same system state. In this situation it is the description of the whole rather than the parts that is important. Further, there is little gain in producing a separate semantic description for analysis purposes, though it may be useful to derive a separate syntactic specification for syntactic analysis.

3.　Interactor Specification

User interfaces can be specified as a collection of interacting agents using an agent-based language (Abowd 91). A set of agents is identified that together comprise the system and its environment. Agents have state, operations upon that state and may respond to and initiate events. Agents can be combined to form larger (more complex) agents. In an interactive system, some agents are presented to users.

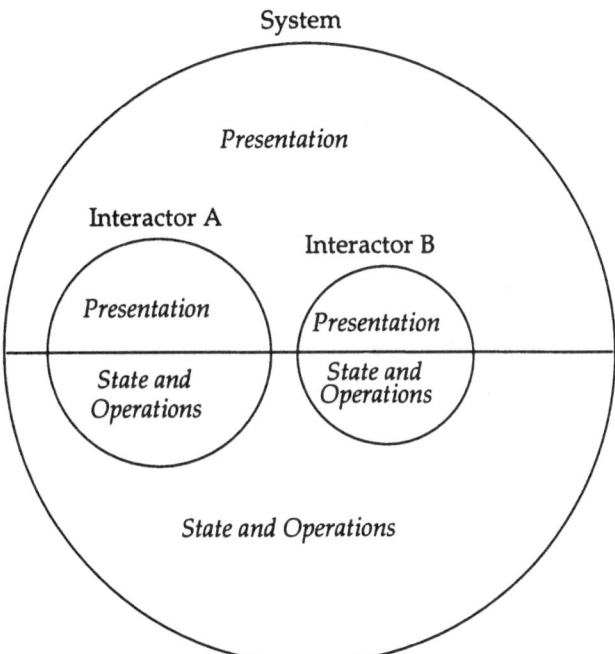

Figure 2: Combining interactors

The agent and its presentation together define an *interactor* (Coutaz, Nigay & Salber 95). Each agent specifies a corresponding interactor. An interactor has a presentation aspect that reflects the internal state of the application (Duke & Harrison 93) (i.e., as defined by the corresponding agent). Defining the presentation aspects of interactors is a design concern. Figure 2 depicts a user interface consisting of a single interactor that is composed of two sub-interactors.

The interactor specifications (agents) define the logical organisation of information presented by the user interface and therefore provide a starting point for design of the presentation. The structure of an interactor-based specification (i.e., choice of agents) does *not* force the structure of a corresponding implementation. So, an implementation based on such a specification need not use agents as a structural mechanism.

The user interface specification is derived from a more abstract system-oriented specification. User interface specification encompasses a range of abstractions that can be ordered according to a refinement relationship (Duke & Harrison 95) as depicted in Figure 3:

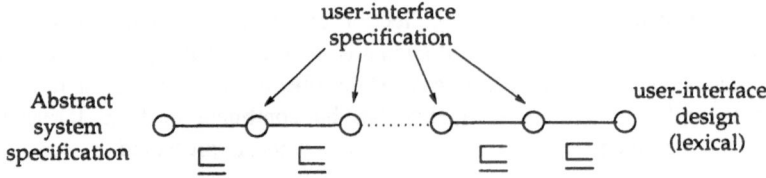

Figure 3: Refinement relationship between specifications

Our goal in refining a user interface specification is to identify those parts of the specification that correspond to common, re-usable interface components (widgets). Identifying such correspondence simplifies producing a design of the user interface's presentation because the presentation (input and output behaviour) of widgets is usually well understood.

Interactors allow us to structure the specification according to the logical organisation of information provided by the interface. Grouping related data and operations in this way inherently simplifies the object interactions in the specification. Additionally, because interactors group related data and operations, an interactor specification provides clues to the designer as to how the interface implementation's structure ought to appear *to the user*.

4. Choosing a Notation

In this section we compare Object-Z to other formal notations for specifying user interfaces. Object-Z (Duke, Rose & Smith 94), an object oriented extension of Z (Spivey 92), can be used as a notation for interactor-based specification. A brief description of Object-Z is provided in Appendix A. Z has been applied previously to the specification of interactive systems (Sufrin 82, Sufrin & He 90, Duke & Harrison 95). Our approach differs from Z (and other state-based calculi such as VDM) primarily because Object-Z enables us to make full and direct use of interactors as a structural mechanism for our specifications. Because Object-Z is object oriented, it can be used to structure specifications as systems of agents. Such a description naturally parallels the presentation of the interface and provides a convenient basis for design of the interface's presentation.

Although Object-Z operations can describe partial traces for the system, the sequence in which operations may occur is not explicit. Supplementary process-based descriptions can be used to clarify the allowable sequences of operations. We provide a CSP (Hoare 85) description of interactor syntax as an aid to the reader in understanding the sequencing of operations defined by the Object-Z specification. A brief introduction to CSP is provided in Appendix B. The CSP description could be used to analyse syntactic properties. We use CSP because event-based algebras have better scalability than either grammars or diagrammatic methods such as state-transition networks (Green 86).

We do not rely on a separate syntax description because we believe the separation of syntactic and semantic concerns to be problematic. We use Object-Z to describe both interface semantics and syntax. Describing both syntax and semantics using Object-Z allows us to emphasise their relationship more effectively than if their descriptions were separated. In addition, we believe that state-based notations have better scalability than process algebras.

Abowd has developed an object oriented notation that is conceptually similar to Object-Z (Abowd 91a). Abowd's notation is a hybrid of Z and CSP (Abowd 91b). Similar interactor-based methods have been developed using Modal Action Logic (Duke & Harrison 96), Petri nets (Palanque 94), LOTOS (Paternò & Faconti 92, Paternò 94) and VDM with CSP (Fields, Harrison & Wright 94a, Fields, Harrison & Wright 94b). Recent work by Paternò has investigated structuring LOTOS interactors using task analysis (Paternò 96). In each case, we believe that Object-Z's predicate calculus (inherited from Z) offers more flexible and powerful operators for expressing the static (state) and dynamic properties of the system. Further, Object-Z's schema calculus enables the succinct expression of relationships between interactors in the specification. When compared to Abowd's notation, Object-Z is more flexible (Abowd only permits the combination of whole interactors, rather than the combination of interactor operations). Similarly, the notations of Duke and Harrison or Fields, Harrison and Wright, do not provide facilities for communication between interactors that match the flexibility of those for Object-Z. Furthermore Fields, Harrison and Wright split syntactic information across the VDM and CSP descriptions.

In Section 5, we develop a case study based on a generic "Web Browser". A Web Browser is a program that provides a user perceivable representation of the information provided by the World Wide Web ("the web"). We apply interactors as a structural mechanism for reducing complexity.

5. Case Study

The current extensive use of the Web motivates its choice as an area for study. Each year, Web usage multiplies and this trend appears likely to continue. In this section we present a specification of a user interface for a generic Web Browser. Our specification is divided into several interactors. For each interactor, the specification is in two sections: the first section defines the semantics of the interactor using Object-Z[7]; the second explicitly defines syntax using CSP. The Dexter model of hypertext (Halasz & Schwartz 94) provides a starting point from which part of the state of a Web Browser may be defined because much of the data manipulated by a Web Browser is hypertext. However the Dexter model is far more complex than the hypertext models actually used by most existing Web Browsers because the Dexter model provides many additional capabilities such as bi-directional links between pages. In this specification, we use only a few central ideas from the Dexter model. Our model is similar to other (simplified) models of hypertext, e.g., (d'Inverno & Priestley 95, Wang, Holden & Hitchcock 93). In particular, we regard our hypothetical system as operating on data whose structure can be treated as consisting of components organised into groups called *pages*. Only one page is accessible by the user at a time. We only deal with the *http* (hypertext) aspects of the web, so each link within the Web is to another component in the web. A Web server determines how data in the Web is interpreted. Web servers retrieve data for a given Web location. We model Web locations by the given type *URL*.

We only deal with the http server because the activities supported by other servers (such as ftp) are so similar. The http server maps Web locations to viewable pages. We model a single Web server thread that handles a single mapping request at a time and can be stopped at any time. In our model, pages are retrieved in their entirety before being passed to the client object. Note that the Web server does not define an interactor, i.e., the server is hidden (it does not have any presentation) and is accessed only via interactors which define user accessible operations.

WebServer

$pages : URL \rightarrow Page$
$currentreq : \mathbb{P}\ URL$

$\#currentreq \leq 1$

Stop

$\Delta(currentreq)$

$currentreq' = \varnothing$

Request

$\Delta(currentreq)$
$url? : URL$

$currentreq = \varnothing$
$url? \in \text{dom } pages$
$currentreq' = \{\ url?\ \}$

CurrentReq

$url! : URL$

$url! \in currentreq$

ServePage

$\Delta(currentreq)$
$dest! : Page$

$currentreq \neq \varnothing$
$\exists\ c : currentreq \bullet dest! = pages(c)$
$currentreq' = \varnothing$

---

[1]   The Object-Z specifications comprising the case study have been checked using the Wizard type-checker that was developed by the Software Verification Research Centre at The University of Queensland.

A *TextComponent* is represented by a sequence of characters. A *GraphicComponent* is represented by one or more pictorial regions in the Browser's display. We are not concerned with the internal details of text and graphic components. A component is either a text component or graphic component.

$$Component == TextComponent \cup GraphicComponent$$

We model a page as consisting of one or more components. Some components may be anchors. An anchor is a component whose selection leads to an alteration of the currently viewed page. We regard the mappings between pages as uni-directional, although other researchers have modelled such links as bi-directional. The current component of the page indicates the location within the page that the user is viewing. Selecting a component that is an anchor produces the URL to which that anchor refers.

Page

$contents : \text{seq}_1\ Component$
$anchors :\ Component \nrightarrow URL$
$curr : \mathbb{N}_1$
Δ
$component :\ Component$

$\text{dom}\ anchors \subseteq \text{ran}\ contents$
$component =\ contents(curr)$
$curr \le \#contents$

PreviousComponent
$\Delta(curr)$

$curr > 1 \Rightarrow curr' = curr - 1$
$curr = 1 \Rightarrow curr' = curr$

NextComponent
$\Delta(curr)$

$curr < \#contents \Rightarrow curr' = curr + 1$
$curr = \#contents \Rightarrow curr' = curr$

ComponentToURL
$source? :\ Component$
$url! : URL$

$source? \in \text{dom}\ anchors$
$url! =\ anchors\ (source?)$

The *Navigator* interactor provides the user's interface to the pages and components that form the web. Initially the navigator views the user's "home" page. The user has a current page within the Web which can be altered by the user clicking on an anchor component. The user's interactions with the system build a sequence of locations within which the user can move backward and forward.

$$RequestType ::= Jump \mid\ Forward \mid\ Back$$

Navigator
$\lceil$(*CurrLocn, Forward, Back, OpenLocation, LinkClick,*
        Stop, NextComponent, PreviousComponent)

| *home* : *URL*

_____

history : seq$_1$ *Component*
curr : N_1
currpage : *Page*
request : **P** *RequestType*
web : *WebServer*

INIT
history = ⟨*home*⟩
curr = 1
currpage = *web.pages(home)*
request = ∅

_ForwardRequest_____
Δ(*request*)
url! : *URL*
_____
curr < # *history*
url! = *history* (*curr* + 1)
request' = { *Forward* }

_BackRequest_____
Δ(*request*)
url! : *URL*
_____
curr > 1
url! = *history* (*curr* − 1)
request' = { *Back* }

_JumpRequest_____
Δ(*request*)
_____
request' = { *Jump* }

_CurrLocn_____
current! : *URL*
_____
current! = *history* (*curr*)

_RecordForward_____
Δ(*curr, request*)
_____
request = { *Forward* }
curr = *curr* + 1
request' = ∅

_RecordBack_____
Δ(*curr, request*)
_____
request = { *Back* }
curr = *curr* − 1
request' = ∅

_RecordJump_____
Δ(*history, curr, request*)
url? : *URL*
_____
request = { *Jump* }
history' = (1 .. *curr* ◁ *history*) ⌢ ⟨*url?*⟩
curr' = *curr* + 1
request' = ∅

_____

Forward ≙ *ForwardRequest* ‖ *web.Request*
Back ≙ *BackRequest* ‖ *web.Request*
OpenLocation ≙ *JumpRequest* ∧ *web.Request*
LinkClick ≙ *JumpRequest* ∧ (*currpage.ComponentToURL* ‖ *web.Request*)
DisplayJump ≙ *web.ServePage* ∧ (*currpage.CurrentReq* ‖ *RecordJump*)
DisplayForward ≙ *web.ServePage* ∧ *RecordForward*
DisplayBack ≙ *web.ServePage* ∧ *RecordBack*
Stop ≙ *web.Stop* ∧ [Δ(*request*) | *request'* = ∅]
NextComponent ≙ *currpage.NextComponent*
PreviousComponent ≙ *currpage.PreviousComponent*

Navigation within the Web is restricted by the proviso that the user cannot backtrack further than the first location viewed in the current session (defined by *head history*) and cannot move forward past the last location (defined by *last history*). A new location can be added to the history sequence, either by the user clicking on a hyperdata link (*LinkClick*) or specifying the page explicitly (*OpenLocation*). *OpenLocation, LinkClick, Forward* and *Back* each lodge a request with the Web server that is serviced after a non-deterministic delay. At any time the user can invoke the operation *Stop* to halt service of the Web server's current request. Note that *DisplayJump, DisplayForward* and *DisplayBack* are not user invoked operations. A corresponding user interface design would not associate any lexical equivalent with these operations. Instead, we regard these operations as invoked internally.

The syntax of the *Navigator* interactor, for navigation between Web pages, is modelled using CSP. We choose not to model the manipulation of the current component within the current page because the syntax involving movement between components is clear and adding it to the page navigation syntax would reduce clarity. We also do not include the operation *CurrLocn* because that operation can be invoked at any time. It is not dependent on the prior sequence of operations. Further, *CurrLocn* is used only for communicating with the *HotList* interactor, which we describe below. It is not available to the user. We provide a CSP model of the interactor syntax to explain the syntactic behaviour that the Object-Z captures. In addition, a supplementary description of syntax allows the reader to concentrate on purely semantic issues of individual operations without concern for what global sequences of operations are valid or invalid.

α **NAVIGATOR** = { *Forward, Back, OpenLocation, LinkClick* }

NAVIGATOR = END_0

$END_0 = x:$ { *LinkClick, OpenLocation* } $\rightarrow END_1$

$END_{j>0} = x:$ { *LinkClick, OpenLocation* } $\rightarrow (Stop \rightarrow END_j \ \square \ END_{j+1}) \ |$

$\qquad Back \rightarrow (Stop \rightarrow END_j \ \square \ WITHIN^j_{j-1})$

The user can navigate forward through the sequence of locations until they are viewing the last location in the sequence. Likewise, the user can navigate backward until they are at the first location in the sequence. A click on an anchor alters the sequence so that the new Web location becomes the last element in the sequence (i.e., the page most recently accessed).

$WITHIN^j_k = Forward \rightarrow (Stop \rightarrow WITHIN^j_k \ \square \ WITHIN^j_{k+1}) \ |$

$\qquad Back \rightarrow (Stop \rightarrow WITHIN^j_k \ \square \ WITHIN^j_{k-1}) \ |$

$\qquad x:$ { *LinkClick,OpenLocation* } $\rightarrow (Stop \rightarrow WITHIN^j_k \ \square \ END_{k+1})$

$WITHIN_j^j = END_j$

$WITHIN_0^j = Forward \rightarrow (Stop \rightarrow WITHIN_0^j \;\square\; WITHIN_1^j)\,|$

$\qquad\qquad$ x: { *LinkClick, OpenLocation* } $\rightarrow (Stop \rightarrow WITHIN_0^j \;\square\; END_1)$

We introducé a *VisitableList* interactor, which forms the basis for several interactors. A visitable list allows the selection and retrieval of a Web location.

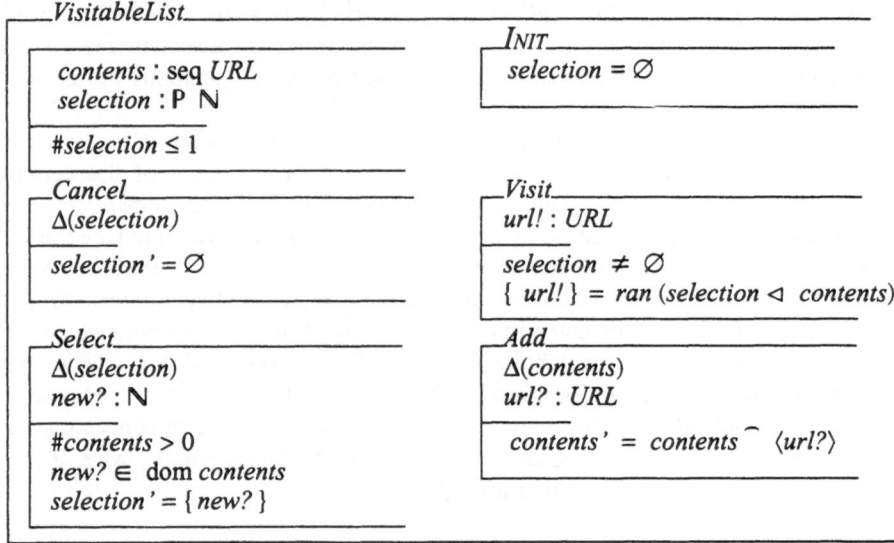

The history list interactor is simply a visitable list. As the user traverses the Web via the navigator interactor, Web locations are added to the history list.

```
___HistoryList_____
  VisitableList
_____
```

The history list interactor allows the user to select and view components from a list of previously accessed components. Until a selection has been made, the operation *Visit* is unavailable. The corresponding CSP description follows:

α **HISTORY** = { *Select, Visit, Add, Cancel* }

HISTORY = *Select* → *SELECTED_HISTORY* |

$\qquad\qquad$ *Add* → *HISTORY* |

$\qquad\qquad$ *Cancel* → *HISTORY*

$$SELECTED\_HISTORY = Select \rightarrow SELECTED\_HISTORY \,|$$
$$Visit \rightarrow SELECTED\_HISTORY \,|$$
$$Add \rightarrow SELECTED\_HISTORY \,|$$
$$Cancel \rightarrow HISTORY$$

The hotlist interactor is a visitable list for which the user controls the addition and deletion of elements.

```
┌─HistoryList─────────────────────────────────────────────
│ VisitableList
│ ┌─DeleteSelection──────────────────────────────────────
│ │ Δ(contents, selection)
│ │ ──────────────────────────────────────────────────
│ │ ∃ n : selection • contents' = squash ({ n } ◁ contents)
│ │ selection' = ∅
│ └──────────────────────────────────────────────────────
└──────────────────────────────────────────────────────────
```

The corresponding CSP specification is similar to that for the *HistoryList* interactor, but also allows the user to delete the current selection from the list.

The Web Browser may be defined by instantiating interactors whose behaviour corresponds to the classes defined above. We promote operations of the instantiated interactors to the top level. In effect, the Web Browser is a system level interactor composed from instances of *Navigator*, *HistoryList* and *HotList*.

```
┌─WebBrowser──────────────────────────────────────────────
│ ┌──────────────────────────────────────────────────────
│ │ navigator : Navigator
│ │ history : HistoryList
│ │ hotlist : HotList
│ │ web : WebServer
│ │ ────────────────────────────────────────────────
│ │ navigator.web = web
│ └──────────────────────────────────────────────────────
│
│ Forward ≘ navigator.Forward
│ Back ≘ navigator.Back
│ NextComponent ≘ navigator.NextComponent
│ PreviousComponent ≘ navigator.PreviousComponent
│ HistorySelect ≘ history.Select
│ HistoryCancel ≘ history.Cancel
│ HotListSelect ≘ hotlist.Select
│ HotListCancel ≘ hotlist.Cancel
│ HotListDeleteSelection ≘ hotlist.DeleteSelection
│ OpenLocation ≘ navigator.OpenLocation ‖ history.Add
│ LinkClick ≘ navigator.LinkClick ‖ history.Add
```

HistoryOpenLocation ≅ *history.Visit* ‖ *navigator.OpenLocation* ‖ *history.Add*

HotListOpenLocation ≅ *hotlist.Visit* ‖ *navigator.OpenLocation* ‖ *history.Add*

AddCurrent ≅ *navigator.CurrLocn* ‖ *hotlist.Add* [*current? / url?*]

Stop ≅ *navigator.Stop*

Operations on interactors may be effected programmatically, rather than by user interaction. For example, operations such as *history.Add* and *navigator.CurrLocn* are not directly accessible by the user. Such operations are invoked by other interactors in the system. In that case, the operations do not have a lexical description. Also, because we are specifying rather than designing, we do not indicate how the user invokes operations such as *LinkClick*. For example, a design based on an architecture derived directly from the specification might give control to the *navigator* interactor. However our specification is not concerned with this.

The class *WebSystem* models a site with a population of Browsers and a single Web server. From a user's perspective, the Web server is multi-threaded; each such server thread is modelled by the *Web* attribute of each Browser. A separate server thread is associated with each Browser. The system permits a flexible number of concurrent Web Browsers with dynamic instantiation and termination of Browsers. Note that we elide most of the operations of *WebSystem* because they are simply a promotion of the operations available on instances of the class *WebBrowser*.

WebSystem

browsers : P *WebBrowser*

∀ b_1, b_2 : *browsers* • $b_1 \neq b_2 \Rightarrow b_1.web \neq b_2.web$

INIT

browsers = ∅

OpenBrowsers

Δ(*browsers*)

browser? = *WebBrowser*

---

browser? ∉ *browsers*

∃ *browser* : *WebBrowser* •

  browser? = *browsers* ∪ { *browsers* }

CloseBrowser

Δ(*browsers*)

browser? = *WebBrowser*

---

browser? ∈ *browsers*

browser' = *browsers* \ { *browser?* }

SelectBrowser

browser? : *WebBrowser*

---

browser? ∈ *browsers*

Forward ≅ *SelectBrowser* • *browser?.Forward*

Back ≅ *SelectBrowser* • *browser?.Back*

..

..

Stop ≅ *SelectBrowser* • *browser?.Stop*

The specification can be used to check user interface properties however, because our specification is only small and the focus of the paper is specification, rather than analysis of properties, we do not consider the derivation of interface properties in depth. Fields et al. (Fields, Wright & Harrison 94) have identified three classes of errors defined as properties of the sequences of events required to perform a task:

1. omission of events (or whole sequences of events);
2. substitution of events (one for another);
3. reversal of two events (or two sequences of events).

To prevent undesirable traces of events occurring, additional interface moding may be required. For example, the *Navigator* interactor does not permit the user to invoke *OpenLocation* unless they have first selected a URL to open. This implies that an open is not possible unless an URL has been supplied by the user (implicitly, a bad URL will produce an error message). Where moding is not desired, it may be sufficient to simply provide more information to the user (i.e., regarding the consequences of a user action) (Fields, Wright & Harrison 94). After recognising the absence of moding, the designer can take steps to ensure sufficient information is available to the user. A specification of a user interface provides a designer with the capacity to analyse fundamental properties of the system such as moding.

An Object-Z specification also assists the designer in identifying a potential implementation structure. The applicability of design patterns can be related to aspects of an Object-Z specification for the system (Hussey & Carrington 96a). A design pattern is a flexible solution to a recurring class of design problems that can be customised to suit each particular context (Gamma, Helm, Johnson & Vlissides 94). Patterns divide design solutions into their elementary parts that can be later recombined and reused (Viljamaa 95). Aspects of Object-Z's structure that prove useful for specification (e.g., separation of state from operations and the class construct) also provide guidance toward useful designs. Because Object-Z user interface specifications (using the techniques described in this paper) have a common structure, patterns can assist in translating Object-Z specifications to implementations.

6. Conclusions

The case study demonstrates that formal methods are useful for describing the syntax and semantics of user interfaces. Web browsers are complex systems for which a precise formal model provides valuable documentation. Further, the case study shows the utility of interactor-based specification and, more specifically, the usefulness of Object-Z as a formal notation for interactor-based specification.

The approach taken produces a clear distinction between *specification* concerns and *design* concerns. In particular, we distinguish between:

*   how to display the system state and obtain input, and

- what is displayed, the available operations and the effects of such operations on what is displayed.

Because user interface specification is not concerned with lexical issues, a user interface specification is an abstract specification of the system itself from the user's perspective. The user interface specification provides a view (the view provided by the interface to the user) of a potentially much larger system.

Such a specification provides an accurate mechanism for communicating the characteristics of a user interface from a designer to an implementer. The effort required to produce such a formal specification is well spent; the exercise is inherently useful for requirements analysis and the product is clear and succinct documentation of the user interface.

The specification demonstrates some key aspects that distinguish an Object-Z user interface specification from other Object-Z specifications of the system:

- Our focus is on the user interface therefore we only describe what is necessary to illuminate the perceivable functions of the user interface.
- The specification describes the model that a user could construct of the system from interaction with the user interface, i.e., the specification formalises the anticipated user model.
- Agents are used to encapsulate key aspects of system behaviour that are associated with the interface's presentation.
- Operations on agents can be used to define user tasks.

By defining the presentation for each agent, an interactor-based Object-Z *user interface design* can be derived from an Object-Z specification. Because Object-Z is used as a software engineering design notation, Object-Z specification and user interface design provides a bridge between software engineering and human computer interface concerns. An Object-Z user interface design may be used to construct a prototype user interface for evaluation of the system's lexical properties. The Object-Z specification permits evaluation of preliminary syntactic and semantic issues without concern for the lexical issues that dominate human computer interface implementation and we believe this separation of concerns is helpful.

There are many issues that have not been considered in this chapter but which are suitable for further research. We have not fully considered the proof of either syntactic or semantic properties from a user interface specification. Neither have we considered notations for user interface design; this is the subject of our current research. Object-Z shows promise as a notation for expressing the visual structure of the user interface (as interactors); however we believe that description of the visual appearance of interactors remains informal.

Acknowledgements

We thank Wendy Johnston for the *Wizard* type-checker that was used to type-check our Object-Z specification.

Appendix A: Modelling Using Object-Z

In an Object-Z description, a class is defined by a named box encapsulating a visibility list, state, initialisation and operations. A simple example class defining a stack of natural numbers appears below:

$$
\begin{array}{l}
\underline{\quad Stack\qquad\qquad\qquad} \\
\hline
\begin{array}{l|l}
\begin{array}{l}
contents : \text{seq } URL \\
\Delta \\
top : \mathbb{N} \\
\hline
top = last\,(elements)
\end{array}
&
\begin{array}{l}
\underline{\quad INIT\qquad} \\
elements = \langle\rangle \\
\\
\underline{\quad Top\qquad} \\
top! : \mathbb{N} \\
\hline
top! = top
\end{array} \\
\\
\begin{array}{l}
\underline{\quad Push\qquad} \\
\Delta(elements) \\
num? : \mathbb{N} \\
\hline
elements = elements'\,\widehat{}\,\langle num!\rangle
\end{array}
&
\begin{array}{l}
\underline{\quad Pop\qquad} \\
\Delta(elements) \\
num! : \mathbb{N} \\
\hline
elements = elements'\,\widehat{}\,\langle num!\rangle
\end{array}
\end{array}
\end{array}
$$

The visibility list (prefixed by ↑) defines those operations and attributes that are visible to clients of the class. If there is no visibility list, all operations are visible. The state schema is un-named and contains attribute declarations and a constraining invariant. Some attributes may be dependent on other attributes (i.e., their value is always derivable from those other attributes). Such dependencies are denoted by a Δ on a separate line preceding the dependent attributes (e.g., top). The nature of this dependency is captured by the class invariant. The initialisation schema is labelled *INIT* and defines the initial state of instances of the class.

An operation schema is divided into two parts. The upper part defines the context of the operation including inputs and outputs. The Δ-list defines those state attributes that may be altered by an operation. State variables not listed in the Δ-list are unchanged by that operation. The lower part defines a predicate relating the initial and final states of the operation.

Classes may inherit from other classes. Inheritance results in a merger of state, *INIT* and operation schemas with the same name. For example, we define a new stack class that can return its size:

$$
\begin{array}{l}
\underline{\quad NewStack\qquad\qquad\qquad} \\
\hline
Stack \\
\underline{\quad Size\qquad\qquad\qquad} \\
size! : \mathbb{N} \\
\hline
size! = \#elements
\end{array}
$$

A class may be instantiated. For example, the declaration *stack: Stack* defines an object stack of type *Stack*. The polymorphic operator (↓) defines the type of an object as either the specified base class or any class that inherits from the base class. Operations applied to such an attribute must be polymorphic, i.e., regardless of the actual class of the object, the operation must be defined. For example, the declaration *stack:* ↓*Stack* defines an object *stack* that can be an instance of any class that inherits from *Stack*. We can define a set of stacks as follows:

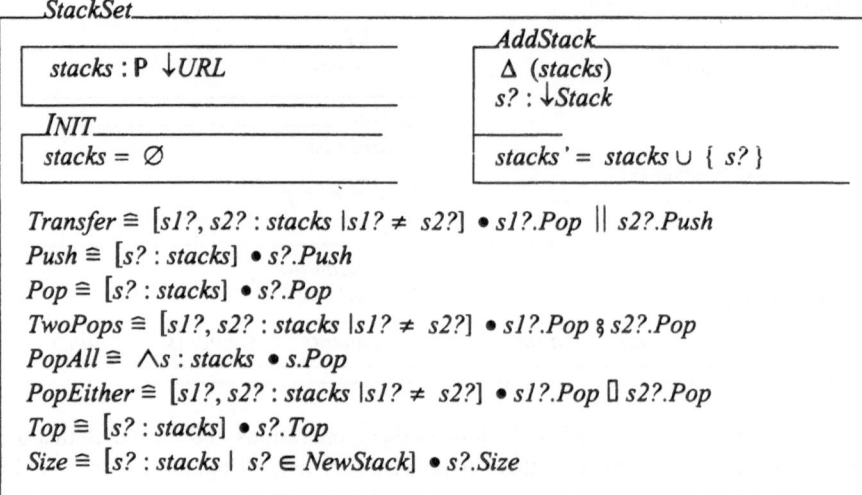

Operations and attributes of class instances may be accessed. For example, the term *s.elements* denotes the value of the attribute elements of *s* while the term *s.Push* denotes the operation *Push* applied to *s*. Operations may be combined using a calculus that extends the Z schema calculus [27], including conjunction (∧) and sequential composition (⨟). Object-Z provides two further operators:

- concurrency (‖) that conjoins operation schemas (i.e., merges state and predicates) and identifies inputs with outputs having the same base name. We illustrate concurrency in the operation *Transfer* that selects two stacks, pops one stack and pushes the result on the other.
- angelic choice (▯) that selects one of two operations according to which can be performed. If both operations can be performed, a non-deterministic choice is made between the two. We illustrate angelic choice in the operation *PopEither* that pops either of two selected stacks.

Operators may be applied over a set of instances, e.g., the operation *PopAll* specifies an operation in which all instances in the set *stacks* are subject to the operation *Pop*. The meaning is the same as $s_1.Pop ∧ s_2.Pop ∧ ...$ for all $s_1, s_2, ...$ in the set *stacks*.

Appendix B: Modelling Using CSP

This appendix describes the subset of the CSP language used in this paper to specify the syntactic behaviour of interactors.

To describe the patterns of behaviour of an object, it is necessary to describe the kinds of events that are of interest to the object and choose a different name for each kind of event. For example, a simple vending machine may participate in two kinds of events:

> **coin** the insertion of a coin
> **choc** the extraction of a chocolate

Each name denotes a class of events of which there may be many occurrences separated in time. The set of names of events for a particular object is the *alphabet* of that object. It is logically impossible for an object to engage in an event that is outside of its alphabet. However the converse does not hold. An object may never engage in an event although it is a part of the object's alphabet.

The patterns of behaviour of an object are a *process* and the alphabet of the object is the alphabet of its corresponding process. The alphabet of a process **P** is denoted α**P**. If x is an event and **P** is a process then:

$$(x \rightarrow P)$$

describes a process that first engages in the event x and then behaves as described by the process P. For example, a simple vending machine is defined as follows:

$$\textbf{VMS} = (coin \rightarrow (choc \rightarrow \textbf{VMS}))$$

Many objects allow their behaviour to be influenced by interaction with the environment. If x and y are distinct events then $(x \rightarrow P \mid y \rightarrow Q)$ describes a process that initially engages in either x or y and whose subsequent behaviour is determined by the choice of first event (**P** if the first event was x, **Q** if the first event was y).

For example, a more complicated vending machine may offer a choice of goods:

$$\textbf{VMC} = coin \rightarrow (choc \rightarrow \textbf{VMC} \mid toffee \rightarrow \textbf{VMC})$$

If a process can engage in one of several events but then proceeds uniformly, we use a shorthand notation. In general, if B is a set of events and **P** is a process then $(x: B \rightarrow P)$ defines a process that first offers a choice of any event in B and then behaves like **P**. For example a vending machine that accepts either 20 cent or 50 cent coins but only ever gives one chocolate would be defined as follows:

$$\textbf{VM2050} = coin: \{ 20c, 50c \} \rightarrow (choc \rightarrow \textbf{VM2050})$$

Choice may also be defined as occurring between processes. The operator $\square$ permits the environment to control which of two processes will be selected, based on the first event in each process. For example, we may offer a customer a choice between our three vending machines:

VendingArcade = VMS ☐ VMC ☐ VM2050

Where the first event of each process is the same, the choice between the processes is non-deterministic.

Chapter 9:
Modelling Clients and Servers on the Web Using Interactive Cooperative Objects

1. Introduction

This chapter presents the use of the Interactive Cooperative Objects (ICO) formalism for specifying the basic behaviour of a Web Browser. According to the case study presented at the beginning of this book, some of the basic actions such as selecting an URL for browsing, interrupting an ongoing transfer or going back to the previously seen pages are modelled. Other aspects, such as scrolling a visualised page or managing bookmarks are not taken into account in the specification. We also focus on the client/server interaction between the Web Browser and the HyperText Transfer Protocol (HTTP) server, and the HTTP protocol itself, that governs the communication between clients and server is partially modelled.

The various models are described within the framework of the Interactive Cooperative Objects (ICO) formalism (Bastide & Palanque 90). The Web client is an interactive application, and as such is modelled by an ICO featuring a presentation part and a behaviour modelled by an high-level Petri net. The HTTP server is not interactive and is only used internally by the Web client.

The verification of models is achieved by using the techniques provided by the Petri nets theory. On the one hand, the analysis provides results concerning the dialogue structure and its influence on the interface behaviour. On the other hand, the formal client server protocol used for describing communication between objects is used for the formal analysis of the cooperation between clients and servers.

The chapter is organised as follows: section 2 describes the ICO formalism, in which a high-level Petri net model is used for modelling the object's behaviour. Section 3 presents a case study to demonstrate the use of the formalism on a Web Browser application. We precisely show how using the ICO formalism it is possible to describe the behaviour of a Web client, a Web server and the http protocol ruling their communication. Section 4 contains a discussion about the benefits of using the ICO formalism for the design of interactive applications.

2. The ICO Formalism

The Cooperative Objects (CO) formalism is a generic formalism dedicated to the modelling of concurrent and distributed systems. The main characteristic of CO is that the behaviour of objects and their cooperation are modelled within the framework of the High Level Petri Nets (HLPN) theory.

The Cooperative Objects formalism has been presented in (Bastide & Sibertin 91, Bastide 92), and several of its theoretical underpinnings can be found in (Sibertin 94). The CO formalism has been extended by Palanque in (Palanque 92) to form the Interactive Cooperative Objects (ICO), encompassing user-related concerns such as the presentation, and the relationship between the presentation and the dialogue behaviour. ICO have also been extended to model the "human" side of the human-computer interaction, describing task models and user models (Palanque et al. 95). We will present here only the main features of the formalism, and the syntactical notations necessary to understand the treatment of the case study.

The goal of ICO is to allow the main features of object languages to be efficiently used in the field of interactive systems. More precisely, we wish to provide an efficient notation which allows the concurrent aspects of complex systems to be described in such a way that concurrency can be modelled inside the objects themselves as well as between objects. The specification of an ICO class contains its *interface* (the word interface is used in the "programming language" meaning, i.e. the list and signature of the methods it offers), its *behaviour*, modelled by a high-level Petri net and called the ObCS (Object Control Structure (Hood 89)) and its *presentation*, modelled by a mathematical relation between the ObCS and the set of interaction widgets that compose its external look. The ObCS defines the inner control structure shared by all instances of the class. The ObCS states the availability of methods according to the inner state of the object, and conversely the effect of methods execution on the object's state.

Obviously, even in a distributed system, purely sequential and algorithmic concerns remain very important. Thus ICO do not aim at replacing conventional object languages, but can more adequately be considered as a host language for sequential OO languages such as Eiffel, C++ or Java. The current implementation of ICO is developed in C++, and the remainder of this chapter will use C++ notations.

The integration of Cooperative Objects with a language such as C++ is performed in the following way: ObCSs are described by High-Level Petri Nets (HLPN), and the tokens that constitute the marking of the net can hold information, instead of being dimensionless entities like in conventional Petri nets. In the current implementation of ICO, the value of a token is a n-tuple of typed values, those values representing either:

- Any C++ type (native type, class instance or polymorphic pointer);
- A reference to another ICO in the system.

Transitions in the net contain a precondition part and an action part, that are able to manipulate the tokens involved in the firing according to their type. Two quite different kinds of actions may be represented:

- A block of C++ code, which is executed sequentially and in mutual exclusion with other transitions in the ObCS. This code can make use of C++ objects involved in the firing of the transition, call their methods, dynamically create new C++ objects, etc. This allows ICO to be for an easily integrated with existing class libraries, and insures that ICO are interoperable with more conventional approaches. For example we describe in (Bastide & Palanque 90) how to integrate ICO with a User Interface Management System (UIMS).
- An *invocation* of another ICO, i.e. the call of a method it offers; this call is executed in a concurrent and non-blocking way. The classical invocation strategies described by G. Booch (Booch 94) are available (synchronous rendezvous, asynchronous message sending, time-out rendezvous), and each of these strategies is formally defined in terms of HLPN. The fact that both the inner behaviour of objects and their communication primitives are modelled by HLPN allows the system of communicating ICO to be formally modelled in terms of HLPN only.

2.1 Relationship Between Interface and Behaviour

The interface part of a ICO class gives the list of services provided by the instances of this class, and their signature. This is essentially the same information that is provided by the IDL definitions of CORBA systems (Corba 91).

The behaviour of the instances is given by a HLPN. This behaviour is related to the interface definition in the following way:

- For each service given in the interface, the ObCS net contains one *Service Input Port* and one *Service Output Port* that are places dedicated to a special purpose: the service input port is meant to receive the service invocations along with their input parameters, while the service output port is the channel through which the service results will be provided by the object. A service input port can only have output arcs in the ObCS, and conversely a service output port can only have incoming arcs.
- The processing associated to a service is modelled by one or several macro-transitions related to the service's input and output ports. The transitions connected to the service input port are called *Accept Transitions*, while the transitions connected to the output port are called *Return transitions*.

Figure 1 illustrates an excerpt of an ICO class definition. Only one service is described, *aService*, taking an integer as input parameter and returning a string. The associated behaviour is described in the ObCS: the subnet comprised between aService *accept* and *return transitions* (not detailed) is meant to compute a return string r according to the input parameter p.

The interface and ObCS together fully define the behaviour of instances: a service request will begin executing when one of its associated *accept transitions* is enabled by the current marking of the ObCS. Conversely, the execution of a service is modelled by the occurrence of the associated macro-transitions, which states the side-effect of the execution of the service on the object.

The variables on the arcs act as formal variables for the transition. The action of the transition is to call the service *aService* on the object bound to variable *s*, providing as a parameter the integer bound to variable *p*.

Class *aServer {   // (excerpt)*
Interface
                aService(p: int): string;
ObCS

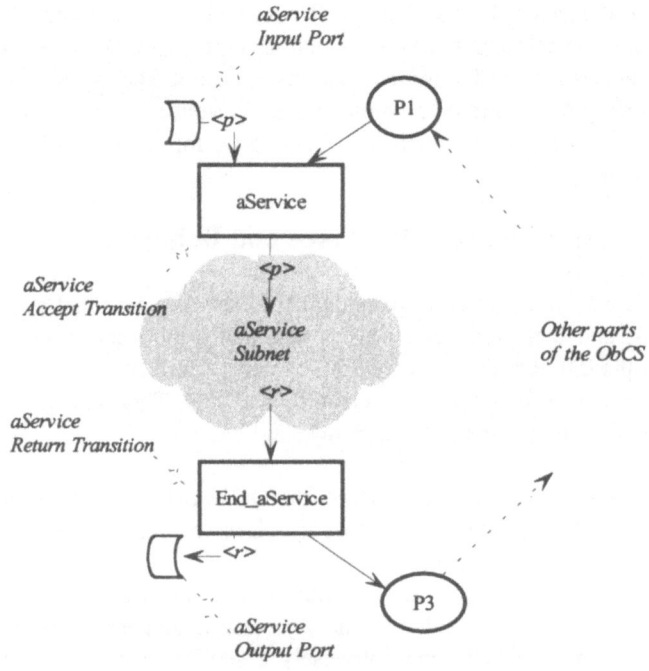

Figure 1: Syntax of a ICO class definition

}

2.2 Invocation Modes and Their Semantics

The ObCSs are meant to describe the "server" behaviour of objects (i.e. what their synchronisation constraints are) but also their "client" behaviour (i.e. how they request services from other Interactive Cooperative Objects in the system).

The communication between Interactive Cooperative Objects is syntactically expressed using the conventional dot notation in the ObCS transitions.

Such a service invocation is illustrated in Figure 2: the class described here acts as a client of the *aServer* class is described in Figure 1. The ObCS descriptions include the definition of the places' type: for example, place PB is defined to hold references to instances of the *aServer* class, while the tokens contained in place PC will be 3-tuples holding an integer, a reference to an instance of *aServer* and a string.

*Class **aClient** { // (excerpt)*
Interface
> *// ...*

ObCS   *// Definition of the places' type*
> *PA: <int>*
> *PB: <aServer>*
> *PC: <int, aServer, string>*

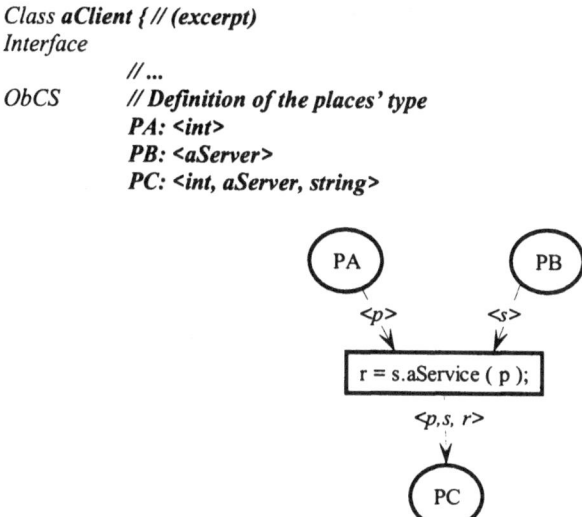

Figure 2: Synchronous rendezvous

}

    A transition whose action is the invocation of another Interactive Cooperative Object is called an *invocation transition*. The default semantics for such a call is the *synchronous rendezvous*, whose operational semantics is described in Figure 3.

    The semantics of the synchronous rendezvous is given within the framework of high-level Petri nets, by enhancing the ObCS nets of both the client and the server of the rendezvous. Although the designer of the net only sees the ObCS descriptions as given in Figure 1 and Figure 2, the nets, before being actually executed in the running system, are expanded as detailed hereafter.

2.2.1 Client-side semantics of synchronous rendezvous

The following transformations have to be applied to each invocation transition:

- The invocation transition is considered as a macro-transition extending from the *request transition* to the *complete transition*. The *request transition* constructs a parameter token, including the original parameters of the service, the identity of the caller (variable *this*) and a globally unique call-identifier. This token is deposited in the *Invocation Parameter port*.
- A *waiting place* is introduced between the request transition and the complete transition. The presence of a token in this place indicates that a call is in progress.
- The results from the service call will be returned to the client in its *Invocation Return Port*. The arrival of a return token will enable the *complete transition*, and terminate the service call on the client's side. It is important to note that the

variable *id* is present on both input arcs of the *complete transition*: the transition is only enabled if a substitution is possible between the token values held in the *Waiting* and *Return Port* places, meaning that the same id is found in both tokens: this construct is necessary to allow a client to issue concurrently several invocations, to enable the client to match the results it receives with the parameters it has initially provided, and to avoid a result to be given to the wrong client.

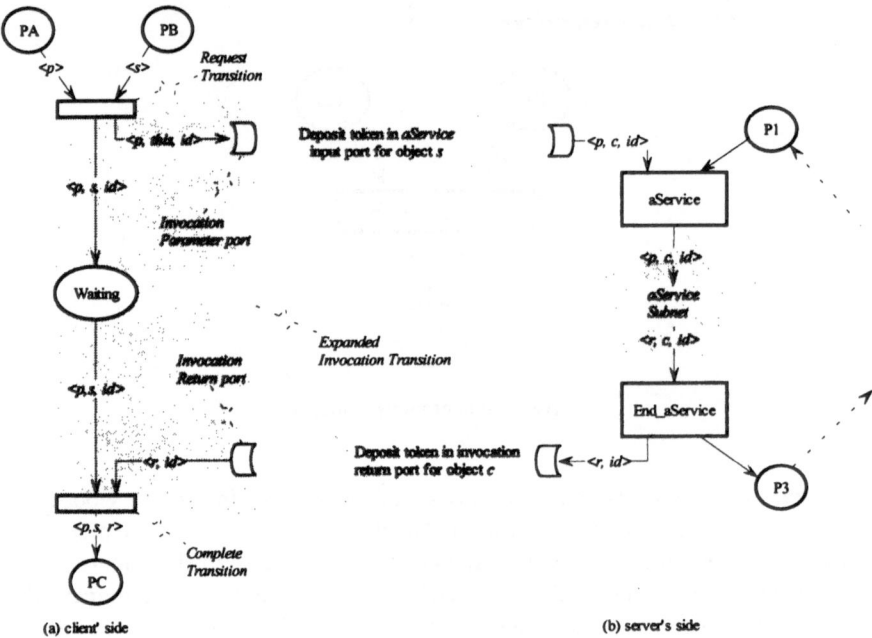

Figure 3: Operational semantics of synchronous rendezvous

2.2.2 Server-side semantics of synchronous rendezvous

On the server's side, the structure of the net is not altered, but only the definition of the places' type and the inscriptions on the arcs. The only requirement for the server is to keep both the client's identity and the call-id within the service subnet, so that the results of the service can be properly routed back to the caller. The synchronous rendezvous is thus implemented as two unidirectional asynchronous message sending.

Only one primitive is required, and supposed to be provided by the implementation environment: the ability to deposit a structured token in a place of a remote Interactive Cooperative Object. This primitive is used to transport both the parameters and the results of an invocation. In the current implementation, this primitive is provided by a CORBA compliant system, which takes care of the marshalling and unmarshalling of call arguments, and of the routing of tokens.

However, other implementations could be easily substituted, such as Java RMI (Remote Method Invocation) or lower level solutions based on sockets.

Other invocation strategies can be described in the same way: the time-out rendezvous allows the client to specify the amount of time it is prepared to wait for the result of the call, and to take a corrective action if the result is not provided within this time limit.

2.2.3   Client-side semantics of asynchronous rendezvous

Sometimes, the client may chose to simply ignore the possible results of a service, and to proceed as soon as the invocation has been issued, without any acknowledgement. This strategy is called asynchronous invocation, and its syntax and operational semantics are illustrated in Figure 4.

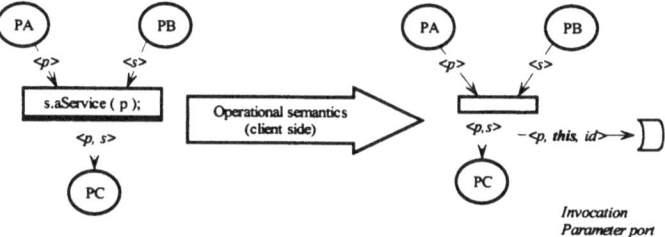

Figure 4: Asynchronous invocation and its operational semantics

It must be noted that whatever invocation strategy is chosen, it only has an impact on the structure of the client's ObCS: the structure of the server's ObCS is not modified, and any service can thus be called with any invocation strategy.

2.3 Presentation

The ICO formalism includes special features to describe the interaction between the user and the system. Special services are distinguished in the interface of an ICO class as *user services* i.e. services that can be triggered interactively by the user through the use of some input device, or some conventional user interface element. The interaction in the direction user → system is modelled by the *Activation function,* defined as follows:

- The presentation of the user interface is defined by a structured set of widgets (**Wid**) which can be constructed using the kind of graphical presentation editor found in most UIMS. Each widget is able to react to a predefined set of events (called **Evt**), triggered by the user.
- The activation function (ACT) associates to each couple (widget, user action) one and only one of the services offered by the ICO class.

$$ACT:\ (Wid \times Evt)\ \rightarrow\ Serv$$

Conversely, interaction in the direction system → user is modelled by the *Rendering Function*. While the activation function is event-driven, the rendering function is state-driven. This fact characterises the *predictability property* of interactive systems, stating that the portion of the system state that is relevant to the user must be visible at any stage of interaction.

Thus the ICO formalism models the rendering function as follows:

- The widgets in Wid offer a predefined set of output primitives WidOut (such as enabling/disabling, text output, ...). The implementation of these primitives heavily depends on the programming environment.
- The rendering function Rnd associates to each reachable state of the system a set of output primitives dedicated to the rendering of this state

$$Rnd: \quad Marking \quad \rightarrow \quad P(WidOut)$$

Petri nets do not present an explicit enumeration of all the reachable states, but on the contrary, model states by state variables (called *places*) and a distribution of tokens in these places, which is called the *marking* of the net. This local modelling of states allows to partition the rendering functions between the places of the ObCS nets.

An interface component modelled as an ICO is an object whose services can be triggered interactively by the user, through interactions with widgets. The sequencing and synchronisation constraints for these services are expressed in the ObCS.

As stated before, transitions relate to the object's services, stating their availability, and user services relate to widgets through the activation function. Thus the active or inactive state of the widgets may be known by looking at the ObCS's marking: the fact that no transition associated to a service is enabled by the current marking means that this service is not currently available to the user. This must be shown by greying out or otherwise inactivating the related widgets.

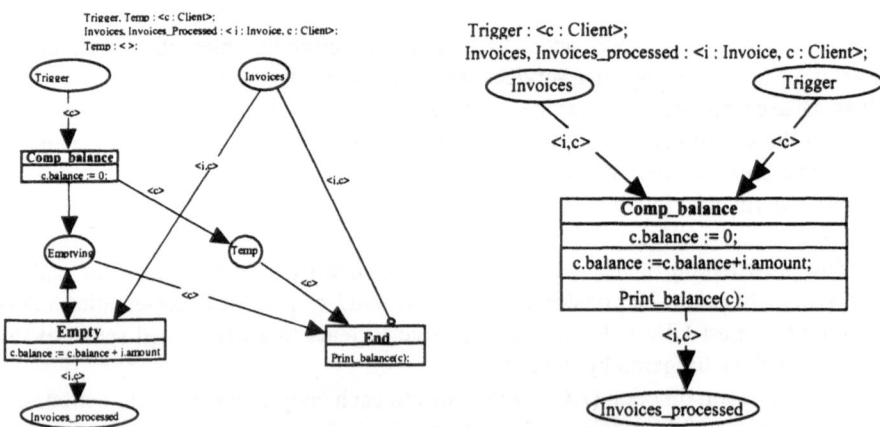

Figure 5: Emptying arc and its abbreviation

2.4 Abbreviation

We use **emptying arcs** which are represented by double arrows (see right hand part of Figure 5), whose semantics is formalised in (Palanque 92). Such arcs allow a transition to remove all tokens at once, whatever their number, from an input place and to put them into an output place. After the occurrence of a transition with emptying arcs, the input place is empty and the output place has gained all the tokens of the input place. Emptying arcs are a useful extension for modelling **multicasting**, where a same service call is performed on several destination objects.

2.5 Architecture

Along with the ICO formalism we have proposed an architecture which aims at organising the objects according to their role within the interactive system. We have identified two main kinds of objects:

- Non interactive Objects (NICOs) bear the core semantics of the application, including the application's database, if any, functions for achieving the needed computations, accesses to a printer device, and so on; they do not deal with user interaction and are shared by all ICOs.
- Interactive Objects (ICOs) support the application's user interface; they define the dialogue structure, and maintain the coherence between the state of the NICOs and what is shown to the users by the Presentation; each opened window in an application is associated to an instance of an ICO Class.

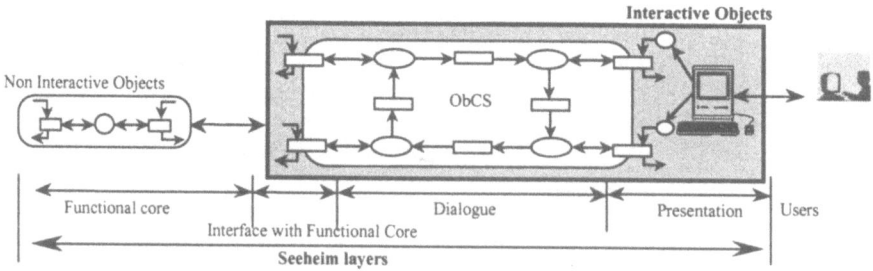

Figure 6: The architecture of an interactive system modelled by ICOs

This architecture shows the relationships between the environment and the system. Indeed, the arrow from the user to the ICOs represents how a user can act on the system (this is usually done by means of dedicated input devices such as a keyboard or a mouse). The arrow in the other direction represents how the system provides information to the user.

3. The Case Study

In order to model the case study we use two different classes of objects: the Web client and the Web server. Event though most of the parts of the classes can be defined in an independent manner, several parts (such as the ones implementing the communication between the classes) must be defined jointly. This part corresponds to the HTTP client-server protocol that rules communication on the Web.

3.1 The Web Server

This class does not correspond to an interactive system as it can only be accessed through other classes such as the Web client. It offers only one service: to provide the client with a requested page. The definition of the Web server class is given in Figure 7. The server only offers one service (named **Request**) to its environment. This service can be requested several times concurrently. This is modelled in Figure 7 by the place Possible_Connections, which holds the number of possible concurrent connectons. The place *Files_Served* models the set of pages that are available in a given server. The service *Request* takes as an input parameter the URL to serve, and returns a value of type *HTTPConnection*, along with the size of the requested file. The connection will be written by the Web server, and read by the Web client.

Class HTTPServer { // (excerpt)
Interface
        Request(aUrl: Url): <conn: HTTPConnection, size: int>
ObCS   *// Definition of the type of the places*
        Possible_connexions: <>
        Files_served: <aUrl: Url, aFile: File, aSize: Real>
        Serving: <aConnection: HTTPConnection, aFile: File>

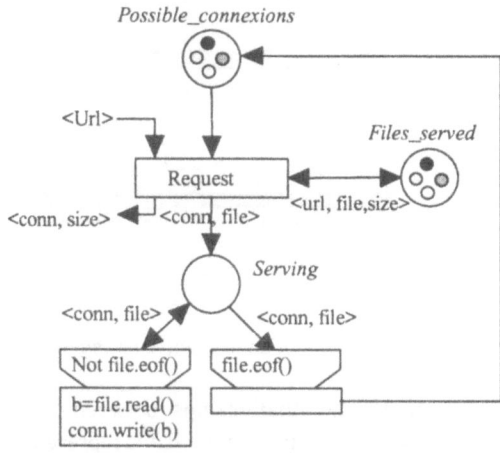

}

Figure 7: The definition of the class WebServer

The class HTTPServer is complemented by the class Connection, which models the data transfer between Web server and Web client and acts as an intermediate buffer. This is a simplification of the actual data transfer that takes place between a

Web server and a Browser, in that the number of read (performed on the client side) will always match the number of writes (on the server side), whereas in reality those numbers might differ.

Class *Connection {*
Interface
                // ...
ObCS   // *Definition of the type of the places*
                Buffer: <aBuffer: String>

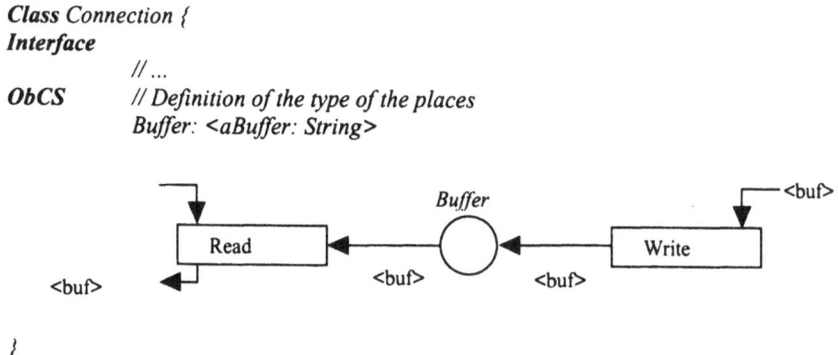

}

Figure 8: The connection class

3.2 The Web Client

This class is a full fledged ICO as users can interact with it. The presentation part of the Web client class is given in Figure 9, while its specification is given in Figure 10. In the case study we will only model the actions available directly through the manipulation of buttons on the Web client's window. The handling of actions available in the menus is not presented for space reasons.

According to the specific features of the case study (see the beginning of the book), the model presented in Figure 10 does not take into account the use of scroll bars for browsing within a page, however all the other aspects have been taken into account.

The Web client class is modelled in Figure 10. This class features several services which are described in its interface. The ObCS of the class must be read as follows:

In the initial state the places *Home_page* and *UrlSelected* hold a token. The value of this token corresponds to the URL of the home page of the Web client. From that state the user can either click on the Home button or type a new URL using the EditURL transition. Otherwise the user can wait for the transition GetPage to be fired (this transition is greyed as it is a macro transition). This firing will remove the token form the place *URLSelected*, extract from the home page all the links to other pages and display them. For each link a token will be set in the place *DisplayedURLs*. When the page is displayed, the URL is put in the place *HistoricBack*. As stated in the case study description, all the URLs are considered to be displayed, as scrolling is not modelled.

The history mechanism is modelled using two stack places *HistoricForward* and *HistoricBack*. As they are actually macro places they are represented respectively in dark and light grey. Those places drive the availability of the services Back and Forward. Back is only available when the content of at least two URLs has been displayed by the Browser. This is modelled by the double incoming arrows from the place *HistoricBack* to the transition Back. If Back is triggered by the user, the older of the last two URLs is displayed (sent to the place *URLSelected*) while the last one displayed is sent to the place *HistoricForward*. At that stage (and only now) the transition Forward is available. If the user triggers this service, the last URL is displayed again and set again in the *HistoricBack* place.

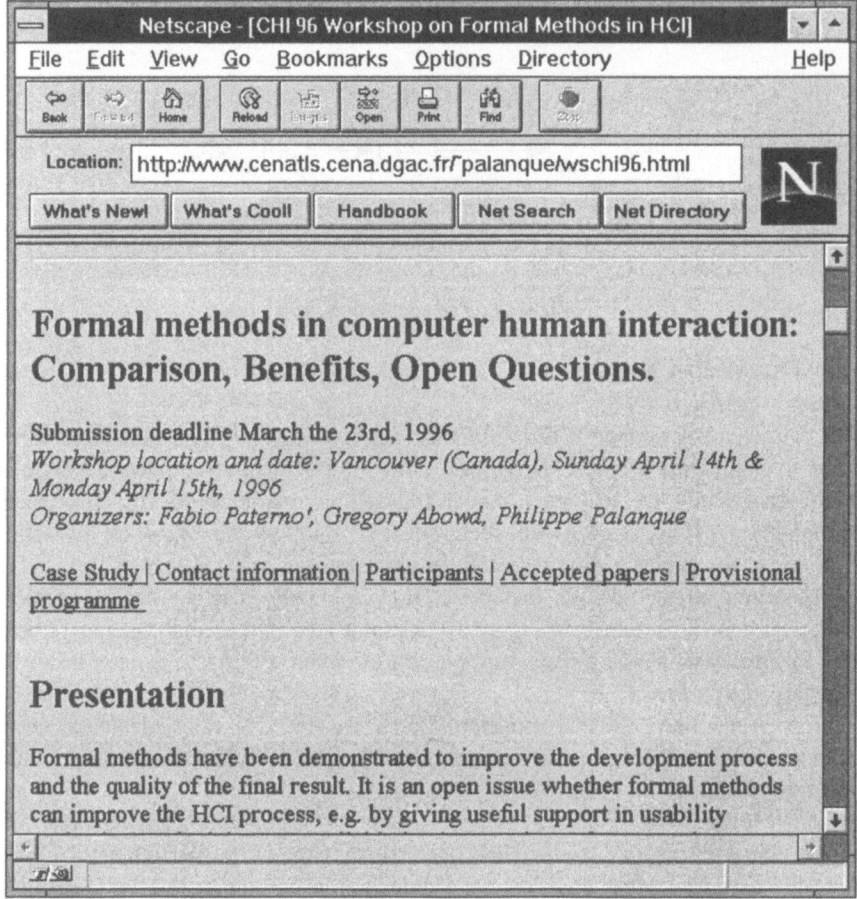

Figure 9: The presentation part of the Web client

The dotted arrow between the macro-transition GetPage and the service Stop means that the availability of the latter is conditioned by the inner stage of the page retrieval process (this is detailed in Figure 11).

Class WebClient
Services

> Home;-- select the home page of the browser
> Back;-- go to the page previously seen
> Forward; -- go to the next page in the stack of the pages previously seen
> GotoUrl(x: string);-- Select a URL on the screen
> EditUrl(x: string); -- Edit the URL of a page in a box EditText

ObCS

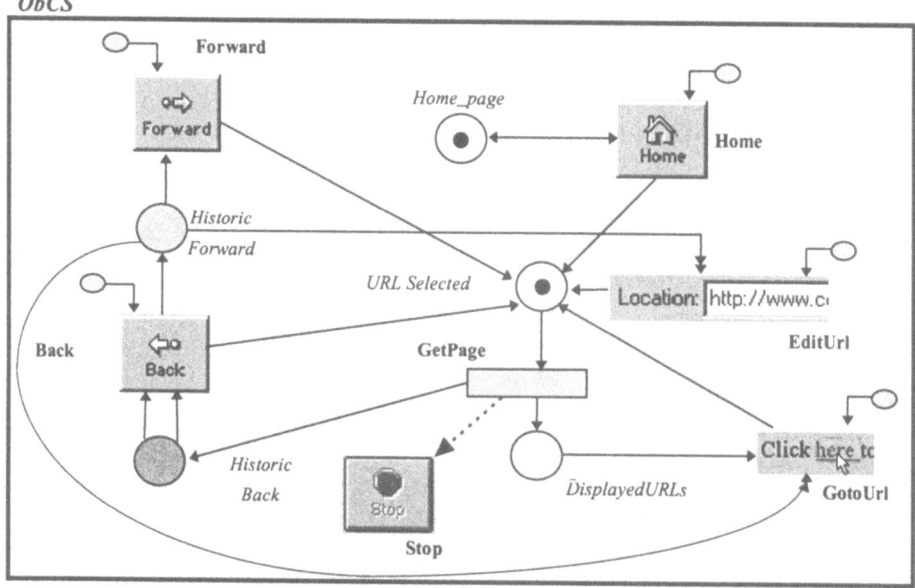

Figure 10: Definition of the class WebClient

There are two emptying arcs in that figure (see section 0) from place Historic Forward, one to transition EditUrl and the other to transition GotoUrl. This models the fact that when one of these transition is triggered, all the tokens from the place *HistoricForward* are removed. As a consequence the transition Forward is no more available.

The services interactively triggered by the user (e.g. Forward, Back, Home, etc.) are represented by button-shaped transitions, to stress the fact that they have to be related to some element of the Presentation part of the ICO. Note that this is only a graphic convenience, and does not preclude on the actual input device associated with the service.

3.3 Refinement of the Specification

We will now provide a finer grained refinement of the initial WebClient specification, first by detailing the macro-transition GetPage, then by making more precise the behaviour of the history mechanism.

The macro transition GetPage models the detailed interaction between the Web server and the Web client, and show how the intermediate HTTPConnection is used on the client's side.

Class *aClient { // (excerpt)*
Operation
              ExtractUrl(aBuffer: String)
              ContainsUrl(aBuffer: String): Boolean
Interface
ObCS   *// Definition of the type of the places*
              Buffer: <aBuffer:String, aSize: Real>
(See Figure 11).
}

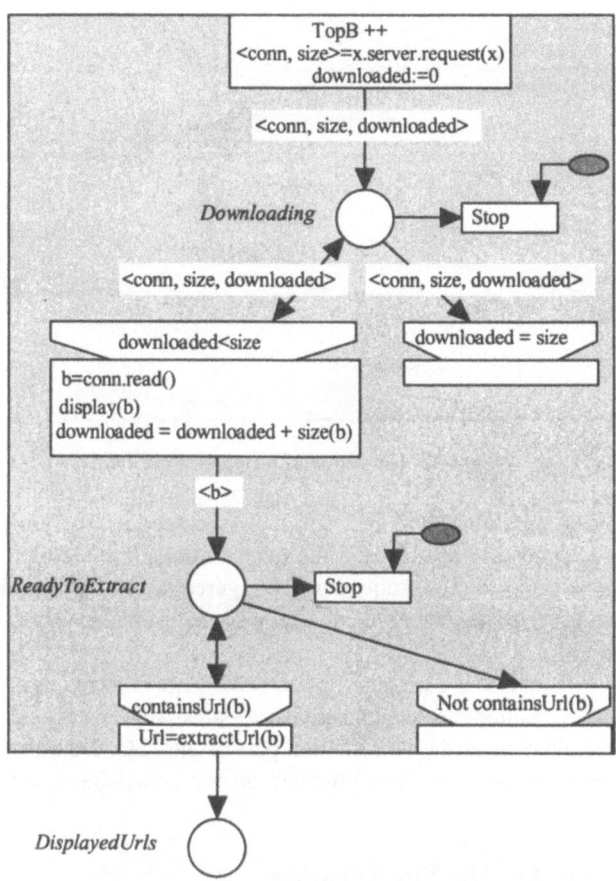

Figure 11: Macro-transition GetPage

The macro-transition detailed in Figure 11 shows how the Web client sends the request for an URL to the Web server, and receives in answer an instance of HTTPConnection. This instance is read (using method Read) until all of the file has been downloaded. The macro also shows at which steps the Stop command is available through the user interface.

Figure 12 gives a more detailed model of the history mechanism, showing that stack-like data structures are reasonably easy to model using high-level Petri nets. The detailed net essentially shows how to maintain two distinct counters representing the top of the forward and backward history, respectively. This is done by using two integer variables TopB and TopF counting the number of tokens in the places *HistoriBack* and *HistoricForward*.

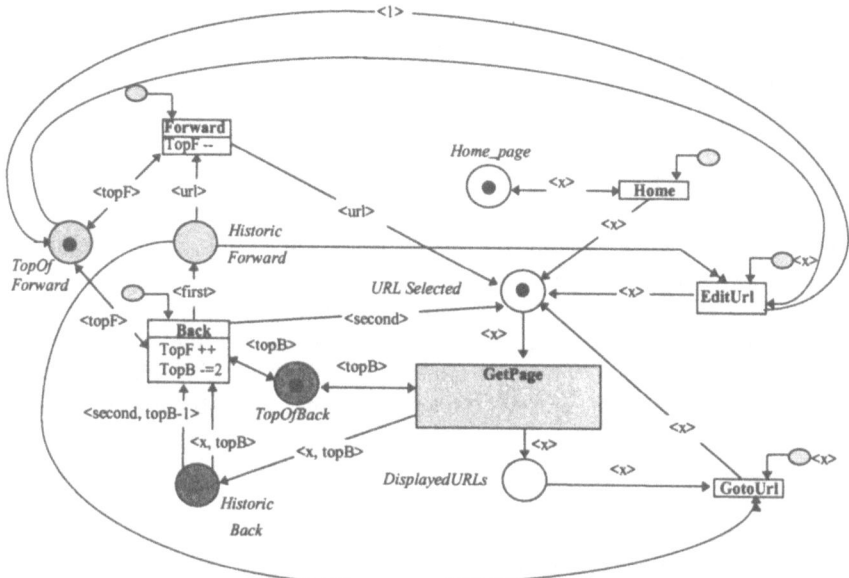

Figure 12: A refined model of the history mechanism

4. Discussion

4.1 Modelling Benefits

Modelling the behaviour of an event-driven application by means of ICO offers several benefits.

- The graphic (but still formal) modelling, allows an easy communication between designers, programmers and user. Moreover, the descriptions are explicit as all the possible states and operations are clearly shown to the reader,
- A single formalism may be used at different steps of the application development life-cycle. For drawing up the application specifications proving correctness of models and simulating them (it may even be used at the implementation step, by means of a Petri Net interpreter),

- A full description of the interface control structure including causal dependencies between the application services, i.e. dealing fully with the concurrency inside the application and between several applications,
- The composition mechanism enables the application models to be designed according to a bottom-up approach. But, refinement mechanisms also exist allowing a top-down approach to be followed. Moreover, this mechanism allows yet completely designed elements to be reused which is one of the main difficulties in software engineering.
- Modelling the behaviour of a system may be done from the state point of view (what are the reachable states and the transitions between them) or from the operation point of view (what are the operations and their pre/post conditions). Both of these points of view are useful for different purposes, and the ICO formalism (through Petri Nets) enables one to be adopted as well as the other.

4.2 Formal Analysis

In this section we will present the kind of verification that can be done using the ICO formalism. Most of this verification is based on the Petri net theory which provides tools and techniques for the verification of properties over Petri net models.

We have already presented how these results can be applied to interactive systems (Palanque & Bastide 95a, Palanque & Bastide 95b), so we only present here the principles of the verification that can be made over an ICO-based specification.

4.2.1 Unitary validation

This validation studies the behaviour of a single ICO, making a "good cooperation" assumption upon its relationships with other objects, that is: the servers used by the ICO are always able to process all its requests, and its clients send as many requests for its services as it may process. The dialogue properties we want to check are those specified in the application's interface requirements. These properties may relate: either to sequences of commands e.g. each update command may be followed either by a save command or by a cancel command; or to states that must or must not be reachable e.g. a list box may be able to contain any number of items above a given minimum. The main properties that can be proved using Petri net theory are: the absence of deadlock, the predictability of a command, the reinitiability, the availability of a command, among others (see (Peterson 81) for more details on the properties themselves). When modelling an interactive system, unitary validation enables to prove that the dialogue of each window is designed in such a way that it meets the basics requirements in HCI design (for example for all the widgets, there is always a sequence of commands that will make it available to the user, user-driven style of dialogue, etc.).

4.2.2 Cooperation validation

This validation studies the behaviour of a set of ICOs according to the way they cooperate through the client/server relationship. It shows whether the objects cooperate in such a way that each server fulfils the needs of its clients, that is whether the cooperation preserves the objects' behaviour properties set out by the unitary validation. Cooperation validation concerns ICO cooperation that can be seen in two different ways: cooperation with the user (through user services) and cooperation between ICOs. The former ensures that the user's requests may be satisfied by the application's functional kernel and that the ICO's presentation reflects the state of the functional kernel; the latter is needed if an application may open several windows that can cooperate together (for example a user's action in a window can affect the availability of interactors in another window).

4.3 User Centered Modelling

Using the ICO formalism two different kinds of user centered modelling have been investigated: task analysis and task modelling. The use of the same formalism for both tasks and system modelling allows us to provide designers with additional features such as verification of conformance between task models and system models.

4.3.1 Task modelling

Task modelling is accomplished within the ICO formalism by constructing a task model in the form of an object class, which is a client of the ICO classes that model the user interface of the system. These task classes therefore request any number of the services published by the user interface classes. The ObCS of a task class is as usual given by a high-level Petri net. It is therefore easy to represent the usual primitives found in most of the usual task modelling formalisms, e.g. sequence, alternative, parallelism and synchronisation. Petri nets also provide an elegant representation of non-determinism, which proves to be particularly useful in the field of task modelling.

The cooperation verification techniques described in § 4.2.2 can also be used for verifying that the actions triggered in the task classes correspond to actions offered by the system classes, and that the sequences of these actions in the task model is coherent with the sequencing of actions in the system model. The composition mechanisms offered by Petri nets allow tasks to be modelled at various levels of abstraction, starting from high level models where complex user goals are represented by macro-transitions, and further refining these models to the point where elementary actions on the interface devices are represented.

Figure 13 illustrates an excerpt of a possible task model relative to the system model presented in Figure 10. The user as a set of URLs he/she whishes to visit. He first starts the browser, which triggers automatically the display of the home page. The user is the able to request one of the desired URLs, and later will undeterministically choose to go back to the start page, or to request another URL.

Using the ICO formalism two different kinds of user centered modelling have been investigated.

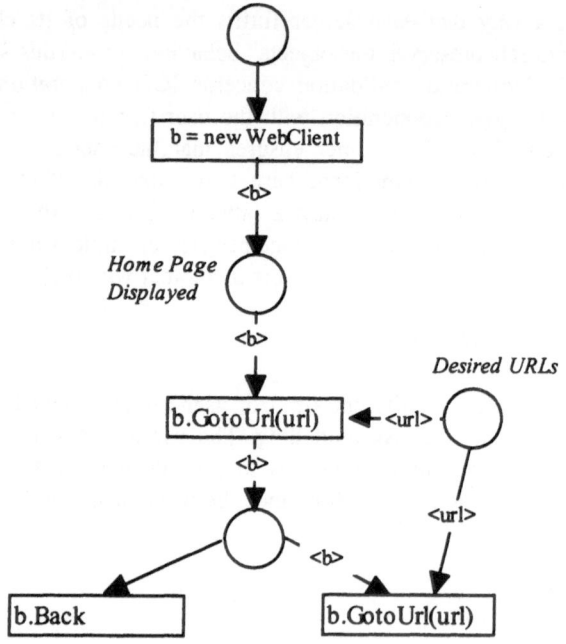

Figure 13: Excerpt of a task model

4.3.2 User modelling

Then we have investigated two different ways of embedding user modelling in the specification of an interactive system.

- **Generic user model:** such models as for instance the human processor has been proposed in the early eighties by Card, Moran and Newell in (Card et al. 83) In this model the user is modelled as a set of three processors interacting together and for each processor cycle temporal values are given (minimum, mean and maximum). This information can be related to both tasks and system models thus allowing to do some performance evaluation on the couple user-system (see next section).
- **Specific user model:** we have shown in (Moher et al. 96) that the precise modelling of the internal behaviour of a user can help in designing better systems. This user modelling is done using HLPN. In a user model places represent type of information the user can embed and the tokens in those places the information they know. Transitions are associated to cognitive actions performed internally by the users such as learning an information or forgetting it as well as external actions such as providing an information or performing physical actions on a physical device (like keyboard or mouse).

4.4 Performance Evaluation

The use of a formal model for task modelling results in the same advantages as formal system modelling but, as the task model describes the sequences of actions the user will have to perform in order to reach a given goal, it is very important to compute some performance evaluation on the model. This is fully supported using stochastic or timed Petri nets[8] as they have been used for a long time for performance evaluation of systems and a lot of theoretical work is available in this area.

The kind of analysis results that can be done on the task model is:

- number of actions the user has to perform in order to reach the goal,
- the number and the length of cycles in the models,
- if some actions have to be performed by the user under temporal constraints (such as entering a password within a given amount of time) it is possible to compute the frequency of those actions and to prove that the temporal constraints are consistent, i.e. they do not contradict each other.

Another kind of quantitative analysis is related to the complexity of the tasks the user has to perform. This is done by automatically building the marking graph of the Petri net and computing complexity measures on it. For example the number of nodes (corresponding to the number of states in the task model) the number of actions (corresponding to the number of arcs with different labels) and the length of the path to come back to the initial state are associated with weights in order to have a quantity of complexity of the task model. This quantity is used within the design life-cycle to decide whether or not the task and system models meet the requirements.

Besides, it is possible to include in the Petri nets models the values of the human processor model described in (Card et al. 83) about the human performance while interacting with a computer. This is really important as it is related to the actual behaviour of the user interacting with the system. Computing performance evaluations on the tasks models labelled with these values allows us to have precise information about the cost for the user of achieving a task.

4.5 Automated Implementation

We have presented how Petri nets integrate in the process of designing modern interactive software. Petri nets might be used only for the specification phase, allowing requirements for the control structure of interactive systems to be stated in a concise, complete and non ambiguous manner. With the help of automated

---

[8] Timed Petri nets are a dialect of basic Petri nets where time is added on transitions, places or arcs of the Petri net, thus allowing quantitative temporal behaviours in the models to be described (see Palanque & Bastide 95).

implementation techniques, Petri nets can be retained throughout the development process, until the development phase.

Obviously, the compiled solution will be much more efficient in terms of execution speed. The interpreted solution is time consuming, since the task that consists in checking which transitions are enabled in the ObCS net is computationally intensive. This drawback must be weighted, however, by the fact that this computation occurs in the interval of time between user-generated events, which is large with regards to machine efficiency. The ObCS nets are object-structured, and usually remain very simple, addressing the usual complaint about Petri nets being unstructured. The interpretation process can thus be made efficient enough to provide response times compatible with user expectations.

An advantage of the interpreted solutions is that the net structure is preserved at run-time, thus allowing for debugging facilities (e.g. animating the net representation during user activity). Moreover, the fact that the net structure is available at run-time allows for run-time reasoning about user interaction in terms of the dialogue model itself. We have explored ways to provide contextual help from this representation, for example (Palanque et al. 93b). With the interpreted solution, the ICO formalism is amenable to a "model-based UIMS" environment, where the interface model is preserved until run-time.

5. Conclusion

In this chapter we have presented how the ICO formalism can be used for the modelling of a well known distributed interactive system: a Web Browser and a server class. It has also been shown that it is possible to formally describe the HTTP protocol that handles the communication between clients and servers.

The next step is to show that the client class and the server class have a coherent behaviour according to the HTTP protocol. This can be proven using formal analysis techniques provided by Petri nets. The fact that the ICO formalism is based on the object-oriented approach allows for dynamic instanciation of objects to be handled thus (for instance) corresponding to the possibility of the user handling several Web clients at the same time and adding or removing Web clients at run time.

Acknowledgement

The authors would like to thank Egbert Schlungbaum for the precise review he did on the first version of this paper.

Chapter 10:
Development of a WWW Browser Using TADEUS

1. Introduction

Users expect advanced interactive applications to be easy-to-use and easy-to-learn. Today users expect to be able to sit down and use software without spending their time reading manuals. But such user interfaces are hard to design and implement. Different studies have shown that an average of 48% of the code of an application is devoted to the user interface, and that about 50% of the implementation time is devoted to implementing the user interface portion (Myers & Rosson 92). As user interfaces become easier to use, they become harder to create. User interface developers need tools which provide a rich support for the development of advanced user interfaces.

Over the last years several tools were created to support user interface developers, e.g. Toolkits, User Interface Management Systems, Interface Builders, User Interface Development Environments. In his state of the art report B. Myers has introduced a classification of these user interface software tools (Myers 95). It is based on the way user interface developers can specify the layout and the dynamic behaviour of a user interface. There are *language-based tools* (they require the developer to program in a special-purpose language), *interactive graphical specification tools* (they allow an interactive design of the user interface), and *model-based generation tools* (they use a high level model or specification to generate the user interface automatically).

The user interface development still remains difficult and time consuming when using language-based or interactive graphical specification tools because they support the specification of either the dynamic behaviour or the layout in an easy way but rarely both parts at one time. These tools support the user interface implementation rather than task-oriented or user-centred design. One goal of model-based generation tools is to meet these limitations.

The basic idea of the model-based approach is that user interface development can be entirely supported by declarative models at a high level of abstraction. These models are at the centre of model-based user interface development as well as the model-based tools supporting this approach. Due to their formal structure the declarative models have several uses:

- They are used to specify all characteristics of the desired user interface such as user tasks, application domain objects, dialogue behaviour, and presentation characteristics. The user interface developer (as the user of model-based environments) specifies *what* features the interface should have, rather than writing programs that specify *how* to make the computer exhibit the desired behaviour.
- They are used to implement the executable user interface software automatically.
- They are used to build an environment of comprehensive tools to support the user interface developer during the whole life cycle of the user interface, e.g. (graphical) model editors, automatic check of the conceptual user interface design for consistency and completeness, design critics and advisors, automatic generation and implementation.
- They are used to build additional service components for the user, such as intelligent help with several different forms. This is an inherent feature of model-based environments that user interface developers specify the declarative models to generate user interfaces *and* these additional user support tools. These tools come for free, that is without any additional expense from user interface developers because the necessary information for their development is already specified in the declarative models and the model-based environment contains the necessary tools to support their generation.

TADEUS (*TA*sk-based *DE*velopment of *US*er interface software) is a task-oriented and model-based approach to user interface development of interactive software systems (Elwert & Schlungbaum 95, Schlungbaum & Elwert 96). This chapter describes the application of TADEUS to develop a Netscape-like Web browser. Because the main purpose of TADEUS is the development of *interactive systems* we do not describe the development of a server.

This chapter is based on the presentation at CHI'96 workshop (Schlungbaum 96). It is organised as follows. The next two sections briefly introduce the TADEUS approach and the Dialogue graphs as a pre-requisite for reading the 4th section. This is the main section of this chapter and it describes the development of a Web browser by means of TADEUS in detail. The paragraphs of the 4th section correspond to the TADEUS procedure. The case study example is developed in two steps in order to show the way to extend a given specification of an interactive system by means of TADEUS. A discussion of related work, a summary on case study work, and some remarks on future developments conclude this chapter.

2. TADEUS Approach - Brief Overview

The TADEUS approach is a task-oriented and model-based approach to the development of interactive software systems. Their user interface and application core can be developed independently by means of TADEUS. The user interface developer's work, following the TADEUS approach, is supported by the TADEUS system. Its architecture and the data flow of the user interface development procedure are shown in Figure 1.

The user interface development process is divided into three stages: the requirements analysis and specification, the dialogue design stage, and the automatic generation of the user interface prototype (Elwert & Schlungbaum 95):

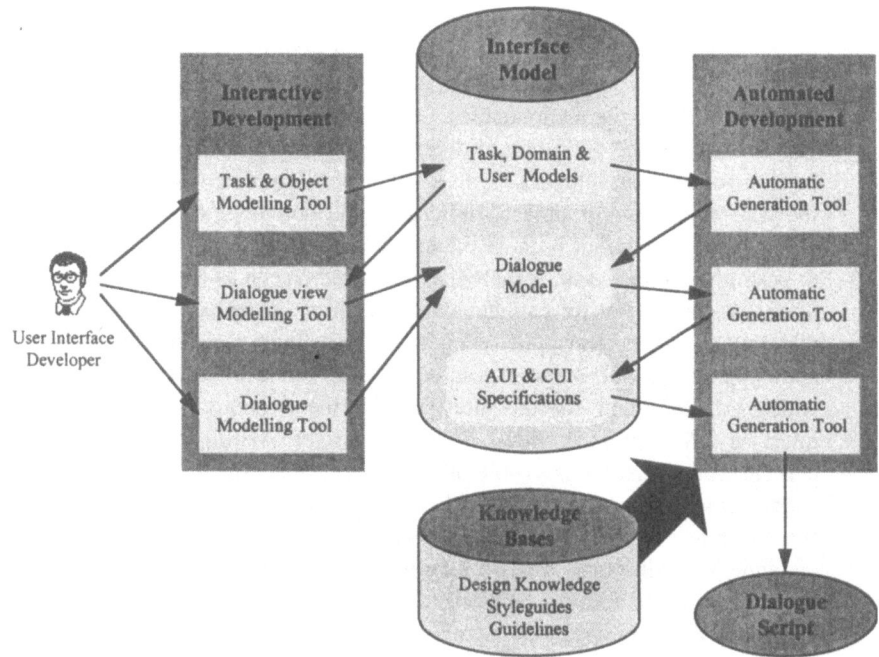

Figure 1: TADEUS: Tool architecture and data flow of user interface development procedure

1) The current state of TADEUS enables user interface developers to specify four declarative models in order to generate the desired user interface as depicted in Figure 1. After requirements analysis the developer creates the task, domain, and user models which are the basis of subsequent development of the interactive and noninteractive parts of interactive applications. The task model represents a hierarchical structure of the tasks the user plans to carry out using the interactive system. Like TKS (Johnson 92) each task representation includes a goal, a procedure to achieve this goal, preconditions and effects, and subtasks with an ordering. The domain model represents the important entities (objects with attributes and methods) of the application domain using an object model known from object-oriented analysis methods like OMT (Rumbaugh et al. 91). The user model describes prospective users in terms of roles and their relations to the tasks they perform.

2) During the dialogue design stage the user interface developer creates the dialogue model. The dialogue design includes manual, computer-aided, and automatic steps.

Two levels of dialogue are distinguished in the TADEUS dialogue model: the navigation and the processing dialogue. The *navigation dialogue* describes the sequencing between different task-oriented presentation units called dialogue views. It can be specified by means of Dialogue graphs (Schlungbaum & Elwert 95, Schlungbaum & Elwert 96a). The *processing dialogue* deals with the description of the dialogue within a dialogue view including the realisation of state changes on the level of user interface objects. All parts of processing dialogue could be generated automatically, but in order to improve the generation result the user interface developer can provide additional presentation information using interaction tables.

The first step is the definition of dialogue views. Usually, this step is carried out by user interface developers. A *dialogue view* is a collection of tasks defined in the task model and/or objects defined in the domain model. These tasks and objects are put together because the user needs their user interface representation to perform a certain task. A dialogue view can be seen as a class definition. That means a dialogue view can have one or more instances. One instance of a dialogue view becomes one window of the final user interface during the automatic generation stage. A dialogue view instance has essential properties which are important for the modelling of the dynamic behaviour of a user interface. A dialogue view instance can be *visible*, which means the corresponding window is visible on the screen. A dialogue view instance can be *active*, which means the corresponding window is visible and possesses the input focus (all user interactions are directed to objects inside this window). Finally, a dialogue view instance can be *manipulable*, which means the corresponding window is visible and can be activated. Furthermore, a dialogue view has some properties which influence its layout generation. These include the dialogue view character (e.g., primary, secondary or dialogue box view), and the dialogue view object representation (e.g., container or data view).

The next dialogue design steps include the design of the navigation and processing dialogues. At the request of the user interface developer, the TADEUS system generates the default interaction table for each dialogue view and transitions between the dialogue views. The user interface developer can then refine and modify the generated specifications of navigation and processing dialogues.

3) The third stage is the automatic generation of the prototype of the final user interface from: the specified models, a software ergonomics knowledge base, and auxiliary interaction with the dialogue designer in order to request non-specified information. There are two internal declarative models (the abstract and concrete user interface specifications) which are created during the automatic generation procedure. The user interface developer cannot access them. The result of the generation procedure is a dialogue script file for an existing UIMS, e.g. the ISA Dialog Manager (ISA GmbH, Stuttgart, (Fähnrich & Kärcher 91)).

3. Dialogue Graphs - Brief Introduction

Dialogue graphs are a formal and visual specification for dialogue modelling (Schlungbaum & Elwert 96b). The dialogue specification of graphical user interfaces requires a notation capable of expressing the following: concurrence between different windows, multiple instances of a window type, modal dialogue situations and dynamic creation of user interface objects. Furthermore, it should be possible to construct a user interface prototype directly from the specification.

Coloured Petri Nets (CPN) (Jensen 91) can be used to specify the mentioned properties of graphical user interfaces. However, many user interface developers are unaccustomed to CPN, and several authors argue that it is better to use a simpler notation like condition/event-nets (Janssen 93). Conceptual difficulties result from the complexity of CPN elements such as node functions, guard functions, arc expressions, transition functions, and colour functions. For this reason we developed an abstraction called Dialogue graphs, that is more suitable and understandable for the user interface developer than CPN while remaining expressive enough for dialogue modelling. Dialogue graphs use a simple directed graph notation that hides the more complex graphical structure of a CPN while preserving the CPN properties for dynamic modelling.

Dialogue graphs make it easy to specify the concurrence of window-oriented user interfaces. Furthermore, they include resources to specify modal dialogue situations (e.g., appearance of an error message, file selection dialogue), to refine dialogue views in a hierarchical structure, to specify the dynamic creation of user interface objects, to handle multiple instances of windows, and to reuse predefined sub-Dialogue graphs (e.g., standard dialogues such as file handling). This section introduces these elements of Dialogue graphs that are used for the explanation of the Web browser example. The interested reader may find a more complete description of Dialogue graphs and their formal specification in (Schlungbaum & Elwert 96b).

3.1 Structural (or Static) Modelling

A Dialogue graph consists of nodes and directed arcs between these nodes. Each node represents a dialogue view. Each arc represents possible interactions between the connected dialogue views.

Dialogue views are drawn as circles or ellipses labelled with a name. There are single (non-modal), multi (non-modal), modal and complex views. The modal view is a starting point for a modal dialogue. If the user achieves this dialogue view by an interaction he must first complete this modal dialogue in order to continue the other dialogue. A complex view allows the dialogue designer to refine a dialogue view. The non-modal views contain neither refinement (unlike the complex view) nor interaction limitations (unlike the modal view). The difference between a single and a multi view is that a single view has only one instance but the multi view can have one or more instances. The instances of a multi view all have the same layout characteristics but they represent different objects of the same type. For example, users can use more than one instance of a HTML viewer. The multi view in this example represents the viewers in general. Each HTML viewer is an instance of this multi view, and each instance contains an object (the concrete HTML page). Furthermore, there is an end node which does not represent any dialogue view (drawn as a black point). This node is necessary to complete the graph structure.

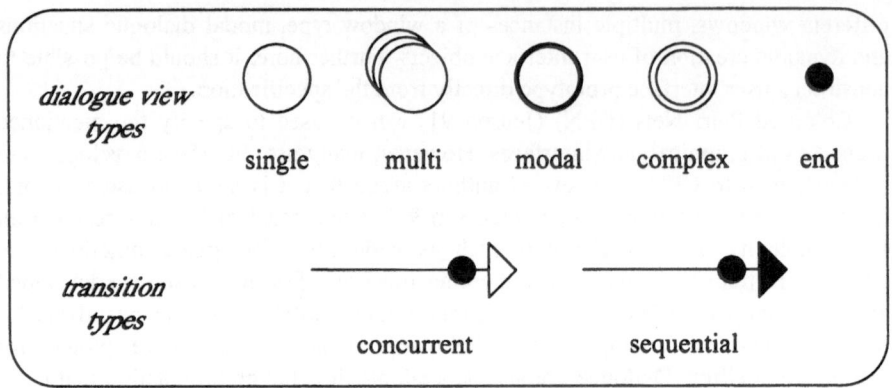

Figure 2: Dialogue views and transitions of a Dialogue graph

The user can navigate between dialogue views by interactions represented by *directed transitions*. Transitions may be concurrent or sequential. The representation of dialogue views and transitions are shown in Figure 2.

Definition 1:
A Dialogue graph is defined as a directed graph DG=(DVT,DV,TT,T,Nm,n) with:

DVT   {single, multi, modal, complex, end} is a set of dialogue view types.
DV   is a finite set of nodes, called dialogue views: $\forall dv \in DV$: TYPE(dv)$\in$DVT.
TT   {concurrent, sequential} is a set of transition types.
T   is a finite set of transitions: T$\subseteq$DV×DV; $\forall t \in T$: TYPE(t)$\in$TT.
Nm   is a finite set of names.
n   DV$\cup$T$\rightarrow$Nm is a label function.

3.2 Behavioural (or Dynamic) Modelling

3.2.1 Marking of dialogue views

In order to specify the state of a user interface, Dialogue graph views are marked. The marking of a dialogue view describes its state. The total state of the modelled user interface is the aggregate of these dialogue view markings. The properties of dialogue view's dynamic behaviour are encoded in tokens:

- activity (a)   describes whether a view instance has the input focus or not,
- visibility (v)   describes whether a view instance is visible or not,
- manipulability (m) describes whether a view instance is manipulable or not by the user.

These properties are modelled by tokens and their value. Furthermore each instance of a dialogue view possesses an identifier, the 4th token. This token is necessary to differentiate multiple instances of a dialogue view. The view instances may be known at design time or created at run time dynamically. All four tokens form a tuple that resides in a dialogue view. The tuple exists for each instance of a dialogue view and describes the state of the dialogue view instance. The existence of tuples on a dialogue view with particular token values is controlled by the following *existence rules*:

- Only one dialogue view instance can be active in the Dialogue graph at the same time. That means only one tuple with an a-token can exist in the Dialogue graph.
- If a dialogue view instance is active then it is also visible and manipulable.
- If a dialogue view instance is visible and manipulable then this dialogue view instance can become active through an user interaction.
- If a dialogue view instance is visible but not manipulable then it cannot be activated. That means a modal dialogue view is active.
- A non-marked dialogue view in the Dialogue graph means that there is no instance of the view.

Definition 2:
Marking of views is defined as a finite set TU with: TU⊂Σ, Σ is the finite set Σ=A×V×M×Id | A={a,_}, V={v,_}, M={m,_}, Id={0,...,n} | n∈N.

In consideration of the existence rules there are some valid examples of marking tuples:

- (a, v, m, Id) active instance of a dialogue view,
- (_, v, m, Id) visible and manipulable instance of a dialogue view,
- (_, v, _, Id) all other visible instances of dialogue views, if a modal dialogue is activated.

3.2.2 Complete definition of a Dialogue graph

The definition of the general Dialogue graph extends Definition 1 and considers Definition 2:

Definition 3:
A Dialogue graph is a tuple DG=(DVT,DV,TT,T,Nm,n,Σ,TU,C,M_0,INI,Ω,GF,TF) with:

DVT   {single, multi, modal, complex, end} is a set of dialogue view types.
DV   is a finite set of nodes, called dialogue views: ∀dv∈DV: TYPE(dv)∈DVT.
TT   {concurrent, sequential} is a set of transition types.
T   is a finite set of transitions: T⊆DV×DV; ∀t∈T: TYPE(t)∈TT.
Nm   is a finite set of names.
n   DV∪T→Nm is a label function.
Σ   Σ=A×V×M×Id | A={a,_}, V={v,_}, M={m,_}, Id={0,...,n} | n∈N.
TU   is a finite set of marking of views TU⊂Σ.
C   DV→TU is a colour function, which maps each view into a set TU.

M_0 is a finite set, which contains for each $dv \in DV$ the initial marking $m_0 \in M_0$, $m_0 \in TU$

INI $DV \rightarrow M_0$ is an initialisation function, which maps each view into a set $M_0 \subset TU$.

Ω is a finite set of interaction events. $\omega \in \Omega$ can be external (user interaction) or internal (application event).

GF   is a guard function and maps each transition $t \in T$ into an expression of type Boolean. The expression evaluates to TRUE, if the pre-conditions described in the control rules are satisfied. Pre-conditions include the marking on source and destination views and the occurrence of the assigned interaction event $\omega \in \Omega$.

TF $TU \rightarrow TU$ is a transition function, which can be assigned to t, $t \in T$ and is executed if t occurs; TF_t denotes TF assigned to the transition t, $t = (dv_i, dv_j)$ and TF_t has an effect on all $dv \in DV \backslash \{ dv_i, dv_j \}$.

The specification of a Dialogue graph requires the definition of the graph structure *and* of an initial marking. At least one node (e.g., dialogue view) must be marked in order to specify the initial state of the desired user interface.

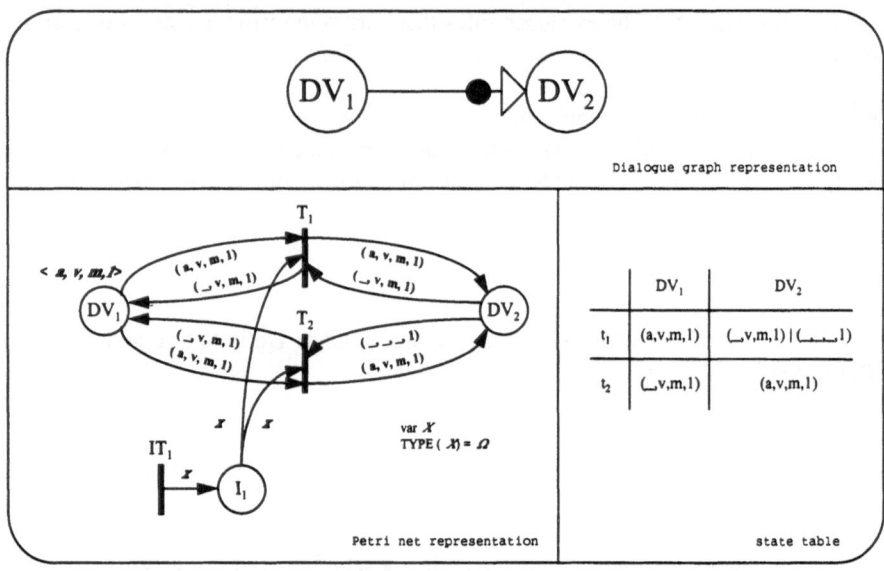

Figure 3: Concurrent transition

3.2.3 Semantics of dialogue graph transitions

The transitions of a Dialogue graph describe explicitly the change of visibility. The change of activity is not expressed by a special transition in the Dialogue graph. It is described implicitly without any loss of information because this property is very clearly recognisable by means of the simulation tool.

$TF_{modal-in}$ $\{(\_,v,m,X)\} \rightarrow \{(\_,v,\_,X)\}$, $X \in$ Id is assigned to all transitions t, $t \in T$
     with t=(dv_i,dv_j), $dv_i,dv_j \in DV$, TYPE(dv_j)=modal.

$TF_{modal-out}$ $\{(\_,v,\_,X)\} \rightarrow \{(\_,v,m,X)\}$, $X \in$ Id is assigned to all transitions t, $t \in T$
     with t=(dv_i,dv_j), $dv_i,dv_j \in DV$, TYPE(dv_i)=modal.

3.3.2 Multi view with concurrent transition

The existence of the multi view demands a specialisation of the concurrent transition into an Id-preserving concurrent transition from a single to a multi view and between two multi views, and an Id-losing concurrent transition from a multi to a single view. In Figure 6 we explain the multi view in combination with a concurrent transition from a single to a multi view. The behaviour of this transition is similar to the concurrent transition. After the related user interaction, the dialogue views V_1 and V_2 are visible. An important property of this transition is the possibility to create more than one instance of the dialogue view V_2 dynamically at runtime. Each instance of dialogue view V_2 represents one object (instance-window) of a related class. The user interaction that fires the transition is connected with the selection of an object in dialogue view V_1 at runtime.

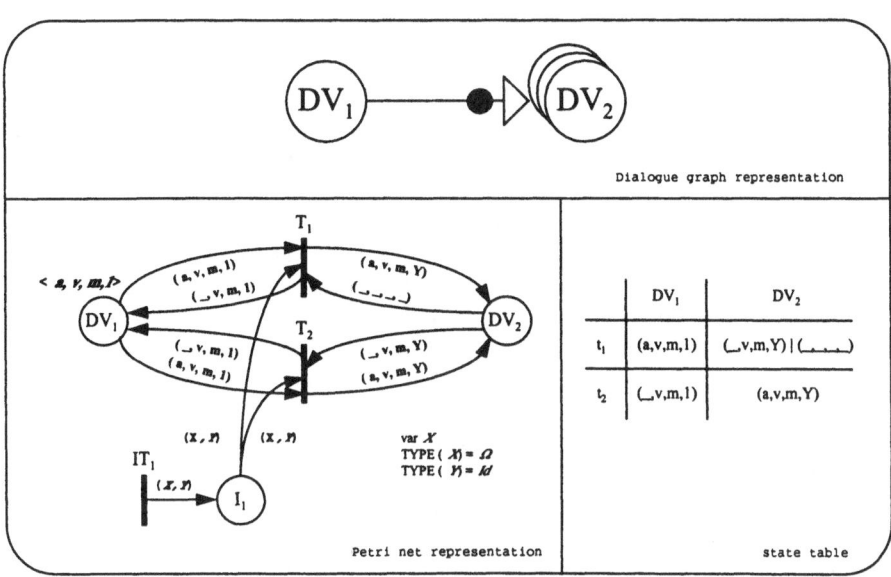

Figure 6: Concurrent transition from a single to a multi view

3.3.3 End node

The dialogue designer can describe the closing of a user interface by the usage of the end node. This node does not represent any actual view of the desired user interface. The end node is always connected via a sequential transition with the view where the closing is initiated. The behaviour of a sequential transition with a end node can be described as follows. Its source view is active. If this transition fires, the current dialogue view instance will be deleted with all other existing dialogue view instances. Therefore, the transition function $TF_{closing}$ is defined which removes the tokens from all other visible view instances which are not connected by the transition to the end node.

Definition 5:
Definition of the transition function $TF_{closing}$:

$TF_{closing}$ $\quad$ $\{(\_,v,m,X)\} \rightarrow \emptyset$, $X \in Id$ is assigned to all transitions t, $t \in T$ with $\quad$ $t=(dv_i,dv_j)$, $dv_i,dv_j \in DV$, $TYPE(dv_j)=end$.

3.4 Types of Dialogue Graphs

In general, a Dialogue graph is defined as a directed graph. In order to specify the navigation dialogue user interface developers can use an *Abstract Dialogue graph*. This is a Dialogue graph with no loops. A general Dialogue graph can include loops which can be interpreted as a representation of the processing dialogue inside a dialogue view. All single, multi and modal dialogue views should include a description of processing dialogue.

4. Specification of a WWW Browser

4.1 Requirements Analysis and Specification

The task-oriented development of interactive systems is primarily focused on the analysis of the user and on the elaboration of the real and complete tasks the user plans to perform by means of the interactive system to be developed (Lewis & Rieman 93). In contrast, traditional requirements analysis looks at abstract and partial task elements. Furthermore, an inherent trait of task-oriented development is the iterative design of the user interface and the system. It is seldom that the first design of a user interface is a complete success. Several iterations are usually required. The model-based automatic generation of the user interface supports user interface developers during this iterative procedure. In this section we demonstrate how this can be done if user interface developers use TADEUS.

The TADEUS system provides modelling tools for expressing the results of the requirements analysis. It does not support the activities of the requirements analysis itself. As result developers create the task, domain and user models.

The development of our Web browser is divided into two parts. First we specify a very simple browser with a minimum of functionality. In a second step we extend the first specification with a history mechanism in order to show how the model-based approach deals with an evolutionary development of interactive systems. Let us start with the elaboration of the tasks the user plans to perform by means of a very simple Web browser:

- The user can start to use the Web browser. In this case a viewer will always be opened and either an empty or predefined page will be shown. This task is not included into the specification of the Web browser. This is a necessary step users have to perform before they can use the browser but it is not a task the browser has to support. It simply defines the initial state of the Web browser.
- The user can view HTML documents in different ways: GoToURL
  ◊ The user can view any HTML document by giving the name of the URL or by following a link inside the current document: NewURL
  ◊ The user can view a predefined HTML document, the so-called home-page: Home
  ◊ The user can interrupt the procedure of loading an HTML document at any time the operation is in progress: Stop
- The user can keep the current viewed HTML document: KeepDocument
  ◊ The user can save it to a file: SaveToFile
  ◊ The user can print it: SaveToPrinter
- The user can finish the use of the browser at any time: Quit

This list only indicates the high-level tasks the user plans to perform using the simple Web browser. As depicted in Figure 7 these tasks build a hierarchy. This list represents *what* users plan to do and not *how* they will perform these activities. For example, the task NewURL can be carried out in several ways. The subtasks of the KeepDocument tasks obviously need some parameters (e.g., filename, filelocation, fileformat, printername). On the other hand, especially for tasks like the subtasks of KeepDocument the user interface styleguides include standard designs. As we will see in the further development steps of our Web browser TADEUS offers predefined subdialogues which user interface developers can include in their design. That means, so far there is not any need to refine these tasks (e.g., SaveToFile, SaveToPrinter).

One of the next task modelling steps is to identify task attributes (e.g., is_repeatable) and the temporal relations between the different subtasks (e.g., sequence, choice). The notation of temporal relations between the subtasks of one task in TADEUS is based on the temporal relations defined for the UAN (User Action Notation, (Hartson & Gray 92, Hix & Hartson 93). Most of the tasks of our simple Web browser are repeatable, the attribute is_repeatable is set to true (the thick border of task representations in Figure 7). The temporal ordering of the subtasks fits into the Choice operator: at any time users can select one of the available subtasks. After the selected subtask is completed all subtasks of one subroot are available again because the subroottask is_repeatable.

It is necessary to discuss the Stop task in more detail. This task should be available for users only if one of the other subtasks of the task GoToURL is in progress. The procedure of loading an HTML document can be very time consuming (e.g., due to a high load on the net). Then users should be able to terminate this task by means of the Stop task. That means, in our case Stop can terminate the Choice of NewURL, Home. But there are some difficulties with the Stop task. The temporal operators of the UAN do not allow the correct specification of this task's behaviour. First of all, there is no operator to specify that one task can terminate another one like the Exclusive ordering operator in Mastermind (Browne et al. 97). Furthermore, the Stop task should be available only while one of the other tasks is in progress. As shown in Table 2 we use additional preconditions and effects to specify such complex application dependent behaviour in TADEUS. The preconditions and effects use the state of the application and because of that we have to specify parts of the domain model before we can finish the initial task model of the simple Web browser.

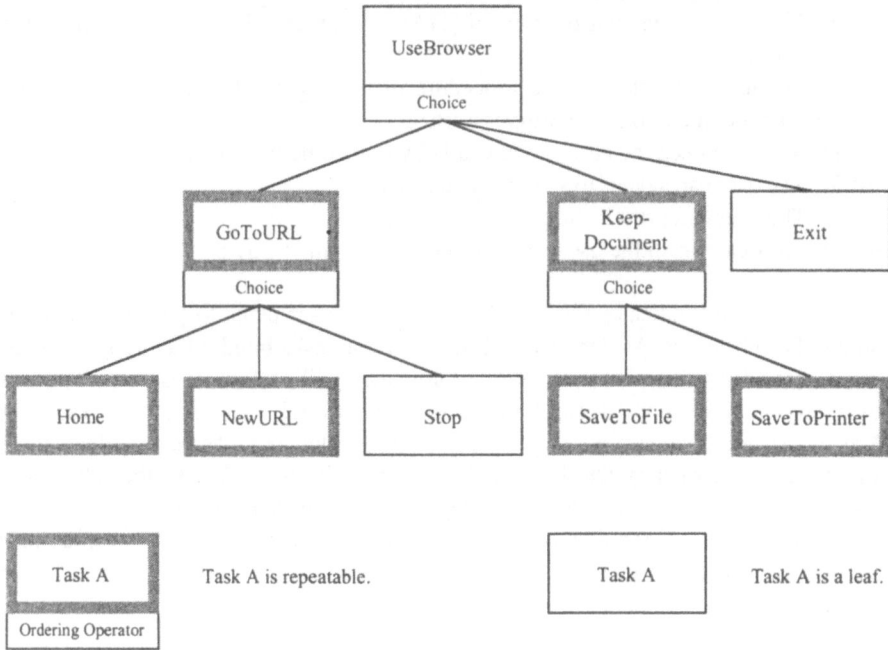

Figure 7: Task model: task hierarchy of the simple Web browser

After knowing the tasks the user likes to perform with our simple Web browser we define the domain model of this simple Web browser, which is shown in Figure 8. Using the OMT notation (Rumbaugh et al. 91) it describes one class - the Browser - with its attributes and methods. Two attributes of the Browser class (LoadProgress, LoadInterrupted) represent its state and can be used to describe the complex relations between the high level tasks. The attribute CurrentURL contains the name of the URL actually shown in the Web browser. Furthermore, for each leaf task in our task hierarchy the Browser class includes a method which is invoked if the user performs the corresponding task.

The following tables refine the specification of the task model. The task hierarchy (see Figure 7) only indicates the tasks a user plans to perform and describes their ordering. But a complete task description requires that user interface developers specify which method of a domain object will be invoked in order to achieve the goal of the corresponding task. As one example, Table 1 presents the specification of the Home task. If the user selects the Home task the method Home of the `Browser` class is invoked. The additional comments are hints for the application designer that this method has to worry about some feedback - the attribute `LoadProgress` must be continually updated. As we will see below this attribute is very useful for another part of the desired user interface. The additional precondition explains that this task is always available and the effect sets a necessary precondition of the `KeepDocument` subtasks.

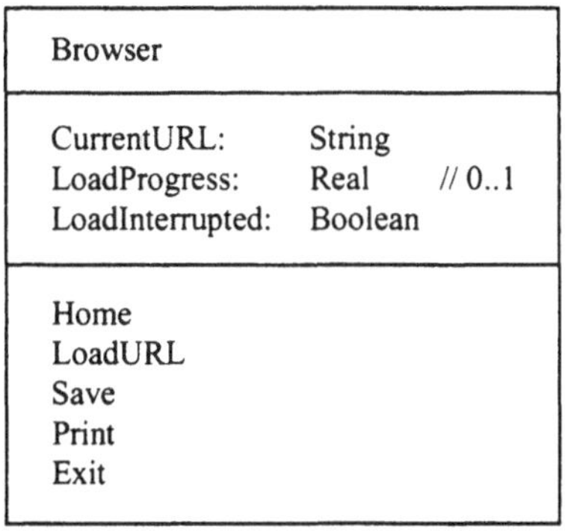

```
Browser

CurrentURL:        String
LoadProgress:      Real      // 0..1
LoadInterrupted:   Boolean

Home
LoadURL
Save
Print
Exit
```

Figure 8: Domain model: class description of the simple Web browser

As mentioned above, we have some trouble specifying the exact behaviour of the `Stop` task if only using the temporal relation operators. As shown in Table 2 the precondition of the `Stop` task enables this task only, if another `GoToURL` subtask is in progress. The effect of invoking the `Stop` task is that the current active task will be terminated. The `LoadInterrupted` attribute keeps this information.

Table 3 explains another feature of the TADEUS task model editor. If user interface developers specify some task-specific information (e.g., a precondition) at a node with subnodes then all subnodes will have the same attribute. In the example of Table 3 all subtasks of the `KeepDocument` task will have the precondition that the loading of an HTML document was successful (e.g., not terminated).

Task	Home
Preconditions	TRUE
Effects	Browser.LoadInterrupted := FALSE
Objects	Browser
Do	Browser.Home // Feedback: LoadProgress == 0 start of the method // 0..<1 while in progress // 1 end of the method

Table 1: Specification of the Home task

Task	Stop
Preconditions	Browser.LoadProgress _ 1
Effects	Browser.LoadProgress := 1 Browser.LoadInterrupted := TRUE
Objects	Browser
Do	// Terminate currently active task

Table 2: Specification of the Stop task

Task	KeepDocument
Subtasks	SaveToFile, SaveToPrinter
Ordering	Choice
Preconditions	Browser.LoadInterrupted := False
Effects	
Objects	Browser

Table 3: Specification of the KeepDocument

4.2 Dialogue Design

After user interface developers finished the work on the task and domain models they can start the dialogue design steps and create the dialogue model.

4.2.1 Identification of dialogue views

The user interface developer can define dialogue views using either the task or the domain model. As depicted in Figure 9, we demonstrate this using the task model. The developer defines one dialogue view Browser for the simple Web browser. Furthermore, the developer includes some predefined dialogue views in order to support the NewURL, SaveToFile and SaveToPrinter tasks: the modal dialogue views OpenURL, SaveDoc and PrintDoc.

The user interface developer must next specify some attributes for each dialogue view (the default value is shown in italics):

- dialogue view type: *single*, multi, modal or complex view;
- dialogue view character: *primary*, secondary or dialogue box view;
- dialogue view object representation for a primary or secondary view: container or *data* view.

For the case of our example, the developer could use the defaults for the dialogue view Browser and the description of the predefined dialogue views. Table 4 gives a combined description of these attributes.

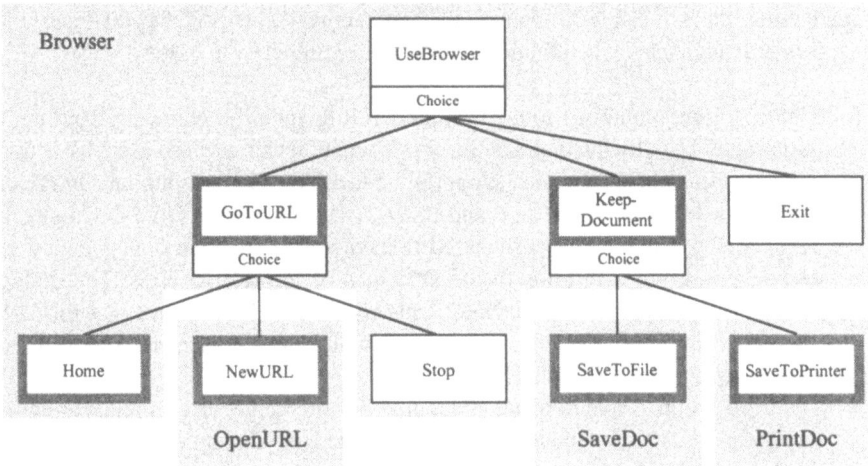

Figure 9: Identification of dialogue views for the simple Web browser

dialogue view name	Browser	OpenURL	SaveDoc	PrintDoc
dialogue view type	single	modal	modal	modal
dialogue view character	primary	dialogue box	dialogue box	dialogue box
dialogue view object representation	data			

Table 4: Combined dialogue view description tables

4.2.2 Design of navigation dialogue

The navigation dialogue describes the dialogue between the different dialogue views and can be specified by means of an Abstract Dialogue graph. This includes two steps. The transitions between the nodes (e.g., dialogue views) and the initial marking of the Dialogue graph must be specified. The Abstract Dialogue graph for the simple Web browser is shown in Figure 10. It can be automatically generated. The main dialogue view is connected with each of the modal dialogue views by a concurrent transition and from each modal dialogue view leads a sequential transition back to the main dialogue view (see Figure 5). The initial state of the Web browser application is that the main window will be active.

4.2.3 Design of processing dialogue

The processing dialogue deals with the description of the dialogue within a dialogue view. Generally, the dynamic behaviour and the presentation of processing dialogue could be generated automatically, but in order to improve the generation result the user interface developer can provide additional presentation information using interaction tables. Table 5 shows the interaction table of the dialogue view `Browser` which can be automatically created in 3 steps:

- The first group conforms to the task model. It includes all leaf tasks from the left to the right. Usually the dialogue form is a function call because users have to call an application function which supports the task they are carrying out. In the case of the `NewURL`, `SaveToFile` and `SaveToPrinter` tasks, the function call is changed to navigation, because there is a navigation to another dialogue view.
- The second group conforms to the attributes of the related class. The dialogue view object representation attribute is instance view. This means, that inside this view the values of the object attributes should be represented. The automatic procedure includes all attributes.
- The third group is added using styleguide information. For example, styleguides require that it is always possible to invoke some Help dialogue.

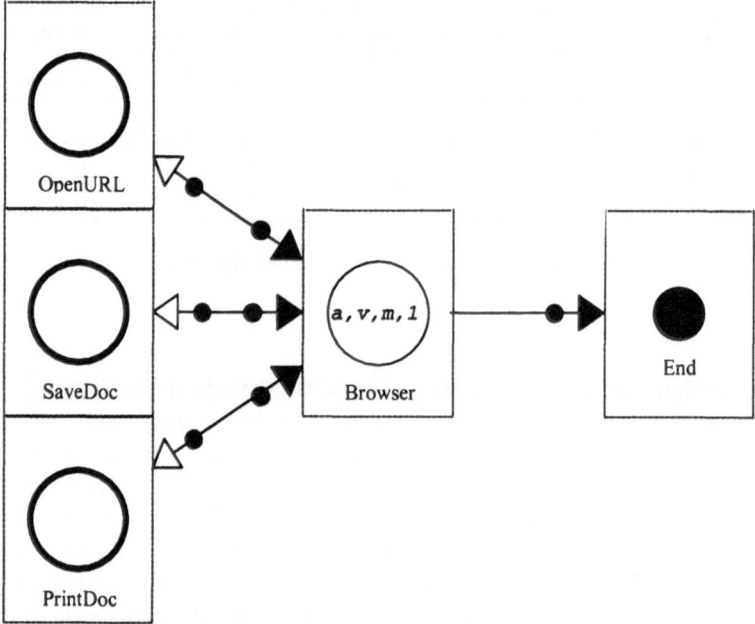

Figure 10: Dialogue model: Abstract Dialogue graph of the simple Web browser

The user interface developer can change the automatically generated interaction table in order to improve the input data for the subsequent automatic generation of the final user interface prototype.

transition	dialogue form	group	position in group
Home	function call	1	1
NewURL	navigation	1	2
Stop	function call	1	3
SaveToFile	navigation	1	4
SaveToPrinter	navigation	1	5
Exit	function call	1	6
CurrentURL	data output	2	1
LoadProgress	data output	2	2
LoadInterrupted	data output	2	3
Help	function call	3	1

Table 5: Interaction table of the dialogue view Browser (automatically generated)

The interaction table of the dialogue view Browser must be changed because there is no hint for the generation of a text output interaction object which will visualise the HTML document. There are some function calls (e.g., Exit and Help) and object attributes (e.g., LoadInterrupted) which do not have to be represented inside the main view. They are shown with a grey background in Table 5. The user interface developer can change the position of the user interface objects which represent the corresponding transitions at the user interface in order to achieve a more convenient layout for the user. Furthermore, the developer can assign a new presentation label to each user interface object (default is the name of the transition). The modified interaction table is shown as Table 6.

transition	dialogue form	group	pos. grp	presentation label
Home	function call	1	1	
NewURL	navigation	1	2	Open
Stop	function call	1	5	
SaveToFile	navigation	1	3	Save
SaveToPrinter	navigation	1	4	Print
CurrentURL	data output	2	1	Location
LoadProgress	data output	4	1	' '
CurrentDoc	data output	3	1	' '

Table 6: Modified interaction table of the dialogue view Browser

4.2.4 Verification of usability properties using Dialogue graphs

Dialogue graphs allow some usability properties of the desired user interface to be checked. There are two possibilities for doing this check: a simulation tool or a formal analysis tool.

If a Dialogue graph consists of a small number of nodes (dialogue views; no more than 10) it is sufficient to use the simulation tool of the Dialogue graph editor in order to compare the designed user interface behaviour with the expected one. To allow developers to recognise the state of the Dialogue graph at a glance we code the states of dialogue views with only one instance by colour. The presence of activity can be expressed by a red coloured background on the view icon. The presence of visibility can be coded by blue colour and non-manipulability by grey. With the simulation tool, the developer can go step by step through the Dialogue graph and can compare the current with the desired behaviour. The development of the simulation tool is complete pending extension to handle multi and complex views.

If the number of nodes is larger than 10 user interface developers need tool support to analyse the Dialogue graph. An equivalent Coloured Petri Net can be constructed for each Dialogue graph. Using the state graph it is possible to check the reachability of all dialogue views (windows in the final user interface), the absence of deadlocks (the user can always carry out an interaction, independently of the previous ones), the liveness (from a dialogue view each interaction can be repeated after a finite number of interactions), and the number of opened windows the user needs to perform a certain task.

Because of the small number of dialogue views in our dialogue model, it is sufficient to use the simulation tool of the Dialogue graph editor in order to compare the designed behaviour of the Web browser's user interface with the expected one. This will be done using the extended specification of the Web browser below.

4.3 Generation of the User Interface Prototype

The development of the dialogue model and the generation of the user interface prototype are closely related. The completeness of the dialogue model influences the required effort for the generation of the user interface and its quality. Missing information in the dialogue model must be supported by the user interface developer in response to questions during the generation procedure.

In TADEUS the desired user interface is primarily generated from the dialogue model which consists of two parts the Dialogue graph and interaction tables. Additionally, information represented in the task and domain models is used during the generation procedure. The presentation layout of the user interface is generated using the interaction tables and the domain model. The dynamic behaviour of the user interface is generated using the Dialogue graph and the task model. The complete procedure for generating user interface code was described elsewhere (Elwert & Schlungbaum 95, Schlungbaum & Elwert 96a). Here we present the result of the automatic generation: Figure 11 contains the layout of the user interface. It requires some additional explanations. The first group includes five buttons to realise the certain method invocations or the navigation to the dialogue boxes. The second group includes an (invisible) field for string output with a label. Unlike a real Netscape browser our specification does not include the possibility modifying the URL in the location field. The third group contains a Canvas widget only, because the ISA Dialog Manager does not offer any HTML viewer. The fourth group contains an output field for real numbers with an empty label. The ISA Dialog Manager does not offer any other progress indicator widgets.

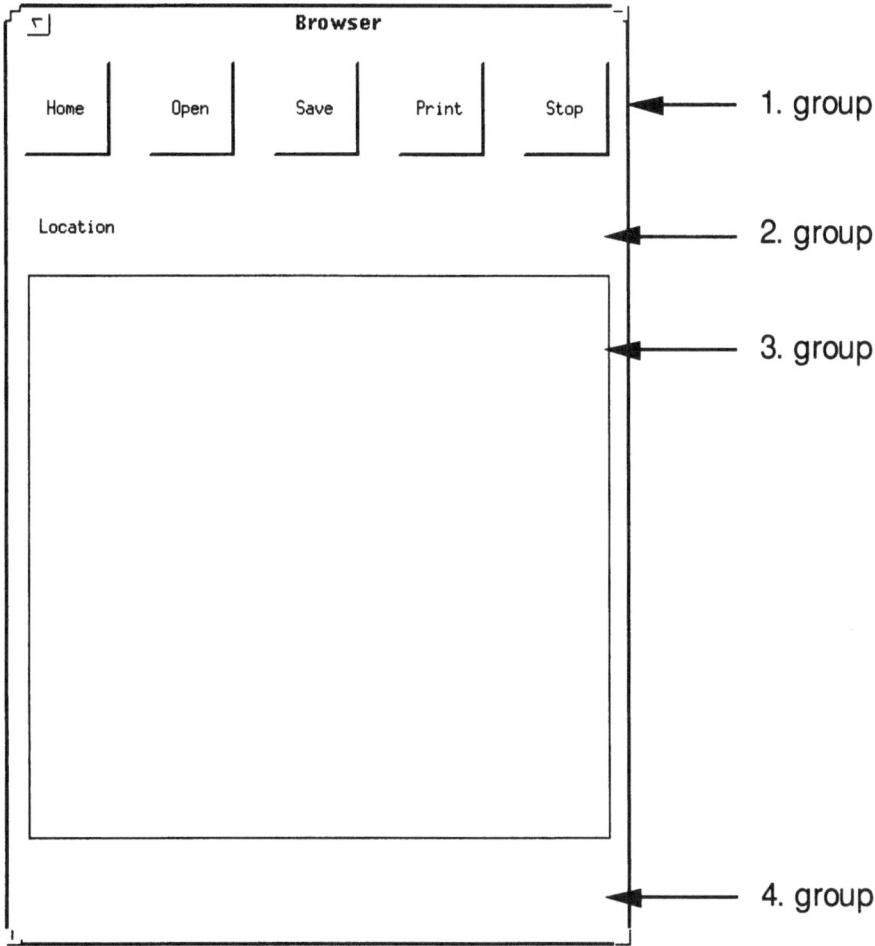

Figure 11: Layout of the simple Web browser

4.4 Extending the Simple Web Browser with a History Mechanism and Bookmark Management

The simple Web browser allows the user to type in a URL and to view the corresponding HTML document. As we know from our own experience such a working style is not sufficient. In this paragraph we add a history mechanism and bookmark management to the simple Web browser in order to demonstrate how user interface developers can use TADEUS for an iterative development of an interactive system. Furthermore, the extended Web browser allows the use of multiple copies of the browser.

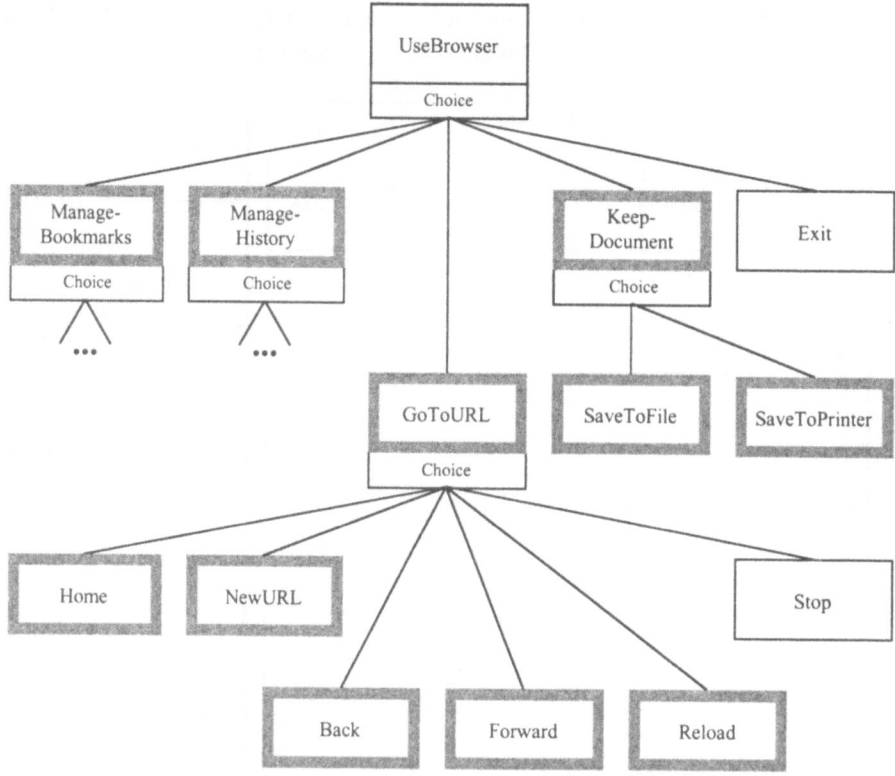

Figure 12: Task model of the extended Web browser

According to the TADEUS methodology we first have to elaborate the additional tasks the user plans to perform using the extended Web browser (for short: Web browser):

- The user can view HTML documents in different ways: GoToURL
  ◊ The user can view the previously viewed HTML document: Back
  ◊ If the Back task was performed at least once, then the user can view the next document according to the state of the session history: Forward (The Forward task is essentially an Undo of the Back task.)
  ◊ The user can reload the document of the current URL: Reload
  • The user can manage the session history and the bookmarks[9]: ManageHistory, ManageBookmarks

---

[9]The subtasks of these tasks will not be described in this chapter due to the limited space.

Task	Back
Preconditions	History.CurrentPosition > 1
Effects	Viewer.LoadInterrupted := FALSE History.CurrentPosition := History.CurrentPosition - 1
Objects	Viewer
Do	Viewer.Back // Feedback: LoadProgress == 0 start of the method // 0..<1 while in progress // 1 end of the method

Table 7: Specification of the Back task

Task	Forward
Preconditions	History.CurrentPosition > History.CurrentPosition
Effects	Viewer.LoadInterrupted := FALSE History.CurrentPosition := History.CurrentPosition + 1
Objects	Viewer
Do	Viewer.Forward // Feedback: LoadProgress == 0 start of the method // 0..<1 while in progress // 1 end of the method

Table 8: Specification of the Forward task

Task	Home
Preconditions	TRUE
Effects	Viewer.LoadInterrupted := FALSE History.CurrentPosition := History.CurrentPosition + 1
Objects	Viewer, History
Do	Viewer.Home // Feedback: LoadProgress == 0 start of the method // 0..<1 while in progress // 1 end of the method History.AddElement

Table 9: Modified specification of the Home task

After finishing the extension of the task and domain models we can start to adapt the dialogue model. The first step is to review the existing dialogue views and to add new ones. In this example all existing dialogue views are kept for the specification of

The user interface developer can use the existing task model and add the r tasks. The resulting task model is shown in Figure 12.

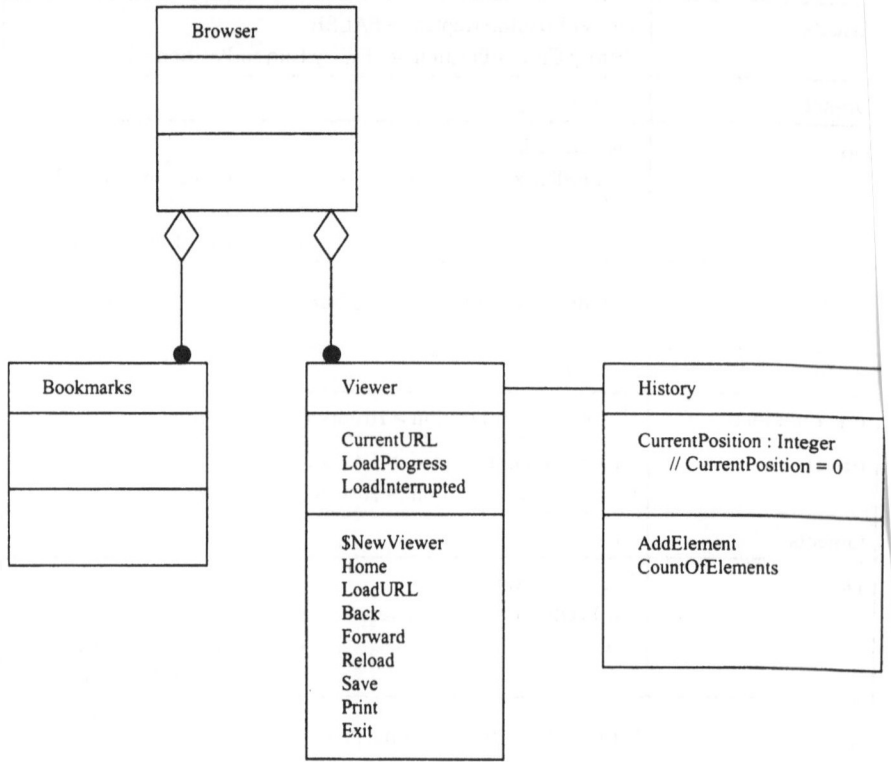

Figure 13: Domain model of the extended Web browser

It is obvious that the Back and Forward tasks need some preconditions to define when these tasks are available for the user. Therefore we have to extend the domain model to that shown in Figure 13. The most remarkable difference between both domain models is the splitting of the former undivided Browser class (see Figure 8) into an "empty" Browser class and a new Viewer class. The Browser class becomes a shape for different services of a Web browser. This decision eases the addition of further services like the Bookmarks now or an Emailer or a Newsreader later on. Furthermore, there is a close connection between the Viewer and the History. As in the task model we only present the information necessary for this chapter in the domain model.

The refinement of the Back and Forward tasks is shown in Tables 7 and 8. The preconditions of these tasks use the history mechanism. Of course, the other GoToURL subtasks influence the history mechanism too. Table 9 presents the modified specification of the Home task as one example.

the extended Web browser. The GoToURL subtasks Back, Forward and Reload will be added to the Browser view. The dialogue view type attribute of the Browser view has to be changed in order to support multiple instances of the viewer window. To support the subtasks ManageBookmarks and ManageHistory we define two new dialogue views. The extentended Dialog graph is shown in Figure 14 and the view attributes in Table 10.

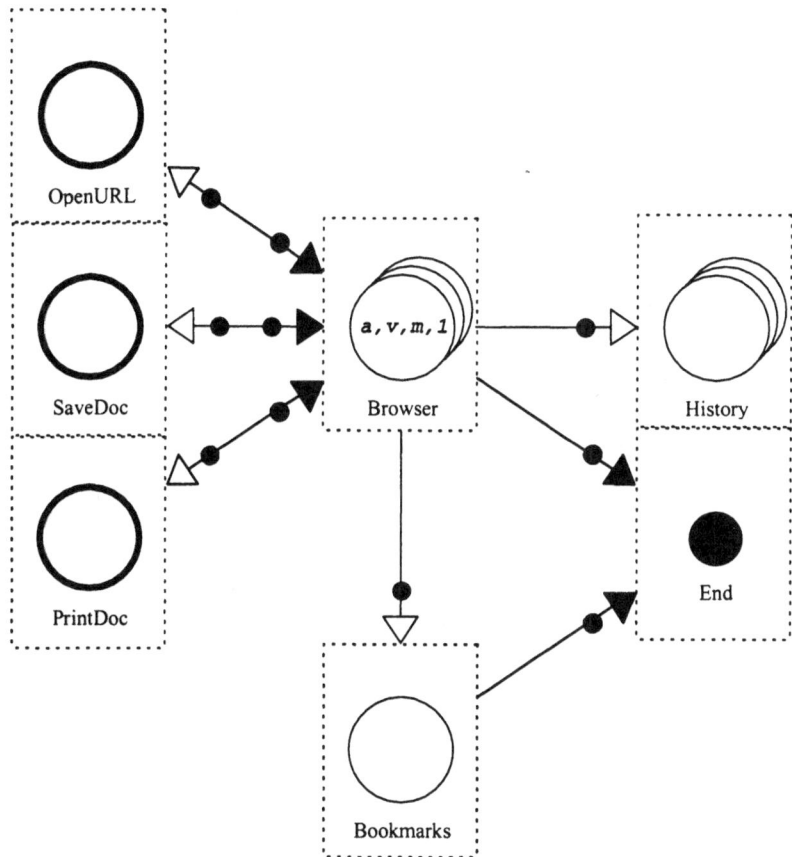

Figure 14: Dialogue model: Dialogue graph of the Web browser

dialogue view name	Browser	History	Bookmarks
dialogue view type	multi	multi	single
dialogue view character	primary	secondary	primary
dialogue view object representation	data	data	data

Table 10: Dialogue view description tables of the new dialogue views

Table 11 shows the new interaction table of the dialogue view Browser after adding the new GoToURL subtasks. Now the user interface developer has to adapt this interaction table (e.g., to define the group information of the new elements) in order to improve the expected result of the automatic generation procedure.

transition	dialogue form	group	pos. grp	presentation label
Home	function call	1	1	
NewURL	navigation	1	2	Open
Stop	function call	1	5	
SaveToFile	navigation	1	3	Save
SaveToPrinter	navigation	1	4	Print
CurrentURL	data output	2	1	Location
LoadProgress	data output	4	1	' '
CurrentDoc	data output	3	1	' '
Back	function call			
Forward	function call			
Reload	function call			

Table 11: Extended interaction table of the dialogue view Browser

After user interface developers have finished the work on the dialogue model they can use the simulation tool of the dialogue model editor in order to check the Dialogue graph. Some snapshots of such a simulation and the automatically generated layout of the extended Web browser may be viewed on the WWW (URL: http://www.informatik.uni-rostock.de/~schlung/FormalMethods_HCI).

5. Related Work

As mentioned in the introduction, one of the basic ideas of model-based user interface development is the use of declarative models which can be understood as a formal specification. Instead of writing large procedural programs, user interface developers specify sets of facts (e.g., the declarative models) in order to describe the features of the desired interactive system explicitly. Over the last decade several model-based environments have been developed which can be distinguished in their use of declarative models. Environments of the first generation like UIDE (Foley et al. 88, Foley & Sukaviriya 95), MECANO (Puerta et al. 94), AME (Märtin 96) and JANUS (Balzert 94, Balzert et al. 96) usually use only an application or domain model to generate the running user interface. Environments of the second generation like ADEPT (Johnson et al. 95), MasterMind (Browne et al. 97, Szekely et al. 95), Mobi-D (Puerta 96), TRIDENT (Bodart et al. 95), GENIUS (Janssen et al. 93), FUSE (Lonczewski & Schreiber 96) and TADEUS use sets of declarative models (e.g., task, domain, user, dialogue and/or presentation models) whereby each of these models emphasises a certain aspect of the desired user interface. Furthermore, the shift from the first to the second generation is connected with developments like emphasis of task-centred user interface development, explicit dialogue modelling, away from the full automatic generation of the desired user interface towards a comprehensive tool support of the user interface developer's work. The interested reader may find a more comprehensive overview on model-based user interface software tools in (Schlungbaum & Elwert 96a).

In his chapter, Fabio Paterno presents a further approach to task-centred user interface design - the TLIM method (Paterno 97). It includes four elements: the use of user task specification as an abstract specification of the interactive system, the use the LOTOS notation to describe both temporal relationships among tasks and software components of the interactive system, the use of the interactor concept as an abstract model for software objects with interact with users and the use of model checking techniques to reason about the resulting specification. The application of the TLIM method supports the evaluation of usability properties of the specified interactive system.

Explicit dialogue modelling is an important step during model-based user interface development. In consensus with D. Harel (Harel 88) such dialogue modelling techniques should be visual formalisms: *visual*, because they are to be generated, comprehended, and communicated by humans; and *formal*, because they are to be manipulated, maintained, and analysed by computers.

In the early stages of user interface management systems transition networks, grammars or events were used to specify the dialogue component (Green 86). The transition networks and their extensions are well known, frequently used visual dialogue specifications. They tend to emphasis the states of the user interface and the sequence of transitions from one state to another. Certainly, transition networks are unsuited to the description of window-oriented and graphical user interfaces. They are useful and powerful for the specification of non-graphical user interfaces, but they have to be modified in order to handle direct manipulation within a user interface. Jacob (Jacob 86) extends state transition diagrams by multiple parallel diagrams. However, the global relations of concurrent dialogues cannot be visualised by this approach.

A further approach to visual specification of user interfaces is the use of Petri nets or Petri net based techniques, like the event graphs (Roudaud et al. 90), the Petri net objects (Bastide & Palanque 90, Palanque et al. 95, Palanque & Bastide 97), or the dialogue nets (Janssen 93, Janssen et al. 93, Janssen 96). Compared to the user interface specification with transition networks, the advantage of Petri nets is that they already have a concept for the specification of concurrence in the basic form. That is needed for the description of window-oriented graphical user interfaces. Another important point of all these approaches is that the user interface software code can be directly created by using the dialogue specification.

Event graphs can be used to describe the dynamic visibility of objects within a graphical user interface. Compared with Dialogue graphs, the specification with event graphs is more expensive and is not so easily surveyed, because the places of the event graph are not in correspondence with the user interface objects. There are not means for dialogue structuring and for visualisation of global relations between separate event graphs describing one user interface.

Petri net objects are more powerful for the description of the general object flow and object manipulation. But they are more complex than event graphs and less suited to the earlier design phases. Like Dialogue graphs Petri net objects are based on high-level Petri nets and so the dynamic creation of user interface objects is natural to model.

Dialogue nets are similar to event graphs. Compared with event graphs, they offer some extensions like hierarchical dialogue structuring, declaration of modal dialogue windows, declaration of macros of dialogue structures, and dynamic creation of user interface objects by dynamic repeated execution of sub nets. But multiple instances of a window and the dynamic creation of user interface objects are difficult to represent because the dialogue nets are based on condition/event nets, which work with a single unnamed token only. Furthermore, the dialogue nets do not allow the refinement of modal views. One intention of our work on Dialogue graphs was to meet these shortcomings. The Dialogue graphs extend the dialogue nets. The modelling of multiple window instances and the dynamic creation of user interface objects was simplified and becomes more natural for the user interface developer because the CPNs provide a more powerful basis for the modelling of these features of a graphical user interface. Dialogue graphs do not restrict the refinement of modal dialogue views. The graphical representation of Dialogue graphs is simpler as of dialogue nets since they preserve the Petri net representation.

6. Conclusion

6.1 Summary on Case Study Work

The goal of this chapter was to answer most of the questions raised in the case study description (see introduction of this book). Because the main purpose of TADEUS is to support the development of interactive software systems, we addressed the specification of a Web browser.

The model-based specification of an interactive software system in TADEUS requires at least that user interface developers specify a task, a domain and a dialogue model. The domain and task models use well-known notations. The dialogue model uses the new Dialogue graphs notation which only includes a few specification constructs. One of the their special features is the sophisticated modelling of multiple instances of user interface windows and the dynamic creation of user interface objects caused on the powerful CPN basis. Due to their formal basis, Dialogue graphs allow a formal analysis of the specified user interface pending the realisation of the corresponding formal analysis tool. The implementation of the user interface is done by automatic generation of a dialogue script file for an existing UIMS from the specified declarative models. The implementation of the interactive application is beyond the TADEUS approach.

The Web browser was specified in two steps, first a very simple one and, second an extension of the simple with a history mechanism in order to demonstrate the evolutionary development of a model-based user interface.

6.2 Future Developments

We are currently completing the development of the TADEUS system. One topic of special importance and active current work is the implementation of all features of the dialogue modelling tool. The development of the simulation tool is complete pending extension to handle multi and complex views. A further step is the realisation of the formal analysis tool.

The integration of a user model to support the development of individual user interfaces is another future direction of the TADEUS project. This adaptation of a user interface can take place during design time or during run time. The paper (Schlungbaum 97) explores a first concept of individualisation during design time. It exploits the usage relation between the task and the user models which describes which task a certain user plans to carry out using the desired interactive system. In the context of the development of user interfaces like the Web browser interface a user model could help to generate different user interfaces which correspond to the level of experience of the user (e.g., novice vs. expert user), to the context of usage the Web browser (e.g., PC or workstation vs. WebTV-box environment).

Acknowledgements

The author would like to thank Thomas Elwert, Kurt Stirewalt and the anonymous reviewer for their detailed and helpful comments on an earlier version of this chapter.

Chapter 11:
Algebraic Specification of a World Wide Web Application Using GRALPLA

1. Introduction

GRALPLA is an algebraic specification language developed at the University of Granada (Spain). This language combines constructive algebraic specification with a graphic formal model (the graphic objects theory). The goal of its development is to generate a specification method, which can be used to specify interactive systems. During the last five years, this language has been applied to several case studies, in an attempt to evaluate its usability, and to solve its limitations by including several new features. A prototyping tool has been developed for the language, which can generate C++ prototypes from the specification text.

This chapter illustrates the specification of an ideal NetScape-like web browser and a html page server using GRALPLA. The advantages and limitations of the method are also discussed. This chapter describes the specification of a case study using GRALPLA. The case study is about the specification of an ideal NetScape-like web browser and a html page server.

The next section contains a brief description of the specification languages. The third section describes the specification of the case study using GRALPLA, and shows the methodology that was employed to develop it. Section 3 demonstrates how to reason on the specification to derive useful specification properties. Section 4 discusses the principles used to carry out a prototype from the specification. Section 5 addresses the evaluation of the method. A whole listing of the specification is given in appendix A.

2. The Specification Language

At present a large number of formal notations and methods have been developed (Faconti & Paterno 90, Palanque & Bastide 94). However there are some strong limitations that discourage their general use. One of these limitations is the difficulty of generating a correct implementation from a satisfactory specification following a step by step method. Our work has focused on the development of executable prototypes from algebraic specifications. The goal is to obtain prototypes written in high level language, which can be refined to produce efficient implementations. The use of algebraic specification poses some advantages:

- It describes the system as a hierarchy of types, which can be mapped to class hierarchy in an object oriented language. This implies carrying out an architectural design of the system.
- It does not fix the data structures used to implement the types. The behaviour of the types is described using axioms over the type functions.

During the last few years we have implemented these ideas in an algebraic specification language, which we call GRALPLA (from GRaphic ALgebraic Prototyping LAnguage). This language supports the definition of abstract data type hierarchy, error management, specification of graphic information and specification of processes and synchronisation. A tool has been designed to check the structure and completeness of specifications, and to generate prototypes in C++. These prototypes can be used as a first version of the system that will be developed. The remainder of this section describes the main characteristics of this language, and the desired features of the case study. A detailed revision of GRALPLA can be found in previous publications (Torres & Clares 94, Torres et al. 96).

The specification of a system using GRALPLA consists of a collection of modules, each one specifying a data type. The specification of every type consists of an interface (a collection of functions) and a set of conditions that hold the objects of the defined type, expressed as a set of axioms on the type functions. The text of a type definition contains the following sections: header, dependencies, constructors, functions, axioms and synchronisation. A syntactically correct type specification is composed by a sequence of these components in the order described. The structure and semantics of constructors and functions are the usual in any algebraic specification language, as they describe the signature of the type.

Axioms have a fixed structure. An axiom is an equation specifying the value of one result of a function, after it has been applied to another function. They are interpreted as directional equations: what appears on the left hand side can be carried out as explained on the right hand side. Both sides of the axioms must be of compatible data types. This interpretation of the axioms is essential in the generation of prototypes, given that we use the object functional history as implicit representation of the system's state. Informally, the functional history of an object is the sequence of functions, which can change the object state in a way not describable by other functions, which have been applied to the object. This representation allows us to implement a prototype from the specification. Of course not every function call must be stored in the functional history (Mallgren 82, Gea & Torres 94).

From a conceptual point of view, functions can be classified in three groups: constructors, generators (which generate new object states) and queries (which do not modify the object state). The behaviour of constructor and generator functions can be defined using axioms. They can be described in term of others functions. In this case, the state of the object after applying the function is equivalent to the state obtained applying the function sequence appearing in the right hand side of the axiom. When this is not the case, the function is considered a basic function, whose behaviour can not be derived from other functions, and which generate new object states. Only basic functions are conceptually needed to keep track of the object state, and therefore they are the only function calls stored in the functional history (Gea 97).

The specification language allows the definition of inheritance relationships, template types and graphic types. A specification might designate a type from which the actual type inherits its behaviour, which, in turn, implies that the type inherits all functions defined by its supertype. The behaviour of these inherited functions can be redefined, and a parameter list can be included to define generic types.

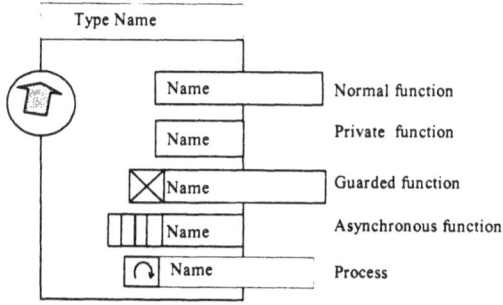

Figure 1: Notation used to draw the system structure

Graphic types have a graphic representation, which can be defined for every constructor, or using specific axioms. We use a precise mathematical definition of graphic objects, defining object properties without imposing any representation. In this abstract view of graphic objects, we might change their representation (depending on the application structure) and the specification remains valid (Torres & Clares 93 and 94). Graphic representations are defined using functions for inquiring their properties at each point. The functions used represent the graphic appearance, or aspect, as well as the object extension, or presence. Aspect and presence are defined as point functions on the space. Some basic graphic types are included in the notation (point and line), which allows the construction of more complex pictures using graphic operations: sum, Boolean operation and product (Torres & Clares 93). Graphic objects have a common interface, which includes the point inclusion test (to detect whether a point *is_in* an object).

We can use two different methods to describe the graphic representation of an object. The first one is to define its aspect and presence functions. In this way, changes in the graphic component can be described adding axioms for aspect or presence functions. The description of the graphic representation may also be done by using a previously defined graphic object as an abstract description (see page specification). Graphic objects can be operated to define complex representations from simpler ones. Graphic operators include addition, product by scalar, union, intersection, complement, object product, geometrical transformation (Torres & Clares 93). Changes in the graphic representation are specified, in this case, using axioms that change the whole graphic representation, using graphic operators and functions.

To allow the specification of interactive systems, the language includes the definition of asynchronous functions, synchronisation conditions and processes. *Synchronous functions* are invoked following a synchronous procedure call mechanism. These kinds of functions allow us to represent the dynamic creation of processes. A *synchronisation condition* is a Boolean expression that acts as a guard for a function. A *process* is defined as a function that is processed forever. A process function expresses an independent activity within the object, which is performed without the direct intervention of any external agent. These kinds of functions must have a precondition within the synchronisation section, and cannot have any input nor output parameter, except their own type. Note, that although there is notion of time in the formalism, the inclusion of the precondition incorporates reference to events time, that is the time when a specific event occurs which make the precondition true.

The overall structure of the system to be specified is described using the graphic notation shown in figure 1, where the box represents an object type. The notation shows the object's graphic appearance, its public functions and those functions involved in synchronisation restrictions (feedback and interaction process).

This chapter describes the specification of a case study using GRALPLA. The case study is about the specification of an ideal World Wide Web browser and a html page server.

The overall structure of the system to be specified is described using the graphic notation shown in figure 1, where the box represents an object type. The notation shows the object's graphic appearance, its public functions and those functions involved in synchronisation restrictions (feedback and interaction process).

3.   Description of the Specification

The aim of this section is to discuss how the specification of the case study can be derived, we will discuss different approaches and the problems that may appear. We think that this approach may be more interesting than explaining a completed specification. The full text of the specifications is shown in appendix A.

The first step in developing the specification is to make a partition of the system into units that can be defined as abstract data types. For the case study, we can identify two main components: the web server and the web client. A web server is responsible for serving html pages to the clients. Its functionality can be reduced, at the initial approach, to a single operation requesting a page:

> **type** webServer
> **functions**
> > request: webServer, page_id -> page;

A web client is an interactive system. That is, it has operations representing user actions (for instance GoTo, Home or Back). We will begin with a simple client, whose functionality is reduced to these three operations: moving to an URL address, loading the home page and moving back. We will discuss afterward how to incorporate other operations, such as managing link and stop. So, our initial web client has the following interface:

> **type** webClient
> **functions**
>> GoTo: web_client, address, page_id   -> web_client;
>> Home: web_client   -> web_client;
>> Back: web_client   -> web_client;

These operations can change the web_client state, and its graphical representation. We need now to specify some basic types, which are necessary to define the main types. These are: *address*, *page_id* and *page*. An address must identify the web client within the network. A page_id identifies a page within the server. The specification of these types is shown in appendix A.

A page is a sequence of items, which can be graphics, text or links. At this point, we will consider a *page* a graphic object. Its graphic representation shall correspond with the visualisation image of the *page* (we will consider how to incorporate links in the next section). We can consider that addresses and page identifiers are strings, as we do not want to specify the network. So, we will define these types as synonymous with strings.

We also need to define the communication between instances of *webClient* and *webServer*. Of course, we can assume that there exists some kind of connection between them that we do not specify. However, in this way, we cannot reason about the communication process between the client and the server. As we explained above, one of the limitations of our approach is that it is necessary to specify all of the components at the same level of abstraction. We will model a simplified connection between the client and the server using a set of hosts. A *host* has a dictionary of web servers that can be accessed through the network. The servers and the clients are attached to specific hosts. The client host is the host through which the client asks for a specific server. Given that a server can be attached to more than one host, the host must include functions to attach servers to it, and to get a reference to a server giving its address. So the interface of the host can be:

> **type** host;
> **functions**
>> serverRegister: host, address, webServer -> host;
>> getServer: host, address -> webServer;

To complete the specification of this type it is necessary to specify the behaviour of the type employing axioms. To do this, we must begin by finding out which axioms must be included. We must write an axiom to describe the behaviour of every derived function. For the specification of the type host, *getServer* is a derived function (as it is a query function). Function *serverRegister* is basic (as the change of state that it produces on the object cannot be produced with any other combination of functions). So, we must specify the result of calling *getServer* after having call the constructor and the *serverRegister* operation. It is easy to see that this behaviour can be expressed by the following pair of axioms:

host.1:   getServer(host, addrQ) = ERROR("Server unknown");
host.2:   getServer(serverRegister(h,addr,ws),servAddr) = if(addr=servAddr) ws
                                                                      else getServer(h,servAddr);

The first axiom declares that a host with no server attached to it, as it has just been created by the constructor *host*, cannot give any server reference. The second axiom specifies the server reference that must be returned when the function is used after registering some server. This value must be the registered server if its address agrees with those of the searched server. If this is not the case, the result must be the same as if the last *serverRegister* operation had not been performed. Note that in the specification shown in appendix A an error function has been included.

We can now return to the specification for client. First, it is necessary to include its relationship with the host. We can do this in two ways: using parametric types (being the actual host used as parameter the host used to search servers); and using a host as argument for the constructor. We will use the second approach, including also argument to designate the home page. Therefore, the constructor for this type will be:

                webClient: host, address, pageId -> webClient;

We can continue specifying the behaviour of some other functions. When some GoTo has been previously performed, the effect of the *Home* function is equivalent to that of a *GoTo* to the home page; the effect is null in other case. We can express this in the following way: performing a Home is the equivalent of performing a *GoTo* to the 'Home Page'. Therefore, in order to write the axiom, it is necessary to name the 'Home Page'. This can be done by including two new functions, which can be privated, to set and retrieve the Home Page identification:

        private   getHome<Id,Adr>: webClient   -> pageId, address;
        private   setHome: webClient, pageId, address   -> webClient;

Note that we define the getHome function with two return parameters of types pageId and address. The bracketed identifiers after the function name (<Id,Adr>) are the selector's names, which are used to identify each return parameter. The behaviour of this function is trivially expressed by the following axiom:

        client.2: getHome(setHome(client,a,id)).Id = id;
        client.3: getHome(setHome(client,a,id)).Adr = a;

Using the *getHome* function we can write the axiom for *Home* as follows:

        client.4: Home(client) = GoTo(addToHistory(client,a,id),
                                        getHome(client).adr, getHome(client).Id);

We can follow this procedure to complete the definition of the types. Let us now focus on the web server, which must have a set of associated html pages. We have two possibilities to define them: defining the set of pages when we build the server (that is using a constructor that accepts a set of pages), or adding two operations allowing the edition of the list of pages (*addPage* and *removePage*). We will use the second possibility, as it is more realistic:

> addPage: webServer, page, pageId -> webServer;
> removePage: webServer, pageId   -> webServer;

We can express the behaviour of removePage as a function of addPage, using the following axioms:

server.1: removePage(webServer(addr), id)=   webServer(addr);
server.2: removePage(addPage(server, pg0, id0), id) = if(id0=id) server
                          else addPage(removePage(server, id), pg0, id0);

The refinement process must continue until the behaviour of every function, except those necessary to generate new object states, has been completely specified. We will end this discussion by showing how to specify the connection between the client and the server.

The client must connect with the server when a *GoTo* operation is performed. So we need to indicate, using an axiom, that the *GoTo* operation must perform a request on the server. This implies that the *GoTo* operation is not a basic function (note that this implies the change of axiom client.5). We want the client and the server to work in an asynchronous way, consequently the request operation must be asynchronous. This also implies that the requested page must be passed back to the client using another asynchronous call:

> asynchronous receive: webClient, page, address, pageId -> webClient;

The communication scheme is shown in figure 2. The behaviour of the functions is expressed by the following axioms:

client.10: GoTo(client,a,id) = if(getServer(myHost(client),addr) <> NullObject)
                 pendingRequest(client,&request(getServer(
                                 myhost(client),addr),addr,id,ThisObject));
client.11: receive(pendingRequest(client,server),pg,a,id) =
                                 addToHistory(client,pg,a,id);
server.6:   reply(server,addr,id,pg,client) =
                         clearClient(server,&receive(client, pg, addr, id));
server.3:   request(server, addr, id, client) =
                   reply(setClient(server,client), addr, id, findPage(id), client);

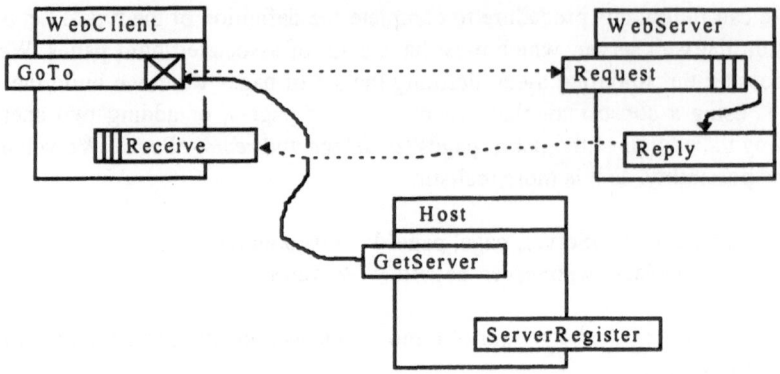

Figure 2: Communication between the client and the server

The first axiom states that performing a *GoTo* is equivalent to storing information about a pending request to a server, whose identification has been got performing a look up in the attached host, and sending the request to the server. The last axiom specifies the semantics for the request operation, which is equivalent to a *reply* with the specified page to the client. The *reply* operation performs an asynchronous call to the *receive* function on the specified client, which is denoted by the prefix &, and clears the reference to the client on the server.

When a call to *receive* is performed on the client, it must add the received html page to its history. Adding the page to the history must change the client graphic representation, this is expressed by the following axiom:

client.7:   graphic_rep(addToHistory(client,pg,a,id)) = pg;

Analysing this part of the specification, we can see that some additional functions have been added, in order to be able to express the types' behaviour using axioms. For instance, the *reply*, *setClient* and *clearClient* operations have been included to be able to incorporate a *&receive*, returning the called client, in the right hand side of an axiom.
The specification can be completed, at this level, disabling the use of user actions on the webClient, while the client is waiting for a page. This can be done by adding the following guards to these functions:

do	GoTo(client,a,id)	when isNotWaiting(client);
do	Home(client)	when isNotWaiting(client);
do	Back(client)	when isNotWaiting(client);

Before extending the specification, to incorporate other required features, we will explain how we can reason about the specification.

4. Verification and Extensions

The verification of algebraic specifications can be carried out by using structural induction over the axioms. Nevertheless, GRALPLA has some additional features that must be taken into account: the use of graphic representation, and the definition of process and synchronisation mechanisms. Within this section, we will briefly discussion how to reason about the specifications (Goguen & Tardo 86, Torres et al. 96). We will also apply the method to prove some properties for the case study specification. The graphic representation of an object is a consequence of the object state, and so we can work with it as defined by a query function. To prove properties about the concurrent components, it is necessary to work with a state representation for the object symbolised as three sequences: performed functions (FH), pending and asynchronous functions (PAF) and blocked function (BF):

$$S = (\text{FH, PAF, BF}) = (f_0\ f_1\ f_2...., g_0\ g_1..., h_0\ h_1 ...)$$

We assume that functions are performed in an atomic way, and that external functions are performed with higher priority than asynchronous functions. Process functions with synchronisation restrictions belong normally to the blocked functions (BF) sequence of the state (they will be moved to the PAF queue when their guarded condition is true). Normally, the PAF queue is empty. When this is not the case (there is some guarded function that has become unblocked, or there is some function pending), a function in PAF (g_0) can be performed. This implies that the system changes to a new state:

$$S' = (\text{FH', PAF', BF}) = (g_0(\text{FH}), g_1...., \text{BF})$$

where $g_0(\text{FH})$ denotes the new functional history, obtained applying, in the conventional sense, g_0 to the previous one. Whenever the state changes, the preconditions of all blocked functions are checked, and if any of them has become true the function is moved to the PAF queue. If no other function is waiting, then it is performed. In this case the state changes to:

$$S'' = (\text{FH'', PAF', BF'}) = (h_i(\text{FH'}), \text{PAF', BF-}h_i)$$

We can use these ideas to reason about the specification. We can, for instance, prove that one state can be reached from another one, or that one property (expressed as an equation) holds for a given state. It is also possible to prove lifeness properties for the specification (Duke et al. 91).

As an example, we will prove that whenever a valid *GoTo* is performed on the client, no user actions will be executed, until the *receive* operation is performed.

To prove this we will find the general structure of the functional history for the type. The only basic functions are the private *webClient*, *addToHistory* and *pendingRequest*. So, in principle, the functional history would be:

$$\text{FH} = \{\ \{addToHistory|pendingRequest|setHome\}^*, webClient\}$$

It is easy to see that *setHome* appears only once in the functional history, as it is a private function that is invoked when the public constructor is used. We will now prove that it is not possible to have more than one *pendingRequest*, and that this must be the last operation in the functional history. To do this, we must see that the *GoTo* operation blocks all the user action on the client. Let us suppose that the object is in the state:

$$S_0 = (FH_0, \{\}, \{\}) = (\; \{\; \{addToHistory\}^*, setHome, webClient\}, \{\}, \{\}\;)$$

Invoking a *Home* operation is equivalent to a *GoTo*, and calling *Back* can remove a *addToHistory* from the functional history. So, the only user operation that can change the structure of this state is a *GoTo*. Let us suppose that a *GoTo* is performed. The GoTo semantic is given by the axiom 11, and assuming that the address is correct and that the host knows it, the new FH will be:

$$FH_1 = \{\; pendingRequest, \{addToHistory\}^*, setHome, webClient\}$$

and a request to the specified server will be executed. For this state, the Boolean function *isNotWaiting* is evaluated to false, and so all the user functions that will be performed would be blocked as their guards are false.

The only external function that can be performed at this state is *receive*. This function changes the state removing the last *pendingRequest* operation, and adding a new *addToHistory*. So the functional history will be again of the form of FH_0. Thus for an object having a state described by FH_0, the only possible functional history transitions are FH_1 and them FH_0. As the initial state is of this type, any object can have a functional history different from these.

For the state FH_0 *isNotWaiting* is evaluated to true, and all the blocked user operation that could have been invoked will be performed sequentially (note that this happens even when the *receive* operation does not correspond with the last *request*: if we want to avoid that we must control this in the axioms for the receive operation).

The remainder of this section is devoted to the extension of the specification. We will address two extensions: including a *Stop* function in webClient and contemplating links.

The *Stop* function represents a user action that must cancel the pending request, if any. This operation must not be blocked while the client is waiting for a html page. Cancelling the pending request is equivalent to removing the pending request mark from the functional history, as axiom 13 establishes that the *receive* operation has no effect when there is no previous pending request. So the behaviour of *Stop* can be expressed by the following axioms:

client.15 stop(pendingRequest(client,server)) = client;
client.16 stop(webClient(h)) = webClient(h);

It is easy to see that this disproves the previous reasoning on the webClient behaviour, as now it is possible to have more than one pendingRequest. This can take place when, for instance, a stop is performed while a request is pending. In this case, if no user operation is performed on the client before the *receive* operation is called, the request is ignored. However, the following scenario may arise:

Action	State
GoTo page1	{ *pendingRequest*, FH_0 }
Stop	{ FH_0 }
GoTo page2	{ *pendingRequest*, FH_0 }
receive page1	{ *addToHistory*(page1), FH_0 }
receive page2	{ *addToHistory*(page1), FH_0 }

In this case, the second *receive* is ignored. The problem can be solved in two different ways: including the page identifier in *pendingRequest*; or adding a cancel operation to the webServer. The second proposal does not resolve the problem always, as we are using asynchronous calls for *request* and *receive*. We have included the first possibility in the specification. It can be seen that axiom 11 has been changed incorporating a check on the received page.

In order to incorporate links, it is necessary to modify the definition of page, to which a list of links can be added. A link can be represented as a reference to a page (a pair address-page identifier), and a graphic object, which describes the link representation within the page. Taking this into account, the specification of a page can be reworked, adding two functions: *addLink* and *getLink*. The graphic representation of the page is equivalent to the addition of the original one and the link's representation. The *getLink* operation receives a point as argument, and looks for a link whose representation includes this point.

We must now add a new operation to the webClient's specification, *SelectLink*, in order to allow the user to handle links. This operation accepts a point as an argument, checks whether the point is on a link's representation within the active page, and in this case, performs a *GoTo* to the link's address. Its behaviour depends on the active page, that is, the last *addToHistory* performed. When there is no active page, the operation is ignored. This behaviour is captured by the following axioms:

client.17: SelectLink(addToHistory(client,pg,a,id),pt)=
   if(getLink(pg,pt).Adr<>NullAddress)
   GoTo(addToHistory(client,pg,a,id),   getLink(pg,pt).Adr,
getLink(pg,pt).Id);
client.18: SelectLink(webClient(h)) = webClient(h);

5. From Specification to Implementation

The GRALPLA specification language has been designed to allow the generation of running prototypes. The prototyping process stems from two ideas: to associate a representation of the object state based on its functional history, and to interpret the axioms as equations defining the behaviour of their left-hand sides as the expressions of their right-hand sides.

Once we can ensure that the specification is correct, we can use our prototype as a first version for the design and implementation process. In this way, we can handle each class from the prototype and substitute it with a more efficient, hand coded, class. Using this method we can work with only one class at any time, carrying out the integration test for the new class with a full correct system, and thus ensuring that the system's next version is also correct. In this way, it is also easier to distribute the work amongst a team.

Every specification module represents an abstract Data Type, and GRALPLA generates a C++ class for it. Therefore the software architecture of the system is decided at specification level. The implementation of every class must preserve its public interface, and must include an explicit representation for the object state. The code for each operation can be derived from the axioms and the object state representation chosen.

6. Conclusion and Evaluation of the Method

In this chapter the specification language GRALPLA has been applied to specify a WWW application. The specification of the case study covers the description of a web server, a web client and a host representing the connection between them. In this section, we will summarise the properties of the specification language and discuss its strengths and weaknesses.

The main goal of GRALPLA is to allow the specification and prototyping of interactive graphic systems, without fixing the internal data structure used for the objects. Thus, GRALPLA specifications are property oriented, as there is no explicit model for the specified object state. The development of prototypes is possible by imposing limitations on the structure of axioms. For this reason, the structure of the specification is rigid, and the expressiveness of axioms is limited, since the syntax for describing them is not as flexible as it is in other algebraic specification languages.

This also makes it necessary to include additional private functions in specifications, which are required to express the system's behaviour. This may occur for two different reasons:

- The non existence of state description on algebraic specification forces us to include some function to set and retrieve the state.
- The specification of an operation that may raise some exception must be done by splitting the operation behaviour into two functions: one with the original behaviour, and the other that performs the operation once the checking has been carried out. This may produce a large number of internal functions.

Another consequence of the simple structures used for the axioms is that the mathematical notation used in GRALPLA is not complex; a strong mathematical background is not therefore required, although it is necessary to develop skill on the notation itself.

GRALPLA uses a formal mathematical notation to describe the graphic representation of objects. This allows us to reason about the graphic appearance of elements, at the expense of using a very abstract notation to describe graphic elements.

The description of the system using a hierarchy of types fixes the system's architecture. This implies the identification of the system's components, which is also a design decision. Although the language incorporates mechanisms to describe interactive systems, which have been powerful enough to describe practical systems, its use sometimes seems unnatural. This is due to the strict semantic structure of the function signature of algebraic specifications.

Appendix A. Specification Text

This appendix contains the specification text for the following types: page_id, address, page, webClient, webServer and host. Some types have been extended on section three, for these types the new functions and axioms are shown in italic, at the end of each specification section.

```
//                                            page_id
object page_id;
        page_id: string    -> page_id;
        NullPageId         -> page_id;
```

```
//                                            address
object address;
        address: string    -> address;
        NullAddress:        -> address;
```

```
//                                            page
graphic object page;

import address, page_id;
        page: string, graphic_object     -> page; // Main constructor
        unknownPage:                      -> page; // Unknown page constructor
```

functions
```
        addLink: page, graphic_object, address, page_id    -> page;
        getLink<Id,Adr>: page, point                       -> address, page_id;
```

axioms
```
    var    pg:     page;        str:    string;       gO: graphic_object;
           addr:   address;     id:     page_id;      pt:     point;
```

page.1   graphic_rep(page(str, gO)) = gO;
page.2   graphic_rep(addLink(pg, gO, addr, id)) = gO + pg;

page.3   getLink(addLink(pg, gO, addr, id), pt).Adr = if   (isin(pt,gO)) addr
                                                         else   getLink(pg, pt).Adr;

page.4   *getLink(addLink(pg, gO, addr, id), pt).Id =*   *if*   *(isin(pt,gO)*
)   *id*

                                                                   else   *getLink(pg, pt).Id;*

page.5   *getLink(page(str, gO)).Adr =*   *NullAddress;*
page.6   *getLink(page(str, gO)).Id =*   *NullPageId;*

//   webClient

graphic object webClient;

import page, pageId, address, webServer, host;

          webClient: host, address, pageId   -> webClient;
private   webClient: host   -> webClient;

functions
          GoTo: webClient, address, pageId   -> webClient
          Home: webClient   -> webClient;
          Back: webClient   -> webClient;
asynchronous   receive: webClient, page, address, pageId   -> webClient;
          Stop: *webClient*   *-> webClient;*
          SelectLink: *webClient, point*   *-> webClient;*
private   getHome<Id,Adr>:   webClient   -> pageId, address;
private   setHome: webClient, pageId, address   ->
webClient;
private   addToHistory: webClient, page, address, pageId   -> webClient;
private   pendingRequest: webClient, webServer, *address, pageId* -> webClient;
private   isNotWaiting: webClient   -> Boolean;
private   MyHost: webClient   -> host;

axioms
   var   client: webClient; server: webServer;   h: host;
          pt: point;   a,a0: address;   pg,pg0: page;
          id,id0: pageId;

client.1   getHome(webClient(h)).Adr = NullAddress;
client.2   getHome(setHome(client,a,id)).Id = id;
client.3   getHome(setHome(client,a,id)).Adr = a;

client.4   Home(client) = GoTo(addToHistory(client,a,id),
                                   getHome(client).Adr,getHome(client).Id);

client.5   webClient(h,a,id) = GoTo(setHome(webClient(h), a, id), a, id);

client.6   graphic_rep(webClient(h))   = NullGraphicObject;

client.7   graphic_rep(addToHistory(client,pg,a,id))   = pg;

client.8   Back(webClient(h))   = webClient(h);
client.9   Back(addToHistory(client,a,id,pg)) = if(client=webClient(myHost(client)))
                             addToHistory(client,a,id,pg)
                    else   client;

client.10 GoTo(client,a,id) = if(getServer(myHost(client),addr) <> NullObject)
           pendingRequest(client, &request(
                   getServer(myHost(client),addr),addr,id,ThisObject), addr, id);

client.11 receive(pendingRequest(client,server,a0,id0),pg,a,id) =
                if(a0=a and id0=id)   addToHistory(client,pg,a,id)
                else   pendingRequest(client,server,a0,id0);
client.12 receive(webClient(h),pg,a,id) = webClient(h);

client.13 isNotWaiting(pendingRequest(client,server)) = false;
client.14 isNotWaiting(webClient(h)) = true;

client.15 stop(pendingRequest(client,server)) = client;
client.16 stop(webClient(h)) = webClient(h);

client.17 SelectLink(addToHistory(client,pg,a,id),pt) =
           if(getLink(pg,pt).Adr<>NullAddress)
           GoTo(addToHistory(client,pg,a,id), getLink(pg,pt).Adr, getLink(pg,pt).Id);
client.18 SelectLink(webClient(h)) = webClient(h);

synchronization
do   GoTo(client,a,id) when isNotWaiting(client);
do   Home(client)   when isNotWaiting(client);
do   Back(client)   when isNotWaiting(client);
do   selectLink(client) when isNotWaiting(client);

//   host
object host;

import address,webServer;

   host: -> host;

functions
            serverRegister: host, address, webServer   -> host;
            getServer: host, address   -> webServer;
            ServerUnknown: host   -> webServer: error("Server unnknown");

axioms

   var   h: host;   ws: webServer;   addr,servAddr: address;

host.1   getServer(host, addrQ) = ServerUnknown(host);
host.2   getServer(serverRegister(h,addr,ws),servAddr) = if(addr=servAddr) ws
                                     else   getServer(h,servAddr);
host.3   ServerUnknown (h) = NullObject;

//   webServer

object webServer;

import address, page, pageId, webClient;

       webServer: address -> webServer;

functions

asynchronous   request: webServer, address, pageId, webClient -> webServer;
                      reply: webServer, address, pageId, page, webClient -> webServer;
                      addPage: webServer, page, pageId   -> webServer;
                      removePage: webServer, pageId   -> webServer;
private   findPage: webServer, pageId   -> page;
private   setClient: webServer, webClient   -> webServer;
private   clearClient: webServer, webClient   -> webServer;

axioms

   var   server: webServer;   client,client2: webClient; pg,pg0: page;
           addr: address;   id,id0: pageId;

server.1 removePage(webServer(addr), id) = webServer(addr);
server.2 removePage(addPage(server, pg0, id0), id) = if(id0=id) server
                         else   addPage(removePage(server, id), pg0, id0);

server.3 request(server, addr, id, client) =
           reply(setClient(server,client), addr, id, findPage(id), client);

server.4 findPage(webServer(addr), id) = unknownPage;
server.5 findPage(addPage(server, pg0, id0), id) =   if(id0=id) pg0
                                    else findPage(server,id);

server.6 reply(server,addr,id,pg,client) =
           clearClient(server,&receive(client, pg, addr, id));

server.7 clearClient(setClient(server,client),client2) = server;

Chapter 12:
TLIM: A Systematic Method for the Design of Interactive Systems

1. Introduction

The TLIM method is the result of some years of research in the area of model-based user interface design, development and evaluation with formal support which has been developed at the User-Centred Design Group of CNUCE.

The main goal is to introduce the user's point of view into the various phases of the design and development of an interactive software application. To this end we believe it is not possible to be based completely on the intuition and the skill of the designer because it can often fail. It is important to have a systematic method which incorporates rules for supporting this work and highlights the main aspects that designers and developers have to take into account.

In particular, various specification levels (such as task, architectural, and implementation) should be considered when reasoning about user interface design, and each of them may require specifications with a relevant complexity. Thus it is important to have methods able to capture in a direct and systematic way the relevant aspects, to find relationships among levels and to structure each of them.

The level of formality depends on the features of the application, the purposes of the specification, the aspects that we want to consider.

This approach can be used both to design and develop new systems and to analyse existing systems. In the latter case it is useful because it allows us to have a better insight into the dialogue which is supported by the considered application, how it is supported, and what the main software components are.

The TLIM method is based on four main elements:

- the use of the ConcurTaskTrees (Paterno' et al. 97) notation, a diagrammatic notation to describe task models with operators for describing temporal relationships obtained by extending the set of LOTOS (ISO88) operators;
- the use of task specification as an abstract specification which can be used to drive the design of the architecture and implementation of interactive software applications;

- the interactor concept as an abstract model for software objects which interact with users, useful for structuring the design and the specification of the user interface software architecture;
- the use of model checking techniques to reason about the properties of the resulting specifications at both task and architectural level.

In this chapter we describe this method and use concepts from it to provide specifications of some aspects of the most popular current interactive application: the WWW environment.

In this type of interactive environment there are three types of components whose instances continuously interact with each other: users, browsers which allow documents written in html or other formats to be continuously loaded and presented, and servers which make these documents available to browsers. The use of a concurrent notation thus becomes very important in giving a precise description of the temporal ordering among possible actions and it provides a useful model to reason about its interactive properties.

The proposed approach starts by considering the possible tasks. The rationale behind this is that task specifications provide a logical description of what the user wants to accomplish. They integrate descriptions of both functional and interactive aspects. Thus they give a framework for analysing and developing the software architecture and for designing and evaluating the user interface. Other examples of proposals which used task-related aspects for similar purposes are: Adept (Wilson et al. 93), Trident by Bodart, Vanderdonckt et al. (Bodart et al. 95), and Sutcliffe and Faraday to design multimedia applications (Sutcliffe and Faraday 94). However, these proposals did not address these concepts by using formal methods to specify and reason about their properties.

The advent of the web has made the use of hypermedia common. This has activated an interesting discussion about which properties can be used to evaluate user interfaces of hypermedia. An example of the metrics proposed is in (Garzotto et al. 95) where the authors use richness, ease, consistency, self-evidence, predictability, readability, and reuse for this purpose on hypermedia documents described by HDM models. However, the identification of the key elements to evaluate this type of environment is still an open issue as is the understanding whether they need different requirements with respect to other interactive environments.

2. The TLIM Method

Creating a direct correspondence between tasks and software components, although insufficient to address all the usability issues, opens up many perspectives in the various phases of the design process. Some research has been developed in this direction but is still at a preliminary stage with respect to the potential results.

UAN (Hartson and Gray 92) is an important contribution as it is a formal notation with concepts very similar to process algebra notations such as LOTOS, CCS and CSP. The main difference is that in UAN the modularization concept is the task rather than the process, which gives a more user-oriented way to structure and analyse the specification. The external description of the user interface is obtained by associating basic tasks with the user actions and system feedback which are needed to perform them. The main goal of UAN is to communicate user interface design in order to discuss possible solutions, whereas we are interested in approaches which support more directly the software design and development process. Thus we have developed an approach which transforms the task specification into an architectural specification which includes both the perceivable behaviour of a user interface and the description of the software part which controls it.

The reasons for choosing task-based approaches in designing Interactive Systems are:

- *The organisation of system functionalities should reflect the user's view of them*, users would thus be facilitated in understanding how to use the system if they can interact with user interface implementations that allow them to make actions which correspond immediately to logical actions and which hide all implementation aspects which are less comprehensible for end users.
- *Task modifications can be immediately implemented*, because if a system has to remove, add or modify the support of some tasks it is easy to locate which part of the system should be modified.
- *Automatic generation of task-oriented help*, maintaining in the implementation the relationships between tasks and interactors allows us, with minimal effort, to generate context-dependent help automatically, structured in a task-oriented way and thus more readable for the user (Pangoli and Paternò 95).
- *Evaluation within the task framework* of the user interactions, we have developed a research (Paternò et al. 95) showing that logs of physical user actions generated during a user session can be analysed by mapping user actions onto actions of the task model of the corresponding application.

We consider a task as the indication of an activity required to reach a desired state modification or to inquiry the current state. Tasks can be described at a semantic level, independent from the tools used to perform them, or at a lower level where designers take into consideration the interaction techniques used to accomplish them.

In the task analysis phase given an application domain the possible tasks are identified. In a task model designers describe the possible tasks and their relationships.

Task-based approaches are an extension of the traditional functional specifications as they describe not only what functionalities should be performed by the application, but also what functionalities are performed by the user and the interactions the user should perform to access the application functionalities and to control them. They may take into account non-functional requirements such as user interruptibility, reversibility, and frequency.

After having developed a theory for user-interaction objects (interactors) (Paternò 94) to give the formal semantics of User Interface Systems, we started to work with the aim to introduce the user point of view in the design and development cycle. To this end we considered task models.

In our approach task specification is performed in a hierarchical way, where abstract tasks are described in terms of more refined tasks, using ConcurTaskTrees which is obtained by extending some LOTOS operators (such as interleaving, enabling, disabling, synchronisation, recursive instantiation) to indicate temporal relationships between tasks at the same level thus giving the possibility to describe concurrent tasks differently from other approaches, such as GOMS (Card et al. 83), which only address sequential tasks. For each task, related objects and actions are indicated. Next, we developed an algorithm which takes as input the task specification and produces an interactor-based specification of a software architecture where it is possible to find a direct correspondence between tasks and the software interactors used to perform them. This transformation can be performed in a tool-supported way: it is not completely automatic as in some points we want to allow designers to express preferences and choices in the design of the software architecture.

The TLIM method for design and development of user interfaces consists of several phases (see Figure 1):

1) An informal phase where user requirements and task analysis are gathered by doing meetings and interviews with the users and domain experts, considering existing documentation, how tasks are performed by the currently available systems and possible new usage scenarios with new technologies;

2) Structuring the ConcurTaskTrees specification of the tasks for the application considered by an hierarchical decomposition where temporal relationships among tasks are indicated along with task performance allocation. This phase is semiautomatic   because   we   have   a   graphical   editor (http://giove.cnuce.cnr.it/task.tgz) which supports the designer's work in the process of performing the task specification and checking whether some information is missing or is provided in a contradictory way.

3) Transformation of the task specification into an interactor-based architectural description which is a logical description, platform-independent, of the software components needed. We have implemented an algorithm which performs part of this transformation and it requires in some points the decisions of the designer in order to perform some choices.

4) Transformation of the architectural description into a LOTOS specification. In order to enrich the analysis of the Interactive System at this level it is possible to specify the user behaviour too as a set of concurrent internal and external actions. The formal specification can be useful to automatically check properties (Paternò 97) which are important for evaluating the design. This part of the method requires designers with a background in formal methods and is more useful for specific application areas such as safety critical systems like air traffic control applications (Paternò and Mezzanotte 95).

5) Transformation of the architectural description into a software prototype in which interactors are modelled as Java objects; during this phase the designer has to take

into account the media available and the user requirements in order to make decisions about the presentations of the interactors and how feedback of the user-generated input should be provided.

6) Another possible evaluation which we can provide is by considering logs of user actions generated during testing of the prototype performed. These are compared with the task model associated with the prototype developed and this analysis indicates user errors and problems in performing the possible tasks thus providing useful information for improving the design of either the task model or the architectural model or both.

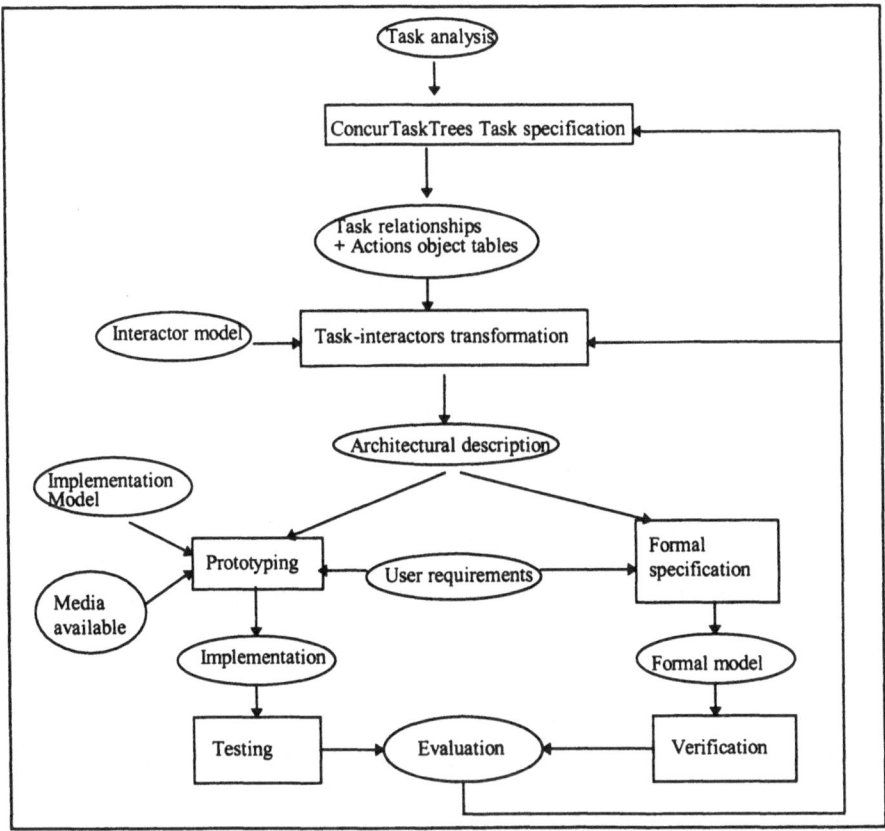

Figure 1: The TLIM method for user interfaces design and development

The diagram in Figure 1 describes the proposed method. Boxes represent transformation processes (such as building a specification, making a transformation from one type of description to another type), ovals represent input elements to the transformation elements.

3. ConcurTaskTrees

We started using LOTOS in our work of formalization of user interfaces. LOTOS is an expressive notation. The main problem has been that since it was developed mainly for another application area (network protocols) there are often recurrent situations in user interface specification which can only be described with quite complex expressions. We thus felt the need to develop a new notation based on this experience which could be more easily used by designers.

ConcurTaskTrees is a hierarchical graphical notation which can be easily understood and allows designers to address medium-large specifications too.

In ConcurTaskTrees it is possible to have four types of tasks depending on their performance allocation: user, system, interaction and abstract. User tasks describe either cognitive activities (such as identifying the most suitable flight for the next travel among a set of flights satisfying the given requirements which have been selected by an interactive application) or activities involving user interactions with the environment (such as receiving information from a colleague). System tasks describe system activities triggered by internal events such as presenting the result of a simulation or information arrived from the network. Interactive tasks require actions from both the user and system (i.e., editing a graph). Abstract tasks need to be further refined in order to give an indication about their allocation.

In ConcurTaskTrees it is possible to specify additional information other than the tree indicating the tasks and the temporal relationships between them. This additional information is useful for documenting the task model and in the process of deriving a corresponding architecture model.

For each task it is possible to indicate the objects that it needs to manipulate in order to be performed and the actions required for allowing different objects to exchange information. The actions are associated with receiving input information which is needed for the object processing, and generating output information which is needed for accomplishing other objects' processing.

The objects are user-perceivable and internal objects which are both manipulated to perform the tasks by using the associated actions.

Perceivable objects are items with which users can interact using their senses, for example menus, icons, windows, voice, sounds, and so on. They can belong to either application or interaction tasks.

Internal objects are entities which belong to the application and which need to be mapped onto perceivable objects to be presented to the user. Examples of internal objects are: the state of the request for a data base, the data contained in the data base.

3.1 Operators for Temporal Relationships

The operators used to indicate the temporal relationships among tasks are:

Interleaving (T1 ||| T2), where actions belonging to two tasks can be performed in any order without any specific constraints. An example is in a word processor application where editing a file and scrolling its contents can be performed in any order;

Choice (T1 [] T2), where it is possible to make a choice between a set of tasks and, once the choice has been made, it has to be terminated and other tasks are not available at least until that time. This operator is useful in the design of user interfaces because often it is important to enable the user to choose from various tasks. An example of this is, when at the beginning of a word processor session, the user is given the possibility to choose whether to open an existing file or a new one.

Synchronization (T1 |[a1, ..., an]| T2), which indicates the actions (a1, ... , an) where two tasks have to synchronise.

Deactivation (T1 [> T2), where the first task is definitively deactivated once the first action of the second task has been performed. This operator was introduced in LOTOS because it allows one to manage error conditions in network protocol connections. This concept is often used in many user interface implementations when the user can deactivate the possibility of performing a set of tasks and activate a new set of possible task accomplishments by a specific action (for example by selecting a button).

Enabling (T1 >> T2), where one task enables a second one when it terminates. An example of this is in a word processor where we have first to open a file and only after this task has been performed is it possible to modify the file.

Enabling with information passing (T1 []>>T2), in this case task T1 provides some information to task T2 other than enabling it. For example, T1 allows the user to specify a query and T2 provides the query result which obviously depends on the information generated by T1.

Suspend-resume (T1 |> T2), this gives T2 the possibility to interrupt T1 and then, when T2 is terminated, it is possible to reactivate T1 from the state reached before the interruption.

Iteration. In the tasks' specification we can have some tasks with the * symbol next to their name. This means that the tasks are performed in a repetitive way: when they terminate the performance of their actions automatically starts to be executed again from the beginning. This continues until the task is deactivated by another task.

Finite Iteration (T1(n)), this is used when designers know in advance how many times a task will be performed.

Optional tasks ([T]), this gives possibility of indicating that the performance of a task is optional. Optional tasks are indicated in between squared brackets. We have optional tasks when we fill in a form and there are some fields which are mandatory other which are optional. For example, when we make a query to a flight database we must give departure and arrival towns and we also have the option to provide indications about our preferences (smoking, vegetarian diet, ...).

Recursion, in our diagrammatic notation we give the possibility to provide recursive tasks' specifications which usually describe tasks which, for each recursion, provide the possibility of performing the recursive tasks with the additional possibility of some new possible interaction, until some task interrupting the recursion is performed.

4. ConcurTaskTrees Specification of Tasks in a Web Session

In this work we describe how the TLIM method can be used to analyse an existing application (the web environment in this exercise). TLIM can also be used to design and develop new applications from scratch.

More specifically in this case we consider a subset of the tasks which can be accomplished in a web session:

- Loading a remote resource;
- Activating an additional browser;
- Saving a bookmark;
- Closing an instance of a browser without closing the others;
- Stopping loading;
- Reloading;
- Modifying options and bookmarks;
- Editing a URL

Tasks are described in a hierarchical way. The most abstract tasks are those most related to the application domain and to the semantic aspects. The lower levels are more oriented to describing the interaction techniques available to support the performance of the semantic tasks.

In hierarchical task specifications the root is not particularly meaningful, it mainly represents a starting point. In our example at the first level we find a generic abstract task associated with a session for interacting with WWW which can be disabled by a specific *Close application* task. This task will close all the browsers activated by the user.

The first problem that we have in building our task model is how to express the possibility that the user can activate multiple instances of the browser and each of these instances is independent from the others: it can be closed at any time without effects on the others. ConcurTaskTrees allows designers to express these situations by using recursive expressions.

In Figure 2 we show how the user at the beginning of the session can perform the *Browsing* task which is composed of two main subtasks: one (*Manage session*) describes the possibilities during the session, the other allows the user to close it. Additionally there is the *Multiple browsing* task which allows the activation of an additional browser. Its first subtask is *Sel new browser*. After its performance we obtain the enabling of a new instance of the *Interact with WWW* task and we obtain a situation with a concurrent independent use of two browsers. If this possibility is not selected by the user we remain in the initial situation during which the user can perform various subtasks in a single browser environment until s/he closes the browser. Whereas if the possibility of multiple browsers is selected then these instances are independent, each with its own instance of the close task and so they can be closed independently of each other. Obviously this recursive possibility can be performed multiple times so as to obtain multiple browsers active.

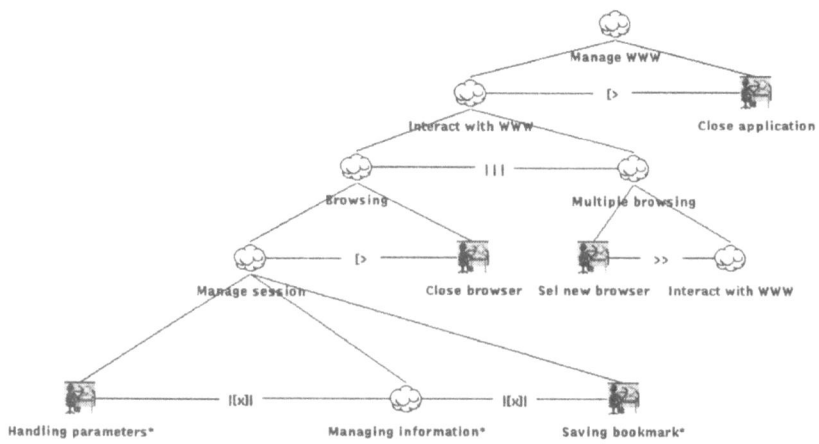

Figure 2: The first levels of the task tree

In this task tree we can note that there is a session which can be closed by a specific task (*Close browser*). This is expressed by the disabling operator ([>). Managing a session is a task which can be performed various times before the session is closed and it consists of an interleaving with synchronisation (|[]| operator) between the *Handling parameters* task which can be used to configure the browser (such as the size of the cache or bookmarks), the *Managing information* task which describes the searching, receiving and evaluating information and the *Saving* the *bookmark* of the currently loaded page. All these three tasks are iterative tasks (indicated by an *).

The temporal relationships between tasks give us the precise requirements of the temporal constraints that the user interface implementation should satisfy. In fact, the first level indicates that when the session is active an action for performing the *close application* task should be available for the user so that when the closing procedure is activated the session will actually be closed.

The interleaving with synchronisation between the *Handling parameters*, the *Managing information* and the *Saving bookmarks* tasks indicates that some actions should be available simultaneously to perform the tasks and that these tasks should communicate to exchange information. In fact at the same time in WWW browsers there are pull-down menus which allow users to modify parameters, and menus or hyperdocuments which allow users to select new information to be presented.

Figure 2 describes the most abstract tasks for the WWW case study. For each task we can identify the logical objects which are needed to perform them. They will be described in next paragraphes.

We now consider the basic tasks in Figure 2 and refine them further. In this refinement process we slowly include assumptions about the implementation environment (we will assume that we are using a Netscape-like browser). The result is described in Figure 3.

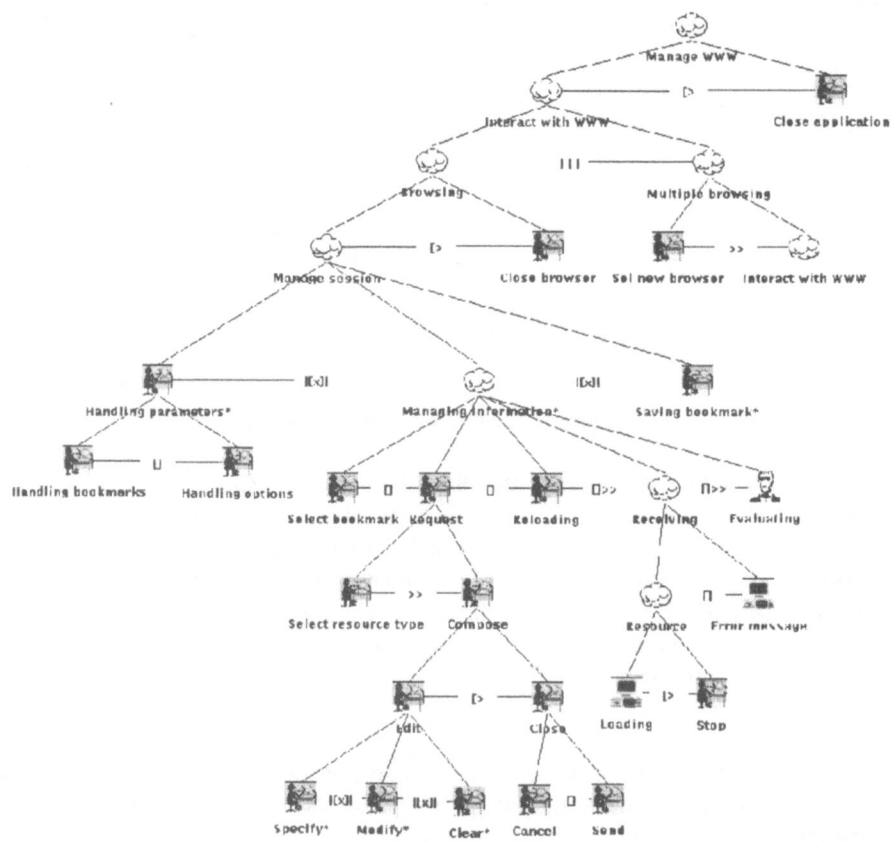

Figure 3: An extended description of the task tree

For example, let us take the *Managing Information* task. Its subtasks are: *Select bookmark, Request, Reloading, Receiving* and *Evaluating*. The first three tasks are in mutual choice. Once one of them is performed then the application starts loading the requested information. The user can stop the loading. Finally the user can evaluate the presentation of the result of the request. In the *Request* task once the user has precisely indicated the type of resource s/he can edit the request until s/he closes this task. Editing consists of interleaving with synchronisation between three repetitive tasks (*specifying* the request, *modifying* it, *clearing* it) which are all possible at any time. The compose task can be closed either definitively by cancelling the request, or by sending it.

5. The Transformation from the Task Model to the Software Architecture Model

The approach for designing a software architecture according to the requirements of the task model is top-down. We start with the hierarchical task specification on one side. Then we consider one level of the task tree and we build the corresponding software architecture. The result is used for building the software architecture corresponding to the next task level until we obtain an abstraction level where each basic task is associated with at least one interactor. However, even when specifying an implementation, such a low level of detail is not needed. The right abstraction level depends on the aspects that designers want to analyse.

In the tasks-to-interactors transformations there are four key elements:

- the identification of the interactors;
- the identification of the connections between interactors so as to allow the information flow needed to perform the tasks;
- the interactor-based architecture should comply with the temporal constraints of the task level so that at any time only the interactors associated with the active tasks are active;
- the allocation of the objects needed to perform the tasks in the corresponding interactors.

The identification of the required interactors depends mainly on the relationships of the object manipulated by the tasks. For each task we identify the objects which are manipulated only by it and we allocate oney related interactor. For the remaining objects we group them in such a way that we put together the objects which are manipulated by the same tasks. Then we allocate one interactor for each group of objects identified.

As mentioned above, a set of operators is used to indicate the temporal relationships between tasks. When we have evaluated all the subtasks of a given task, Tx, we transfer the operators among subtasks to the interactors that we associate with these subtasks. In fact, if Txj and Txj+1 are subtasks of Tx, and subtask Txj is synchronised with subtask Txj+1, then the interactor associated with Txj will be synchronised with the interactor associated with Txj+1.
If the two tasks are interleaving this means there are no constraints between ther related interactors. Iteration involves one task and it implies that the associated interactors have an iterative behaviour. The alternative choice between two tasks is usually obtained on the interactor side by imposing constraints on the actions that the interactors can perform. Sequential enabling between two tasks means that once the first task has performed the last action then the second task is enabled, and this should be maintained at the corresponding interactor level too.

The interactor concept (Paterno' 94) is used to structure the specification: it is a model for software objects which have to interact with users and it can support a bidirectional flow between the user and the application. Instances of interactors can be composed in a hierarchical way along both the input and the output information flow.

The software architecture is designed top-down by sequentially considering the levels in the task tree. Designers can stop this process at different abstraction levels depending on what their purposes are. In any case the software components inherit the temporal constraints of the corresponding tasks.

Note that in the end many types of relationships can be obtained between tasks and interactors:

- the performance of a task can need the use of various interactors,
- a task can be performed by using different alternative sets of software objects,
- an interactor can be used to perform various tasks (for example, one menu interactor can be used to print, save, and open files).

It is very important that the architectural specification satisfies the temporal constraints in the task specification, otherwise the chances of a user making a mistake would increase. In fact, if there were a sequentiality constraint between two tasks because the second needs information which has to be processed by the first, and if the software implementation allowed the two tasks to be performed in parallel, this might cause the user to perform, in this case, the second task without all the information needed.

Since the software specification must not relax the constraints of the task level, likewise it must not add any further constraints which have no reason from the application domain point of view.

5.1 The Transformation from the Task Model to the Software Architecture Model

In Table 1 the objects, their types and the related actions which are associated with the tasks in the task tree are described. We consider most of the tasks but not all just for avoiding a too detailed description.

For example we have the *Manage Session* task which requires both a perceivable object (Pres-browsing) for describing the user interactions and presenting the information received from the network and an internal object (State-browsing) which maintains the state of the browser. Then we have the *Close browser* and the *Sel new browser* tasks which both have a perceivable object for interacting with the user and then communicate to the state of the browser to close it or to create a duplication.

In the next level we find two tasks (*Handling Parameters* and *Managing Information*) both with two perceivable objects and one internal object. In the former one object allows the user to modify the value of some parameters, the other perceivable object shows the current value of the parameters which is stored in the internal object.

In the *Managing Information* task one perceivable object is used to ask for the resource to load in the browser, the other perceivable object is used to present the resource received which is stored in the internal object. In both the tasks for managing bookmarks and options there are three objects (two perceivable and one internal) for presenting the current state, allowing the user to modify it and store it.

Task name	Object name	Obj type	Input Action	OutputAction
Interact with WWW	Session	Perc	Inf. from user Inf. from Network	Inf. to user Inf. to Network
Close Application	Pres-close - session	Perc	Inf. from user	Inf. to Session
Browsing	One-browser	Perc	Inf. from user Inf. from Network	Inf. to user Inf. to Network
Multiple browsing	Multi -browser	Perc	Inf. from user Inf. from Network	Inf. to user Inf. to Network
Manage session	Pres-browsing	Perc	Inf. from user Inf. from Network	Inf. to user Inf.to Network
	State-browsing	Int.	Inf. from Pres-browsing Inf. from Pres-close Inf. from Pres-select	Inf. to Pres-browsing
Close browser	Pres-close	Perc	Inf. from user	Inf. to State-browsing
Sel new browser	Pres-select	Perc	Inf. from user	Inf. to State-browsing
Handling Parameters	Pres-param-state	Per	Inf. from Param-state	Inf. to user
	Pres-param-mod	Perc	Inf. from user	Inf. to Param-state
	Param-state	Int.	Inf. from Pres-param-mod	Inf. to Pres-param-state
Managing Information	Req-information	Perc	Inf. from user	Inf. to Network
	Pres-information	Perc	Inf. from Information	Inf. to user
	Information	Int.	Inf. from Network	Inf. to Pres-information
Handling Bookmarks	Pres-book	Perc	Inf. from State-book	Inf. to user
	Modify-book	Perc	Inf. from user	Inf. to State-book
	State-book	Int.	Inf. from Modify-options	Inf. to Pres-book
Handling Options	Pres-options	Perc	Inf. from State-options	Inf. to user
	Modify-options	Perc	Inf. from user	Inf. to State-options
	State-options	Int.	Inf. from Modify-options	Inf. to Pres-options
Request	Pres-query	Perc	Inf. from user	Inf. to State-query
	State-query	Int.	Inf. from Pres-query Inf. from Pres-reload	Inf. to Network
Reloading	Pres-reload	Perc	Inf. from user	Inf. to State-query

Receiving	Pres-result	Perc	Inf. from Resource	Inf. to user
	Resource	Int.	Inf from Network	Inf to Pres-result

Table 1: Specification of objects and actions associated with tasks

The *Request* task has a perceivable object for allowing the user to formulate the query and an internal object which stores it. The *Reloading* task communicates with this internal object to activate a new request to load the current resource which will be presented by the objects associated with the Receiving task: one internal for communication with the remote server and one perceivable for presenting the information.

5.2 The Identification of the Components

Now we show how the information in the task model can be used to derive the corresponding architecture.

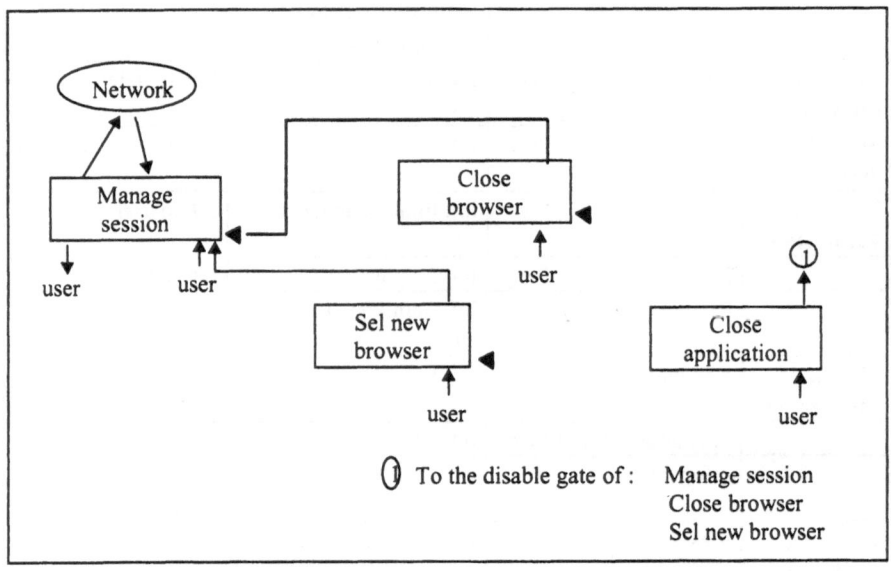

Figure 4: The interactor decomposition corresponding to the first levels of the task tree

The first level of the task tree has significant information to create the Close application interactor which will control the disabling of all the others interactors. The two tasks at the second level operate on different objects and thus they require one different interactor for each of them. Then we consider the next level of the task decomposition which has three new tasks (*Manage session, Close Browser, Select new Browser*) each of which operates on different objects so again we have one interactor for each of them. We have also to indicate that one task object has to be allocated with some internal functional core functionalities. In this case we indicate them by the network application object which is represented by an oval to distinguish it from the interactors which compose the User Interface System. In the next figures we represent interactors by rectangles and composition of interactors for their communication by arrows.

The next task level introduces the need for an interactor for handling parameters and one for managing information. The interactor for the parameters will be decomposed into one interactor for each parameter (bookmarks, options and so on). The interactor for managing information has to be decomposed in multiple interactors. One (or more depending on the level of abstraction) interactor is dedicated to allowing the user to formulate a request. Then there is an internal interactor (Compose) which receives the request and activates the dialogue with the remote server (Network) to load the information requested which is then passed to the interactor (Resource) which has to present it. The Reloading interactor has to communicate with the interactor for composing requests (Compose) which stores the last resource location sent and so can perform that request again.

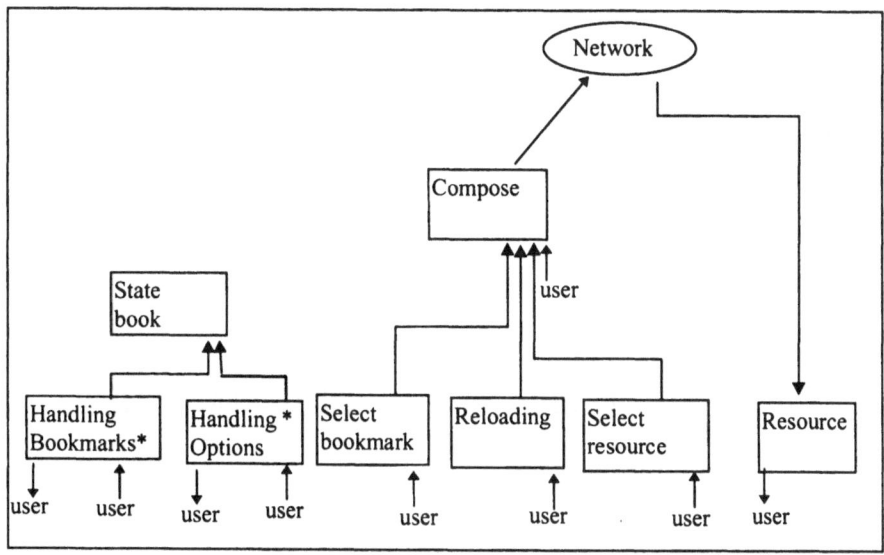

Figure 5: A further level of interactor decomposition

Then we can carry on the structuring of the interactor-based architecture by using information from the task model until we reach the level of detail which is useful for our purposes.

Next picture shows how the automatic tool allows the designer to indicate the preferences in developing the architecture specification. In this case the tool recognises the need to compose two interactors (Handling bookmarks and State book in the example) because they handle objects which communicate in the task model and thus the tool requires indications from the designer about how to perform this communication. This means to choose what type of communication channels of the two interactors have to communicate directly. According to our model each interactor can communicate by eight types of channels depending on the type of information (data, control, activation) and the direction of the information flow.

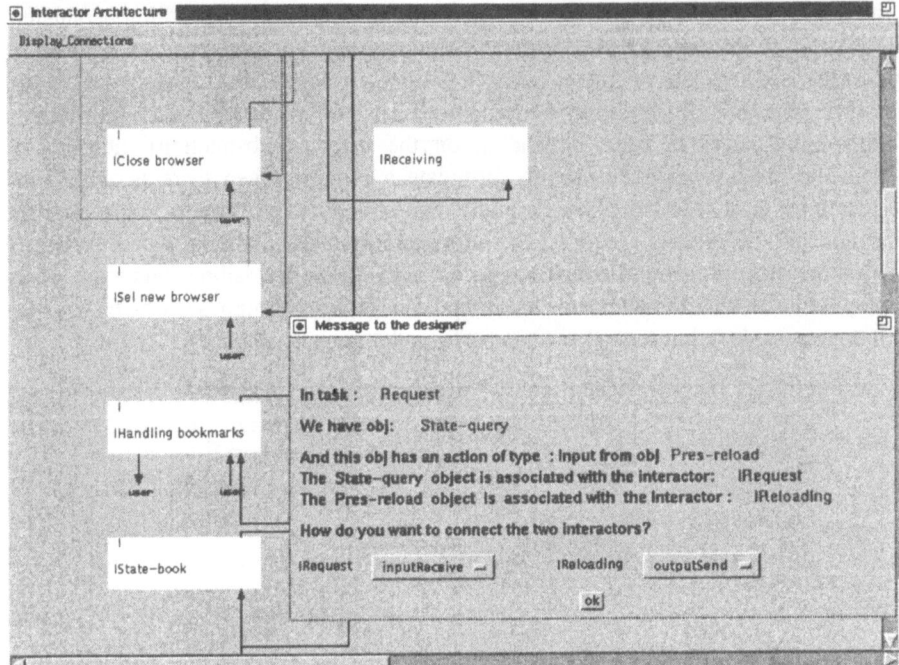

Figure 6: An example of interaction with the tool for task-to-interactor transformation

6. Formal Specification of Properties of the Web

6.1 A Formal Framework for Expressing Interaction Properties

The first approach to formal verification of user interface properties was described in our work (Paterno' 93). After that (Abowd et al. 95) used tools similar to those used by us to verify properties expressed in CTL. This notation has the same power as ACTL but describes state modifications rather than action performance. Chris Johnson has developed some work which starts from a temporal logic specification in order to produce a prototype for the user interface (Johnson 93). He uses temporal logic to provide a complete specification of the system, whereas we use it to summarise specific aspects of interest which are checked on the model of the Interactive System considered obtained by the LOTOS model.

At the University of Waterloo some work has been developed (Bumbulis et al. 96) which has similar goals but uses theorem provers (HOL in this case).

Once we have obtained a specification of the considered system using a structured approach we can verify its properties, using Action-based Temporal Logic (ACTL) (De Nicola et al.93). This notation has been successfully applied to other application areas such as hardware verification. It allows specifiers to reason about the actions which a system can perform. This is very important in Interactive Systems, which are mainly characterised by the actions performed both by the user and the system.

6.2 Demonstration of Properties over the Specification of the Web

Properties on the web specification can be verified with the support of some general purpose tools for formal methods. Once we have obtained the LOTOS specification we can automatically translate it into a corresponding labelled transition system. In order to be transformed the data types specification should be removed from the specification. This means that if ACT ONE (the data algebra part of the Full LOTOS notation) was used in the LOTOS specification it has to be modified so as to obtain an equivalent specification using only the process algebra part. The labels associated with the transitions in the resulting finite state machine are the actions of the LOTOS specification. Then we can use another automatic tool which can receive as input the property to verify and the labelled transition system. It is able, by analysing the automaton, to verify whether or not the specification supports the given property and, in the negative case, it allows the designer to unfold interactively a trace of actions allowed by the specification which does not comply with the given property. It thus gives useful information for understanding why the specification fails to verify it, which can be used to improve the specification itself.

An action-based, branching time temporal logic represents a useful basic framework which stimulates the designer to reason about the possible interactive behaviours which can occur in the various temporal evolutions: it stimulates designers to think about the actions needed to get to the next state, eventually, never, for at least one temporal evolution, or for all the temporal evolutions.

In order to evaluate the usability of an interactive application we can consider two levels of properties:

- properties related to the task's level such as "can this task always be performed?" or "if the user performs this task can s/he then perform this other task?". In the web application, examples can be "can a request to a server always be sent?" or "if the user selects a resource can s/he then print it?"
- properties related to the possible user actions and system feedback such as "if the user performs this action will this specific effect on the presentation of the user interface be achieved?". For example, "if the user selects the print menu item will a dialogue box for specifying specific printing parameters be activated?"

We can now use the possibilities of the ACTL notation to express the main features of a WWW browser. If we consider the possibility to request permanent access to a location:

$$AG<send\_url\_request>true$$

the answer is false because there are some states where a browser does not allow this, for example while the user is accessing a file. If we provide a more flexible property, such as it is always possible to have a temporal evolution during which at some time it is possible to request access to a location:

AGEF<send_url_request> true

then the answer is positive. This means that for this purpose in a browser environment there are no one-way doors: it is not possible for the user to enter in a state from where it is no longer possible to perform the considered task (to request access to a given location). This means that it is not always possible to perform the given task immediately, but it is always possible to activate an interaction which terminates with the accomplishment of the task.

The branching time approach is useful to give a compact indication of the typical behaviour of a web environment where whenever the user makes a request for a html document then it is both possible that the request is satisfied and a new page is presented, and that the new page is not rendered (for example because of network load) and an error message is visualised. This can be expressed by the following formula:

AG[send_url_request] (EF<present_new_data>true & EF<error_message>true)

It is also possible to identify the action which has to be performed in order to be sure that a given effect will be achieved. For example:

AG[send] EF<connect> A[true {true} U {present_new_data} true]

The last property means that if the user sends a request to a server then it is possible that the connection will be activated (connect action). The E operator indicates that this is not always possible, for example the server may be not available. However, if the connection is activated then at least some new data will be presented.

Another important element is that if an error is performed then the user can still perform the desired task. For example, if the wrong url address is specified then an error message will appear. Our formal specification indicates that the following property holds:

AG[error_message] EF<present_new_data> true

This means that whenever an error message appears, it will still be possible to visualise a new page (specified with the correct address).

Another possibility is to express whether some actions can be performed sequentially: once one occurs then in order to get to the next state the other can occur. For example:

AG[send]EX{add_bookmark}true

This is false because in the browser environment, once a request for receiving a resource is sent, some actions have to occur before the user can add a new bookmark (first a button has to be pressed in order to send the request and the bookmark pull-down menu has to be selected).

In ACTL it is also possible to verify if two interactions are task-equivalent: they both allow to perform the same task, for example:

AG[select_netscape_bookmark]   E[{true}{~specify_netscape_url}   U
{send_netscape_url} true]
&
AG[specify_netscape_url]   E[{true}{~select_netscape_bookmark   }   U
{send_netscape_url} true]

This means that a specific URL request can be sent both by selecting a previously stored bookmark and by specifying the interested address using a dialogue box (the & symbol is the logical and between the two parts of the property).

7. Conclusions

In this chapter we have discussed how the TLIM method uses formal concepts to support the design of an interactive application at both task and software architecture levels allowing designers to obtain precise descriptions which can be analysed and discussed for improving the possible solutions.

Besides, we can express action-oriented properties at both levels which indicate in a compact way the main interactive features of the system considered that we are interested in evaluating.

The proposed approach has been discussed by using some aspects of the WWW environment as an example. This approach has been used for different applications including: industrial applications for Enterprise Resource Planning (Breedvel 97 et al.), hypermedia for museum applications (Paterno' and Bucca, 97) and it showed a good scalability for medium-large applications. We have also begun the developing of an application in the air traffic control domain.

The possibility to perform model checking of user interface properties represents an interesting aspect. However, in order to facilitate the use of these techniques it is necessary to improve the user interfaces of the tools for model checking in order to build an environment which can be understandable and useful for a user interface designer. The goal should be to provide the possibility of defining properties to check in such a way as to make their semantics more intuitive even for people without a background in formal methods, such as many user interface designers.

Chapter 13:
Electronic Gridlock, Information Saturation and the Unpredictability of Information Retrieval over the World Wide Web

1. Introduction

In 1980 there were approximately one hundred computers attached to the Internet. In 1990 there were one hundred thousand. In 1994, the number of systems connected to the Internet exceeded one million. A recent estimate placed the number of Internet users at just over twenty-five million (Schofield 94). Hundreds of sites in many different domains provide access to a vast range of information sources. The growth of these information sources and the development of mass-market browsers has encouraged the active participation of new groups of users (Berners-Lee et al. 92).

The very success of distributed computing has, however, exacerbated a range of existing usability problems. For example, retrieval delays have reached a stage where many sites suffer from a form of 'electronic gridlock' (Johnson 95). At peak times it can take thirty or forty minutes to download relatively small files. Other usability problems arise from the sheer volume of information that can be accessed from remote sites (Schofield 94). When users select a link, they have little idea if the information that they have selected will be relevant to their task.

These problems are exacerbated by the unpredictable nature of information retrieval over the Web. Users, typically, cannot predict the time taken to retrieve a file. Server performance varies according to the time of day, local network capacity, the availability of mirror sites etc. Unpredictability arises because many users have little understanding of the underlying technology that supports interaction with the Web. Remote site failures, network bottlenecks and the problems of data fusion have little relevance to their tasks. Unfortunately, it is not possible to engineer out these problems given current technology. In consequence, users are faced with a range of apparently 'bizarre' temporal behaviours when interacting with distributed computer networks. The resulting usability problems frustrate attempts to exploit Internet resources.

1.1 The Problems: Electronic Gridlock

The term 'electronic gridlock' is used to refer to situations in which networks and servers cannot cope with the amount of information that is being requested from them. Recent innovations in caching, including the widespread use of mirror sites, have done much to increase the efficiency of network communications. However, the majority of Internet users still suffer from the "bottlenecks" created by modem and Ethernet connections. As more and more people access a greater and greater volume of data over these low bandwidth systems, there has been an increase in the amount of time that is required to download information (Johnson 95, Johnson & Kavanagh 96). Kuhmann (Kuhmann 89) argues that these retrieval delays have a profound impact upon the quality of interaction with distributed systems. Prolonged periods waiting to retrieve a file frequently lead to frustration and error.

1.2 The Problems: Information Saturation

The term 'information saturation' refers to situations in which users simply cannot cope with the volume of information that can be accessed from remote sites. Hiltz and Turoff (Hiltz & Turoff 85) argue that this problem stems from "information entropy"; electronic documents are insufficiently well structured for users to select the items that they need. This problem affects a wide range of applications, not just Web-based systems. For example, it can often take ten or twenty minutes to extract critical items from the morning's electronic mail messages. The use of in-page indexing and graphical navigation techniques through image maps helps to address these problems for Web users. However, the low marginal cost associated with creating Web documents and the large number of potential authors helps to offset any long-term benefits that these techniques might offer. Search engines also help to address the problems of information saturation but even these systems are being swamped by the difficulty of effectively indexing the millions of documents that are created every day.

1.3 The Problems: Unpredictability

The problems of electronic gridlock and information saturation are made much worse for many users because of the unpredictability of interaction with the World Wide Web. Unpredictability occurs whenever a user cannot determine the consequences of their actions based upon the information presented by the system at the time that they perform those actions (Dix et al. 87). Figure 1 illustrates the way in which the architecture of interaction with distributed information retrieval systems leads to unpredictability.

Browsers translate user requests for information into the communications primitives that are necessary to transfer relevant data from remote servers. These browsers hide the details of the underlying networks from the user. This leads to unpredictability because without this information it is difficult to determine whether a retrieval command will be successful. Remote site failure and communications bottlenecks can delay the transmission of data between the browser and the remote servers. Unfortunately, it is not always possible to isolate users from the underlying communications mechanisms that support Web browsers. Delays can occur when bottlenecks form in the passage of information back to the browser.

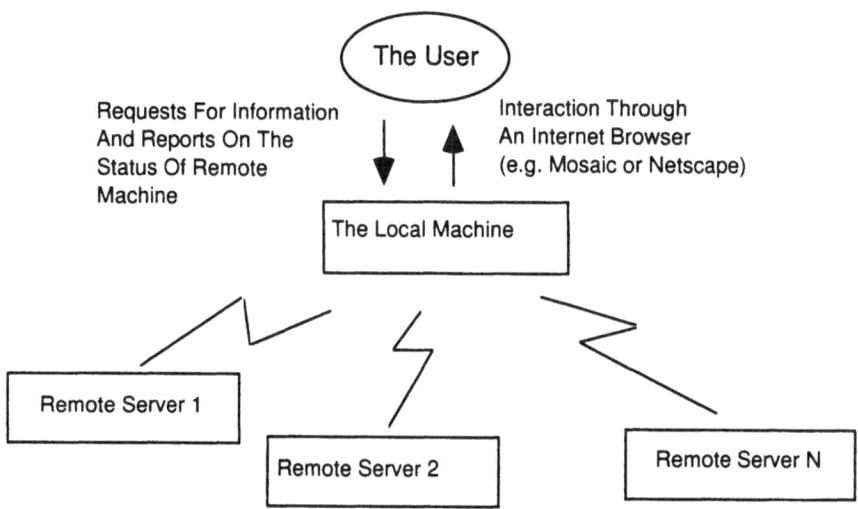

Figure 1: Information retrieval over a distributed network

These problems come and go as the network loading changes over time. From the point of view of the user, it is impossible to predict the effects that such problems will have upon the duration of their retrieval task. The information that they request may be provided relatively quickly if none of these factors intervene. Alternatively, their retrieval task may fail completely if a remote site goes down. Several studies have shown that users find it difficult to complete retrieval tasks under such circumstances, especially if they have a fixed amount of time at their disposal (Pejtersen 89). Other studies have shown that variable delays in system response times lead to frustration and error (Kuhmann 89). It is important to emphasise that these problems are tied both to the temporal behaviour of the network and to the temporal characteristics of the browser. If the interface to the application provides feedback on the rate of information transfer then users may be able to make better predictions about the likely costs of a retrieval as it progresses. However, these problems are also linked to the nature of the requested resource. For instance, users may not be able to predict the time necessary to retrieve a particular file given a simple hypertext label. This chapter argues that designers can exploit formal notations to reason about the presentation techniques that reduce these problems.

2. Analysing Electronic Gridlock

Formal methods provide designers with means of abstracting away from the mass of detailed information that is available on the World Wide Web. Logic can be used to reason about underlying problems, such as electronic gridlock and information saturation, rather than focusing in upon surface characteristics of particular browsers. For example, a Horn Clause notation might be used to represent the interaction between a user's request and a server's response. This formalism is appropriate because it eases the transition between abstract logic requirements and executable prototypes using variants of the Prolog programming environment (Johnson 93, Johnson 94). The following formula states that a resource is retrieved if the user selects an area of text which is linked with that resource. The term *url* stands for Uniform Resource Locator. The *http* addresses that are so familiar to Web users provide examples of these addresses:

display_url(url)⟸
     user_selects(label) ∧ *linked(label, url)*∧   (1)
     fetch(url)∧ *present(url)*

Unfortunately, there is no notion of time in classical logic. The previous Clause fails to capture the potential delay that can occur between the user selecting the label and the resource being returned from a remote machine. This is a significant limitation because retrieval delays have a considerable impact upon the design of Web-based systems. For example, many users will abandon their requests rather than tie up their machine while large files are downloaded. Figure 2 illustrates this point. The graph shows the times that are required to access different lengths of video clips using the Netscape browser on a stable network. As can be seen, the bigger the file, the more time the user needs to complete their task.

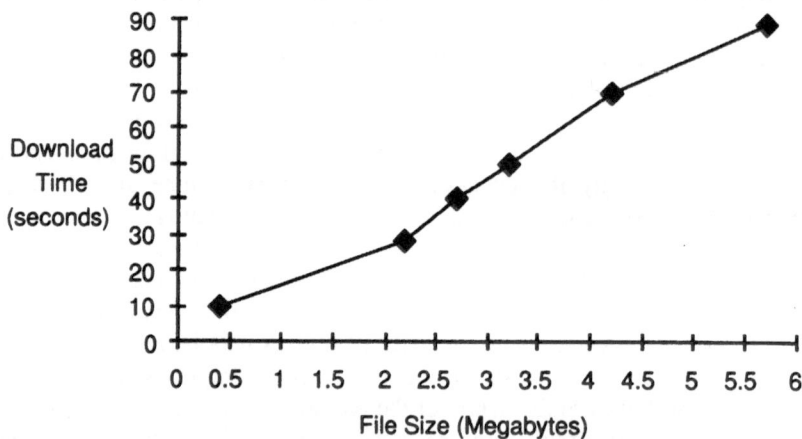

Figure 2: Variable download latency with file size

Several notations can be used to represent the impact of time upon information retrieval. For example, designers might exploit temporal extensions to graphical notations, such as timed Petri Nets. Alternatively, real-time constraints can be introduced into first order logic. For example, the following Clause represents the ninety second delay that might be expected for the largest of the files shown in

Figure 2. The user requests there source at 12:00:00 hrs but it is not presented until 12:01:30 hrs:

$$acceptable\_delay(url, 12\_00\_00, 12\_01\_30) \Leftarrow$$
$$user\_selects(label, 12\_00\_00) \wedge linked(label, url, 12\_00\_00) \wedge \qquad (2)$$
$$fetch(url, 12\_00\_00) \wedge present(url, 12\_01\_30)$$

Such Clauses quantify the real-time delays that occur during information retrieval tasks. In this case the delay was only ninety minutes. This might be deemed "acceptable" for some applications. This might not be the case if delays extended beyond ten minutes. Under such circumstances, designers might consider splitting resources, such as video files, into smaller segments. The following Clause states that delays of ten minutes are considered to be 'unacceptable':

$$unacceptable\_delay(url, 12\_00\_00, 12\_10\_00) \Leftarrow$$
$$user\_selects(label, 12\_00\_00) \wedge linked(label, url, 12\_00\_00) \wedge \qquad (3)$$
$$fetch(url, 12\_00\_00) \wedge present(url, 12\_10\_00)$$

Previous Clauses such as (2) and (3) help to address the problems created by electronic gridlock because they explicitly represent the boundaries for acceptable retrieval delays. If 'average' delays increased beyond these limits then designers must re-design their resources, for instance, by reducing the amount of graphics or by editing audio and video clips. These Clauses also raise a number of further issues. For instance, they do not state the precise conditions under which timings may be taken for 'average' delays. This is a significant limitation because download times vary between different parts of the globe. It would be of little benefit if some users had an *acceptable_delay* but had no interest in a resource while others had to suffer an *unacceptable_delay* for information that they really needed. For example, I can rapidly access meteorological information about Seattle but frequently have great difficulty in accessing information about the West of Scotland. Figure 3 presents the results of a trial that we conducted to illustrate the importance of geographical location for retrieval delays. A number of users were asked to download the same file at approximately the same time of day.

As can be seen from the graph, retrieval delays are determined by the user's location. It is important to note that this does **not** mean that delays are not determined by the user's geographical distance from a resource. Dublin is 200 miles away from Glasgow and yet it takes longer to retrieve the file than Montpellier which is 900 miles away. This is due to a 256kbit line between Ireland and the United Kingdom. If designers were providing a resource for use by Dubliners then the Web page would have to be designed as if Dublin were geographically further away than Montpellier. This implies that any attempt by designers to define acceptable and unacceptable delays must be indexed by the relative position of the user to the resource. Logic provides a means of representing these objectives or criteria for the development of a Web-based system:

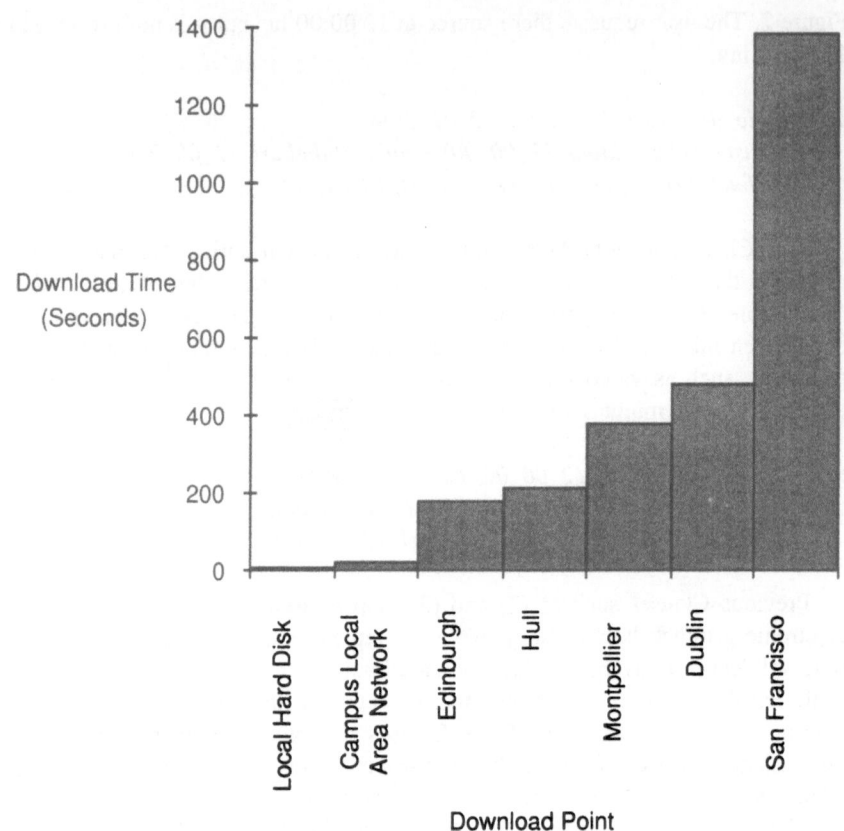

Figure 3: Variable download latency with users' location

unacceptable_delay(url, 12_00_00, 12_10_00, hull)⇐
    user_selects(label, 12_00_00) ∧ linked(label,url, 12_00_00) ∧   *(4)*
    user_position(hull, 12_00_00) ∧
    resource_position(Glasgow, 12_00_00)∧
    fetch(url, 12_00_00)∧ present(url, 12_10_00)

acceptable_delay(url, 12_00_00, 12_10_00, San_francisco)⇐
    user_selects(label, 12_00_00) ∧ linked(label,url, 12_00_00) ∧   *(5)*
    user_position(San_fransisco, 12_00_00) ∧
    resource_position(Glasgow, 12_00_00)∧
    fetch(url, 12_00_00)∧ present(url, 12_10_00)

Too many designers have, perhaps, become preoccupied with the quantity of information that can be accessed over the World Wide Web. Pages have become crammed with complex graphical images, trivial Java Applets and unnecessary frames. As a result, many users feel exasperated at the amount of time that is wasted while huge files are retrieved from distant sites (Johnson 95). Clauses (4) and (5) show how designers can use a formal notation to explicitly represent the temporal and geographical properties that determine 'quality of service'. The introduction of additional features is only justified if users can access particular resources within an acceptable period of time. If these features have to be introduced and response time fall outside *acceptible* limits then designers must consider the use of mirror sites to reduce the impact of physical, or rather network, distance upon retrieval delays. Alternatively, improvements can be made to the supporting infrastructure. For example, the delays between Glasgow and Dublin, shown in Figure 3, are being addressed by the provision of a 512kbit line across the Atlantic.

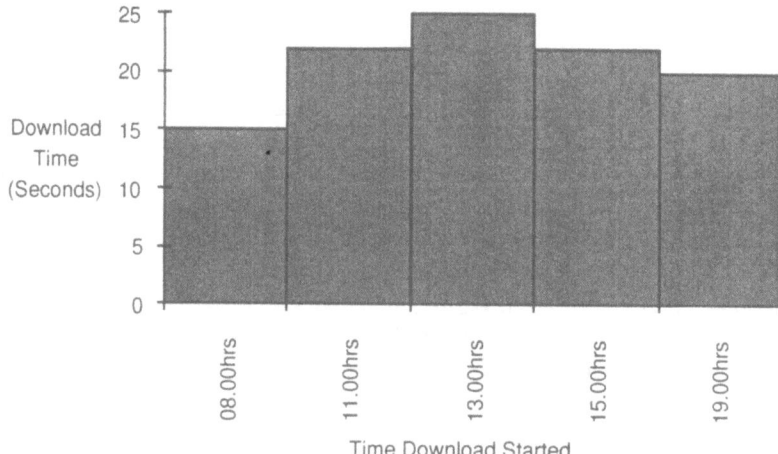

Figure 4: Variable download latency with time of day

There are, however, further issues that must be considered if designers are to address the problems created by electronic gridlock. Figure 4 presents the delays that occur when accessing a video file over the Glasgow University network at different times during the day. Variations stem from both network and server loading. From this it follows that acceptable and unacceptable delays are not only determined by file size and the relative position of the user, they are also determined by the time of day when a request is issued. For instance, a ten minute delay might be quite acceptable at midday when machines and networks are heavily loaded. The same delay might be less acceptable at nine in the morning when less demands are placed on supporting infrastructures:

unacceptable_delay_1(url, 09_00_00, 09_10_00, hull)⇐
    user_selects(label, 09_00_00) ∧ linked(label,url, 09_00_00) ∧   *(6)*
    user_position(hull, 09_00_00) ∧
    resource_position(Glasgow, 09_00_00)∧
    fetch(url, 09_00_00)∧ present(url, 09_10_00)

acceptable_delay(url, 12_00_00, 12_10_00, hull)⇐

$user\_selects(label, 12\_00\_00) \wedge linked(label,url, 12\_00\_00) \wedge$ *(7)*
$user\_position(hull, 12\_00\_00) \wedge$
$resource\_position(Glasgow, 12\_00\_00) \wedge$
$fetch(url, 12\_00\_00) \wedge present(url, 12\_10\_00)$

Clauses (6) and (7) help to specify the boundaries of acceptable and unacceptable delays for particular locations at particular times of the day. If these limits were regularly broken then, as before, designers might consider dividing resources into smaller files with faster access times. The number of graphical images in a page might be reduced. Mirror sites might be provided. However, a number of limitations restrict the utility of Clauses, such as (6) and (7), for reasoning about information retrieval systems. In particular, they only describe fixed intervals of time. Designers would be forced to introduce additional Clauses to specify that delays of eleven minutes, twelve minutes, thirty minutes, one hour... were also unacceptable. Such problems can be avoided by introducing variables to stand for precise moments of time. The following Clause states that for all times, *t*, there is an unacceptable delay in presenting a *url* if the resource is selected at *12:00:00hrs* and presented at *t* and *t* occurs more than ten minutes after *12:00:00* :

$\forall\ t: unacceptable\_delay(url, 12\_00\_00, t, hull) \Leftarrow$
    $user\_selects(label, 12\_00\_00) \wedge linked(label,12\_00\_00) \wedge$ *(8)*
    $user\_position(hull, 12\_00\_00) \wedge$
    $resource\_position(Glasgow, 12\_00\_00) \wedge$
    $fetch(url, t) \wedge present(url, t) \wedge after(12\_10\_00, t)$

The same abstraction techniques can be used to represent a range of geographical locations. This avoids the needless duplication of Clauses such as (4) and (5) for many different points in the globe. The following Clause states that delays of more that two hours are unacceptable at any time, anywhere in the world:

$\forall\ t,t',c: unacceptable\_delay(url, t, t', c) \Leftarrow$
    $user\_selects(label, t) \wedge linked(label, t) \wedge$
    $user\_position(c, t) \wedge resource\_position(Glasgow, t) \wedge$ *(9)*
    $fetch(url, t') \wedge present(url, t') \wedge after(t+2\_00\_00, t')$

The important point about Clauses (8) and (9) is that they force designers to focus upon quality of service issues for Web-based interaction. It is of little use providing rich multimedia resources over the Internet if no user can afford to wait while they download. In this sense, (8) and (9) illustrate how formal notations can be used to establish high level objectives for Internet providers. If such standards cannot be achieved then designers must take specific steps to combat electronic gridlock by splitting resources, reducing multimedia information and constructing mirror sites.

3. Analysing Unpredictability

Our previous formalisations have not captured the tremendous unpredictability that frustrates everyday retrieval tasks. For instance, a request might block owing to site failure, it might be stalled by heavy server loading, it might fail because a resource is missing. In order to capture these various eventualities, we must recruit a notation that can describe a range of alternative futures. For example, Clarke and Emerson's (Clarke & Emerson 82) Computation Tree Logic (CTL) uses a branching model of time to represent a number of alternative traces of possible interaction. The Appendix to this chapter presents a brief introduction to the syntax and semantics of CTL. Figure 5 illustrates the way in which this notation might be applied to analyse unpredictability during interaction with a Web browser. Two possible futures lead from the user selecting the label. In one path the resource is successfully retrieved from a remote site. In another path it cannot be retrieved because the remote site is unavailable. This captures the uncertainty that frustrates attempts to predict the outcome of particular commands.

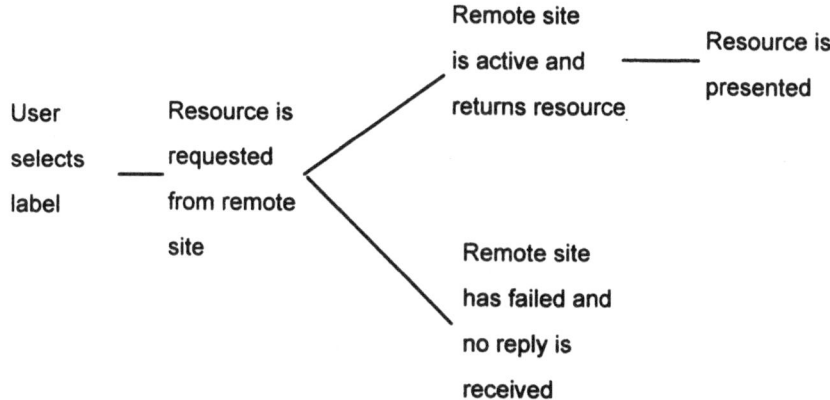

Figure 5: CTL's branching view of possible futures

CTL can be used to specify properties over traces of interaction between a user and a distributed system. For instance, the *AX* quantifier specifies that a particular property is true in the next interval of all possible traces. This provides a means of introducing the sequential information that was missing from Clause (1) without representing a particular moment in time which was a problem in Clauses (6) and (7). The following formularequires that the user selects the label before the corresponding resource is retrieved:

strong_predictability(Url) ⇐ user_selects(Label)∧
*   linked(Label, Url) ∧ AX (fetch(Url) ∧ AX present(Url))*   *(10)*

This formula represents an ideal state of affairs; the resource would be retrieved immediately after it had been requested in every trace of interaction. As we have seen, however, network delays and site failures make it impossible for designers to guarantee that a particular resource will be retrieved immediately after it has been requested. It is only possible to ensure that there are some traces in which a resource is returned immediately after it has been requested. This weaker objective can be represented using the *EX* operator (read as "there exists some next state"):

$$weak\_predictability(Url) \Leftarrow user\_selects(Label) \wedge$$
$$linked(Label, Url) \wedge EX \ (fetch(Url) \wedge AX \ present(Url)) \tag{11}$$

Unpredictability occurs because users cannot determine whether a request will be one of those for which the resource is immediately retrieved. In other words, a browser may behave unpredictably if the user selects a label and it is possible that the resource cannot be retrieved and presented in the next interval:

$$unpredictable(Url) \Leftarrow$$
$$user\_selects(Label) \wedge linked(Label, Url) \wedge \tag{12}$$
$$EX \ not(fetch(Url) \wedge AX \ present(Url))$$

Formal reasoning techniques provide means of re-writing temporal logic Clauses in order to clarify the properties that they describe. For example, a temporal form of De Morgan's law can be applied to the previous formula in order to identify the causes of unpredictability in distributed systems. Informally, the following Clause specifies that unpredictability occurs if the browser fails to fetch the resource referenced by the URL in the next interval or if there exists a subsequent interval in which the browser does not present that resource:

$$unpredictable(Url) \Leftarrow$$
$$user\_selects(Label) \wedge linked(Label, Url) \wedge \tag{13}$$
$$EX \ (not(fetch(Url)) \vee EX \ not(present(Url)))$$

Logic formulae, such as (13), provide a focus for the development of user interfaces to distributed systems. For example, one of the causes of unpredictability was identified as retrieval failure. This occurs when information is not returned to the browser immediately after the initial request; *EX not(fetch(Url))*. Typically, this might be due to high network loading or to the failure of a machine at a remote site. This delay is propagated into the user interface of the browser and can create considerable frustration when using the system (Kuhmann 89). A number of techniques can reduce the impact of such retrieval failures. For instance, browsers frequently warn users as soon as a transmission failure has been detected. In CTL, the *EF* operator (read as 'there exists some future') can be used in combination with the *AX* operator to specify that the user is alerted to a problem if eventually a resource is not retrieved and a warning is presented:

$$failure\_warning(Url) \Leftarrow user\_selects(Label) \wedge linked(Label, Url) \wedge \tag{14}$$

EF (not(fetch(Url)) ∧ AX present(request_failure))

The Mosaic and Netscape browsers both exploit this approach. In Mosaic, the number of bytes read from a remote server is displayed. The Netscape browser presents the percentage of data already received for a particular resource. If failures eventually occur then these numbers remain unchanged. The problem with both of these techniques is that the failure may only be detected well into a transfer. This interval is represented by the *EF* quantifier in Clause (14). Given the distractions of many working environments it can be difficult for users to monitor the precise amount of data that has been transferred from a remote site. Internet browsers, typically, provide additional displays to attract users' attention when connections cannot be made to remote sites. For instance, Mosaic uses the warning 'Unable to connect to remote host'. The results of an initial "think aloud" evaluation show that the warning is easily overlooked by many users and that this can lead to further unpredictability. For instance, novice users frequently respond to transmission delays by re-selecting a label. Rather than repeating the retrieval request, subsequent mouse clicks select the text under the cursor. Given such problems, it is important that designers can exploit logic to identify alternative solutions. For example, designers might specify that users must select a button to confirm warnings about remote site failure. Such techniques reduce the likelihood that users will miss the warning and continue to request unavailable information:

failure_confirmation(Url) ⇐ user_selects(Label)∧
    linked(Label, Url) ∧ EF (not(fetch(Url)) ∧   *(15)*
    AX present(request_failure)∧user_selects(request_failure))

The previous Clause represents a high-level approach that might be implemented in a number of different ways. From this it follows that the use of a logic notation does not guarantee the 'usability' of a particular interface. Some implementations of the formal requirement will be better than others. For example, Netscape v3.0 exploits a variation of the approach advocated in (15). Users are required to click a button labelled **OK** after being presented with the following warning:

Netscape is unable to locate the server: www.giraffe.gla.ac.uk. The server does not have a DNS entry. Check the server name in the location (URL) and try again. The domain name server cannot locate a requested machine.

Most users have little or no idea about the importance of DNS entries. This warning, therefore, causes considerable confusion when learning to use the browser. Other problems have arisen when browsers fail to satisfy the temporal properties described by (15). For example, early versions of the Mosaic browser would only provide warnings of transmission failures if the problem was immediately detected, *EX(not(fetch(Url)))*. The browser would 'hang' if the failure occurred at some mid-point during transmission, *EF(not(fetch(Url)))*. In multi-processing environments, there were few technical reasons for this behaviour and subsequent versions of the browser allow the termination of a request at any point in a transfer. The use of the logic, and in particular the distinction between *EX* and *EF*, captures this problem in a precise and concise way.

The second cause of unpredictability, identified in Clause (13), can be termed presentation delay. This occurs when information is successfully retrieved from a remote site but its presentation is delayed by the demands of processing text, graphics etc. This leads to unpredictability because people cannot determine how long it will take to assemble a page before they select it. Users can be discouraged from exploring Internet resources if they are forced to commit large amounts of time whenever information is requested. A number of techniques can be used to reduce the unpredictability caused by such processing delays. For example, interface designers can provide some indication about the size of remote resources. This does not imply that designers must include the file size of every item that can be accessed from a Web page. For instance, the interface shown in Figure 6 provides schoolchildren with access to videos about the Romans in Scotland. Each clip is accompanied by an indication of the running time which has more meaning for the intended users than a file size measured in bytes.

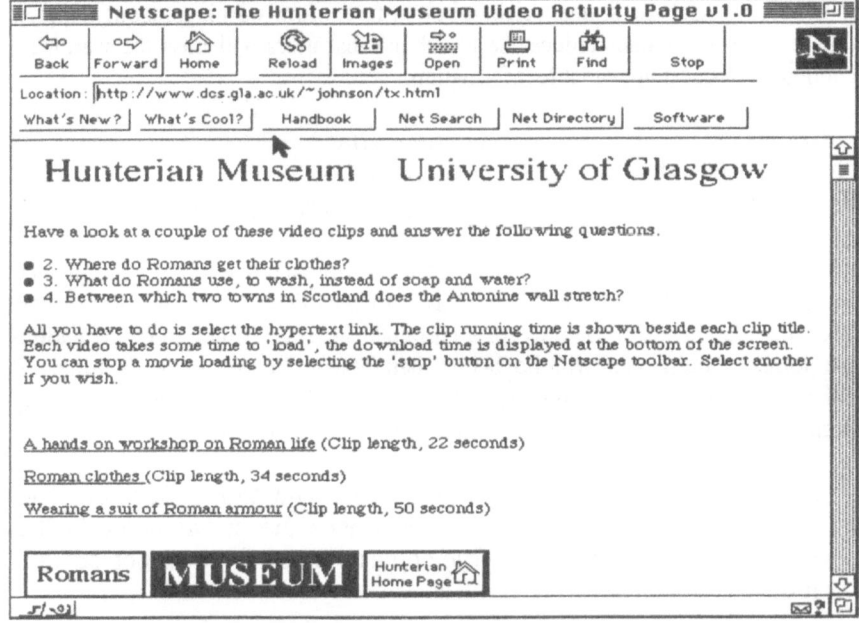

Figure 6: Reducing unpredictability by indicating resource size

As before, logic abstractions can be used to represent generic requirements for Web pages. This is important because, as Figure 6 indicates, the precise means of presenting the size of a resource is determined by the particular characteristics of the user population. File lengths were inappropriate for the school-children accessing this Web page. Users may predict retrieval delays if the size of a resource is presented until the user makes a selection:

$$predict\_delay(Url) \Leftarrow [present\_size(Url)\ Uuser\_selects(Label)] \qquad (16)$$

Other techniques are exploited by the designers of browsers so that users gain a better impression of the likely delays while pages of text and graphics are assembled from remote resources. Mosaic and Netscape process and present the text on a page before displaying any associated images. A temporary icon is presented while the images are processed. This supports predictability. The number of temporary icons gives the user some idea of the amount of time required to retrieve and present all of the information on the page:

$$update(Url) \Leftarrow$$
$$\qquad fetch(Url) \wedge$$
$$\qquad AX((present\_text(Url) \wedge$$
$$\qquad present\_temporary\_icon(Url))\ U\ present\_images(Url)) \qquad (17)$$

One of the benefits of the distributed architecture behind the Web is that the text and graphics in any page may be located on different machines. If the graphics machine goes down then, under the approach described in (17), the browser would 'hang'. It would not be possible to *present_images(Url)* until the machine came back up. By splitting the retrieval and presentation processes, the page can still be viewed even if the temporary icons are all that is available for some of the images. Mosaic and Netscape, therefore, not only support predictability through the use of temporary icons but also provide a high degree of fault tolerance:

$$fault\_tolerant\_update(Url) \Leftarrow$$
$$\qquad fetch\_text(Url) \wedge fetch\_images(Url) \wedge$$
$$\qquad AX(present\_text(Url) \wedge present\_temporary\_icon(Url)\ U \qquad (18)$$
$$\qquad (present\_images(Url) \vee present(request\_failure)))$$

Unfortunately, this approach only addresses some of the problems that are caused by unpredictability. Contextual information about the costs of retrieval are provided after the user has made a commitment to accessing the entire page. This increases the frustration associated with distributed retrieval; temporary icons enable the user to predict that a large amount of time will be wasted while graphical images are needlessly processed by the browser. Further problems occur if the user issues requests to access other resources before the original retrieval is completed. It is difficult to predict when the second request, *user_selects(Label2)*, will be processed:

$$unpredictable\_request(Url2) \Leftarrow$$
$$\qquad user\_selects(Label) \wedge$$
$$\qquad linked(Label,\ Url) \wedge fetch\_text(Url) \wedge fetch\_images(Url) \wedge$$
$$\qquad EF(user\_selects(Label2) \wedge linked(Label,Url2)) \wedge \qquad (19)$$
$$\qquad (present\_text(Url) \wedge present\_temporary\_icon(Url)\ U$$

$$(present\_images(Url) \lor present(request\_failure))))$$

This problem arises because browsers will, typically, hand over the processing of graphics, sound and video to helper applications. Once this has been done, any subsequent interaction will be ignored until the processing has been completed. There is no way for the user to detect this 'hand-over' from the information presented by browsers such as Mosaic and Netscape. This helps to create the 'bizarre' temporal behaviour mentioned in the introduction. Users are unable to predict when their input will take effect because they cannot identify the critical intervals before the helper applications are called. This can be resolved in a number of ways. For instance, all subsequent input might be ignored until the initial request has been completed:

$ordered\_request\_processing(Url, Url2) \Leftarrow$
    $user\_selects(Label) \land$
    $linked(Label, Url) \land fetch\_text(Url) \land fetch\_images(Url) \land$
    $AX(user\_selects(Label2) \land linked(Label2, Url2) \land$ (20)
    $(present\_text(Url) \land present\_temporary\_icon(Url) \land$
    $not(fetch\_text(Url2) \land fetch\_images(Url2)) U$
    $(present\_images(Url) \lor present(request\_failure))))$

The designers of Mosaic and Netscape have adopted an alternative solution. They provide a mechanism for halting a request. This enables users to interrupt the processing of a resource in order to revise their initial selection:

$support\_for\_halt(Url) \Leftarrow$
    $fetch\_text(Url) \land fetch\_images(Url) \land$
    $AX(present\_text(Url) \land present\_temporary\_icon(Url) U$
    $(present\_images(Url) \lor$ (21)
        $present(request\_failure) \lor$
        $user\_selects(halt)))$

This is a partial solution. For instance, the following Clause describes a trace in which the halt request is issued before all of the information is retrieved from the remote servers. Under such circumstances, there will be an inevitable delay while the browser handles the information that has already been requested from other sites:

$ordered\_request\_processing(Url, Url2) \Leftarrow$
    $user\_selects(Label) \land linked(Label, Url) \land send\_request(Url) \land$
    $AX(user\_selects(Label2) \land linked(Label2, Url2) \land$ (22)
    $EF(fetch\_text(Url) \land fetch\_images(Url)))$

This section has used CTL to represent techniques that reduce the unpredictability of Web-based systems. Page designers can provide indications of the size of a remote resource. Browser designers can provide termination mechanisms and support the parallel presentation of text and graphics. It is important to emphasise, however, that these techniques also help to reduce the problems created by electronic gridlock. If users fail to accurately predict the delays that affect a particular request, from a particular geographical location at a particular time of day then termination mechanisms provide an escape route. Similarly, by indicating the size of a resource, designers can help users to judge whether it is worth requesting a file from a particular machine.

4. Analysing Information Saturation

Previous sections have shown how formal methods can be used to represent and reason about the problems of electronic gridlock and unpredictability. In contrast, this section uses the problem of information saturation to identify two critical weaknesses in the application of formal methods. Firstly, there is no means of assessing **why** an interface is appropriate given its formal specification. Secondly, there is no guarantee that the application of formal methods will actually result in more "usable" interfaces.

4.1 Information Saturation and the Creativity of Design

The most irritating feature of the World Wide Web is not, perhaps, that users cannot predict the time that it will take to retrieve a resource but rather that they cannot predict the quality of the resource from its link. In other words, delays would be far less irritating if users could be sure that the final page would be worth the wait. Much of this frustration stems from information saturation. We have reached a point where the sheer volume of information makes it difficult for users to distinguish valuable resources from worthless trivia. For example, many Web pages now provide access to video clips. Most of these clips suffer from extremely poor production quality and inadequate direction. In consequence, many users are reluctant to tie up their machines while large files of poor quality footage are retrieved from remote sites. This problem affected the interface shown in Figure 6.

Initial trials with the page showed that 30-40% of requests were abandoned before they were completed (Johnson & Kavanagh 96). The actual percentage varied with the length of the clip. These results were extremely depressing because a great deal of time, effort and money had gone into the development of the Web site. The videos were produced by a professional crew working for a national broadcaster. They were processed using "state of the art" compression software. In spite of these precautions, many users were still not prepared to wait for the films to download. Users were, however, more likely to complete a retrieval request if they had already downloaded one of our videos and hence were aware of the production standards. It might, therefore, be argued that the design technique described in Clause (16) ought to be strengthened. Not only must designers indicate the size of a resource but they must also provide users with some indication of its quality or value to their task:

display_value_size(Url) ⟸
   [*(present_size(Url)* ∧ *present_value(Url)) U user_selects(Label)]*   *(23)*

For example, Figure 7 illustrates a revised page design for the video interface shown in Figure 6. Thumb-nail icons and descriptive paragraphs are used to indicate the production and compression quality of the associated material. Even if users cannot predict the delays imposed by network loading, our experience with this application shows that designers can affect attitudes to retrieval delays by providing a clear indication of the quality of the resources that users request.

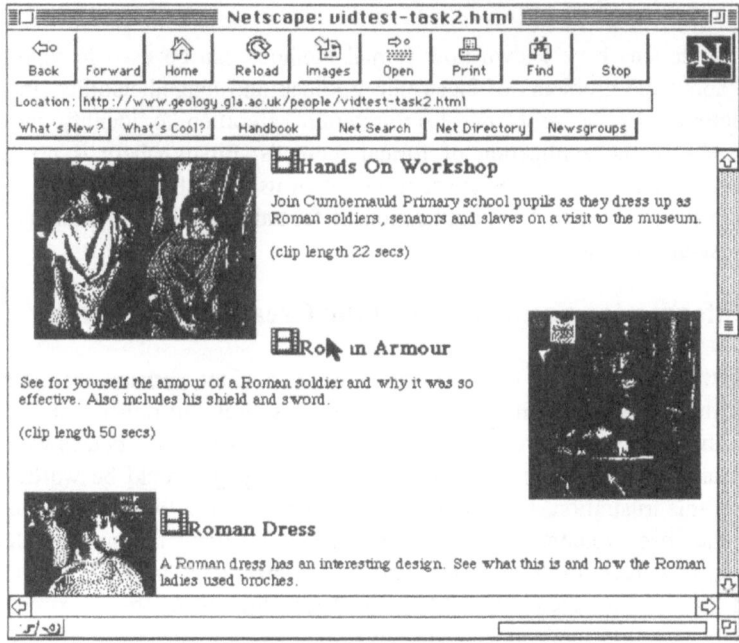

Figure 7: Indicating the quality of remote information

Additional Clauses might be introduced to represent the techniques, such as those used in Figure 7, that satisfy the high-level requirements of Clause (23). For example, the following formula states that the value of the movie located at a particular URL is represented if a *G if* is used to present a screen shot from that movie:

$$present\_value('http://www.dcs.gla.ac.uk/~johnson/mov1') \Leftarrow$$
$$display\_screen\_shot(Gif,http://www.dcs.gla.ac.uk/~johnson/mov1') \qquad (24)$$

This Clause illustrates both the strength and the weakness of formal approaches to interface development. On the one hand, mathematical notations provide designers with means of specifying high-level design objectives. On the other hand, they provide little indication of how this requirement might be satisfied within a particular interface. Further problems stem from the fact that formal specifications, typically, provide an indication of **what** an interface must do. They do not say **why** it must do it. This is significant because it can be difficult for non-formalists to understand why the design of Figure 7 is an improvement over the page layout shown in Figure 6. In previous papers, we have addressed these problems by developing literate specification techniques (Johnson 96, Johnson 96a). This approach uses the semi-formal argumentation of design rationale to support the use of formal methods during systems development. Figure 8 illustrates this approach. Rank Xerox's Questions, Options and Criteria (QOC) notation is used to document the reasons why the previous Clause might be adopted within the design of a particular system. QOC diagrams are built by identifying the key questions that must be addressed during the development of an interactive system (Buckingham Shum 95). In this case, the question is which style of interface best addresses the problems created by information saturation. The options that answer a particular question are then linked to it using the lines shown in Figure 8. The textual interface that satisfies Clause 16 is one alternative that might reduce information saturation. The 'cinematic' interface that satisfies Clauses 23 and 24 is a further alternative. Finally, these options are linked to the criteria that support them, using solid lines, or weaken them, using broken lines. In Figure 8, the cinematic interface is justified by the criteria that it represents both the size and the quality of the remote resources. It is not supported by the argument that the initial screen, shown in Figure 8, will take a relatively short time to download. Additional delays will be introduced by the introduction of the thumb-nail sketches. In contrast, the textual interface of Figure 6 is supported by a short down-load time, it also indicates the size of the remote resource but unlike the cinematic design it does not indicate the production quality of the video. This example, therefore, helps to illustrate the trade-off that is being made when using Clauses such as (23) and (24) to address the problem of information saturation. Users are given some indication of the quality of remote information. This is achieved at the cost of increased retrieval delays from the additional information that provides an indication of this quality on the indexing screen shown in Figure 7.

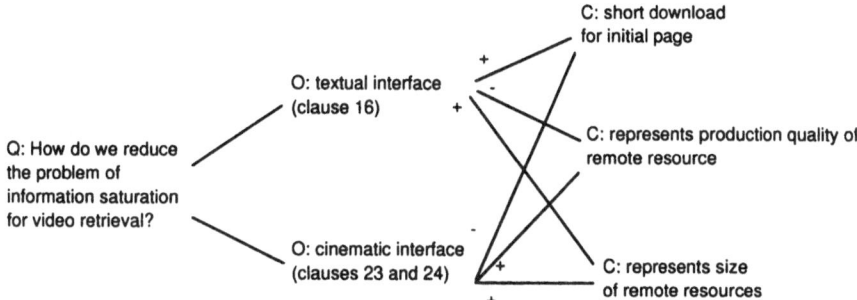

Figure 8: Literate specification for information saturation.

Natural language annotations of the Questions and Criteria provide non-formalists with an entry-point into the Clauses that represent particular Options. In literate specification, these annotations provide the justifications for and against formal design requirements. The interested reader is directed to Johnson (Johnson 96a) for more detail on the application of this approach. It is important to note, however, that both formal and literate specification techniques suffer from a major limitation. Designers have no proof that a particular approach, such as that described by Clauses (23) and (24), will actually improve the 'usability' of an interface.

4.2 Information Saturation and the Evaluation of Design

The interface shown in Figure 7 is intended to reduce the problem of information saturation by using thumb-nail sketches to provide an indication of the quality of a remote resource, *present_value(Url)*. Formal methods provide no means of determining whether or not the page design actually achieves this claimed benefit. In order to provide this evidence, designers must recruit techniques from experimental psychology. For example, Figure 9 present the results from a series of tests that were used to gauge subjective attitudes to the video pages (Johnson & Kavanagh 96).

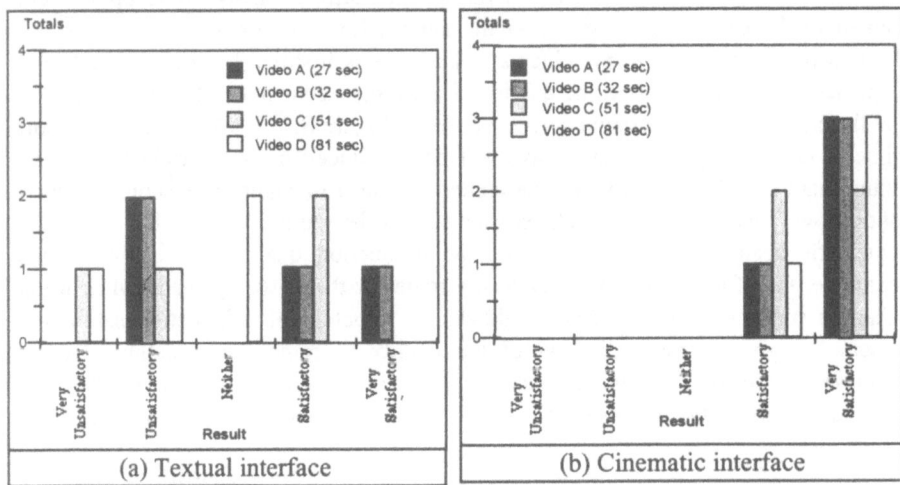

Figure 9: Results of an empirical evaluation of web-based video pages

The chart on the left presents subjective attitudes towards the textual interface shown in Figure 6 for video clips of several different lengths. This page design satisfied Clause (16) because it represented the size of the video resources that it indexed. It did not satisfy Clauses (23) and (24) because it did not provide users with an indication of the production quality. In contrast, the chart on the right shows subjective attitudes to the delays suffered when using the revised page design of Figure 7. As predict edit is possible to see higher satisfaction ratings from the cinematic interface.

Figure 9 illustrates the complementary nature of formal specifications and empirical evaluations. Without empirical evaluation, designers cannot be sure that particular interface techniques will actually support the intended users of an interface. Without formal specification techniques, it is difficult for designers to precisely describe the differences between the various interfaces being tested. In our example, Clauses (16), (23) and (24) characterise the two interfaces that are being evaluated. Unfortunately, there has been no research into the integration of formal and experimental design techniques. In particular, designers have no means of documenting the relationship that exists between the results of an evaluation and the interfaces that are described in the Clauses of a formal specification. We are currently extending literate specification techniques to address this problem. For example, the Questions, Options and Criteria notation can be translated into a form that directly represents the empirical evidence that supports a particular option. Instead of using questions to represent critical design issues, diagrams can represent the usability claims that are made about a particular option. These can then be linked to more detailed descriptions of the empirical techniques that support the claim. Figure 10 presents a Claims, Analysis and Evidence (CAE) diagram for the interfaces shown in Figures 6 and 7.

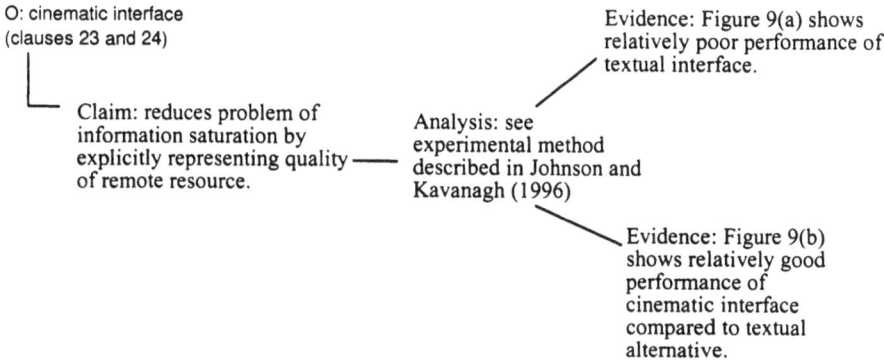

Figure 10: Claim, Analysis, Evidence (CAE) diagram for the video retrieval system

As mentioned, the claim, analysis and evidence links shown in Figure 10 are simple extensions of the literate specification techniques shown in Figure 8. Literate specifications provide a bridge between formal analysis and design rationale. CAE diagrams provide a bridge between formal specifications and empirical evaluations. In short, these complementary techniques are intended to provide a Web of supporting evidence for particular interface design decisions. Figure 11 shows how literate specifications and CAE diagrams can be integrated to provide an overview of our formal and empirical analysis of the Web-based video system:

Future work intends to evaluate the usability of these linking structures for different groups of interface designers. Much of this research will focus upon tool support for the resulting diagrams. It is important to stress, however, that we are less concerned about the particular form of the links than with the pressing need to integrate formal and experimental approaches to interface design. Without abstract, mathematical notations it is difficult to reason about the complexity of interaction with distributed information systems. The problems of electronic gridlock, information saturation and unpredictability cannot easily be understood without some precise and concise means of representing temporal properties. Equally, formal techniques cannot be used to validate particular interfaces once the problems of electronic gridlock, information saturation and unpredictability have been better understood.

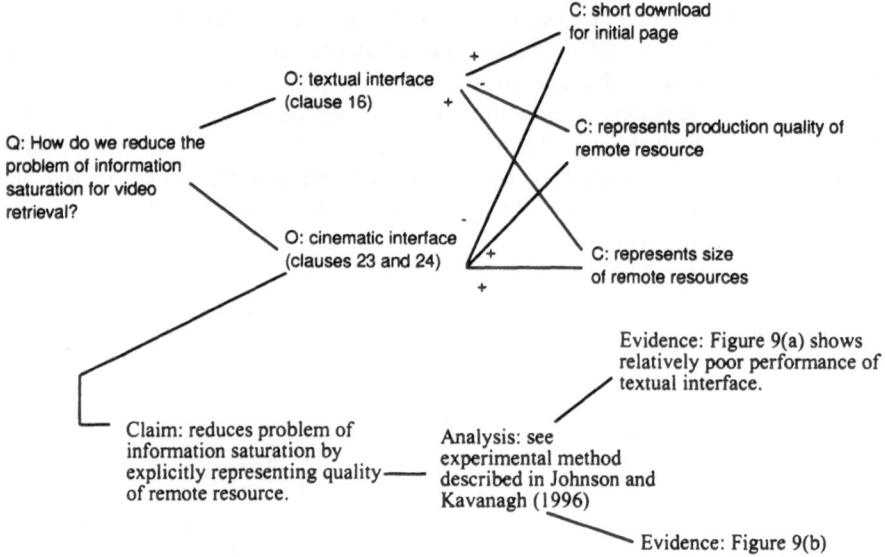

Figure 11: Integrating CAE and literate specification

5. Conclusion

This chapter has argued that the increasing demands upon the world's computing resources has created a problem of 'electronic gridlock'. This occurs when users are forced to wait for long periods of time in order to access remote resources. In contrast, the huge increase in the supply or remote information is creating a problem of 'information saturation'. This occurs when users cannot distinguish high quality resources from a background mass of mediocre material. Communications' failures, network loading and processing overheads all help to compound these problems because people cannot predict the delays that occur during retrieval operations. Most users cannot be expected to have a detailed understanding of network engineering. As a consequence, the temporal properties exhibited by distributed systems often appear to be 'bizarre' and 'unreasonable'. In order for designers to address these concerns, it is important that they are provided with some means of reasoning about the complex temporal properties of user interfaces. This chapter has exploited CTL to examine a range of interaction techniques that can be used to reduce the impact of electronic gridlock, information saturation and unpredictability in distributed systems. For example, the incremental presentation of text and graphics can help users to predict potential delays. Halting mechanisms free users from systems that would otherwise have been tied up by the problems of electronic gridlock.

Representations of the size and quality of remote resources can be used to reduce the frustration that arises from information saturation.

It is important to remember that formal methods are simply tools and like any tool, they are only as good as the person who uses them. It is perfectly possible for designers to specify presentation techniques that exacerbate rather than resolve usability problems. The later sections of this chapter have described a range of techniques that address this problem. Literate specification techniques use formal requirements to document **what** an interface must do. They also provide a rationale that explains **why** such techniques are appropriate. Unfortunately, this approach provides no evidence that the claimed benefits of a particular interface will be satisfied in a particular implementation. We have, therefore, extended our literate specification techniques to include claims, analysis and evidence diagrams. These represent the methods and results of the empirical evaluations that must be recruited to support the formal design of interfaces to distributed information systems.

Acknowledgements

This work was conducted as part of the Temporal Aspects of Usability project SPG9201233, funded by the UK Joint Council Initiative in Cognitive Science and Human Computer Interaction. It was also funded by UK EPSRC grant GR/K69148.

Appendix: Syntax and Semantics of CTL

CTL represents future time in terms of a number of possible sequences of states. Following Clarke and Emerson (Clarke & Emerson 82),our description of CTL uses p to denote an atomic proposition.

p is a formula

$f\_\{i\}$ denotes a formula or sub-formula

$f\_\{1\} \wedge f\_\{2\}$ is a formula denoting conjunction

$\neg f$ is a formula denoting negation

$EX F\_\{j\} f$ is a formula; f is true in the next state of possible future $F\_\{j\}$.

$A[f\_\{1\} U f\_\{2\}]$ is a formula; there exists a prefix for all futures such that $f\_\{2\}$ is true in the last state of the prefix and $f\_\{1\}$ holds at all other states in that prefix.

$E[f\_\{1\}Uf\_\{2\}]$ is a formula; there exists a prefix for a future such that $f\_\{2\}$is true in the last state of the prefix and $f\_\{1\}$ holds at all other states in that prefix.

The semantics of CTL are represented by a model $M = (S, F\_\{1\},...,F\_\{k\}, L)$ where:

S is a countable set of states; $F\_\{i\} \subset S \times S$ is a relation on S giving the transitions over a possible future i ; L is an assignment of true atomic propositions in each state.

Let $F = F\_\{1\} \cup F\_\{2\} ... \cup F\_\{k\}$ and$\forall$ s in S, $\exists$ s' in S (s, s') in F .

A trace is an infinite sequence of states $(s\_\{0\}, s\_\{1\}, s\_\{2\}, ...)$in $S\char94 w$ where $\forall$ $i(s\_\{i\}, s\_\{i+1\})$ in F .

To any structure M and state s *in* S of M there corresponds a tree of possible future states with root labelled $s\_\{0\}$ such that $s \rightarrow s\_\{i\}$ is a branch in the tree iff *(s, s_{i})* *in F.*

$M, s\_\{0\} \vDash f$ denotes that formula f is true in state $s\_\{0\ \}$ of future tree M. The M is omitted if it is understood by the preceding context.

The $\vDash$ relation can be defined inductively:

$s\_\{0\} \vDash p$ iff p *in* $L(s\_\{0\})$;

$s\_\{0\} \vDash \neg f$ iff not *(s_{0} $\vDash$ f)* ;

$s\_\{0\} \vDash f\_\{1\} \wedge f\_\{2\}$ iff $s\_\{0\} \vDash f\_\{1\}$ and $s\_\{0\} \vDash f\_\{2\}$;

$s\_\{0\} \vDash EX F\_\{k\}f$ iff $\exists \, s\_\{1\}$ *in* $S(s\_\{0\}, s\_\{1\})$ *in* $F\_\{k\} \wedge s\_\{1\} \vDash f$;

$s\_\{0\} \vDash A[f\_\{1\}U f\_\{2\}]$ iff for all traces
$\exists \, i \, [i \geq 0 \wedge s\_\{i\} \vDash f\_\{2\} \wedge \forall \, j(0 \leq j \wedge j < i \wedge s\_\{j\} \vDash f\_\{1\})]$;

$s\_\{0\} \vDash E[f\_\{1\}Uf\_\{2\}]$ iff for some trace
$\exists \, i \, [i \geq 0 \wedge s\_\{i\} \vDash f\_\{2\} \wedge \forall \, j(0 \leq j \wedge j < i \wedge s\_\{j\} \vDash f\_\{1\})]$;

$f\_\{1\} \vee f\_\{2\} \equiv \neg \, (\neg f\_\{1\} \wedge \neg f\_\{2\})$;

$f\_\{1\} \Rightarrow f\_\{2\} \equiv \neg f\_\{1\} \vee f\_\{2\}$;

$EFf\_\{1\} \equiv E[true \; U f\_\{1\}]$, in some trace there exists a state where $f\_\{1\}$ is true;

$AGf\_\{1\} \equiv \neg \, EF \neg f\_\{1\}$ states that $f\_\{1\}$ is true for all states in all traces;

$AXf \equiv \neg \, EX \neg f\_\{1\}$ states that $f\_\{1\}$ holds in all next states.

Chapter 14:
From Formal Models to Empirical Evaluation and Back Again

1. Introduction

In this chapter we will describe the results of a study to explore how formal modelling and empirical methods can be linked to provide a complementary approach to design and usability evaluation.

Formal and empirical methods are often seen as alternative and competing approaches to design. This stems from the fact that the approaches are grounded in different disciplines which lead to quite different design philosophies. Within software engineering there is a predisposition to abstraction and top-down design. From the human sciences community there is a predisposition towards prototyping and iterative design.

The value of formal methods is often argued to be control of complexity through abstraction and correctness through formal proof. Formal approaches to interaction modelling may concern themselves with the identification and specification of abstract system properties deemed to have an impact on usability. Issues of consistency can be clearly articulated and proved.

The value of empirical methods is often argued to be the analysis of context of use in all their richness. In this sense empirical evaluation can be regarded as concerned with implementation level usability problems, but this an over-simplification. (Harrison, Roast & Wright 89) produced a formal model of a menu-driven database system. Using the model, they were able to specify an abstract property which they termed a *dialogue cycle*. The model revealed that for certain contexts of use, the database was inconsistent with respect to the cycle property. What was interesting about this study was that subsequent empirical evaluation with users was able to identify which of the inconsistent contexts led to usability problems and which did not. The empirical evaluation also revealed a number of 'implementation-level' usability problems that would not have been captured in any abstract model. But this was considered to be an 'added bonus' and not the central purpose of adding an empirical evaluation component

Harrison et al. viewed the relation between empirical and formal methods as one of hypothesis testing, or claims analysis. This view merits some further consideration. This analogy with scientific method suggests that a formal model serves to articulate a claim about what properties or behaviours of the system lead to improved usability and the empirical analysis functions as an experiment to test the claim. This implies that the empirical evidence can, in some cases, refute the formal model, which is clearly not the case. The model is a model of system properties or behaviour. The empirical data concerns user performance or user perceptions. What the data may do is highlight limitations of the model by identifying other aspects of system behaviour that impact usability, but it does not refute the model.

In this chapter we view the relation between formal model and empirical data in a much more constructive way. We offer a cyclical process of design-by-evaluation where the empirical and formal play complementary roles as means of identifying and expressing usability requirements at both abstract and detailed design levels. The process is presented in Figure 1.

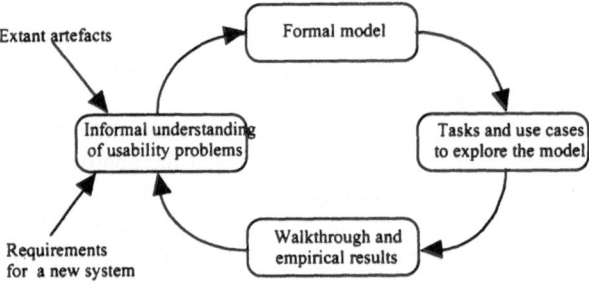

Figure 1: An iterative view of interactive system design

The process can be seen as analogous to a general inductive approach to model building from data of the sort common in human sciences. Inputs to the process might be extant artefacts, requirements for a new system or informal visions of a product. These provide the designers with an informal understanding of usability properties that might be relevant to the final product. This informal conceptual modelling by designers feeds into a formal specification of the system properties and behaviours associated with the conceptual model. The process of formal modelling helps refine the designers' understanding of usability issues and generates, design alternatives or design questions which cannot be decided on the basis of formal modelling alone. These question and options so identified are used to generate a set of use cases or user tasks focused on the modelled properties. These can be evaluated empirically using prototypes.

The evaluation may answer the questions raised by the model and it will also generate new issues at a number of levels of abstraction. Questions raised at abstract levels can be used to fine-tune or extend the model. In some cases they may suggest new formal modelling perspectives that need to be added to those models already specified (Fields, Merriam & Dearden 97). Questions at some intermediate level of abstraction may suggest ways of making the model more concrete and closer to an implementation. Finally, implementation level questions may be accumulated for use later in detailed design. The process then iterates round further cycles of formal modelling and empirical evaluation until no more issues are generated. In this way the formal modelling guides the design of the empirical enquiry which in turn provides the basis for extending the formal model or models in ways informed by usage contexts, while abstracting away from these contexts where appropriate.

Our view of formal modelling and empirical methods is a pluralistic one. We do not espouse the view that there is one multi-purpose formal notation nor one generic approach to data collection. Rather we expect that different models and different empirical techniques will be used to highlight different aspects of design. This is not an unusual position to take in other engineering disciplines but seems more unusual in the HCI formal modelling community (see Fields et al 97 op. cit.).

In this chapter we look at one formal modelling technique, based on action systems, and two approaches to empirical data analysis. The first is the Cognitive Walkthrough (Wharton et al 94), the second Cooperative Evaluation (Monk et al 93). Our choice was one of convenience. It would go against the pluralistic spirit of our approach to address issues of which technique was best.

In this chapter we will report on the results of a study which began by formally modelling key aspects of the Netscape browser concerning history and navigation, showing how these raised a number of usability issues and design alternatives that could not be answered with the modelling framework. We will then show how the empirical work was used to answer some of these questions and extend the modelling further.

The chapter is structured as follows. After an initial, informal exploration of some of the relevant usability issues in Section 2, Section 3 describes the construction of a high-level specification of the general concept of Web browsing, and refines this model a little, by the addition of URL addresses. The modelling activity raises (but does not answer) a number of interesting usability-related questions (particularly when the modeller is faced with a number of design choices or options for modelling). The areas highlighted during the modelling activity as important are investigated in more detail using Cognitive Walkthrough in Section 5 and Cooperative Evaluation in Section 6. In Section 7 the iterative loop is closed by using the findings of the inspection and user testing to feed back into the formal modelling. The model is extended to cover some of the areas that the empirical evaluation showed to be problematic, attempting to throw some light on why this might have been the case, and what a designer might do about it (and in doing so, raising more issues that could be addressed by inspections or empirical observation). Finally, Section 8 makes some concluding remarks and comments on the effectiveness of the three approaches and their integration.

2. An Informal Understanding Of Usability Issues

To begin our look at some of the possible usability pitfalls that might be encountered by a user of the world wide Web, interacting with a browser such as Netscape, we initially document our informal understanding of where the problems might be. The case study that runs throughout this book (see Chapter 2 for a description) has a number of facets: servers and clients, browsing and navigating the Web, concurrency, history mechanisms, managing bookmarks, and so on. In fact the space of Web-related tasks is much larger than this, encompassing authorship and design of Web pages, finding information using search engines, setting preferences in the browser, submitting and sending information using forms, and so on.

In what follows, rather than making an attempt to formalise everything that can easily be formalised and ignoring the rest, we focus our attention on only a few aspects of the problem. The decision about what to formalise and evaluate is based on an informal notion of where in the human-machine system the sources of usability problems might lie, together with our "gut feelings" (as frequent users of Netscape Navigator and the World Wide Web) about the sorts of interactions that are likely to cause problems. This means that some features of Netscape-like browsers are not considered at all (an example is altering the preferences setup), on the grounds that they are either not problematic, or that they do not routinely form a part of typical users' activity.

We are therefore going to concentrate our efforts on browsing and "surfing the Web". Navigation and finding one's way around the Web is highlighted as one collection of tasks where usability problems might emerge from the interaction of the properties of the browser and the browsed pages. In the next section we begin to construct a formal model of some parts of the Web and Web browsing tools that are relevant for navigation.

3. A Formal Model

The next step is to construct a formal model of the essential characteristics of the kind of system that we are considering. This is in common with traditional formal approaches to software engineering, where a model is used to capture the high-level functional requirements for a new system. It also allows us to describe what the business of interacting with the World Wide Web is about independently of any particular implementation of browsing by programs such as Netscape or Mosaic.

Before describing the formal model and introducing the particular formal notation that was chosen, a few introductory remarks are appropriate in order to situate this modelling work in the context of other formal approaches to human-computer interaction. Many of the other chapters in this volume introduce or apply formal notations, so why have we not used one of these? The purpose of this chapter is not to advocate the use of a particular notation or style of specification, but instead to explore the potential for integrating formal modelling of interactive systems *in general* with less formal analysis techniques.

The notation we have chosen is based on Action Systems, and was picked for several reasons which seem to make it a good *exemplar* of formal approaches (if not necessarily a good formal approach!). Firstly, it has a well understood and uncontroversial semantics and theory of refinement (e.g. Back & Sere 94). Secondly, it is relatively neutral in the assumptions it makes about interaction (for example, although the style of specification seems to be very state-based, a correspondence has been established between this kind of specification and the CSP process algebra (Morgan 90). Thirdly, the formalism has previously been applied to interactive systems to look at refinement of interface specifications and formal ways of recording design rationale (Bramwell et al 95, Bramwell 95).

The purpose of the initial formal model (Section 3.1) is to describe, as abstractly as possible, the kinds of features one might expect a networked hypertext system to have, with a particular emphasis on navigation type functions. The abstract specification consists of a definition of the state of a hypertext network and some operations on the state. An interesting observation is that some of the operations cannot be specified abstractly, without making a commitment to a particular design option. Instead, various options for designing these functions can be presented. The notation used is based on Action Systems and has been applied to interactive systems elsewhere (Bramwell et al 95, Bramwell 95). A summary is given in Appendix A.

A second layer of formal description (Section 3.2) is given to show how the process of refinement allows us to make progress from high-level requirements towards actual designs. In this case, refinement proceeds by the addition of a more realistic and implementation-oriented way of accessing Web pages, and along the way, raises some additional usability questions

3.1 An Abstract Model

In the abstract specification, a hypertext network is modelled as a graph whose nodes are of the type *Page* and whose arcs are labelled with elements of type *Link*.[10] This is represented in our specification as the state variable *links*. The user's exploration of this network is represented by a sequence of already-explored pages, *history*, and an index into this sequence, *current*. These three variables together represent the state of the *Hypertext* interactor. Note that at this stage, we make no distinction between what is in the browser and what is a part of the World Wide Web.

In addition to the state variables in the **variables** section, the interactor specification has a **pres** section stating which properties of the state variables are "presented" to the user (see (Duke & Harrison 94) for a more comprehensive account of how the presentation in the interface of state information can be specified). An **invariant** section where invariant properties of the state are defined, and a number of **action** specifications describe the effects that user actions have on the state variables.

The special *init* action initialises the interactor so that the constant homepage is the first page to be viewed. The interactor specification includes the definitions of four other state-changing actions: *goto*, *follow*, *back* and *forward* for jumping to pages, following links from the current page, and moving backwards and forwards in the history respectively. The latter two are fairly simple and are completely specified, but the former two are more complex. The development of the model so far has been fairly straightforward, but in completing the specification of the goto and follow actions (i.e., filling in the "...."), the way forward is less clear as several possible options seem equally sensible.

---

[10]Note that this is a simplified view of the World Wide Web, where the only entities are pages. In reality many types of file may be available on the Web, and a browser can choose to handle different file types in different ways.

The possible design options for following links and going directly to pages can be broken down into two relatively orthogonal aspects: modifying the current location pointer and modifying the history sequence.

interactor Hypertext
variables

links	: Page $\rightarrow$ (Link $\rightarrow$ Page)
current	: $\mathbb{N}$
history	: **seq** Page

pres

page	= history [current];
anchors	= **dom** links(history[current]);

invariant

$$\mathbf{ran(ran}\ links) \subseteq \mathbf{dom}\ links$$
$$\wedge \quad \mathbf{ran}\ history \subseteq \mathbf{dom}\ links$$
$$\wedge \quad history \neq \langle\ \rangle \Leftrightarrow \left(\begin{array}{c} current \in \mathbf{dom}\ history \\ \wedge\ history[current] \in \mathbf{dom}\ links \end{array} \right)$$

action init === history := $\langle \mathbf{homepage} \rangle$; current := 1
action goto? p ===

$$(p \in \mathbf{dom}\ links) \longrightarrow \begin{array}{c} current, \\ history \end{array} : \left[\begin{array}{c} history[current] = p \\ \dots \end{array} \right]$$

action follow? l ===

$$(l \in \mathbf{dom}\ links(history[current])) \longrightarrow goto(links(history[current])(l)))$$

action back ===

$$(current > 1) \longrightarrow current : \left[current = current_0 - 1 \right]$$

action forward ===

$$(current < \#\ history) \longrightarrow current : \left[current = current_0 + 1 \right]$$

3.1.1   Updating the current location

There are two possible ways of defining how the *current* value should be updated (as a result of moving to a new page as part of a *goto* action): either the *current* value is incremented (c1) or *current* is set to point to the end of the old history sequence (c2):

$$c1 === current : \left[current = current_0 + 1 \right]$$
$$c2 === current : \left[current = \#\ history_0 + 1 \right]$$

3.1.2   Updating the history sequence

There are three possibilities for updating the history: the new page can simply be added to the end of the history (h1), the new page is appended to the history with any history after the current page discarded (h2), and the new page may be inserted into the history at the *current* point.

$$h1 ? p === history: \left[history = history_0 \text{^} \langle p \rangle \right]$$

$$h2 ? p === history: \left[history = history_0 [1..current_0] \text{^} \langle p \rangle \right]$$

$$h3 ? p === history: \left[\begin{array}{l} history = history_0 [1..current_0] \text{^} \langle p \rangle \text{^} \\ history_0 [current_0 + 1.. \# history_0] \end{array} \right]$$

This third option might, at first sight, appear a little bizarre as the order of items in the history sequence no longer bears any relationship to the temporal order in which pages were visited. However it does preserve some useful properties: *back* and *forward* behave in a sensible manner, and following links does not result in history items being discarded.

3.1.3 Combining options

A complete specification of the effect the *goto* and *follow* actions have on the *current* and *history* state variables can be gained by combining two of the partial actions, one from each set. In order to select which of the six possible combinations of options for updating the current and history variables, (Bramwell et al 95) suggest that we formalise a number of properties that will help in making a choice. Two such apparently desirable properties are that the history mechanism does not "lose" information and that the back and forward actions behave in an "intuitive" way.

The first property, that pages are not lost from the history, can be defined by saying that any sequence of actions, or "programme" P can be "undone" by a sequence Q consisting only of back and forward actions (a BFProg).

$$\forall P:Prog \quad \bullet \quad \exists Q:BFProg \quad \bullet \quad init;P;Q \equiv_{page} init;Skip \qquad (1)$$

where Prog and BFProg are arbitrary action sequences and sequences of back and forward actions respectively. The equivalence says that two programs are equivalent with respect to the subscripted variables (in other words, the programs are indistinguishable in terms of the effect they have on the subscripted variables). This relationship can be defined more formally by saying that programs P and Q acting on an interactor with a set of internal and presentation variables v are equivalent with respect to a set of variables s, if and only of they are equivalent with variables (v - s) "hidden" as local variables inside a new programme block:

$$P \equiv_s Q \quad \Leftrightarrow \quad \left| var(v - s) \bullet P \right\| \equiv \left| var(v - s) \bullet Q \right|$$

The second property is that the back and forward actions operate in an intuitive way (or in other words that they conform to an intuitive requirement about what "back" and "forward" functions should do). This requirement is captured by the following two properties, which state that the effect of a goto action is "undone" by carrying out a back action, and that the effect of such a back action is "undone" by a forward.

$$\forall P:Prog, \ p:Page \quad \bullet \quad init; P; goto \ p; back \ \equiv_{page} \ init; P; [p \in dom \ links] \qquad (2)$$

$$\forall P:Prog \quad \bullet \quad init; P; back; forward \equiv_{page} init; P; [current > 1] \qquad (3)$$

The assertions shown in curly brackets on the left are to ensure that both sides exhibit the same behaviour when actions are disabled (e.g., attempting to invoke back when the history is empty).

The combined behaviours, and an assessment of them against these properties, is summarised in Table 1. An example of a formal proof of one of these properties (the "intuitiveness" of back, equation 2, for the combination of **c1** and **h2**) is given in Appendix C.

	c1	**c2**
h1	Inconsistent with specification.	No history loss; behaviour of *back* not intuitive.
h2	Netscape-like behaviour; loses history information but *back* and *forward* conform strictly to sequence visited.	Inconsistent with invariant.
h3	No history loss; *back* and *forward* have intuitive interpretations.	Inconsistent with specification.

Table 1: Combining design options

Out of the six possible combinations, it can be seen that three are inconsistent with either the specifications already given for which page should be the current one after a *goto* or *follow* (c1+h1 and c2+h3) or with the invariant constraint that current must be an index into the history (c2+h2). The remaining three options are formally valid and conform to varying degrees with our intuition about how the operations should work and whether or not history information should be discarded. One of the important "usability questions" that arises at this point is:

Several possible behaviours for the history mechanism are presented. Which is easiest to use, results in less confusion for users and matches most closely the tasks being carried out?

The more general point is that the history mechanism is a design issue, and designers will need to know what users will want to do with such a mechanism and how they will employ it.

3.2 A More Concrete Model

The model around which the preceding discussion has been centred is fairly abstract, and can be refined in a number of ways. An interesting observation about the data model of *Hypertext* and the operations that go with it is the fact that the only way of identifying a page is the page itself. In some hypertext systems this is a perfectly valid assumption: the user has no means for identifying pages, and the only means of moving around the text is by following links, starting at a designated "home" page. The *Hypertext* model, however, contains a *goto* action which allows arbitrary pages to be jumped to. In the World Wide Web this type of action is supported by having a unique identifier, or URL for each page on the network, and these identifiers may be used directly by users.

We now extend the model a little by adding URLs as a set of identifiers to locate pages. The World Wide Web can then be modelled as two associations: one between pages and the URLs identifying them (*lookup*), and another between pages and the URLs of the pages to which they are linked (*links*). The *goto* action is now parameterised by the URL of the page to be jumped to. In the Netscape implementation, this corresponds to entering a URL address into the "Location:" field, or using the "Open Location..." dialogue that can be selected from the "File" menu.

interactor Web
variables
lookup	: URL $\nrightarrow$ Page
links	: Page $\rightarrow$ (Link $\nrightarrow$ URL)
current	: N_1
history	: **seq** Page

pres
page	= history[current];
anchors	= **dom** links (history [current]);

action init === history := $\langle$**homepage**$\rangle$; current := 1
action goto? u ===

$$\begin{matrix} \text{current} \\ \text{history} \end{matrix} : \left[\text{u} \in \textbf{dom lookup}, \quad \begin{matrix} \text{history[current]} = \text{lookup(u)} \\ .... \end{matrix} \right]$$

action follow? l ===

$\quad (l \in \textbf{dom} \, \text{links}(\text{history[current]})) \longmapsto \text{goto}(\text{links}(\text{history[current]})(l)))$

The *back* and *forward* actions are just the same as in the *Hypertext* specification and are therefore not repeated. Additionally, all the same choices exist for how the *history* and *current* variables are updated in moving to pages and following links.

3.2.1 Following links

The fact that *links* is a total function means that every page in the range of *lookup* is one for which we can extract the URL links using *links*. It would also be tempting to assert that for every URL in *links*, we can find its corresponding page using *lookup*:

$$\left(\textbf{dom} \cup \textbf{ran} \, \text{links}\right) \subseteq \textbf{dom} \, \text{lookup}$$

It would be very convenient if this were true, since it would mean that any attempt to follow a link or to jump to a page specified by a URL would be certain to succeed. However, this property is not observed by the World Wide Web, due, largely, to its distributed and multi-authored nature. Two reasons why this property might fail to be true are that the page doesn't exist (e.g., the file containing it has been deleted) or that the underlying network is unable to deliver it (in an acceptable period of time). Two "usability issues" that arise from this analysis are:

> *Will users assume the network is an ideal one, like the* Hypertext *interactor, or one prone to failure, as specified in the* Web *interactor?*

> *Will they understand the reasons why an attempt to fo' ~~ a link fails and what to do about it?*

3.2.2 Jumping to pages

The introduction of URLs as a means of identifying pages in the Web has served to make our specification of the *goto* action more realistic: instead of describing the page itself, the user must provide the URL of the page to be jumped to. However, this raises the interesting question of how the user is able to do this. Typically, the user will have in mind some information, and will attempt to view a page containing that information (presumably working under the assumption that the page also contains some related information, not already known to the user). The functions *urls* and *contains* are intended to capture this relationship.

Urls   : Info $\rightarrow$ URL
contains   : (Info $\times$ Page) $\rightarrow$ **B**

The condition for *Urls* to be useful is that any URL discovered from it does indeed refer to a page containing the given information:

$\forall$ i : Info $\bullet$ lookup(urls(i)) contains i

For the information finding process to work effectively, the user must have "access" to the *Urls'* mapping and be able to apply it. Looking at the way in which users actually carry out Web accesses, it becomes clear that there are numerous ways in which *Urls* is implemented by the user, browser-based aids (such as Netscape's bookmarks, or search engines), other artefacts (magazines, newspapers, Email) and rules and conventions of the social system in which the Web is used. The relevant usability issue can be summarised as:

> *How do users identify the URLs of the pages they wish to find? Are there parts of the system or other artifacts that serve as resources to help doing this?*

3.2.3 Formal modelling summary

The formal analysis has highlighted some issues that might be important when considering the design of Web browsers and the Web sites that they provide access to. The issues raised can be broadly categorised into two groups:

- History management and "forward/back" mechanisms.
- Finding one's way around the Web.

It is perhaps unsurprising that these issues are raised, since the formal model does not cover many other aspects of World Wide Web browser usage. However, it is reassuring that the areas that intuitively seem problematic, proved to be a fertile ground for raising questions using formal modelling.

In a pilot study, (Lightner et al 96) found that searching for specific information and locating sites rated high in people's lists of dislikes and difficulties in using the Web. The models suggest that a number of design options may be possible, but provide little help in determining how serious the problems are or which design options are likely to be advantageous. In order to make progress in this area, we turn now to a less formal way of looking at usability.

4. Selecting Tasks and Use Cases

Before conducting any analysis of where usability problems might lie, we can attempt to find a set of tasks that will help, given the understanding developed so far, to probe for possible usability problems. Tasks and usage situations were selected which would allow some of the usability issues raised during the modelling exercise to be explored when users carry out the tasks.

A number of questions have been posed, and the tasks are to answer the questions using information available on the Internet. The questions themselves were part of a Web page, which is the starting point for the tasks. This page also included space for the answer to be entered and gives hints about where on the Web the relevant information may be found. An example question is shown in Figure 2.

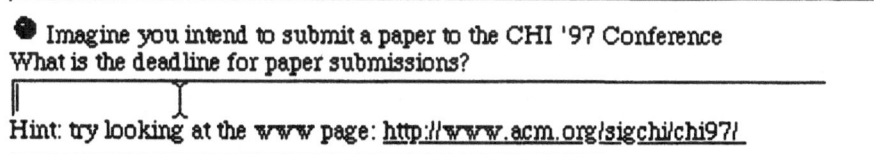

Figure 2: Example question

Even though many of the questions used refer to "real" items of information, it is perhaps inevitable that posing questions of this kind leads to a somewhat artificial set of tasks. However, in order to answer the questions, a number of elements are present (using menus and history, specifying URLs, copying and pasting, interacting with windows), all of which come together in the kinds of real activities that users engage in outside of the usability evaluation set-up. Another feature of the tasks used here that makes them more realistic, is that there are typically many ways of achieving any goal. This fact seems to be an intrinsic feature of the World Wide Web: Web pages are interconnected in many ways; URLs can often be specified by different means; users are provided with a number of "navigation aids" (links, bookmarks, history) to help them get around the Web.

5. Usability Inspection

The formal models above suggested that potential problem areas are in the design of a history mechanism, and in general navigation and page finding. The first of our less formal approaches is to use the Cognitive Walkthrough (Lewis & Rieman 93, Wharton et al. 94) inspection technique that helps designers to find possible usability problems in their designs.

In order to apply the technique, the system itself must be defined to a reasonable level of detail, and may even exist as a prototype or complete system. The intended users and their level of expertise must be known, along with the tasks that they will be carrying out. The analysis, performed by a designer or evaluator, without users present, gives a procedure for envisaging a person's thoughts as they carry out a task using the system, and the problems they might have.

5.1 The Cognitive Walkthrough Process

The Cognitive Walkthrough technique described in (Lewis & Rieman 93, Wharton et al. 94) is a way of inspecting a design to uncover the potential for usability problems. The inputs to the analysis are a description of the design, a set of tasks described in terms of the sequences of actions a user will perform, and an idea of the level of skill and expertise of the expected users.

For each step in a sample task, the evaluators attempt to construct a plausible account of why a user would be able to carry out the step correctly. This involves trying to think of convincing stories about why the users would or would not be able to carry out the step correctly. In doing so, the evaluators try to answer the following questions for each action in the task:

1. Will users be trying to produce whatever effect the action has?
2. Will the users see the control (button, menu, switch, etc.) for the action?
3. Once users find the control, will they recognise that it produces the effect they want?
4. After the action is taken, will users understand the feedback they get so they can go on to the next action with confidence?

5.2 The Analysis

In the analysis, it was assumed that the person carrying out the tasks has a reasonable familiarity with the World Wide Web and the concepts of hypertext in general. A familiarity with the particular browser (e.g., Netscape) that they're using and (as far as is necessary) with the computer platform on which it is running is also assumed. However, they have not previously seen the particular Web sites that the sample tasks will lead them to visit.

5.2.1 Tasks

1	Click hint URL	follow("http://www......./chi97/")
2	Click "The Call"	follow("The Call")
3	Scroll and search for info	
4	Click on the link for "Papers"	follow("Papers")
5	Select text "20 September 1996"	
6	Use "back" return to questionnaire page	back; back; back
7	Select answer space on questionnaire page	
8	Paste text	

Table 2: Action sequence

For each question in the problem task, a sequence of actions was determined that accomplishes the task. The action sequence is, of course, *sufficient* to achieve the goal of answering the question. More importantly, however, it was judged to provide scope for probing some of the usability issues raised earlier (for example, it involves navigation and use of the history). The action sequence for the above task is shown in Table 2, which gives a description of the actions as they would be carried out in a browser like Netscape, as well as the corresponding action (where one exists) in the model of Section 3.

5.2.2 Results

What kinds of answers do we get from the Cognitive Walkthrough inspection? In carrying out the inspection, stories are constructed about why it is plausible to believe that the user will correctly carry out the given sequence of actions. For example, the justification that the first action in the above task will correctly be carried out was:

> The user is advised in the question to "try looking at the www page", Their knowledge of colour coding conventions (assuming a user with some experience of Netscape) suggests that the address text ("http://www.acm.org/sigchi/chi97/") is a clickable link, and the text surrounding the link indicates this is probably the right thing to do. On clicking the link, they immediately move to a clearly titled page, suggesting that they did, indeed, take the right course of action.

Constructing believable stories in which the user was able to perform actions correctly was relatively simple for many of the actions, implying that the steps could be carried out unproblematically. Step 5 (selecting the text which will be the answer), however, revealed one or two interesting points.

> The user sees the text stating that the submission deadline is 20 September 1996 and, assuming they remember what the question is, will recognise that this test is the answer. While an expert user will be familiar with copy and paste facilities, they may not realise that it is appropriate in this context. Furthermore, there is no indication that selecting text is possible. Once a selection has been made, there is no feedback to indicate that it has been copied to the browser's internal buffer, ready for pasting, not, at a later stage, is there any indication of what it was that was selected.

These two fragments, and the rest of the walkthrough demonstrate how a user's ability to correctly carry out the task is dependent on them making use of a large amount of background knowledge. The knowledge required covers a wide range of aspects of the task, including a low-level understanding of how the interface works (e.g., for the copy and paste machinery), task-specific knowledge (e.g., remembering what the question was), and "domain" knowledge (in this case, an understanding of conferences that allows links with labels like "The Call" to be identified as being relevant).

5.3 Usability Inspection Summary

Cognitive Walkthrough seems to work quite well in encouraging designers to think about how well the interface affords individual actions. Its appropriateness seems to be highly contingent on finding use cases to explore particular usability questions, and the ability to write down the actions that constitute a task (as in Table 2). For some tasks, this is certainly valid — the example of altering printing options, given in (Lewis & Rieman 93) is a case where there is really only one way of accomplishing the task, and the walkthrough gives the designer a powerful way of thinking about whether the user will spot it. On the other hand, (May & Barnard 95) report on a study in which Cognitive Walkthrough was compared with other similar methods, such as heuristic evaluation, and claim that the performance of Cognitive Walkthrough is relatively poor, especially given the effort and expertise required.

In the Cognitive Walkthrough analysis, the usability of an interface is judged with respect to the specified task sequence or "plan". It could be argued that the plan itself, or for that matter, the concept of a plan isn't called into question by the analysis. For some types of interaction, this might not be significant, but in situations like Web browsing, where the user has a great deal of freedom to organise the activity, assessing with respect to a pre-determined sequence may be too restrictive. This point is made by Franzke (Franzke 95) who uses a model of exploratory learning, supported by empirical findings, to refine the Cognitive Walkthrough procedure.

In the terminology of Wright et al. (Wright et al. 96), underlying the Cognitive Walkthrough there seems to be an assumption that the user is following a *plan*, albeit *external* and possibly *implicit* one. On this basis, (Fields, Wright & Harrison 97) suggest a framework in which a broader perspective may be considered, allowing alternative cognitive perspectives and strategies for organising work. In the next section, however, we consider observations of users carrying out the tasks, in a way which is not strongly biased towards any particular cognitive standpoint.

6. User Testing

The third approach that we used to try to understand the usability issues was to observe real users performing tasks. The particular technique employed was Cooperative Evaluation, described in (Monk et al. 93). In principle it "sets down procedures by which a designer can work with the sort of people who will ultimately use the software in their daily work, so that they can identify potential problems and their solutions." One of the key advantages of Cooperative Evaluation is that it requires very modest training and can be used by designers with little human-factors expertise. In our study, only one of us had performed Cooperative Evaluation before and the others had no formal human-factors training.

6.1 The Cooperative Evaluation Process

Briefly, Cooperative Evaluation involves a number of users, each of which performs some tasks during a session in the presence of an evaluator. When working on the tasks, the user is encouraged to ask questions about the interaction with the system and the evaluator asks questions about the user's understanding of the system. The user is also helped to verbalise the difficulties they encounter and their problem solving strategies. The procedure should seem natural to the user. The sessions are recorded in one or more ways, typically including written notes of problems encountered and an audio or video recording. In this study, audio recordings were used. Then a summary is made of the observations. In selecting users it is important to find users who are as representative of the actual ultimate users as practical. For this study we selected Computer Science research staff. This was convenient and adequately representative of the users we had in mind. In selecting the tasks it is important to choose realistic everyday activities and to describe them in terms of work goals rather than functions of the system. Thus we asked the users to find information rather than, for example, asking them to "go back four pages". Some of the tasks were those studied using Cognitive Walkthrough and all of them had been performed at least once by the evaluators.

6.2 The Analysis

From written notes of the evaluation, certain key observations emerged. These can be classified as being: reflections on the nature of the study itself, remarks on the low-level operation of the system, remarks on the user's higher-level strategies. The comments in the last two categories are catalogued in Appendix B. One major, if unsurprising, observation relating to the whole study was that the user's success in achieving the top-level goal, answering the question, is dependent not only on effective operation of the software but also on understanding the question and knowledge of the relevant domain. Since we are principally interested in the Netscape interface, we have focused our observations on behaviour which reflects features of the interaction more than on those concerning the understanding and answering of the question.

6.2.1 Comparing Cooperative Evaluation with Cognitive Walkthrough

User 1: We can follow the progress on one of our users through the task described in Table 2, and compare the results of the Cognitive Walkthrough with the kind of information obtained from the Cooperative Evaluation. The user was presented with a Web page containing the question in Figure 2, requiring the deadline for paper submission to be retrieved from the CHI '97 Conference Web site. The following is a list describing some actions and remarks made by the user. Whilst the actions are in temporal sequence, they are not necessarily consecutive. We have annotated these with comments, particularly where the user's behaviour challenges the assumptions made in the story told by the Cognitive Walkthrough.

First, we present the annotated actions for a less experienced user of Netscape. In addition to clarifying the differences between Cooperative Evaluation and Cognitive Walkthrough it is hoped that these abridged sequences give some flavour of the Cooperative Evaluation process.

Action	Comments
To find the CHI '97 Web site, the user said, "if I didn't know [the URL] I would have done a global search" but that the hinted address was presumably the intended site. The URL in the hint was then typed (accurately) into the 'Go To:' entry box in the Navigator frame above the Web page.	The expected action listed in the Cognitive Walkthrough task sequence was to click on the URL text, which was highlighted showing that it was a hyperlink. It seems that the user's initial reaction to the question is to consider using a search engine, presumably a familiar and previously successful approach. On reading the hint, this is seen to be unnecessary but there is no immediate recognition that the text was the link to the indicated page

On finding the CHI '97 home page the user started to read the various entries on the page, searching for a clue as to the correct way to proceed. In this process a link was accidentally activated. When asked by the evaluator what they could do, the user volunteered that they could stop the loading of the unintended page and, when prompted, did this.	It was not anticipated in the Cognitive Walkthrough that the user might mistakenly activate a link. Also there is no modelling of the delay caused by loading pages and therefore no anticipation of the desire to interrupt the loading of unwanted pages.
The user noted that the picture at the top of a page was taking a long time to appear. The user said "....you've got to wait for the graphics to download." When this was queried by the evaluator, the user said, "I'm not sure ..." and described various cues they used to decide whether or not a page was still being loaded. These included the rotating Silicon Graphics logo and the line at the bottom of the window showing increasing percentages.	The user had to assess the completeness of the Web page being viewed. This concept is not described in the model and there are no considerations in the Cognitive Walkthrough of assessing and coping with the varying status of a page.
The user found and activated the links marked "The Call" and "Papers" and found the text "20 September 1996", recognising that this was the information required in order to answer the question.	This served to confirm the assumptions made in the Cognitive Walkthrough.
Having found the information needed to answer the question the user was asked how they intended to return to the question page. The reply was, "I think I might just go....back through the Netscape pages." When asked for alternatives the user suggested, "I could go through 'Previous' on the main screen." but expressed some doubt about exactly what would happen. They then expressed a correct description of the distinction between back and previous, pointing out that previous could never take them right back to the questionnaire.	The assumption that the user's experience of using back would allow them to return to the questionnaire was shown to be valid, although there was a little confusion about the function of previous.

User 2: Next we present annotated actions for a second, more experienced user of Netscape. These include actions which are part of other tasks, not just that of answering the first question.

Action	Comments
The user started by asking questions to clarify the nature of the exercise and how it was to be performed. They expressed surprise at the hint for the first question, which contained a link to an appropriate starting page for finding the required information by exploration, saying "Do you really want me to use this Web page?" When this was confirmed, the user clicked on the link.	The user was immediately aware of the link in the hint and its implication for a low effort route to obtaining the answer to the question. When questioned later the user said that they would normally expect to use a search engine to find specific information such as the answer to a question.
The user started to read the displayed page, explaining, "The first thing that I would try is to see if there are any deadline dates here." When no such information was found, the evaluator asked, "Is there anything that corresponds to this?" and the user replied hesitantly, "I don't know, try probably 'conference overview' and see..." and clicked on the conference overview link.	The user displayed a search strategy of first looking for the required information and then trying to guess which of the available links would be most likely to yield this information. They were correct in their choice.
The evaluator asked, "What was it we were looking for again? Can you remember?" The user used the Netscape 'Go' menu to return to the questionnaire form, and then used the 'Go' menu again to return to the page last visited.	It was not anticipated that the user would return to the questionnaire form page so readily. This experienced user was able to very quickly move from any page to the questionnaire form page and then to switch back and used this low cost strategy frequently rather than trying to remember information in the questions.
When the user had found the deadline date information required to answer the question, this text was selected with a mouse drag, the 'Go' menu was used to return to the questionnaire form page and the mouse middle button was used to paste the text into the appropriate part of the form.	The user was able to use the X selection mechanism as predicted by the Cognitive Walkthrough. The use of the 'Go' menu was an effective and probably superior method of returning to the questionnaire form page than the repeated use of 'Back' suggested for the Cognitive Walkthrough.

When the user found a page where they could not tell which link would take them to the required information, they said, "Well, I think this is not the document [containing the answer information] and I don't know which one of these pointers is, so what I'll probably do is try each one of those." The evaluator asked, "Where are you going to start?" and the user replied, "I'll skip the introduction because I don't think it is going to be there." This implied that they were starting from the top and working down.	The user deliberately elects a systematic trial and error strategy for finding the information in the absence of any useful indicators as to where to look. The order of exploration is driven by the physical appearance of the page, rather than being ordered by the user, but this is modified as the user postpones the exploration of unlikely links. In later questioning, the user claimed that they would use the 'Next' following strategy suggested in the Cognitive Walkthrough if they expected to read substantial parts of the document.
The user was asked about their use of the 'Go' menu in preference to 'Back'. They explained that they used 'Go' because only a single selection would be required, compared with an arbitrary number of 'Back' clicks. However, they qualified this, saying, "But if I remember that the page is just two or three pages back, I'll probably use 'Back'."	In practice, 'Back' was only used to go back one page. This experienced user prefers to use system features rather than relying on their memory of how far they need to go 'Back'.
The user activated the hint link for the Western Isles distillery question and remarked, "Right, I have been on this page." They proceeded, explaining, "Well, if I am not mistaken, I remember there is a kind of active map somewhere in one of these links." The evaluator prompted, "You remember that from last the time that you visited?" and the user replies, "Yes and so if I could remember that I could go to the active map and ... try mainland ... maybe a list of the distilleries or something like that." The user then explored several links, failing to find the active map of Scotland.	The user preferred to use known information about how the information can be obtained rather than reading the current page and trying to find a link which would progress them directly toward the overall goal. The Cognitive Walkthrough cannot, of course, take account of the particular expertise of a particular user.
After a while the evaluator asked, "So did you get anywhere finding that map?" and the user replies, "No and I'm trying to see which of these pointers should I go. Maybe 'reference section'."	The user persisted for a while in the face of difficulty, before eventually returning to a more opportunistic strategy.

| The evaluator asked, "How about the buttons at the top? Did you see them before?", to which the subject replied, "No." | The user was unable to find the link to the remembered page because it was presented in a button bar at the top of the Web page which the user apparently did not recognise as an area to search for links. |

6.2.2 Differences between experience of users

Although we had no true novices in the Cooperative Evaluations, clear differences in behaviour can be attributed to widely differing degrees of experience. In general the less experienced user was less able to take advantage of the available information and features than anticipated in the Cognitive Walkthrough. As commented before, the more experienced user preferred to use browser features rather than relying on their memory or other cognitive functions.

This was illustrated in several different ways. The experienced user used Netscape's navigational features to return to the questionnaire rather than recall question information. When unable to see which of two links had already been explored[11], they used a 'Forward' 'Back' pair to see where they had come back from. A transcript from the Cooperative Evaluation audio recording shows how the user can articulate the history mechanism:

User 2: One of the problems I have with this is sometimes, well this is a kind of list, the 'Go' menu, it loses things, when you ... for example if I try another page here, I cannot ... there is no way to go back to your control room page very quickly.

Evaluator: Why is that? Is that a function of ...?

User 2: This is a kind of the 'Go' menu, the pointers are lists so if you are in this page and you have three pages to go forward but if you decide to take another way, another path, well, call another page, you lose all that path.

Evaluator: And that's lost forever, it's not just a question of it being further away, it's actually gone?

User 2: Yes, it's gone and well sometimes I would like to have both, and maybe by skipping from one of the branches of this tree to another branch of the tree. Suppose that this menu is not a list but a tree, so I could go from this sibling to this sibling.

The user shows a thorough understanding of the history mechanism, including the way that 'Forward' history can be lost. This information enables them to use the history and be confident that they will not lose information unintentionally.

---

[11] The user was exploring links from an image map; normal hypertext links would have changed colour if they had been followed.

However, they are able to express dissatisfaction with the system and show how it sometimes fails to meet the requirements for certain tasks.

6.3 User Testing Summary

The primary advantages of Cooperative Evaluation over the first two techniques rely on the fact that we are not reliant solely on models of the users but have actual users involved. Of course, this is also the disadvantage in terms of effort compared with the other methods. Cognitive walkthrough relies on the notion of a task and relies on being able to describe that task as a simple sequence of actions. When applying the technique, we found that it was sometimes hard to claim that one sequence of actions was better than another. The Cognitive Walkthrough, which has no reliance on such a notion of task, also illustrated the fact that the user does not need to find the "correct" or "best" sequence of actions. Some remarks especially suggest that the user considers a number of possible approaches and that trade-offs are made, for example between efficiency and familiarity. After performing the Cooperative Evaluation, it is more convenient to think of the user finding an adequate method of reaching a goal, rather than following a plan. Also the Cooperative Evaluation shows how hard it is to do a good job with the Cognitive Walkthrough: The first question, asking whether the user will attempt the correct action may be very hard to decide. It may be impossible for the evaluators to avoid making some assumptions which are unreasonable for the users. Two such assumptions were that the user was familiar with the X windows model of overlapping windows and that the user was familiar with the workstation's three-button mouse. These assumptions only proved to be true for the more experienced user.

At another level, the appropriateness of the tasks was challenged by one user, who doubted that they represented typical uses of the World Wide Web. The user pointed out that they rarely used Netscape to retrieve such specific information; more often they would be searching for information on a topic and be collecting a variety of different pieces of information. They said that furthermore, when they *were* looking for such specific information, they would use a search engine which would hopefully provide a link directly to the right page without the need for further navigation and exploration. One of the requirements for a good Cooperative Evaluation is that the user performs genuinely representative tasks, so this criticism might be seen as invalidating the study. However, it was the process of interaction which we particularly wanted to examine and it seemed that our artificial tasks nevertheless produced genuinely representative navigation and exploration behaviour. It was generally the case that the Cooperative Evaluation gathered more information than that directly pertinent to the usability of Netscape and this could be a disadvantage compared with the Cognitive Walkthrough but we did not feel that the information of interest to us was being obscured.

In conclusion, in Cognitive Walkthrough we are biased toward a model of cognition, whereas in Cooperative Evaluation we are free to adopt any model. While we may use the same scheme as Cognitive Walkthrough and use the results of the Cooperative Evaluation to challenge or validate the assumptions made in the Cognitive Walkthrough, we may also adopt some other scheme. Indeed we can explore different hypotheses considering how they might explain the observed behaviour.

7. Integrating with Formal Modelling

The user testing and usability inspection described above raised some questions, and lead to a number of surprises for the evaluators. While interesting, this does not immediately help in generating better designs or design features; indeed, many of the points raised in the Cooperative Evaluation are expressed in terms of the task rather than the design.

In this section, we focus on one particular set of issues that surfaced in the Cooperative Evaluation and extend the formal model of Section 3 in order to be more clear about where the problems lie and to help identify some new design concepts that might mitigate the problems.

The issue, raised by the Cooperative Evaluation, on which this section will be focused is that of the different ways of navigating around a document structure. The evaluation suggested that problems might arise when the user is provided with a number of different ways of navigating around a collection of pages, and this section presents a model that helps to understand more of the relevant issues.

One distinction between navigational features that was highlighted in the evaluation is between features like Netscape's "Back" and "Forward" functions, which allow navigation around the history of the current interaction and the "Next", "Previous", "Up" and similar buttons provided in certain pages to move around the structure of the document. Based on the physical separation between the Netscape buttons and the current page, this difference was recognised and correctly understood by one of the users while trying to return from the CHI'97 pages to the questionnaire sheet:

User 1:　　　...well that's [the previous button] the one for the programme, the one for all the pages and the Web site... I think I'd have to go click back all the way through on the major icon bar up here.

However, the precise meaning of the buttons within a page seemed to be a little more problematic:

User 1:　　　...at the top there's an up navigation button so...if you pressed up it takes you to the previous page.

but later in the same task, as a different page is being displayed

User 1:　　　...there's some command buttons previous next up...so I'm really confused now what previous and up mean don't know what the difference is there

This suggests that an understanding of how the document specific navigation schemes might be organised is worthy of further investigation. The vehicle for this investigation will be a further refinement of our formal model.

7.1 Example: Hierarchically Structured Documents

In this section, as suggested above, we extend the model to look more closely at the navigational structure provided by World Wide Web documents, rather than that provided by the browsing software. In particular, we specify a number of constraints on the structure of nodes and links that restricts us to talking about documents with a hierarchical tree structure. Rather than simply pick an arbitrary scheme for navigating a hierarchically-organised document, we consider first one that is produced as the output of an automatic translator from LaTeX translator, and secondly, a slight variation of the same theme.

7.1.1 The LaTeX2HTML translator

The LaTeX2HTML (Drakos 94) converter generates, from a LaTeX source file, a tree-structured HTML "document", i.e., a set of linked pages. The structure of the tree reflects the hierarchical structure of the document's sections and subsections and the text at each node (*Page*) is the text which would appear in the appropriate section.

We can model such tree-structured document using the following definition:

DocTree == node(Page, seq DocTree)

Each node contains a page and an index of sub-documents. For example a node corresponding to Section 1 would contain an index of links to a collection of pages containing the text and links for subsections 1.1, 1.2, ..., and so on.

Each page generated by LaTeX2HTML has one link for each of the indexed pages plus extra navigational links. These include "Next", "Up" and "Previous" buttons, as in the upper part of Figure 3.

The index links (in the lower part of Figure 3) require that a page be linked to a subpage if it is that sub-page's parent in the document tree. The up button provides an inverse to these index links. This is formally stated by the following requirement for these links to be in the networks *indexlinks* and *uplinks*, both of which are subsets of *links*.

$\forall$page, subpage: Page •

$$
\left(
\begin{array}{l}
\exists\, \text{ind}: \textbf{seq}\ \text{DocTree} \bullet \\
\quad (\text{page}, \text{ind}) \in \text{node} \land \\
\quad \left(\exists\, \text{ind}_1: \textbf{seq}\ \text{DocTree} \bullet (\text{subpage}, \text{ind}_1) \in \textbf{ran}\ \text{ind}\right)
\end{array}
\right)
$$
$\Leftrightarrow \left(\exists\, \text{indexlink}: \text{Link} \bullet (\text{page}, (\text{indexlink}, \text{subpage})) \in \text{indexlinks}\right)$
$\Leftrightarrow \left(\exists\, \text{uplink}: \text{Link} \bullet (\text{subpage}, (\text{uplink}, \text{page})) \in \text{uplinks}\right)$

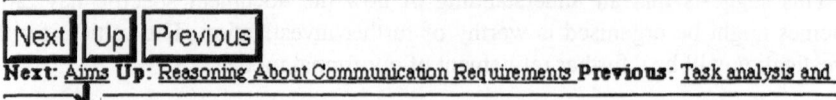

Next: Aims **Up**: Reasoning About Communication Requirements **Previous**: Task analysis and

Communication Link analysis

- Aims
- Procedure
- Data analysis

Figure 3: Navigation buttons and links in a LaTeX2HTML document

To explain the function of next and previous, we will define the notion of a thread through the document, a sequence of the document's pages in the order they would appear in the normal linear document generated by LaTeX:

$$\text{thread}: \text{DocTree} \rightarrow \textbf{seq}_1 \text{ Page}$$
$$\forall\, p:\text{Page}, \text{ind}: \textbf{seq} \text{ DocTree} \bullet$$
$$\text{thread}(\text{node}(p, \text{ind})) = \langle p \rangle^\wedge(^\wedge/(\text{thread} \circ \text{ind}))$$

In general we may use a number of *threads* instead of just a single one, so for the moment we define:

$$\text{threads} == \{\text{thread}(d)\}$$

and go on to define the next and previous links in terms of this. Note that it is not possible to define next and previous using only local information to a node in the document tree because one next link may lead to a large leap within the tree structure. For example node 4 might be the next node after note 3.3.2.

$$\forall \text{page}, \text{nextpage}:\text{Page} \bullet$$
$$(\exists s, t: \textbf{seq} \text{ Page} \bullet s^\wedge\langle\text{page}, \text{nextpage}\rangle^\wedge t \in \text{threads})$$
$$\Leftrightarrow (\exists \text{nextlink}:\text{Link} \bullet (\text{page}, (\text{nextlink}, \text{nextpage})) \in \text{nextlinks})$$
$$\Leftrightarrow (\exists \text{prevlink}:\text{Link} \bullet (\text{nextpage}, (\text{prevlink}, \text{page})) \in \text{prevlinks})$$

Of course, *nextlinks* and *prevlinks* must be subsets of *links*.

A claim that one could make about the usability of such a scheme is that, in order to use the next and previous buttons effectively, the user will have to understand both the tree structure of the document and its linearisation performed by *thread*.

7.1.2   An alternative navigation scheme

An alternative specification of next would only allow the user to move across siblings in the tree, i.e., acting as a short cut for up and then selecting the next link. The potential advantage here is that knowledge burden placed on the user, in order to understand the effect of following a next or previous link, might be alleviated. This is simply because, wherever such a link appears, it has the effect of moving to the next or previous sibling, but never allows moves up or down the hierarchy. This kind of structure can be specified quite simply by amending the definition of *threads*, so as to produce a different collection of linked items.

$$\text{threads} : \text{DocTree} \rightarrow \textbf{seq} \text{ Page}$$
$$\text{threads}\big(\text{node}\big(p, \langle (p_1, n_1), \dots, (p_k, n_k) \rangle \big)\big) =$$
$$\big\{ [p_1, \dots, p_k] \big\} \cup \text{threads}(n_1) \cup \dots \cup \text{threads}(n_k)$$

We can compare these two schemes in a more pictorial way, as in Figure 4.

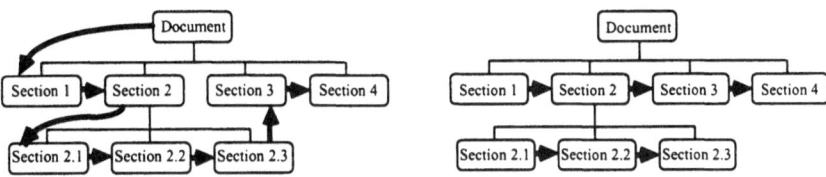

Figure 4: Alternative configurations of "next" links. The dark lines show the "next" links and lighter lines show the document hierarchy (and therefore the "up" and "index" links)

The left hand diagram illustrates the scheme employed in LaTeX2HTML: the entire document is traversable from start to finish using only the "next" links. However, in the right hand diagram, this is not the case. A possible hypothesis about usability is that the left hand system of links may lead to readers of the document being confused when the "next" links lead to a change of level in the hierarchy without them being aware of it. In order to interpret and understand a page correctly, it is often important to understand how it relates to previously read pages. This is made more difficult if a change in level occurs, such as in moving from section 2.3 to section 4. The new model now prompts the analyst to consider a further collection of usability, including:

Will the user understand the different mechanisms and distinguish between them? Do interactions between them cause problems?

How much of the structure of the document or interaction does a user have to know about in order to use the navigation mechanisms effectively or understand the context in which pages retrieved via "next" should be interpreted?

This new collection of issues and usability questions could be used either by a designer in refining the design of the system further, or iteratively in carrying out more empirical studies.

8. Conclusions

We have described an exploration of the use of formal and informal methods in an integrated process of usability evaluation. In the course of this exercise, some aspects of a Netscape-like browser and the underlying World Wide Web network were modelled formally. In constructing the model we were faced with a number of design options, and the formalism was unable to provide much help in selecting the most appropriate ones. These areas of uncertainty about specific design choices were generalised into two broad areas of concern worthy of further investigation: using the browser's history mechanism, and finding one's way around the Web. We applied two usability evaluation techniques to probe more deeply into these areas of concern. The empirical study allowed us to develop a better understanding of what the usability-related issues were, which in turn meant that the formal model could be refined further to cover a problem area in more depth.

The formal modelling activity, the usability inspection and the empirical observation raised some useful questions about Netscape and similar browsing tools, a number of which were not obvious and had not been articulated prior to the study. One could object that, as a study, this exercise was flawed, for example, because of the small number of users used. The point of the study was not, however, to draw any conclusions about Netscape, but to illustrate some of the possible consequences of attempting to use empirical observation, task-centred inspection and system modelling within the same development method.

The process underlying this study consists of both modelling and assessment, used in an iterative fashion. The modelling can be used as a way of capturing the current state of a design, and helping to generate new concepts and design suggestions and to pose questions about the effectiveness of a proposed solution. The assessment techniques can be used in attempts to find the answers to specific questions about usability, or to suggest areas where further modelling and design effort might be fruitfully directed. The models can the be enriched by focusing in on the issues raised by users and designers in the evaluation.

We began this chapter by suggesting that there was a tension between formal modelling and empirically-based approaches to the design of interactive systems. Perhaps the tension we spoke of comes about because researchers in the respective areas feel that their particular approach has some privileged status as a way of understanding usability issues. Researchers in an empirical tradition might argue that data from users is a more veridical source of knowledge about usability since usability is a contextual phenomenon. Formal modellers, in contrast, might argue that a formalisation of usability properties is more veridical since it aims to uncover more abstract, and therefore generalisable, properties, unencumbered by the details of particular contexts of use.

Implicit in the veridicality argument is the idea that there is a best way of understanding interaction and representing usability properties. (Fields, Merriam &

Dearden 97 op. cit.) have argued for a more pluralistic approach to formal modelling, suggesting that different models may be useful for different purposes. In this chapter we have taken this idea a step further by exploring a way in which formal models may be seen in a complementary relationship to empirical data. Each informed by, and informing the other. Our process model is an expression of this complementary, pluralistic approach.

Our explorations have been encouraging and we conclude that there is certainly a useful dialogue to be had between those involved in formal modelling and those concerned with user data. But such pluralistic approaches are not without their overheads. Multiple models, each highlighting different aspects of usability, have to be co-ordinated in such a way that information can be synthesised. Using multiple formal models means that a single notational framework cannot serve as the lingua-franca of the design team. Similarly, representing user data in a way which makes its connection with system models apparent, is a non-trivial methodological issue. But if these problems can be overcome there is much to be gained by a pluralistic methodology in what is, after all, an inter-disciplinary field of research.

Appendix A

The tables below describe some of the formal notation used in the paper for defining types and predicates and constructing action systems.

Types	
$\mathbb{N}$	The set of natural numbers.
$\mathbb{N}_1$	The set of natural numbers greater than zero.
$A \rightarrow B$	Total functions form type A to type B.
$A \nrightarrow B$	Partial functions form type A to type B.
$A \times B$	Cartesian product of A and B.
seq X	The type of sequences of elements of type X (including the empty sequence)

Sets	
$e \in s$	Set membership

Sequences	
$\langle \rangle$	The empty sequence.
$\langle e \rangle$	The sequence with a single element e.
ran s	The range of sequence s (i.e., the set of elements in s)
dom s	The domain of sequence s (i.e., the set of indices of s)
$s \wedge t$	The concatenation of two sequences.
# s	The number of elements in sequence s
s [n]	The nth element of a sequence s
s [m..n]	The sub-sequence of s between m and n (or vice versa if n < m): [s[min(m,n)], ..., s[max(m,n)]]

Action Systems and Refinement Calculus	
name?(args) ===guard $\longrightarrow$ body	Action definition.
vars $\lfloor$ *post* $\rfloor$	Specification statement, with "write frame" *vars* (set of variables that are altered by the statement) and a post-condition *post* (a predicate defining the state after the statement has executed).
vars [*pre, post*]	Specification statement, with write frame *vars* pre-condition *pre* (defining the conditions under which the postcondition must be satisfied), and a post-condition *post*.
P ; Q	Sequential composition.
v := expr	Assignment.
$\lfloor$var v • P$\rfloor$	A programme block with body P and local variables v.

Appendix B

As an example of the kinds of information a Cooperative Evaluation might provide, we include some of the conclusions drawn from two sessions. In the first, our user was relatively unfamiliar with the use of the Netscape browser and with the windowing system under which it was running. In the second, the user had much more expertise in using the browser and X Windows.

User 1

Low-level operation

- There was no copy and paste to transfer the answer text to the fields of the questionnaire form.
- The bookmark facility was used by the user in order to return easily to the questionnaire form page. (Note: The history list could have been used to perform the same function.)
- The difference in colour between followed and unexplored links was noted by the user and exploited in the later parts of the exercise. The fact that this pair of colours varied from one Web page to another did not seem to affect performance.
- After initially typing the hint URLs into the "Go To:" entry box, the user accidentally activated one of these links and noted that this was the intended means of navigation.
- The user was not sure of the status of a page which claimed to have been loaded completely but which showed incomplete graphics.
- The user was not sure when the page had been adequately loaded for a link to be followed. A fear was expressed that premature activation of a link would lead to

errors but where the delay was extreme the user was prepared to attempt following a link from an incomplete page.

- The user was unfamiliar with the X Window System being used and did not know how to bring windows to the fore.
- The user was unfamiliar with the multi-button mouse and activated unintended functions by using the middle button, where the left button would have given the expected behaviour.
- One particular link did not lead to another Web page but activated a dialogue box which the user found surprising and then confusing.
- Pages were opened in new windows rather than the current one by accident, perhaps because the user was not aware of the difference between the different mouse buttons.
- The user accidentally killed all windows and thus Netscape itself when attempting to kill spares.
- Downloading a file exposed the UNIX file system at an unexpected moment.
- Downloading a file lead to even more "where am I now?" orientation activity.
- There was some understanding of the differences between back, up and previous, apparently based on where the relevant button appeared in the Web page or as part of the unchanging Netscape interface display.
- It was not clear whether the user was aware of the difference between forward and following a previously followed link. (Note: the latter deletes any forward history.)

High-level strategies

- Strategy blending. The user articulated a plan which was subjected to modification as it was followed. The plan following and semantic matching strategies were being blended.
- Lots of opportunistic label following was observed in contrast to possible methodical plan following, for example the phrase "computer science" was used to match a link.
- The user was frequently required to perform "where am I now?" orientation.

User 2

Low level

- Copy and paste was used for all the answers.
- The history list was used repeatedly to travel back from a page being studied, to the questionnaire form, the first entry in the history list, and to return from there to the studied page, the last entry. This allowed the user to refresh their memory of the question.
- The difference in colour of followed and unexplored links was exploited.
- When navigating with an image map, where colour remains unchanged, the user was unable to recall which of two links had been followed and used a 'forward; back' sequence in order to discover which page they had just come 'back' from.

- The user had a policy of not using next and previous buttons on Web pages. The stated reason was that it is better to use back and forward if possible because these take advantage of the cache.
- The user volunteered an accurate and comprehensive explanation of the history mechanism. They explained the implications of this for losing forward history and described exactly how this would occur.
- The user repeatedly overlooked an image map button bar to the top of several pages (it linked to the page they were seeking). The evaluator asked, "How about the buttons at the top? Did you see them before?", to which the user replied, "No."
- The history mechanism was only ever used to move one step forward or back or to move all the way forward or back.
- The user used their own recall of what was in the history list rather than reading the titles in the history menu.
- Back was used when exploring, e.g. try a link, go back, try another page, go back, etc. Then forward was then used to undo a back: "Forward into the past rather than back to the future."
- Several times the user dragged the cursor back and forth between the adjacent 'Go' and the 'Bookmarks' buttons causing the history menu and the bookmarks menu, respectively, to appear alternately. These are both menus of links (there are no other pull-down menus of links in the interface), raising the possibility that some confusion arose. The bookmarks menu was never used.

High level

- At one site the user remarked that they had visited these pages before. They recalled a page containing a map of Scotland which would allow them to obtain information about specific distilleries, information required to answer the question. They elected to try to find this page as a strategy for accomplishing the task. In practice they failed to find this page despite considerable exploration but were eventually able to opportunistically use a link to a Western Isles map. This is another instance of strategy blending.
- Because of the user's confidence in using the history mechanism, they chose to switch to the questionnaire and back frequently rather than struggling to recall information in the question.
- The user appeared to perform atomic interactions very rapidly and without any apparent need for deliberations. In contrast, they carefully selected strategies, such as exhaustive exploration, invariably augmented by ordering, and elimination.
- Navigation techniques, such as 'forward; back' to reveal the source of a 'back' transition, seemed to be well rehearsed rather than devised "on the spot".
- When questioned, the user claimed that they only used next as part of a strategy to read through every part of a document (sub-document). They explained that forward would be useless for this task.

Appendix C

We present a proof that the "back" equation holds for the combination of **c1** and **h2**. Note that the actions in the trace are interpreted as **if** statements in a program.

$$|\text{var anchors, current, history, links} \bullet \text{init; P; goto p; back}\|$$

$\equiv$ expanding action definitions

$$
\begin{aligned}
&|\text{var anchors, current, history, links} \bullet \\
&\quad \text{init; P;}
\end{aligned}
$$

$$
p \in \textbf{dom}\,\text{links} \longrightarrow
\begin{matrix} \text{current,} \\ \text{history,} \\ \text{anchors,} \\ \text{page} \end{matrix} :
\begin{bmatrix}
\text{history[current]} = p & \text{(goto)} \\
\wedge \;\; \text{current} = \text{current}_0 + 1 & \text{(c1)} \\
\wedge \;\; \text{history} = \text{history}_0\,[1..\text{current}_0]^\wedge\langle p\rangle & \text{(h2)}
\end{bmatrix} ;
$$

$$
\text{current} > 1 \longrightarrow
\begin{matrix} \text{current,} \\ \text{anchors,} \\ \text{page} \end{matrix} :
\begin{bmatrix} \text{current} = \text{current}_0 - 1 & \text{(back)} \end{bmatrix}
$$

$\equiv$ guarded command equivalent to asserting condition in postconditions

$$
\begin{aligned}
&|\text{var anchors, current, history, links} \bullet \\
&\quad \text{init; P;}
\end{aligned}
$$

$$
\begin{matrix} \text{current, history,} \\ \text{anchors, page} \end{matrix} :
\begin{bmatrix}
p \in \textbf{dom}\,\text{links} \\
\wedge \;\; \text{history[current]} = p \\
\wedge \;\; \text{current} = \text{current}_0 + 1 \\
\wedge \;\; \text{history} = \text{history}_0\,[1..\text{current}_0]^\wedge\langle p\rangle
\end{bmatrix} ;
$$

$$
\text{current, anchors, page} :
\begin{bmatrix}
\text{current}_0 > 1 \\
\wedge \;\; \text{current} = \text{current}_0 - 1
\end{bmatrix}
$$

$\equiv$ coalesce sequential composition

$$
\begin{aligned}
&|\text{var anchors, current, history, links} \bullet \\
&\quad \text{init; P;}
\end{aligned}
$$

$$
\begin{matrix} \text{current, history,} \\ \text{anchors, page} \end{matrix} :
\begin{bmatrix}
p \in \textbf{dom}\,\text{links} \\
\wedge \;\; \text{history[current}_0 + 1] = p \\
\wedge \;\; \text{current}_0 > 0 \\
\wedge \;\; \text{current} = \text{current}_0 \\
\wedge \;\; \text{history} = \text{history}_0\,[1..\text{current}_0]^\wedge\langle p\rangle
\end{bmatrix}
$$

$\equiv$ contract frame and simplify postcondition

$$
\begin{aligned}
&|\text{var anchors, current, history, links} \bullet \\
&\quad \text{init; P;}
\end{aligned}
$$

$$
\text{history} :
\begin{bmatrix}
p \in \textbf{dom}\,\text{links} \\
\wedge \;\; \text{history} = \text{history}_0\,[1..\text{current}_0]^\wedge\langle p\rangle
\end{bmatrix}
$$

$\equiv$ history is in specification frame but is local so "forget" it and its postconditions

$$|\text{var anchors, current, history, links} \bullet \text{init; P;} [p \in \textbf{dom}\,\text{links}]\|$$

Chapter 15:
A Component-Based Approach Applied to a Netscape-Like Browser[12]

1. Introduction

A wide variety of toolkits[13] have been developed to allow user interface designers to prototype and build graphical user interfaces (GUIs) rapidly. Unfortunately it is usually difficult to verify that GUIs built with such toolkits behave as intended (in the sense that they possess certain formally expressed properties); this is of concern for safety- and security-critical applications. In this chapter we describe an approach to structuring GUI-based applications that helps address this issue and illustrate its possible use in the validation of behavioural properties. The approach that we propose can be adapted for use with most existing toolkits.

One technique often used for gaining confidence in GUI implementations is testing (Quinn, Ware & Spragens 93). However, testing on its own is usually not adequate for safety- and security-critical applications. There is always the possibility that an untested case will produce an error. In this chapter we present and illustrate through examples a complementary approach to detecting faults in GUIs. Our approach is based on specifying GUIs in a component-oriented (Nierstrasz, Gibbs & Tsichritzis 92; Rice & Seidman 94) fashion; as a hierarchy of interconnected component instances. From such descriptions we automatically derive both prototypes (implementations) for experimentation and a variety of corresponding formal models suitable for mechanical reasoning. Mechanisation is important for two reasons: not only does it increase confidence in the validations performed (Garland, Guttag & Horning 90), but it also has the potential for reducing the amortised cost of the validation effort. GUIs are not static, they evolve over time. Indeed, it is likely that a significant fraction of the total GUI development effort will be expended after

---

[12] The work described here has been supported by the Natural Sciences and Engineering Research Council of Canada (NSERC), the National Research Council of Brazil (CNPq) and Sybase Inc.

[13] We use the term toolkit to refer not only to interface libraries such as Motif (Open Software Foundation, 1991) but to tools such as Visual Basic Microsoft Corporation, 1993) and Tk/Tcl (Ousterhout, 1994) as well.

the initial implementation. If models are automatically generated, then producing new models as GUIs evolve will require little effort. If reasoning is also mechanised, then there is a chance that subsequent verifications will be able to reuse at least portions of previous ones.

In this chapter we describe a component-based approach for building graphical user interfaces and illustrate through examples how this approach can be applied to a Netscape-like browser. Our approach combines formal techniques and rapid prototyping for user interface development in which a single specification is used for constructing both implementations (prototypes) for experimentation and models for reasoning. First, we describe primitive application components and discuss how the implementations and corresponding reasoning models for these components can be obtained. Then we show how to use IL (an interconnection language) to specify the graphical user interface and describe how we can automatically generate implementations and models suitable for formal reasoning from the IL descriptions. Finally, we consider the validation of this user interface and discuss the kinds of properties that we can prove in this approach.

1.1 A Summarized Description of our Approach

Ideally we would like to derive formal models (suitable for mechanical reasoning) directly from GUI implementations. Unfortunately, the structure of most GUI implementations makes this a difficult task. Our solution (Bumbulis, Alencar, Cowan & Lucena 95, Bumbulis, Alencar, Cowan & Lucena 96) is to introduce the necessary structure as follows:

1. Devise a component-oriented formalism for describing GUIs. This consists of fashioning a set of primitive components and devising an interconnection language (IL[14]) for assembling them. The exact nature of this formalism will depend on the GUI toolkit(s) that we are interested in using.[15]
2. Construct implementations (and corresponding models) for each of the primitive components introduced in the first step. The presentation primitives will typically be specializations and aggregations of the primitives (widgets) provided by the underlying GUI toolkit(s).
3. Rather than directly implementing GUIs using the underlying toolkit(s), specify them using IL and from these descriptions generate implementations. The advantage of this approach is that we also can automatically generate models suitable for formal reasoning from the IL description.

We restrict our attention to callback-based GUI toolkits. This is not a serious limitation as most commercially available toolkits (including the Motif (OSF/Motif 91) UI toolkit) are callback-based.

Our idea is to use a component-oriented formalism, much like those proposed for structuring distributed systems (in particular Darwin (Darwin Overview 94)), for IL.

---

[14] The reader should be aware that this acronym also refers to Intensional Logic.

[15] For economic reasons, most GUIs are constructed using some toolkit (Myers, 1994).

However, in our case the components will be widgets and functions, not processes, and connections will represent bindings of functions to call sites, not FIFO communications channels. While component-oriented formalisms have long been popular for addressing reusability and ease of use concerns, their attraction for us is the prospect of being able to construct models easily for corresponding implementations. If we can model interconnection then we can construct models for composite components given models for each of their constituent components and a description of their interconnection. If we have models for each of the primitive components, then we can automatically generate a model for any implementation. While such a representation can serve as a basis for reasoning about various presentation aspects of the user interface, for example layout evaluation (Sears 93), our interest lies in reasoning about user interface behaviour.

Fashioning suitable presentation components from the widgets provided by callback-based toolkits will require little work: a wrapper that provides a new interface to the existing functionality is probably all that will be required. Using widgets as components simply involves following the convention that callbacks are restricted to calling interface functions (methods) supplied by components. Application functionality, rather than being embedded in callbacks, is now encapsulated in *application interface* components.

We will illustrate our approach using one possible choice for IL; in the remainder of this chapter we will use the name IL to denote this particular formalism. We will implement presentation components using Tk/Tcl (Ousterhout 94) toolkit widgets and model implementations as terms in *higher-order logic* (Gordon 86) as mechanised by the HOL system (Gordon & Melham 93).

Throughout this chapter we will illustrate by examples how our approach can be applied to a Netscape-like browser application. A general description of this application was provided in the introductory chapter of this book. The extensive local and wide-area networking, particularly the emergence of the World Wide Web as a publishing and distribution media and the adoption of a WIMP (windows, icons, menus, pointers) style of graphical user interfaces, are some of the reasons why this application has become so relevant. In order to be comprehensive, we will present some fragments of our model for this application in a very detailed way. Note that we deal with implementation models, which are programming-logic models of the system, and that these models are, in general, very complex.

2. Fashioning a Component-Oriented Toolkit

In this section we sketch our proposed approach to structuring GUI-based applications and indicate how the basic components of the sample application can be structured. Our approach involves devising a component-oriented formalism for describing GUIs and fashioning a set of presentation primitives for it from the presentation primitives provided by some existing (callback-based) toolkit. Rather than directly implementing GUIs using the existing toolkit, we now specify GUIs using the newly introduced formalism and generate implementations from these descriptions.

We describe IL, one possible formalism for this purpose, discuss how to fashion a set of IL presentation primitives, and demonstrate how to generate implementations from IL descriptions. We first start by discussing the run-time organisation of callback-based toolkits: not only will this motivate some of the features of IL, but it will also motivate our approach to modelling.

2.1 An Interconnection Language: IL

IL is an interconnection language, much like those proposed for structuring distributed systems (in particular Darwin (Darwin Overview 94).) However, IL components will represent widgets, not processes, and IL connections will represent the binding of procedures to call sites, not FIFO communications channels.

An IL description of a GUI consists of one or more component definitions. A component definition minimally consists of a name. For example,

```
component Button
```

defines a component named **Button**. This button can be, for instance, the one associated with the action to clear the location area that contains the actual http address.

Components act as templates from which instances are created. A unique name must be provided for each instance as it is declared. For example,

```
b:Button
```

declares a **Button** named **b**.

Each component instance makes a number of named ports available for binding. Each port has a *polarity: input* (<) or *output* (>); only ports of opposite polarity may be bound together. The ports provided by a component are specified when the component is defined. For example,

```
component Button clicked>
component  Textfield  clear<  setValue<  entered>
changed>
```

defines two components **Button** and **TextField**. **Buttons** provide an output port named **clicked** and **TextFields** provide input ports named **clear** and **setValue** as well as output ports named **entered** and **changed**. This specification describes the Clear button and the Location textfield that contains the http address. Instances **b** and **t** of these components can be declared with the **clicked** port of **b** and the **clear** port of **t** bound as follows:

```
b:Button t:TextField
   b.clicked → t.clear
```

This configuration is depicted in Figure 1. Often we will show only bound ports in such diagrams.

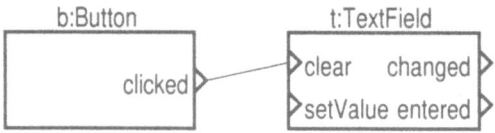

Figure 1: One-to-one binding

Figure 2: A push button

IL component definitions only determine how instances can be interconnected; they do not provide a description of instance behaviour. This must be done using other means: Sections 2.2 and 3 discuss, in some detail, the generation of implementations and models from IL descriptions, respectively. In short, we will implement component instances using widgets, with output ports corresponding to callbacks and input ports corresponding to actions.

Figure 3: A text entry field

Given this interpretation, an IL description can also be viewed as a dataflow diagram with bindings representing the flow of events between components. Events are introduced as a result of an action by the user (or environment); these events then flow from one component to another, being transformed as they go. For example, **Buttons** and **TextFields** could be used to describe the interfaces of push buttons and text entry fields, such as those shown in Figures 2 and 3. In the implementations shown, push buttons generate a (unit[16]) value at their **clicked** port when they are clicked. The appearance of a value at the **clear** port of a text entry field clears the field's value; a string appearing at the **setValue** port sets the field's value to that value. The value of a text entry field is generated at its **entered** port whenever the enter key is pressed (while it has focus) and at its **changed** port whenever its value has changed, either as a result of activity at the **clear** or **setValue** ports, or as a result of user input and subsequent loss of focus. When connected, as in Figure 1, a button push clears the value of the text entry field.

IL's binding rules allow a number of output ports to be connected to a single input port, but disallow the converse: at most one input port can be connected to an

---

[16] The unit type has only one value.

output port. One can always, however, define different output ports in a component and connect them to input ports in different components. These binding rules are a direct consequence of our desire to implement component instances using widgets, with output ports corresponding to callbacks and input ports corresponding to actions. At most one action can be registered with a callback. Furthermore, events on output ports are not supposed to have side effects on the component state.

Events can be modified as they flow through a binding with the use of functions called *filters*. For example:

```
B:Button t:TextField
b.clicked -[x => "default"] → t.setValue
```

applies a constant function (with value "**default**") to the values that flow from **b.clicked** to **t.setValue**: whenever a value x is produced at **b.clicked** the value "**default**" is presented to **t.setValue**. If a push button and a text entry field (as previously described) are connected as above then clicking the push button will result in the text entry field being set to the string "default."

The body of a filter is not restricted to constants; simple expressions can also appear. These expressions are built from constants, variables, a tuple building operator, and function applications. Only Boolean, natural number, and string constants are provided. All IL functions are unary (nullary functions can be expressed as functions on the unit type, functions of arity greater than one can be expressed as functions on tuples). IL provides no predefined functions: as with primitive components, functions must be defined using other means.

Besides ports, components can make available a number of functions called *observers* (@). Observers only provide a view of an instance's state: they are not allowed to modify it. This is the main difference between observers and ports. Further, observers can only be referenced in filters. The observers and ports provided by an instance form its interface. Observers are specified when a component is defined. For example:

```
component   TextField   clear<   setValue<   entered>
changed> value@
```

provides another definition of **TextField**; one which provides an observer named **value**. The corresponding graphical depiction is shown in Figure 4.

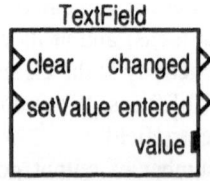

Figure 4: Observers

When queried, the **value** observer provided by a text entry field (as shown in Figure 3) returns the field's value.

2.1.1 Parameters

Parameters are used to configure and supply initial values to component instances. Parameter declarations are supplied when a component is defined. For example, the definition of a **Button** could be extended with parameters for specifying the placement and label of instances as follows:

```
component Button(x,y,label)
```

Actual parameters must be supplied during component instantiation:

```
b:Button(40,5,"Clear")
```

The other buttons in the application are also modelled in a similar way. The expressions that can be used to supply actual values are essentially those that can be used for the bodies of filters. Also allowed as parameters are component names: these will be useful for specifying the layout of the resulting user interface. We place a restriction on the use of such parameters: the relation on component instances R defined by $a R b$ iff b is a parameter of a must form a partial order. This will allow us to create instances before their reference.

2.1.2 Composite components

Composite components consist of an interconnected collection of simpler components; they provide a means of structuring IL descriptions. The definition of a composite component consists of an interface definition, just as for primitive components, along with a body consisting of a number of component instantiations and port bindings. The definition of a simple composite component is shown below: Figure 5 provides the corresponding graphical depiction.

```
component Main {
        b:Button t:TextField
        b.clicked → t.clear }
```

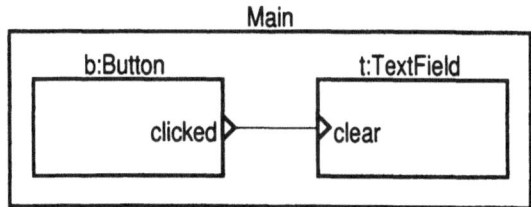

Figure 5: A composite component

An IL description of a user interface simply consists of a collection of component definitions. By convention, the user interface described is an instance of the component named **Main** (that is, the ClearField component). In this case, the above IL description models the Clear button and the Location http address textfield by instances *b* and *t* of the Button and Textfield components respectively. The interconnection between these two components is modelled by binding the output port *clicked* of the Clear button instance to the input port *clear* of the Location textfield instance.

In the same way, we can model buttons that are associated with the execution of some more complex program, like the one (GO) that returns the contents of a page (http address). Figure 6 contains the IL description of a one-button instance of a button bar. The state of the button provides a visual indication as to whether the execution has been completed or not. In this case the buttons are either enabled or disabled. Figure 7 contains a graphical depiction of Figure 6.

```
component Button enable< click>
component Launcher execute< done>

component Main {
        b: Button
        l: Launcher
        b.click → l.execute
        l.done → b.enable
}
```

Figure 6: A one-button button bar

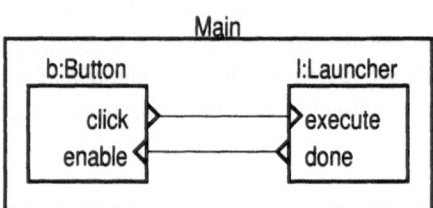

Figure 7: Graphical depiction of Figure 6

Thus, composite components and component parameterisation are essential tools to describe the structure of the application.

2.1.3 Fashioning primitives

There are two parts to the task of fashioning primitives: devising interfaces for the primitives, and implementing them using the widgets provided by some existing (callback-based) toolkit. We will defer the discussion of fashioning interfaces for primitives to Section 2.3. The task of implementing the primitives is closely related to that of generating implementations.

2.2 Generating Implementations

Implementations are required for both components and instances. We will implement instances using widgets, with output ports corresponding to callbacks and input ports and observers corresponding to actions. Components are templates for constructing instances: they will be implemented (essentially) as procedures that build and return widgets. Implementations must be provided for primitive components, they will be generated for composite components.

The details of constructing implementations will depend on the toolkits and languages that we are interested in using. In the following sections we will outline how one might generate implementations for Tk/Tcl to demonstrate the feasibility of our approach.

2.2.1 Tk/Tcl-based implementations

We first provide a brief introduction to Tk, a callback-based toolkit for building X[17]-based GUIs. A comprehensive description of Tk/Tcl can be found in (Ousterhout 94). While the architecture of the Tk toolkit is conventional, Tk differs from most other toolkits in that it is embedded in a high-level scripting language (Tcl) rather than a more conventional programming language, such as C. As a result, Tk is able to hide many of the language and resource management details that similar C-based toolkits are forced to expose.

Implementing Instances and Components. Tk/Tcl does not provide any complex data types, only strings. Rather than allocating memory for dynamically created objects we must instead create new global variables. Procedures as well as variables can be created at run time: we will take advantage of this when constructing instance implementations. We will assign each instance a unique name and use this to form the names of the variables and procedures used to implement the instance. If x is the name assigned to an instance, then an array named x will be used to hold the state of the instance and procedures with names of the form $x:y$ will be used to represent its ports (both input and output) and observers. Deciding upon a representation for values is straightforward: Tcl already provides suitable representations for Boolean, numbers and tuples (lists).[18] Instance names will be used to represent handle values. We will implement components as procedures that build instances; these procedures will take as a parameter the name to be assigned to the newly created instance.

```
component Main {
  f:Window(154, 46)
  t:TextField(f, 2, 2, 150, 20)
```

---

[17] X Window System.

[18] i.e., Tcl provides conventions for encoding these kinds of values as strings.

```
b:Button(f, 47, 24, 60, 20, "clear")
b.clicked → t.clear
}
```

Figure 8: A simple IL description

Figure 8 shows a simple IL description, a version of Figure 1 in which the presentation components have been parameterized. **TextFields** and **Buttons** now take as parameters the name of the container in which they are to be placed, the x and y co-ordinates of their top right corner (relative to the origin of the container), and their width and depth. **Buttons** have an additional parameter for specifying the text to be used in labelling the button. **Windows** are top level containers: the only parameters they provide are for specifying their width and depth.[19]

Figure 9 shows one possible implementation for **Buttons: Button:new** is a procedure that builds **Button** instances. The first two lines of **Button:new** make accessible the arrays representing the instance and the container in which it is to be placed through the local variables **n** and **p**, respectively.

```
proc Button:new {name parent x y w h label}{
upvar #0 $name n
upvar #0 $parent p
set n(button) $n(stem).$name
button $n(button) -text $label -command
                        "$name:clicked {}"
place $n(button) -in $p(widget) -x $x -y $y -width
                        $w -height $h
proc $name:clicked {value}{}
}
```

Figure 9: A Button implementation

We follow the convention that arrays representing container instances have elements named **widget** and **stem** that hold the name of the Tk widget implementing the container and a string that is to be used as a prefix for the name of any Tk widget that is to be placed in the container, respectively.[20] The next line constructs a name for the Tk **button** widget that will implement the **Button** and saves it in the element named **button**. A **button** widget is then created, and subsequently placed in the appropriate container. The final line constructs a stub for the **clicked** output port. If the **clicked** port is subsequently bound, then another procedure with the same name as the stub will be created, effectively replacing the stub.

Figure 10 shows a possible implementation for **TextFields**. It is similar in style to the **Button** implementation of Figure 2. Note that the creation of a **TextField** instance involves constructing procedures for each of the input ports and observers.

---

[19] The window manager is responsible for their placement.

[20] A Tk widget must be a descendant of the outermost container widget that contains it.

The **bind** command associates Tcl statements with events. For example, when the **entry** widget implementing the **TextField** instance loses focus, the procedure **TextField:out** will be invoked.

Generating Tk/Tcl implementations for composite components is not difficult. The generated code simply has to invoke routines to build the constituent instances and then construct procedures for any output ports that have been bound. Note that container instances must be built before any instances appearing in the container. In the case of Figure 8, the **Window** instance must be built before either the **Button** or **TextEntry** instances. The restrictions placed on component parameters in Section 2.1.1 ensure that this is always possible. Names for each of the constituent instances are formed by appending the name of the instance to the name given to the composite component. The code generated for Figure 8 is shown in Figure 11.

2.3 Fashioning Interfaces for Primitives

The idea of describing user interfaces as a static hierarchy of interconnected component instances is not new. In particular, a number of user interface construction tools and systems have been based on component-oriented visual programming languages (VPLs). These tools describe user interfaces essentially as static directed graphs: the nodes of a graph representing components and the arcs representing the flow of data between them.

```
proc TextField:new {name parent x y w h} {
upvar #0 $name n
upvar #0 $parent p
set n(entry) $p(stem).$name
entry $n(entry) -relief sunken
place $n(entry) -in $p(widget) -x $x -y $y -width $w
                                -height $h
set n(value) [$n(entry) get]
proc $name:setValue {value} "TextField:set $name
                                \$value"
proc $name:clear {value} "TextField:set $name \"\""
proc $name:value{value} "upvar #0 $name n; return
                                \$n(value)"
bind $n(entry) <FocusOut>  "TextField:Out $name"
bind $n(entry) <Key-Return>  "TextField:Out $name;
                                $name:entered {}"
proc $name:changed {value} {}
proc $name:entered {value}  {}
}

proc TextField:set {name value} {
upvar #0 $name n
$n (entry) delete 0 end
$n(entry) insert 0 $value
```

```
if {$n(value) != $value} {
set n(value) $value
$name:changed {}
}
}

proc TextField:Out {name} {
upvar #0 $name n
set value [$n(entry) get]
if {$n(value) != $value} {
set n(value) $value
$name:changed {}
}
}
```

Figure 10: A possible Textfield implementation

```
proc Main:new {name} {
Window:new $name:f 154 46
TextField:new $name:t $name:f 2 2 150 20
Button:new $name:b $name:f 47 24 60 20 "clear"
Proc $name:b:clicked {value} "$name:t:clear
                                        \$value"
}
```

Figure 11: Generated Tk/Tcl code for the example

One attraction describing user interfaces in this fashion is that user interface construction essentially consists of wiring parts together, requiring little or no programming in a conventional programming language. Such tools and systems have been made available not only by the research community (Fabrik (Ingalls 88)), but by commercial vendors as well (PARTS Workbench (Digitalk 94), Visual Age (IBM 94), Visual AppBuilder (Plain 94)).

We can take advantage of this work when fashioning primitive components: we can base their interfaces on those provided by the primitives of existing systems. If we base them on those provided by a commercially available system, we have some assurance that they will be workable in practice. While each of the above mentioned systems interprets components and connectors differently, one of the commercially available systems, PARTS Workbench, uses an interpretation similar to ours.

3. Modelling User Interface Behaviour

Formal reasoning is done in the context of some formal system. The formal system that we use is higher order logic as mechanised by the HOL system:[21] HOL terms

---

[21] In particular, HOL88 Version 2.02.

are used to model behaviour, HOL formulae are used to express properties to be validated and the HOL deductive apparatus is used for reasoning. This section expands on the first of these points, the process of modelling user interface behaviour using HOL terms.

In the proposed framework, models, as well as implementations, must be supplied for each of the primitive components; some notation must be provided for expressing these models. Our approach is to express user interface behaviour using a simple non-deterministic language, modelling components essentially as a collection of code fragments. We define the semantics of this language by defining HOL predicates corresponding to the various statements.

It is generally accepted that user interfaces are best described as *reactive systems* (Harel & Pnueli 85); what is of interest is how they interact with their environment. If we are to model user interface behaviour with programs, we must express their semantics in a way that allows reasoning about intermediate states of computation. This rules out a number of approaches commonly used for modelling programs, including state transformers (Plotkin 79), relations (Guerreiro 80) and predicate transformers (Dijkstra & Scholten 90). All of these approaches are concerned only with reasoning about input-output behaviour.

The behaviour of a reactive system is usually modelled as either a sequence of actions or a sequence of states. While it is possible to translate an action-based description into a state-based one (Wang & Abowd 94) and vice versa,[22] often one form of description is more appropriate than the other. Abowd and Dix (Abowd & Dix 94) argue, however, that for user interface modelling neither form of description is entirely satisfactory: while some user interface phenomena are more naturally modelled with actions, a state-based approach is more appropriate for others.

Our approach is to model behaviour as an alternating sequence of states and events (actions) called *runs*. This will give us the flexibility to use whichever form of description is more appropriate. We will identify programs with sets of runs, each run representing a possible computation. A variety of sequence-based approaches to modelling programs have appeared in the literature (Hoare 78, Kuiper 81, Lukkien 92, Brink 92 & Tredoux 92). They differ in the kinds of sequences used and the manner in which they are constructed. Our approach to constructing sequences is most closely related to those presented in (Lukkien 92, Tredoux 92); however, these approaches all model behaviour using state sequences.

This section proceeds as follows. After describing the language we will use and its mechanisation, we discuss how it can be used to model components.

3.1 A Simple Language

We express behaviour using a notation based on Nelson's extension (Nelson 89)[23] of Dijkstra's guarded command language (Dijkstra 76). It is best viewed as a simple, non-deterministic, programming language. Statements (programs) in the language are also referred to as *commands*. Each statement has associated with it a predicate

---

[22] These translations are usually done to take advantage of existing tools.

[23] Nelson's extension allows for partial commands and drops the law of excluded miracle.

that describes the possible states in which the statement can be activated. This predicate is referred to as the statement's *guard*. Only three primitive statements are provided: **skip** (do nothing), **abort** (loop forever), and **assign** E (when activated in state s, results in a state $E\ s$). These primitives never fail, i.e., they can be activated in any state.

The **assign** statement simultaneously updates all state variables; single variable updates are implemented by having E fix all variables but the one of interest. More complex statements can be built using a number of operators. Operational definitions of the fundamental operators are as follows: $c_1\ []\ c_2$ (activate either c_1 or c_2), $c_1\ ;\ c_2$ (activate c_1, then activate c_2), $P \rightarrow c$ (activate c if in a state where P is true and fail otherwise) **do_od** c (activate c until it fails). More conventional programming language constructs can be built from these. For example, "**if** P **then** c_1 **else** c_2" can be expressed as $(P \rightarrow c_1)\ [](\neg P \rightarrow c_2)$ and "**while** P **do** c" can be expressed as **do_od** $(P \rightarrow c)$.

To define the semantics of this notation we define what happens if a program written in this notation is executed by a machine. Executing a statement in the program causes a change to the machine's internal state. The meaning assigned to a program is the set of all state sequences (finite or infinite) that may result from the program's execution.

To handle events, we augment this notation with an operator for flagging their occurrence: **atomic** $x\ c$ flag the occurrence of event x (the command c expresses the effect of x). Our execution sequences are now state sequences interspersed with events. To simplify manipulation, we will represent these execution sequences with an alternating sequence of states and events, using a distinguished event τ for padding. We refer to these sequences as *runs*.

Rather than providing a concrete syntax for our notation we will instead identify statements with the HOL predicates that model them. The HOL pretty printer and parser will let us write statements in a relatively natural fashion. The predicates that we will use to model statements are best thought of as defining sets of runs. We will explicitly construct these sets for each of the primitive statements; the various operators for constructing more complex statements will be defined in terms of set operations. Before we can construct these definitions we first need to define runs.

3.2 Modelling Runs

A run consists of a start state followed by a (finite or infinite) sequence of actions, each action consisting of an event-state pair. The polymorphic nature of the HOL type system will allow us to define runs without any further knowledge of states or events. We represent runs in the obvious fashion: a pair whose first element holds the start state and whose second element holds the subsequent actions. The only difficulty in constructing this representation is that the HOL system,[24] as distributed, does not provide a suitable sequence type so we are forced to first construct our own.

In the following text $< s_0,\ e_0,\ s_1,...,\ e_n,\ s_n >$ and $< s_0,\ e_0,\ s_1,... >$ will denote finite and infinite runs, respectively. We define a number of functions and operations on

---

[24] HOL88 Version 2.02.

runs: **start** *e* returns the first state of the run *e*, **idle** *s* returns the run $< s >$ consisting of a single state *s*, **step** *s e s''* returns the run $< s, e, s' >$, and **diverge** *s* returns the run $< s, \tau, s, \tau,... >$. The distinguished event τ is used as a placeholder for internal (hidden) events. We say that two runs e_1 and e_2 are (composable) if the first run is finite and the initial state of the second run is identical to the final state of the first. The operator '•' is used to splice two runs together.

3.3 Commands

We can now define the semantics of commands. We model commands as sets of runs: the definitions that we will introduce make heavy use of the functions and predicates defined in the previous section. Recall from Section 3.1 that the guard of a command is a predicate that describes the possible states in which the command can be activated. If we model commands as sets of runs, each run describing a possible behaviour, then the guard of a command is just the set of all states that start some run in the command. The function **grd** maps a command to its guard:

Definition 1: $\vdash \forall cs.$ **grd** $c\ s = (\exists e.\ c\ e \wedge (\textbf{start}\ e = s))$

The semantics of the primitive statements are defined by explicitly describing the sets of runs that model them.

Theorem 1: $\vdash \textbf{skip} = (\lambda e.\ \exists s.\ e = \textbf{idle}\ s)$

Definition 2: $\vdash \forall e.\ \textbf{abort} = (\lambda e'.\ \exists s.\ e' = \textbf{diverge}\ s)$

The statement **assign** *E*, when activated in a state *s*, results in the state *E s*. We model assign *E* as the set of runs of the form $\langle s, \tau, E\ s \rangle$, for some state *s*.

Definition 3: $\vdash \forall E.\ \textbf{assign}\ E = (\lambda e.\ \exists s.\ e = \textbf{step}\ s\ \tau\ (E\ s))$

We define the semantics of the various operators by modelling as operations on sets.

Definition 4: $\vdash \forall c_1\ c_2.\ c_1\ [\!]c_2 = c_1 \vee c_2$

Definition 5: $\vdash \forall P\ c.\ P \rightarrow c = (\lambda e.\ P\ (\textbf{start}\ e) \wedge c\ e)$

Definition 6:
$\vdash \forall c_1\ c_2\ e.\ \$ \ ;\ c_1\ c_2\ e = c_1\ e \wedge \neg\ \textbf{finite}\ e$
$\vee\ (\exists e_1\ e_2.\ c_1\ e_1 \wedge c_2\ e_2 \wedge \textbf{composable}\ e_1\ e_2 \wedge (e = e_1 \bullet e_2))$

The command **do_od** *c* activates *c* until no longer possible. We define the semantics of **do_od** in parts:

Definition 7:

$\vdash (\forall c.\ \textbf{iter}\ c\ 0 = \textbf{skip}) \wedge (\forall c\ n.\ \textbf{iter}\ c\ (\textbf{SUC}\ n) = \textbf{iter}\ c\ n\ ;\ c)$

$\vdash \forall c.\ \textbf{finrep}\ c = (\exists n.\ \textbf{iter}\ c\ n\ ;\ (\neg\ (\textbf{grd}\ c) \to \textbf{skip}))$

$\vdash \forall c\ e.\ \textbf{iterw}\ c\ e = (\exists f.\ (\forall i.\ c\ (f\ i) \wedge \textbf{composable}\ (f\ i)\ (f\ (\textbf{SUC}\ i))) \wedge (e = \textbf{inf\_fjoin}\ f))$

$\vdash \forall c.\ \textbf{infrep}\ c = \textbf{iterw}\ c\ ;\ \textbf{abort}$

$\vdash \forall c.\ \textbf{do\_od}\ c = \textbf{finrep}\ c\ []\textbf{infrep}\ c$

In the above definition '∃' is just '∃' "lifted" to work on predicates: for all b, $(\exists i.\ R\ i)\ b = (\exists i.\ R\ i\ b)$. In general, a bolded logical connective denotes the corresponding Boolean connective lifted to work on predicates.

The statement **finrep** c contains all of the runs that result from a finite number of activations of c and **infrep** c contains all of the runs that result from an infinite number of activations. The use of **abort** in the definition of **finrep** is needed to handle cases such as **do_od skip**. The **atomic** operator introduces events and elides intermediate states.

Definition 8:

$\vdash \forall x\ c.\ \textbf{atomic}\ x\ c = (\lambda e.\ \exists e'.\ c\ e' \wedge (e = (\textbf{size}\ e' \prec \omega$
$\Rightarrow \textbf{step}\ (\textbf{start}\ e')\ x\ (\textbf{final}\ e') \mid \textbf{diverge}\ (\textbf{start}\ e'))))$

The command **atomic** $x\ c$ is modelled as the set of all runs of the form $\langle\ s,\ x,\ s'\ \rangle$ such that $\langle\ s,\ \ldots,\ s'\ \rangle$ is a run of the original command c together with runs of the form $\langle\ s,\ \{\tau,s\}^{\omega}\ \rangle$, one for each state s that starts an infinite run in c.

3.4 Generating Models from IL Descriptions

In this section we describe how we can generate models for the behaviour of a user interface given its IL description. The procedure that we will follow for constructing models is analogous to the one outlined for constructing implementations in Section 2.2: we first generate models for each of the composite components and then instantiate the model of a distinguished component, **Main**, to arrive at a model for the user interface. We begin this section by discussing the semantics that have been given to notations for describing user interface behaviour, and then discuss the approach that we take. Next we illustrate our approach to modelling components: recall that components are templates for building instances; similarly, our component models will serve as templates for constructing models of instances. While models are provided for the primitive components, they must be generated for the composite components from their IL description. We finish this section with a description of how this is done.

3.4.1 Modelling user interfaces

User interfaces are best described as reactive systems, what is of interest is how they interact with their environment. A wide variety of notations have been used for formally specifying user interface behaviour; good surveys of the various notations can be found in (Abowd, Bowen, Dix, Harrison & Took 89) and Harrison & Duke

94). All of these approaches treat the user interface as an entity whose state undergoes a series of transformations as a result of interactions with the environment (user.) These interactions are commonly referred to as events. In a number of these notations the state of the user interface is described as consisting of two components: an externally visible part and a local, hidden portion.

The semantics given to these notations are sequence-based, user interface behaviour being modelled as a set of sequences of some form. Both event sequences (Paternò & Mezzanotte 94) and state sequences (Systa 94, Duke & Harrison 94) have been used: the choice of representation depending on the tools available and the properties to be validated. There have also been a number of approaches based on sequences containing both states and events (Wang & Abowd 94, Abowd, Wang & Monk 95). While they provide a more natural representation (Abowd & Dix 94), there is little tool support for these approaches. Mechanical validation of models expressed in this fashion usually involves a further translation to a purely state-based description (Abowd, Wang & Monk 95). We will model user interface behaviour using sequences of alternating states and events; however, the approach we take allows us to use HOL to validate properties directly.

We model the behaviour of a user interface with a set of runs, each run describing a possible sequence of interactions with the user. Each event in a run marks the occurrence of an environment-initiated interaction such as the click of a button; the subsequent state change indicates the user interface's response. We describe user interfaces with pairs (I,c) where I is a predicate describing the initial state of the user interface and c is a command expressing its subsequent behaviour. We define the behaviour of a user interface described in this fashion to be the command $I \rightarrow$ **do_od** c. Recall that the guard operator '$\rightarrow$' restricts the states in which a command can start: $I \rightarrow$ **do_od** c consists of the runs in **do_od** c that start in I. Component instances are described in a similar fashion. Each component instance has an associated command that describes how the environment can interact with that instance. For example, commands associated with **Buttons** describe what happens when they are clicked; commands associated with **TextFields** describe what happens when they are set to a value. The command used to describe a user interface simply consists of a choice between the commands associated with the instances comprising the user interface.

If $c_1, \ldots, c_n$ are the associated commands, the behaviour of the user interface is described by the command $I \rightarrow$ **do_od** $(c_1 \, [] \ldots [] c_n)$. The commands associated with component instances will be expressed as a choice between a number of statements of the form **atomic** x c. Recall that such a statement consists of a set of runs of the form $\langle$ **start** e, x, **final** e $\rangle$, where x is an event and e is some run in c.[25] Statements of this form can be viewed as rules: a user initiated action x in a state satisfying **grd** c[26] will result in a transition to the state arrived at by executing c.

We will now illustrate this with examples. As our aim is primarily to illustrate how our approach can be applied, we will use simple examples that are easily

---

[25] Assuming that all runs in c are finite.

[26] Recall that **grd** c is just the set of all start states of runs in c. If c is expressed as $P \rightarrow c'$ for some total command c', then **grd** c is just P.

described and manipulated and that are related to the sample application. Our first example is the user interface described in Figure 12.

```
component Window(width, height)
component TextField1(parent, x, y, width, height)
                                       set< changed>
component TextField2(parent, x, y, width, height)
                                       set< changed>

component Main {
  f:Window(170, 220)
  d:TextField1(f, 5, 5, 160, 160)
  s:TextField2(f, 5, 165, 160, 60)
  s.changed → d.set
  d.changed → s.set
}
```

Figure 12: A simple IL description

In this case we have two textfields connected so that one has the same string value as the other. This situation corresponds to the fact that the textfield value related to the Location http address and the one that appears in the dialogue box related to the button GO have to be the same. To simplify matters, instead of dealing with the strings themselves that correspond to the http addresses we will deal with the values associated with these strings. The implementations of the components presented here are similar in style to the **Button** and **TextField** implementations described in Section 2.2.1. We are also assuming that **TextField1** and **TextField2** provide only layout parameters.

Before we can proceed further we must decide upon representations for values, states, and events. We are free in our choices; the definitions and theorems of the previous sections do not constrain us in any way. We will identify Booleans, numbers, strings, and tuples with values from the corresponding HOL provided type. Handle values will be represented with **VOID**, the unit value:[27] we make no use of handle values in our models. We will represent states with tuples of values, each component holding the value of a variable. In the case of the current example we will model the state of the user interface with a pair of numbers, the first representing the value of the first textfield and the second representing the value of the second one. Another choice often made is to represent states with mappings from variables to values. However, this representation has some drawbacks for our purposes: 1) a single type must be chosen a priori for representing all values, and 2) it requires reasoning about variable names. We will represent events with (essentially) pairs whose components identify the type and value of the event, respectively.

Noting that the initial value of **TextField1** and **TextField2** is the blank value (which we are assuming to be an arbitrary value), we can model the behaviour of this

---

[27] **VOID** is the only value of the **unit** type.

part of the user interface with a statement of the form $(\lambda s.\ s = (0,0)) \rightarrow$ **do_od** $(c_{\text{textfield2}}\ [\!]\ c_{\text{textfield1}})$, where $c_{\text{textfield2}}$ and $c_{\text{textfield1}}$ are statements characterising the possible behaviour resulting from a single interaction initiated by the user involving the textfield1 and the textfield2, respectively.[28] A possible expression for $c_{\text{textfield2}}$ is $\exists v.$**atomic** (**numEv** '*s*'*v*) (*sets v*), where **numEv** '*s*'*v* is an event[29] that indicates that the textfield2 has been set to the value *v* and *sets v* is a command that modifies the state to reflect this fact. Note this expression can be viewed as a shorthand for (**atomic** (**numEv** '*s*' v_1)(*sets* v_1)) [\!](**atomic** (**numEv** '*s*' v_2)(*sets* v_2)) [\!]... where the v_i enumerate the possible values to which user can set the textfield2, and the e_i denote the corresponding events.[30] A similar expression $\exists v.$**atomic**(**numEv** '*d*' *v*)(*setd v*) can be used for $c_{\text{textfield1}}$. We can express the functions *sets* and *setd* as follows:

> *sets* v = if $(\lambda(v1,\ v2).\ v1 \neq v)$ (**assign** $(\lambda(v1,\ v2)\ .\ (v,\ v2))$; setd v)
> setd v = if $(\lambda(v_1,\ v_2).\ v_2 \neq v)$ (**assign** $(\lambda(v_1,\ v_2)\ .\ (v_1,\ v))$; *sets v*)

where **if** has the following definition: **if** B c = $(\neg B \rightarrow$ **skip**) [\!] (B $\rightarrow$ c). The meaning of sets v can be stated as "if the value of the textfield2 is not equal to v then set its value to v and then execute '*setd v*'; otherwise, do nothing.[31] " The command sets v has a similar interpretation. Note that the resulting model is just the set of all runs of the form:

$$\langle\ (0,0),\ (n_1,v_1),\ (v_1,v_1),\ (n_2,v_2),\ (v_2,v_2),\ ...\ \rangle$$

where each n_i is either '*s*' or '*d*' and each v_i is some number.

3.4.2 Modelling components

We need to devise a way of modelling components such that 1) we can automatically construct models for composite components from their IL description (i.e., given models for each of the constituent components and a description of how they are interconnected) and 2) we can easily construct a command expressing user interface behaviour, such as described in the previous section, from such models. Our solution is to model each component C with a predicate **C**. The predicate **C** will take a number of parameters, including one for each parameter, port and observer provided by the component. In particular, if C has interface:

```
component C(p1,...,pm)x1... xn
```

---

[28] Recall that in HOL predicates are simply Boolean-valued functions.

[29] The function **numEv** takes a string (identifying the type of event) and a number and produces an event.

[30] Recall that '∃' is just '∃' "lifted" to work on predicates: for all b, $(\exists i.\ Ri)\ b = (\exists i.\ R\ i\ b)$.

[31] Recall that **assign** takes a function that updates the state as a parameter; for example, **assign** $(\lambda(v_1,\ v_2).(v,\ v_2))$ sets the value of the first component to v.

(each x_i being of the form 'x_i*<', 'x_i*>' or 'x_i*@') then the predicate modelling **C** will be of the form:

C i c s q e p1... pm x1*... xn* .

Ignoring all but the first two parameters for the moment, **C** is defined so that **C** *i* *c* will be true iff *i* and *c* specify the initial state and subsequent behaviour of instances of that component, respectively. Given such a predicate for the component **Main**, we can easily construct a command that expresses user interface behaviour. For example, many of the theorems of interest will be of the form:

$$\vdash \forall i\ c.\ \text{Main}\ i\ c \Rightarrow P\ ((\lambda s.\ s = i) \rightarrow \text{do\_od}\ c)$$

for some predicate **P**. Such a theorem states that if *i* and *c* describe the initial state and subsequent behaviour of the user interface described by **Main**, then $(\lambda s.\ s = i) \rightarrow$ **do_od** *c* possesses the property *P*, i.e., *P* is a property of the user interface described by **Main**.

We will express the predicates representing components essentially as a set of code fragments: one for each input port and observer (in the case of **TextField2**, just **set**) and one for expressing the behaviour of an instance. For example:

TextField2 i c s q e parent x y width height set changed =
(set = (λv. if (q (λn.$\neg$ (n = v))) (assign (s (λn. v)) ; changed v)))
$\wedge$(i = 0)
$\wedge$(c = ($\exists$v. atomic (numEv e v) (set v)))

Figure 13: A model for **TextField2**

Figure 13 contains the definition of a predicate suitable for modelling **TextField2**. The first conjunct provides a definition for the input port **set**. In general, the code fragment associated with an input port will be expressed as a function that takes a single parameter and returns a command. The second conjunct defines the initial state of texfield2 instances. For more realistic components, the expression defining the initial state would involve (parameters representing) component parameters. The final conjunct defines a command that expresses the possible behaviour of **TextField2** instances.

One complication that must be addressed is that each component instance has a separate state. Our solution is to parameterize the code fragments with two functions (*s* and *q* above) that transform local state assignments and predicates into global ones, respectively. The predicates that we use to model components take these functions as their third and fourth parameters; these functions will be discussed in more detail in the next section. Another complication that arises is the need to distinguish events generated by different instances of the same component. Our solution to this is to augment the component models with an additional parameter (*e* in the above definition) that will serve as a name for component instances. This name is then used to generate any event names required. The function **numEv** takes such a name (instead of a string) and a number and produces an event from it.

3.4.3 Generating models for composite components

In the approach that we propose the definitions for the predicates modelling composite components must be generated from their IL descriptions. We illustrate how this can be done by example. The HOL code generated from the IL description of Figure 12 defines the predicate shown in Figure 14. While the term defining Main looks unwieldy, it is simple to generate and can be easily manipulated using HOL. It corresponds to the behaviour of the two connected textfields. The terms that we use to define predicates such as **Main** are expressed as a number of conjuncts: one for each of the constituent instances, one for each of the ports and observers provided by the composite component (in this case there are none), and one each for describing the initial state and subsequent behaviour of instances of the composite component. The state of a composite instance is represented with a tuple, each component holding the state of a different constituent instance.

Main i c s q e = $\exists$i1 c1 i2 c2 set2 i3 c3 set3.
Window i1 c1(λf. s (λ (v1, v2, v3). (f v1, v2, v3)))(λP. q (λ(v1, v2, v3).P v1))
      (CONS 1 e) 170 220
$\wedge$ TextField2 i2 c2 (λf. s (λ(v1, v2, v3). (v1, f v2, v3))) (λ P. q(λ (v1, v2, v3). P v2))
      (CONS 2 e) VOID 5 5 160 160 set2 set3
$\wedge$ TextField1 i3 c3 (λf. s (λ(v1, v2, v3). (v1, v2, f v3))) (λP. q(λ(v1, v2, v3). P v3))
      (CONS 3 e) VOID 45 165 160 60 set3 set2
$\wedge$ (i = (i1, i2, i3))
$\wedge$ (c = c1 [] c2 [] c3)

Figure 14: A model for **Main** components

In the current example, the state of a **Main** instance is represented with a triple (v_1, v_2, v_3), with the components v_1, v_2, and v_3 holding the states of the constituent **Window**, **TextField2** and **TextField1** instances, respectively. The third and fourth parameters passed to the predicates **Window**, **TextField2** and **TextField1** enforce this representation. The functions passed as the third parameters are used to extend state assignments.[32] In general, we will use a function of the form:

$$\lambda f. \ s(\lambda \ (v_1, ..., v_n). \ (v_1, ..., fv_k, ..., v_n))$$

for this purpose. If f is a state assignment function then:

$$\lambda(v_1, ..., v_n). \ (v_1, ..., f \ v_k, ..., v_n)$$

---

[32] State assignment functions appear, for example, as parameters of **assign** operators.

extends f to act on the kth component of an n-tuple. The function s (provided as the third parameter of the predicate modelling the composite component) extends this function to act on the global (user interface) state. The functions passed as the fourth parameters are used to extend predicates similarly. In general, these functions will be of the form

$$\lambda P. \quad q(\lambda(v_1, ..., v_n) . \quad P \; v_k) \quad .$$

The effect of these functions can be observed by rewriting the term defining **Main** with the definitions of **Window, TextField2**, and **TextField1** and then beta-expanding.[33] The resulting (equivalent) definition for **Main** is shown in Figure 15. We are still left with a set of conjuncts, only now each is simply an equation that defines a variable. Note that the code fragments have been modified to operate on the appropriate state components; also note that the layout parameters have disappeared. We form event names from the names assigned to component instances.

> **Main** i c s q e = ∃i1 c1 i2 c2 **set2** i3 c3 **set3**.
> (i1 = **VOID**)
> $\wedge$ (c1 = F)
> $\wedge$ (set2 = (λv. if (q (λ(v1, v2, v3). $\neg$ (v2 = v)))
> **assign** (s (λ(v1, v2, v3). (v1, v, v3))) ; **set3** v)))
> $\wedge$ (i2 = 0)
> $\wedge$ (c2 = (∃v. **atomic** (**numEv** (**CONS** 2 e) v) (**set2** v)))
> $\wedge$ (set3 = (λv. if (q(λ(v1, v2, v3).$\neg$ (v3 = v)))
> **assign** (s(λ(v1, v2, v3). (v1, v2, v))) ; **set2** v)))
> $\wedge$ (i3 = 0)
> $\wedge$ (c3 = (∃v. **atomic** (**numEv** (**CONS** 3 e) v) (set3 v)))
> $\wedge$ (i = (i1, i2, i3))
> $\wedge$ (c = c1 [] c2 [] c3)

Figure 15: Term obtained by rewriting Figure 14 with the definitions of Window, TextField2 and TextField1, and beta-expanding.

For convenience, we name instances with lists of natural numbers; we generate names for the constituents of a composite instance by using the HOL-supplied function **CONS** to prepend a unique number to the name assigned to the composite instance.

In terms corresponding to constituent instances, each parameter that represents an input port or observer is instantiated with a unique (existentially quantified) variable. Parameters representing output ports are instantiated with terms involving these variables. For simple connections involving no filters, this term is simply the variable associated with the input port.[34] Filters are represented with HOL functions; recall

---

[33] `TextField1` is modelled with the same predicate as `TextField2`; `Windows` are modelled with the predicate **Window** *i c s q e width height* = (i = VOID) $\wedge$ (c = F).

[34] Recall that output ports can be bound to at most one input port.

that filters and observers, as well as IL functions, are not allowed to modify state. If there is a filter attached to an output port, then we instantiate the corresponding parameter with $i \circ f$, where i is the variable associated with the input port and f is the function modelling the filter.[35] If an output port is left unbound, we use the term $\lambda v.$**skip** instead. The effect of these instantiations becomes evident upon rewriting with the definitions of the constituent components, as can be seen in Figure 15.

Existentially quantified variables are also generated for capturing the initial state and behaviour of each of the constituent instances. These are then used to construct expressions for the initial state and subsequent behaviour of the composite instances.

4. Validation

We express the properties to be validated as predicates on sets of runs. Validating that a user interface model possesses a property P entails proving a theorem of the form

$$\forall i\ c.\ \mathbf{Main}\ i\ c\ (\lambda f.\ f)\ (\lambda P.\ P)\ [\ ] \Rightarrow P\ ((\lambda s.\ s = i) \to \mathbf{do\_od}\ c)$$

where **Main** is a predicate modelling the user interface. The approach we take to constructing proofs for such theorems involves mechanising a logic for each family of properties of interest. This consists of devising a suitable representation for these properties and deriving a set of inference rules from the run-based semantics that we have given to commands.

We illustrate our approach with two simple classes of properties: state invariants and safety properties that have been expressed in a rule-based fashion.

The proofs that we construct will make use of a forward reasoning predicate transformer **sp** that has the following operational semantics: if c is a command, then for any set of states (i.e. state predicate) P, **sp** c P is the set of states in which execution of c can terminate if started from a state in P. This predicate transformer was introduced by Francez in (Francez 77) and is referred to as the strongest postcondition predicate transformer by Dijkstra and Scholten in (Dijkstra & Scholten 90). Given our representation of commands, **sp** can be expressed as follows:

Definition 9:
$\vdash \forall c\ P.\ \mathbf{sp}\ c\ P = (\lambda s.\ \exists e.\ P\ (\mathbf{start}\ e) \wedge c\ e \wedge \mathbf{finite}\ e \wedge (\mathbf{final}\ e = s))$

A state s satisfies **sp** c P iff we can find a finite run e in c that starts in P and terminates in s. The reader should note that equations comprising inductive definitions of **sp** are used to simplify expressions involving **sp**.

Unfortunately, the equation for assignment statements is complicated (Dijkstra & Scholten 90): **sp** (**assign** E) $P = (\lambda s.\ \exists s'.\ Ps' \wedge (s = Es'\ ))$. However, we can simplify this expression by carefully choosing our representation of state predicates.

---

[35] We use '$\circ$' to represent the HOL-supplied function for function composition.

Definition 10: $|\text{-} \; \forall s \; P. \; \mathbf{xs} \; (s, P) = (\lambda t. \; (t = s) \wedge P)$

We introduce a function constant **xs** for representing state predicates. Note that a predicate of the form **xs** (s, P) is true of at most one state, s, depending on whether P is true or not. In such predicates we will refer to the terms s and P as path expressions and path conditions, respectively. Note that all state predicates can be expressed in terms of **xs**:

Theorem 2: $|\text{-} \; \forall P. \; P = (\exists s. \; \mathbf{xs} \; (s, P \; s))$

4.1 State Invariants

In this section we illustrate one approach to proving that a user interface model, constructed as described in a previous chapter, maintains a state invariant. We first define what it means for a predicate to be held invariant by a command.
Unfortunately, proving that commands maintain invariants directly from this definition is impractical. As a result, we next introduce a number of theorems that let us take a syntax-directed approach to constructing such proofs. We end this section with an illustrative example.

We say that a state predicate Q **holds** on a run e if it is true of every state in e:

Definition 11: $\vdash \forall Q \; e. \; \text{holds} \; Q \; e = (\forall i. \; \neg \text{size} \; e \prec i \supset (i \prec \omega \supset Q \; (\text{st} \; e \; i)))$

The definition of **holds** is complicated slightly by the fact that we use **Inums**, not **nums** (natural numbers) to index the states in a run. A state predicate Q is held invariant by a command c if it holds on all runs in the command. This notion of invariance can be expressed using the predicate **sinv**:

Definition 12: $|\text{-} \; \forall Q \; c \; P. \; \text{sinv} \; Q \; c \; P = (\forall e. \; c \; e \supset (P \; (\text{start} \; e) \supset \text{holds} \; Q \; e))$

The formula **sinv** $Q \; c \; P$ is true iff Q holds for all runs in c that start in P. We will refer to the predicates P and Q as the pre-condition and invariant of such a formula. A state predicate Q is held invariant by a command c iff **sinv** $Q \; c \; T$ is valid; in particular, proving that a user interface maintains an invariant Q reduces to proving a goal of the form:

$$\forall i \; c. \; \mathbf{Main} \; i \; c(\lambda f. \; f) \; (\lambda P. \; P) \; [\;] \supset \mathbf{sinv} \; Q \; (\mathbf{xs} \; (i, T) \rightarrow \mathbf{do\_od} \; c) \; T$$

where Main is a predicate modelling the user interface.

Rather than trying to prove goals (with conclusion) of the form **sinv** $Q \; c \; P$ directly from the definition of **sinv**, we instead make use of a collection of inference rules. These rules are used in a backwards fashion, to decompose complex goals into a number of simpler goals. We write these rules as follows:

$$\frac{G_1 \cdots G_n}{G}$$

Such a rule can be interpreted as *"To prove that G holds, it is sufficient to prove that G_1 through G_n hold."* We express these rules as HOL theorems, with the HOL logical (**Boolean**) connectives serving as meta-logical operators for the object logic.[36] For example, we can express the above rule with HOL theorem:

$$\vdash G_1 \supset ... \supset G_n \supset G$$

Rather than postulating such theorems as axioms, we instead prove their validity using the definition of **sinv**; this eliminates the chance of introducing inconsistency. While we only require implicational theorems for our rules we will often prove equivalence. Equational theorems are more convenient to manipulate in HOL; in particular, they can be used as rewrite rules. In order to simplify goals involving **sinv** we use rules that, for example, strengthen the invariant, weaken the pre-condition, or simplify the commands which appear in the goal.

4.1.1 An example

We now give a simple example of how these rules can be applied. We will verify that the two textfields of the user interface of Figure 12 have the same http address at all times; whenever one is changed, the other changes accordingly. The first step is to generate a model of the user interface from its IL description (shown in Figure 12) and the models of its constituent components.[37] The resulting predicate is shown in Figure 14. Next, we must express the property to be validated in terms of this model. The second and third state components of the model hold the value of the TextField2 and TextField1, respectively. We need to show that in all states of all possible behaviours of the user interface of these two values remain the same. That is, we have to show that the predicate $\lambda(t, u, v).u = v$ is held invariant by any command that models the behaviour of the user interface. In particular, we have to prove the validity of the following formula:

$\forall i$ c. **Main** i c $(\lambda f.\ f)$ $(\lambda P.\ P)$ [ ] $\supset$ **sinv** $(\lambda(t, u, v).\ u = v)$ (**xs** (i, T)
$\rightarrow$ **do_od** c) T

We construct the proof using the HOL subgoal package. We start by initialising the goal stack with the above formula which is shown to be true.

---

[36] The lifted Boolean operators serve as the connectives of the object logic.

[37] The model for **TextField2** can be found in Figure 13; **TextField1** is modeled similarly. **Windows** are modelled as essentially having no state and no associated command: **Window** *i c s q e width height* = $(i =$ VOID$) \land (c = \mathbf{F})$.

4.2 Reactive Properties

Currently user interface specifications are primarily used as media for discussion; the most convincing use of dialogue specification techniques to date being the analysis and redesign of existing GUI implementations (Duke & Harrison 94). While progress has been made with regard to the specification of user interfaces and the validation of such specifications, the issue of constructing implementations that meet such specifications has yet to be satisfactorily addressed. Two approaches currently being investigated are the formal refinement of user interface specifications (Bramwell, Fields & Harrison 95) and the direct generation of user interfaces from specifications (Palanque, Bastide & Senges 94). This section presents yet another possible line of investigation. By giving a semantics to user interface specifications that is compatible with the semantics assigned to our models we can verify if implementations (models) satisfy specifications. In particular, we will express the semantics of user interface specifications in terms of sets of runs. Following Lamport (Lamport 89), we view such specifications as safety properties: an implementation (model) satisfies such a specification iff every possible behaviour of the implementation is contained in the specification. In this section we illustrate how such an approach can be mechanised.

4.2.1 Expressing properties

We need to express specifications as HOL terms. The representation we choose depends on the specifications of interest: it should be easy to express these specifications using our representation. For simplicity, we restrict our attention to specifications expressed in rule-based notations. Examples of such notations include Olsen's Propositional Production Systems (PPS) (Olsen 90, Abowd, Wang & Monk 95) and York interactors (Duke & Harrison 94).

We note that the rules in such specifications can be viewed as defining the transition relation of an automaton. A set-theoretic definition of an automaton is a four-tuple (S, E, Q, N), where S is a set of states, E is a set of events, $Q \subseteq S$ is a set of initial states, and $N : S \times E \times S \rightarrow bool$ is a transition relation on the current state, transition label (an event), and next state. By using type variables to denote the sets of events and actions, we can represent an automaton with a HOL pair (Q, N). Constructing a transition relation from a rule-based specification is simple: each rule in the specification becomes a disjunct in the term defining the transition relation. Note that in the definition of such terms we have access to both the current and next state values.

We express the behaviour of an automaton as a set of **runs**:

Definition 13:
|- $\forall$Q N. **runs** (Q, N) = (λe. Q (**start** e) $\wedge$ ($\forall$i. i $\prec$ **size** e $\supset$ N (**st** e i) (**ev** e i) (**st** e (**SC** i))))

The set of runs defined by an automaton (Q, N) consists of all runs e that start in Q and do not violate the transition relation N; i.e., every state-event-state triple appearing in e must satisfy N.

4.2.2 Satisfaction

We say that a model implements a specification if the observable behaviour of the model is consistent with the (observable) behaviour described by the specification. We need to make the notions of observable behaviour and consistency precise. We express observable behaviour in terms of traces; the trace of a run serves as a description of the features of interest of the run. We have a number of choices as to what we wish to consider observable: just the events, just the (observable portion of the) states, or some combination. For simplicity, we consider the observable behaviour of a run to consist only of the environment-initiated actions appearing in the run. We define the **trace** of a run to be the sequence of events appearing in the run, and extend this definition to sets of runs:

Definition 14:
$\vdash \forall e.$ **trace** $e =$ **mk_seq** (**ev** e, **size** e)
$\vdash \forall c.$ **traces** $c = (\lambda x. \exists e.\ c\ e \wedge (x =$ **trace** $e))$

We say that the observable behaviour of a model is consistent with the behaviour described by a specification iff all traces of the model are also traces of the specification. To show that a command c is consistent with a specification (Q, N) we have to show that the formula:

$[\ ] \vdash$ (**traces** $c \supset$ **traces** (**runs** (Q, N)))

is valid.

Unfortunately, directly proving the validity of such formulas is not feasible; we need to devise an approach that can take advantage of the structure of the formulas. The approach we take involves finding a function f that maps model states to specification states. If f is such a function we say that the mapping of a run $e = \langle s_0, x_1, s_1, \dots \rangle$ by f, **stmap** f e, is the run $\langle f s_0, x_1, f s_1, \dots \rangle$. Intuitively, a command c will implement a specification (Q, N) iff all runs in c, when mapped, have start states in Q and follow N. We now make this notion precise. We say that a run e follows a transition relation N under a mapping f if every state-event-state triple appearing in **stmap** f e satisfies N. Similarly, we say that a command c follows a transition relation N under f if every run e in c follows N under f. We express this in terms of the predicate **follows**:

Definition 15:
$\vdash \forall t f c P.$ **follows** $t f c P = (\forall e.\ c\ e \supset P$ (**start** $e) \supset$
$\qquad (\forall i.\ i \prec$ **size** $e \supset t\ (f\ ($**st** $e\ i))\ ($**ev** $e\ i)\ (f\ ($**st** $e\ ($**SC** $i)))))$

The formula **follows** $t \; f \; c \; P$ is true iff all runs e in c that start in P follow t under f. We refer to the predicate P in such formulas as the pre-condition of the formula. A command c follows a transition relation N under f iff **follows** $N \; f \; c \; \mathbf{T}$ is valid. We say that a command c satisfies a specification (Q, N) under a mapping f if all runs in c, when mapped by f, start in Q and follow N:

Definition 16:

$\vdash \forall Q \; N \; c.$ **fsat** $(Q, N) \; c = (\exists f. [\;] \vdash (\mathbf{grd} \; c \supset (Q \circ f)) \wedge \mathbf{follows} \; N \; f \; c \; \mathbf{T})$

Recall that for any command c, **grd** c is the set of all start states of runs in c. If we can show that c satisfies (Q, N) then c implements (Q, N):

Theorem 3:

$\vdash \forall Q \; N \; c.$ **fsat** $(Q, N) \; c \supset [\;] \vdash (\mathbf{traces} \; c \supset \mathbf{traces} \; (\mathbf{runs} \; (Q, N)))$

As a result, the goals of interest will be of the form:

$\forall c.$ **Main** $i \; c \; (\lambda f. \; f) \; (\lambda P. \; P) \; [\;] \supset$ **fsat** $(Q, N) \; (\mathbf{xs} \; (i, \mathbf{T}) \rightarrow \mathbf{do\_od} \; c)$.

Most of the effort in proving such goals will be in proving that a formula involving **follows** holds. As with state invariants, rather than trying to prove the validity of formulas of the form **follows** $t \; f \; c \; P$ directly from the definition of **follows**, we instead make use of a collection of (mostly syntax-directed) rules. These rules allow us to simplify goals involving **follows** by, for example, weakening the pre-condition, or simplifying the commands that appear in the goal.

4.2.3 An example

We now give an example of applying the approach to prove a particular safety property. As before, the intent of the example is to indicate how our approach can be applied. Figure 6 contains the IL description of a one-button instance of a button bar. Clicking the button launches a program; the state of the button (enabled or disabled) provides a visual indication as to whether an execution is pending. Figure 7 contains a graphical depiction of Figure 6. The user interface described in Figure 6 consists of a button and a launcher. Buttons are either enabled or disabled; they can be clicked only when enabled. The buttons we use are unusual in that they disable themselves after being clicked: they must be re-enabled before they can be clicked again. Such buttons can be implemented easily using more traditional buttons. Launchers are application interface components that execute programs. They can be associated with programs such as the one that returns the content of a page. Many other buttons can be modeled in a similar way. A launcher executes a program upon receipt of an event at its execute port;[38] it generates an event at its done port when there is some visible indication that the program has started. Our launchers allow at most one pending

---

[38] A more realistic Launcher component would provide a parameter for specifying the program to be run.

execution at any given time: after initiating a program launch a client must wait for the subsequent done event before initiating the next launch. We wish to verify that this is indeed the case for the user interface described in Figure 6.

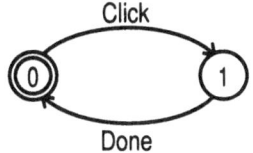

Click

Done

Figure 16: A specification for Figure 6

More specifically, we wish to verify that this user interface implements the specification shown in Figure 16.[39] We would like to verify that all interactions of this user interface with the environment can be described as an alternating sequence of click and done events that starts with a click.

The first step is to generate a model of the user interface from its IL description and the models of its constituent components. Figure 17 shows our model for buttons:

$\vdash \forall$ i c s q e enable click. **Button** i c s q e enable click =
$\quad$ (enable = **assign** (s (λn. **T**)))
$\quad \wedge$(i = **T**)
$\quad \wedge$(c = q (λn. n) $\rightarrow$ **atomic** (**Click** e) (**assign** (s (λn. **F**)) ; click))

Figure 17: A model for Buttons

The state of a button consists of a Boolean flag that indicates whether the button is enabled or not; initially the flag is true. The model for **Launchers** is shown in Figure 18:

$\vdash \forall$ i c s q e execute done. **Launcher** i c s q e execute done =
$\quad$ (execute = **assign** (s (λn. **T**)))
$\quad \wedge$(i = **F**)
$\quad \wedge$(c = q (λn. n) $\rightarrow$ **atomic** (**Done** e) (**assign** (s (λn. **F**)) ; done))

Figure 18: A model for Launchers

The state of a launcher consists of a Boolean flag that indicates whether there is a pending execution or not; initially the flag is false. The predicate generated from the IL description of Figure 6 is shown in Figure 19. The state of the user interface is represented with a pair; the first and second components holding the state of the button and launcher, respectively.

$\vdash \forall$ i c s q e. **Main** i c s q e =
$\quad (\exists i_1 \; c_1$ enable$_1$ $i_2 \; c_2$ execute$_2$.

---

[39] The choice of **0** and **1** for state labels is purely arbitrary.

Button i_1 c_1 $(\lambda f.\ s(\lambda(v_1,\ v_2)\ .\ (f\ v_1,\ v_2)))\ (\lambda P.\ q\ (\lambda(v_1,\ v_2).\ P\ v_1))$
    (CONS 1 e**)** enable$_1$ execute$_2$
$\wedge$**Launcher** i_2 c_2 $(\lambda f.\ S\ (\lambda(v_1,\ v_2)\ .\ (v_1,\ fv_2)))\ (\lambda P.\ q(\lambda(v_1,\ v_2).\ P\ v_2))$
    (CONS 2 e**)** execute$_2$ enable$_1$
$\wedge(i = (i1,\ i2))$
$\wedge(c = c_1\ []c_2))$

Figure 19: The HOL definition generated from Figure 6

In these models lists of integers are used to represent events; the first element identifying the type of event (click or done) and the remaining elements identifying the component(s) associated with the event. The functions **Click** and **Done** have the following definitions:

$\vdash\forall n.$ **Click** $n =$ **ext (CONS** 0 $n)$
$\vdash\forall n.$ **Done** $n =$ **ext (CONS** 1 $n)$

Next, we must express the specification shown in Figure 16 as a HOL pair $(I,\ N)$ where I is a state predicate describing the possible initial states and N is a transition relation expressing the possible subsequent behaviour. We use $\lambda n.\ n = 0$ for I: 0 is the only start state. We express the transition relation in terms of a number of disjuncts, each corresponding to a single transition or rule:

$\vdash\forall u\ x\ v.$ **N** $u\ x\ v =$
    $(u = 0) \wedge (\exists n.\ x =$ **Click** $n) \wedge (v = 1)$
    $\vee(u = 1) \wedge (\exists n.\ x =$ **Done** $n) \wedge (v = 0)$

Each disjunct is expressed as the conjunction of three terms: the first describing the pre-condition, the last the post-condition, and the middle term the possible events that could label the transition (rule.) Here we are not concerned with the component names associated with events because of the simple nature of the model: for each event, there is only one associated component. While this definition is easy to construct, the following theorem (proved as a consequence of the definition) is more useful:

$\vdash\forall n.$ **N** 0 **(Click** $n)$ 1 $\wedge$ **N** 1 **(Done** $n)$ 0

To show that our model implements this specification it is sufficient to show the validity of the following formula using the results of the previous section:

$\forall c.$ **Main** $i\ c\ (\lambda f.\ f)\ (\lambda P.\ P)$ $[\ ] \supset$ **fsat** $((\lambda n.\ n = 0),\ N)$ $($**xs** $(i,\ T) \rightarrow$ **do_od** $c)$

We construct a proof of its validity using the HOL subgoal package. We start by initialising the goal stack with the previous formula which is shown to be true.

5. Conclusions

Verifying that user interfaces behave as expected is gaining importance: more and more security- and safety-critical applications are providing sophisticated graphical user interfaces. Component-based tools and toolkits are becoming increasingly popular for user interface construction, in part because they facilitate rapid prototyping. In this chapter we have described an approach to addressing the issue of ensuring that graphical user interfaces behave as expected, and illustrated through examples how the approach can be applied to a netscape-like browser application. Our approach involves describing a user interface as a hierarchy of interconnected component instances. Associated with each component is a formal model (or models) that captures the features of interest. Rather than analysing the properties of a user interface directly, we analyse the properties of the associated model. This approach requires that the process of component interconnection be modelled as well. Given such a method, we can generate a model for any user interface given only models for the primitive components and a description of their interconnection. In our approach, user interfaces are described using an interconnection language and both implementations and formal models are generated from such descriptions.

Using our approach, the user interface designer does not have to be an expert in formal specification; indeed, the designer need not even be aware of the particular notation being used. As far as the designer is concerned, user interface construction simply consists of connecting components together. There is no restriction on the formalisms used to express models, or their uses. There is no need to maintain separate representations of models and implementations. Generating models and implementations from the same description helps ensure that models accurately reflect implementations as user interfaces evolve. The approach can be adapted for use with almost any existing user interface tool or toolkit.

By describing and applying IL to model parts of the application model, we have indicated the kinds of constructs that we have to structure the graphical user interface. In our case, once the primitive IL descriptions for the components have been built, we can potentially generate implementations from these models, and eliminate much of the burden associated with the implementation process. The adoption of a component-based approach also results in specifications that are less difficult to modify: the changes are more localised and the primitive visual and application components can be available. We have also shown how we can verify properties related to the application. Two kinds of properties have been considered: state invariants and safety properties.

Note that we have not formalised the relation between IL descriptions and its associated implementations in Tk/Tcl. This can be done by using a conventional programming logic refinement process (such as the one provided by the Floyd-Hoare logic). However, as we have used Tk/Tcl only to exemplify our approach and because the transformations from IL descriptions to user interface implementation languages can be addressed by conventional techniques for program refinement using a programming logic, we have decided not to address this issue here.

However, our approach does not cover all aspects of the web browser application. Non-preemptiveness, such as the ability to exit and stop at any time, can not be directly modeled in our approach because of the representation adopted. Since the behaviour is characterised by events followed by sequences of actions, one has in general to wait for all the actions associated with an event to be executed. Our current approach does not allow modelling of concurrency among various servers and various browsers.

References

Abadi M. & Lamport L. (1992) An old-fashioned recipe for real time. Technical Report 91, DEC Systems Research Center.

Abowd G. & Dix A. (1994) Integrating status and event phenomena in formal specifications of interactive systems. In Proceedings for ACM SIGSOFT'94, New Orleans.

Abowd G. (1991a) Formal Aspects of Human Computer Interaction. PhD thesis, Oxford University Computing Laboratory; Trinity College.

Abowd G. (1991b) Formal descriptions of user interfaces. Colloquium Digest, 192:7/1−7/3.

Abowd G., Bowen J., Dix A., Harrison M & Took R. (1989) User interface languages: a survey of existing methods. Technical Report PRG-TR-5-89, Oxford University Computing Laboratory Programming Research Group.

Abowd G., Coutaz J. & Nigay L. (1992) Structuring the Space of Interactive System Properties. In Proceedings of the IFIP TC2/WG2.7 on Engineering for Human-Computer Interaction, Ellivuori, Finland, 1992, pp. 113-128.

Abowd G., Wang H. & Monk A. (1995) A formal technique for automated dialogue development, Proceedings Designing Interactive Systems'95, August, pp.219-226, ACM Press.

ANSI/IEEE Standard 729-(1983) Software Engineering Standards. IEEE, New york, 1989.

Aslett M. J. (1991) A Knowledge Based Approach to Software Development: ESPRIT Project ASPIS. North Holland.

Atlee J. & Gannon J. (1993) State-based model checking of event-driven system requirements. IEEE Transactions on Software Engineering, 19(1), pp. 24-40.

Ayers E. & Stasko J. (1995) Using graphic history in browsing the World Wide Web. Proceedings of the Fourth International World Wide Web Conference, http://www.w3.org/pub/Conferences/WWW4/papers2/270/, Boston.

Back R., & Sere K. (1994) From action systems to modular systems, in (Naftalin et al. 1994), pp. 1–25.

Balzert H. (1994) Das JANUS-System - Automatisierte, wissensbasierte Generierung von Mensch-Maschine Schnittstellen. Informatik Forschung & Entwicklung 9, 1, pp. 22-35.

Balzert H., Hofmann F., Kruschinski V. & Niemann C. (1996) The Janus application development environment / Generating more than the user interface. In: Vanderdonckt J. (ed.): Computer-Aided Design of User Interfaces, Namur University Press, pp. 183-205.

Bass L., Coutaz J. (1991) Developing Software for the User Interface. SEI Series in Software engineering, Addison-Wesley, New York.

Bass L., Little R., Pellegrino R., Reed S., Seacord R., Sheppard S. & Szezur M.R.. (1991) The Arch Model: Seeheim Revisited, User Interface Developers' Workshop, April 26, Version 1.0.

Bastide R, Sibertin-Blanc C. (1991) Modelling a flexible manufacturing system by means of Cooperative Objects. Proceedings of IFIP conference CAPE'91 on computer applications in production and engineering.

Bastide R. & Palanque P. (1990) Petri nets with objects for the design, validation and prototyping of user-driven interfaces. In: D. Diaper, D. Gilmore, G. Cockton, B. Shackel (eds.), Proceedings INTERACT'90, Elsevier Science Publishers (North-Holland), pp. 625-631.

Bastide R. & Palanque P. (1995) A Petri net based Environment for the Design of Event-Driven Interfaces. Proceedings of the 16th International Conference on Petri nets, Torino, Italy, Lecture Notes in Computer Science n° 935, pp. 66-83, Springer-Verlag.

Bastide R. (1992) Cooperative Objects: A formalism for modelling concurrent systems. Ph.D. Thesis, University Toulouse III, France (in french).

Beaudouin-Lafon M. & Karsenty A. (1992) Transparency and Awareness in a Real-Time Groupware System. In proceedings of ACM Symposium on User Interface Software and Technology UIST'92, ACM Press.

Ben-Ari M. (1993) Mathematical Logic for Computer Science, C.A.R. Hoare Series Editor, Prentice Hall International Series in Computer Science, pp. 200-244.

Berners-Lee T.J., Cailliau R. & Groff J.-F. (1992) The World Wide Web, Computer Networks And ISDN Systems, (25):pp. 454-459.

Bieber M., Vitali F., Ashman H., Balasubramanian V. & Oinas-Kukkonen H. (1997) Fourth Generation Hypermedia: Some Missing Links for the World Wide Web. International Journal of Human Computer Studies (forthcoming).

Bodart F., Hennebert A.-M., Leheureux J.-M., Provot I., Sacré B. & Vanderdonckt J. (1995) Towards a systematic building of software architectures: the TRIDENT methodological guide. In Palanque P. & Bastide R. (eds.): Design, Specification and Verification of Interactive Systems. Wien: Springer, 1995, pp. 262-278.

Bodart F., Hennerbert A., Leheureux J. & Vanderdonckt J. (1996) A Model-based approach to Presentation: A Continuum from Task Analysis to Prototype, Proceedings DSV-IS'95, Springer Verlag, pp.77-94.

Booch G. & Rumbaugh J. (1995) Unified Method for Object-Oriented Development, Documentation Set Version 0.8, October.

Booch G. (1994) Object-Oriented Analysis and Design with Applications, Benjamin/Cummings.

Botafogo R.A. & Shneiderman B. (1992) Structural analysis of hypertexts: identifying hierarchies and useful metrics. ACM Trans. on Info. Systems, 10(2):142-180

Bowen J. P. & Hinchey M. G. (1995) Ten Commandments of Formal Methods. IEEE Computer, 28(4), pp. 56–63.

Bramwell C. (1995) Formal aspects of the Design Rationale of Interactive Systems, PhD thesis, Dept. of Computer Science, University of York.

Bramwell C., Fields B. & Harrison M. (1995) Exploring design options rationally, in P. Palanque and R. Bastide, eds, Design, Specification, Verification of Interactive Systems'95, Springer Computer Science, Springer Wien New York, pp. 134–148. URL: http//www.cs.york.ac.uk/~bob/papers/dsv95/spec.ps

Breedvelt I., Paterno' F., Severiins C. (1997) Reusable Structures in Task Models, Proceedings DSV-IS97, Springer Verlag, Granada, Spain..

Brink C. & Rewitzky I. (1992) Modelling the algebra of weakest preconditions. South African Computer Journal, 6, pp. 11-20.

Brown P.J. (1990) Assessing the quality of hypertext documents. In: Rizs, A.; Stritz, N. & André, J. (Eds.) Hypertext: Concepts, Systems and Applications Cambridge, Great

Britain, Cambridge University Press. /Proceedings of ECHT'90 Versailles, France, November 1990/ pp.1-12

Browne T., Davila D., Rugaber S., & Stirewalt K. (1997) Using Declarative Descriptions to Model User Interfaces with MASTERMIND. (in this book).

Buckingham Shum B. (1995) Analysing The Usability Of A Design Rationale Notation. In T.P. Moran and J.M. Carroll (eds.) Design Rationale Concepts, Techniques And Use, Lawrence Erlbaum, Hillsdale, New Jersey, United States of America.

Bumbulis P., Alencar P., Cowan D. & Lucena C. (1995) Combining formal techniques and prototyping in user interface construction and verification. In DSV-IS'95: 2nd Eurographics Workshop on Design, Specification and Verification of Interactive Systems, France, June 7-9, Springer Computer Science Series, Springer-Verlag.

Bumbulis P., Alencar P., Cowan D. & Lucena C. (1996) Validating properties of component-based graphical user interfaces. In DSV-IS'96: 3rd Eurographics Workshop on Design, Specification and Verification of Interactive Systems, Namur, June 5-7, Springer Computer Science, Springer-Verlag, pp.347-365.

Card S., Moran T. & Newell A. (1983) The Psychology of Human-Computer Interaction, Lawrence Erlbaum, Hillsdale, N.J.

Carr D. (1994) Specification of interface interaction objects. Proceedings of ACM CHI'94 Conference on Human Factors in Computing Systems, pp. 372-378.

Carr D. (1995) A Compact Graphical Representation of User Interface Interaction Objects. University of Maryland, Department of Computer Science, Ph.D.

Carr D. (1996) Toward more understandable user interface specifications. Design, Specification, and Verification of Interactive Systems '96. F. Bodart & J. Vanderdonckt (Eds.) Springer-Verlag, pp. 141-161.

Catledge L. & Pitkow J. (1995) Characterising browsing strategies in the World-Wide Web. Proceedings of the Third International World Wide Web Conference, http://www.igd.fhg.de/www/www95/papers/, Darmstadt, Germany.

Clarke E.M. & Emerson E.A. (1982) The Design And Synthesis Of Synchronisation Skeletons Using Branching Time Temporal Logic. In D. Kozen (ed.) Logic of Programs 1981, 52--71, Lecture Notes in Computer Science n° 131, Springer Verlag, Berlin, Germany.

Cockburn A. & Jones S. (1996) Which way now? Analysing and easing inadequacies in Web navigation. International Journal of Human Computer Studies, **44**.

Coleman D. et al. (1994) Object-oriented development: the FUSION method. New Jersey, USA, Prentice Hall, Englewood Cliffs

Conklin J. (1987) Hypertext: an introduction and survey, IEEE Computer, **20**(9), pp. 17–41.

Corba (1991) The Object Management Group, Common Object Request Broker: Architecture and Specification, OMG document n° 91.12.1.

Coutaz J. & Balbo S. (1991) Applications: A Dimension Space for User Interface Management Systems. In Proceedings of CHI'91 Conference, New Orleans, April 27-May 2, 1991, pp. 27-32.

Coutaz J. (1987) PAC, An Object Oriented Model for Dialogue Design. In proceedings of the IFIP conference INTERACT'87, pp.431-436. North Holland.

Coutaz J., Nigay L. & Salber D. (1995) Agent-Based Architecture Modelling for Interactive Systems. Technical Report SM/WP53, LGI-IMAG, Grenoble, April. ESPRIT BRA 7040 Amodeus-2.

Darwin Overview (1994) Imperial College of Science, Technology and Medicine.

Degani A. & Kirlik A. (1995) Modes in human-automation interaction: Initial observations about a modelling approach. In Proceedings IEEE International Conference on Systems, Man and Cybernetics, pp. 3443-3450. IEEE Press.

DeNicola R., Fantechi A., Gnesi S. & Ristori G. (1993) An Action Based Framework for Verifying Logical and Behavioural Properties of Concurrent Systems, Computer Networks & ISDN Systems, North-Holland,.**25**, 7, Februrary 1993, pp.761-778.

Diaper D. (ed.) (1989) Task Analysis for Human-Computer Interaction. Ellis-Horwood.

Digitalk. (1994) PARTS Workbench User's Guide.

Dijkstra E. & Scholten C. (1990) Predicate Calculus and Program Semantics, Springer-Verlag, New York.

Dijkstra E. (1976) A Discipline of Programming, Prentice Hall, New Jersey.

d'Inverno M. & Priestley M. (1995) Structuring Specifications in Z to build a Unifying Framework for Hypertext Systems. In Z User Meeting '95, pp. 81–102. Springer-Verlag.

Dix A. & Runciman C. (1985) Abstract models of interactive systems. People and Computers: Designing the Interface, Cambridge University Press, pp. 13-22.

Dix A. (1991) Formal Methods for Interactive Systems, Academic Press.

Dix A., Harrison, M., Runciman C. & Thimbleby H. (1987) Interaction Models And The Principled Design Of Interactive Programs. In H.K. Nichols and D. Simpson, editors, Proceedings Of The First European Software Engineering Conference, Lecture Notes in Computer Science n° 289, pp. 118-126, Springer Verlag.

Dix A., Mancini R. & Levialdi S. (1996) Alas I am undone - Reducing the risk of interaction? HCI'96 Adjunct Proceedings, Imperial College, London, pp. 51–56.

Dix A., Mancini R. & Levialdi S. (1997) Communication, action and history. Proceedings of CHI'97, Atlanta, USA, ACM Press, pp. 542–543.

Drakos N. (1994) From text to hypertext: A post-hoc rationalisation of LaTeX2html, in The Proceedings of the First World Wide Web Conference, CERN, Geneva, Switzerland. URL: http://cbl.leeds.ac.uk/nikos/doc/www94/www94.html

Duke D. & Harrison M. (1993) Abstract Interaction Objects. Computer Graphics Forum Conference Issue, 12(3), pp. 25–36.

Duke D. & Harrison M. (1993) Abstract interaction objects. Computer Graphics Forum, 12(3):pp. 25-36. Conference Issue: Proc. Eurographics'93.

Duke D. & Harrison M. (1994) A theory of presentations, in (Naftalin et al. 1994), pp. 271–290.

Duke D. & Harrison M. (1994) Connections: From a(v) to z. Technical Report System Modelling/WP29, Department of Computer Science, University of York.

Duke D. & Harrison M. (1994) From formal models to formal methods. In Software Engineering and Human-Computer Interaction: ICSE'94 Workshop on SE-HCI: Joint Research Issues, Lecture Notes in Computer Science n° 896, pp. 159-173, Springer-Verlag.

Duke D. & Harrison M. (1995) Interaction and Task Requirements. In P. Palanque and R. Bastide, editors, Design, Specification and Verification of Interactive Systems '95, pp. 55–75. Springer.

Duke D. & Harrison M. (1995) Mapping user requirements to implementations. Software Engineering Journal, pp. 13–20.

Duke D., King P., Rose G. & Smith, G. (1991) The Object-Z Specification Language. Version 1. Software Verification Research Centre. Department of Computer Science. University of Queensland. Australia. Technical Report N.91-1.

Duke R., Rose G. & Smith G. (1994) Object-Z: a Specification Language Advocated for the Description of Standards. Technical Report 94–45, Software Verification Research Centre, Dept. of Computer Science, The University of Queensland.

Ellis C.A, Gibbs S.J. & Rein G.L. (1991) Groupware, Some Issues and experiences, in Communications of the ACM, **34**, 1, pp. 39-58.

Ellis C.A. & Gibbs S.J. (1990) Concurrency Control in Groupware Systems. In proceedings of ACM SIGMOD'89 Conference on the Management of Data, 1989, ACM, New York.

Elwert T. & Schlungbaum E. (1995) Modelling and Generation of Graphical User Interfaces in the TADEUS Approach. In: P. Palanque & R. Bastide (eds.): Designing, Specification, and Verification of Interactive Systems. Springer Verlag, pp. 193-208.

Emerson E.A. & Srinivasan J. (1988) Branching Time Temporal Logic, in «Linear Time, Branching Time and Partial Order in Logics and Models for Concurrency», Lecture Notes in Computer Science n° 354, Springer-Verlag, pp.123-172.

Enjalbert P. & Michel M. (1984) Many sorted temporal logic for multi-processes systems. MFCS 84 (Prague), Springer, Lecture Notes in Computer Science n° 176.

European Space Agency "HOOD Reference Manual," issue 3.0; ESA, ref. WME/89-173/JB; Sept. 1989

Faconti G. & Paterno F. (1990) An Approach to the Formal Specification of the Components of an Interaction. EUROGRAPHICS.

Fähnrich K-P. & Kärcher M. (1991) The ISA DIALOG MANAGER: Requirements for User Interface Management Systems. In: H.J. Bullinger (ed.) Human Aspects in Computing: Design and Use of Interactive Systems and Work with Terminals. Proceedings HCIInternational'91 (Stuttgart) Amsterdam: Elsevier, pp. 259-264.

Fidge C. (1994) Adding real time to formal program development. In FME'94: Industrial Benefit of Formal Methods, Lecture Notes in Computer Science n° 873, pp. 618--638. Springer Verlag.

Fields B., Harrison M. & Wright P. (1994a) From Informal Requirements to Agent-Based Specification. SIGCHI Bulletin, 26(2), pp. 65–68.

Fields B., Harrison M. & Wright P. (1994b) Modelling Interactive Systems and Providing Task Relevant Information. In Fabio Paterno, editor, Interactive Systems: Design, Specification and Verification–1st Eurographics Workshop, pp. 253–266. Springer-Verlag.

Fields B., Merriam N. & Dearden A. (1997) DMVIS: Design, Modelling and Validation of Interactive Systems. In Proceedings, Design, Specification, Verification of Interactive, Springer Computer Science, Springer Wien New York. URL: http//www.cs.york.ac.uk/~bob/papers/dsvis-97.ps

Fields B., Wright P. & Harrison M. (1994) Applying Formal Methods for Human Error Tolerant Design. In R. N. Taylor & J. Coutaz, editors, ICSE Workshop on SE-HCI: Joint Research Issues, Lecture Notes in Computer Science, pp. 184–195. Springer-Verlag.

Fields B., Wright P. & Harrison M. (1997) Objectives, strategies and resources as design drivers, in Proceedings of Interact'97 (to appear). URL: http//www.cs.york.ac.uk/~bob/papers/interact97.ps

Foley J. & Sukaviriya P. (1995) History, Results, and Bibliography of the User Interface Design Environment (UIDE), an Early Model-based System for User Interface Design and Implementation. In: F. Paterno (ed.): Interactive Systems: Design, Specification and Verification. Berlin: Springer, pp.3-14.

Foley J. & van Dam A. (1995) Computer Graphics: Principles and Practice, Addison-Wesley, Reeding, Mass.

Foley J., Gibbs C., Kim W. & Kovacevic S. (1988) A Knowledge-based User Interface Management System. In: E. Soloway, D. Frye, S. Sheppard (eds.): Human Factors in Computing Systems. Proceedings CHI'88. New York: ACM Press, pp.67-72.

Fortes R.P.M. & Masiero P.C. (1991) A language for a Statechart specification and its analyser. (In Portuguese) Technical Report ME-91/01, ICMSC-USP (http://www.icmsc.sc.usp.br/~renata/WWW/LES.html)

Fortes R.P.M. (1996) Analysis and evaluation of hyperdocuments: an approach based on the structural representation. (In Portuguese) Phd. Thesis, IFSC-USP, São Carlos - SP, Brazil

Francez N. (1977) A case for a forward predicate transformer. In Inf. Proc. Lett., **6**, 6, pp. 196-198.

Franzke M. (1995) Turning design into practice: Characteristics of display-based interaction, in Proceedings, Human Factors in Computing Systems — CHI'95' ACM SIGCHI, pp. 421–428.

Gamma E., Helm R., Johnson R. & Vlissides J. (1994) Design Patterns: Elements of Reusable Object-Oriented Software. Addison-Wesley.

Garland S., Guttag J. & Horning J. (1990) Debugging larch shared language specifications. In IEEE Transactions on Software Engineering, **16**, 9, pp. 1044-1057.

Garzotto F., Mainetti L. & Paolini P. (1995) Hypermedia design, Analysis and Evaluation Issues, Communications of the ACM, **38**, 8, August, pp.74-96.

Gea M. & Torres J.C. (1994) Object Oriented Prototyping of Graphic Application from Algebraic Specification. Fourth Eurographics Workshop on Object Oriented Graphics, Sintra, Portugal.

Gieskens D. & Foley J. (1992) Controlling user interface objects through pre- and postconditions. Proceedings of the ACM CHI'92 Conference on Human Factors in Computing Systems, pp. 189-194.

Goguen J.A. & Tardo J.J. (1986) An introduction to OBJ: a language for writing and testing formal algebraic Program Specifications. Software Specification Techniques. Addison Wesley.

Gordon M. & Melham T. (1993) Introduction to HOL: a theorem proving environment for higher order logic, Cambridge University Press, New York.

Gordon M. (1986) Why higher-order logic is a good formalism for specifying and verifying hardware. In Formal Aspects of VLSI Design: Proceedings of the 1985 Edinburgh Workshop on VLSI, pp. 409-417, North-Holland.

Gram C. & Cockton G. (1996) Ed., Design Principles for Interactive Software. Chapman & Hall.

Green M. (1983) Report on Dialogue Specification Tools. In G. E. Pfaff, editor, User Interface Management Systems: Proceedings of the Workshop on User Interface Management Systems held in Seeheim, FRG, pp. 9–20. Springer-Verlag.

Green M. (1986) A Survey of Three Dialogue Models. ACM Transactions on Graphics, **5**, 3, pp. 245-275.

Gruber T. (1996) What is an ontology? http://www-ksl.stanford.edu/kst/what-is-an-ontology.html

Guerreiro P. (1980) A relational model for nondeterministic programs and predicate transformers. In Proceedings of the 4th International Colloquium on Automata, Languages and Programming, Lecture Notes in Computer Science n°83, pp. 136-146, Springer-Verlag.

Halasz F. & Schwartz M. (1994) The Dexter Hypertext reference model. Communications of the ACM, 37(2), pp. 30–39.

Halasz F. & Schwartz M. (1990) The Dexter hypertext reference model. In: Moline, J.; Benigni, D.; Baronas, J. (Eds.) Proceedings of the NIST Hypertext Standardization Workshop, NIST Special Publication 500-178. Washington: U.S. Government Printing Office, pp 95-133

Harel D. & Pnueli A. (1985) On the development of reactive systems. In Logics and Models of Concurrent Systems, vol. 13 of Series F: Computer and System Sciences, pp. 477-498, Springer-Verlag.

Harel D. (1988) On visual formalisms. Communications of the ACM **31**, 5, pp. 514-530.

Harel D. & Naamad A. (1996), The statemate semantics of statecharts. ACM Transactions on Software Engineering and Methodology, **5**, 4, pp. 293-333.

Harel D. (1987) Statecharts: on the formal semantics of Statecharts. In: Proceedings of the 2nd IEEE Symposium on Logic in Computer Science, Ithaca, NY, pp.54-64

Harrison M. & Duke D. (1994) A review of formalisms for describing interactive behaviour. In Software Engineering and Human-Computer Interaction; ICSE'94 Workshop on SE-HCI: Joint Research Issues, vol. 896 of Lecture Notes in Computer Science, pp. 49-75, Springer-Verlag.

Harrison M., Roast C. & Wright P. (1989) Complementary methods for the iterative design of interactive systems, in G. Salvendy and M. Smith, eds, Designing and Using Human-Computer Interfaces and Knowledge-Based Systems, Elsevier, pp. 651–658.

Hartson R. & Hix D. (1993) Developing User Interfaces - Ensuring Usability Through Product and Process, John Wiley & Sons, Inc., New York, pp. 147-184.

Hartson R. & Gray P. (1992) Temporal Aspects of Tasks in the User Action Notation Human Computer Interaction, 7, pp.1-45.

Hatzimanikatis A.; Tsalidis C. & Christodoulakis D. (1995) Measuring the readability and maintainability of hyperdocuments. Software Maintanance: Research and Practice, **7**, pp. 77-90

Hayes I. J. & Sanders J. W. (1995) Specification by interface refinement. Formal Aspects of Computing, 7, 4, pp. 430--439.

Hayes I. J. (1992) Specification Case Studies. Series in Computer Science. Prentice Hall International, second edition.

Hiltz S.R. & Turoff M. (1985) Structuring Computer-Mediated Communication Systems to Avoid Information Overload. Communications of the ACM, 28: pp. 680-689.

Hix D. & Hartson R. (1993): Developing User Interfaces - Ensuring Usability Through Product & Process. New York: J. Wiley & Sons.

Hoare C. A. R. (1985) Communicating Sequential Processes. Series in Computer Science. Prentice Hall International.

Hoare C. A. R..(1978) Some properties of predicate transformers. Journal of the ACM, 25(3), p.461-480.

HOOD (1989) HOOD Reference Manual, issue 3.0. European Space Agency, ESA, ref. WME/89-173/JB; Sept. 1989.

HTML   http://www.w3.org

Hussey A. & Carrington D. (1996a) Applying design patterns to Object-Z specifications of user-interfaces. Software Verification Research Centre TR96-30, The University of Queensland.

Hussey A. & Carrington D. (1996b) Using Object-Z to specify a web browser interface. In J. Grundy & M. Apperley, editors, OzCHI '96–The Sixth Australian Conference on Computer-Human Interaction, pp. 236–243. IEEE Computer Society Press.

IBM (1989) Systems Application Architecture, Common User Access. Advanced interface design guide. Package SDK Windows - June 1989.

IBM (1994) .VisualAge: Concepts & Features.

Ingalls D. (1988) Fabrik: A visual programming environment. In Proceedings OOPSLA'88 ACM SIGPLAN Notices, vol. 23, no. 11, pp 176-190.

ISO (1988) Information Processing Systems - Open Systems Interconnection - LOTOS - A Formal Description Technique Based on temporal Ordering of Observational Behaviour. ISO/IS 8807, ISO Central Secretariat.

Jacob R. (1986) A specification language for direct-manipulation user interfaces. ACM Transactions on Graphics, 5(4), pp. 283-317.

Jacobson I., Christerson M., Johnson P. & Overgaard G. (1992) Object-Oriented Software Engineering, Addison-Wesley Publishing Company.

Jambon F. (1996) Erreurs humaines et interruptions, PhD Thesis, Laboratoire de communication langagière et d'interaction personne-système - IMAG - Université Joseph Fourier - Grenoble I.

Janssen C. (1993) Dialognetze zur Beschreibung von Dialogabläufen in graphisch-interaktiven Systemen. In: K.-H. Rödiger (ed.): Software-Ergonomie'93 Von der Benutzungsoberfläche zur Arbeitsgestaltung. Stuttgart: Teubner, pp. 67-76.

Janssen C. (1996) Dialogentwicklung für objektorientierte, graphische Benutzungs-schnittstellen. Berlin: Springer. (Diss. A, Universität Stuttgart, 1995).

Janssen C., Weisbecker A. & Ziegler J. (1993) Generating User Interfaces from Data Models and Dialogue Net Specifications. In: S. Ashlund, et.al. (eds.): Bridges between Worlds. Proceedings InterCHI'93. New York: ACM Press, pp. 418-423.

Jensen K. (1990) Coloured Petri nets: A high level language for system design and analysis. In G. Rozenberg, editor, Advances in Petri Nets, volume 483 of Lecture Notes in Computer Science, pp. 342-416. Springer Verlag.

Jensen K. (1991) Coloured Petri Nets: A High Level Language for System Design and Analysis. In: K. Jensen, G. Rosenberg (eds.): High-level Petri Nets. Berlin: Springer, pp. 44-119.

Johnson C. & Kavanagh J. (1996) Electronic Gridlock. In H. Thimbleby and A. Blandford (eds.) Adjunct Proceedings of HCI'96.pp. 78-89. British Computer Society.

Johnson C. (1993) A probabilistic Logic for the Development of Safety-Critical Interactive Systems, International Journal of Man-Machine Studies, **38**, 2, pp. 333-351.

Johnson C. (1993) A Formal Approach To The Presentation of CSCW Systems. In J.L. Alty, D. Diaper and S. Guest, editors, People And Computers VIII, pp. 335-352, Cambridge University Press.

Johnson C. (1993) A probabilistic logic for the development of safety-critical, interactive systems. in Int. Journal of Man-Machine Studies n°39, pp.333-351.

Johnson C. (1994) The formal analysis of Human-Computer Interaction during accident investigations. in People and Computer IX, ed. by G. Cockton, S.W. Draper and G.R.S. Weir, Cambridge University Press pp. 285-300.

Johnson C. (1995) Time and the Web: Representing and Reasoning about Temporal Properties of Interaction with Distributed Systems. In M. Kirby ,A. Dix and J. Finlay (eds.), People and Computers X, pp. 39-50, Cambridge University Press.

Johnson C. (1996) Literate Specification: Using Design Rationale to Support Formal Methods in the Development of Human Computer Interfaces, Human Computer Interaction Journal, **11**, 4.

Johnson C. (1996a) Literate Specification. Software Engineering Journal, **11**, 4, pp. 225-237.

Johnson P. (1992) Human-Computer Interaction. London: McGraw-Hill.

Johnson P., Johnson H. & Wilson S. (1995) Rapid Prototyping of User Interfaces Driven by Task Models. In: J. Carroll (ed.) Scenario-Based Design. London: John Wiley & Son, pp. 209-246.

Jones C.B. (1990) Systematic Software Development Using VDM. Prentice Hall International, second edition.

Kuhmann W. (1989) The Stress Inducing Properties Of System Response Times, Ergonomics, (32)3, pp. 271-280.

Kuiper R. (1981) An operational semantics for bounded determinism equivalent to a denotational one. In J.W. de Bakker and J.C. van Vliet, editors, Algorithmic Languages, pp. 373-398. IFIP, North Holland.

Lamport L. (1989) A simple approach to specifying concurrent systems. In Communications of the ACM, pp. 32-45.

Lamport L. (1994) The Temporal Logic of Actions, ACM Transactions on Programming Languages and Systems, **16**, 3, pp.872-923.

Lewis C. & Rieman J. (1993) Task-centered User Interface Design - A Practical Introduction. University of Colorado, Boulder. (This shareware book is available at ftp.cs.colorado.edu)

Lewis C., Polson P., Wharton C. & Rieman J. (1990) Testing a walkthrough methodology for theory-based design of walk-up and use interfaces. In J. C. Chew and J. Whiteside, eds, Proceedings of CHI '90: Human Factors in Computing Systems pp. 235-241. ACM.

Lightner N., Bose I. & Salvendy G. (1996) What is wrong with the world-wide web?: a diagnosis of some problems and prescription of some remedies, Ergonomics **39**(8) pp. 995–1004.

Lonczewski F. & Schreiber S. (1996) The FUSE-System: An Integrated User Interface Design Environment. In: J. Vanderdonckt (ed.): Computer-Aided Design of User Interfaces. Namur University Press, pp. 37-56.

Lukkien J. (1992) An operational semantics for the guarded command language. In Mathematics of program construction: international conference, vol. 669 of Lecture Notes in Computer Science, pp. 233-249, Springer-Verlag.

Mallgren W.R.(1982) Formal specification of interactive graphics programming languages. MIT Press.

Manna Z. & Pnueli A. (1989) The anchored version of the temporal framework, in «Linear Time, Branching Time and Partial Order in Logics and Models for Concurrency», Lecture Notes in Computer Science n° 354, Springer-Verlag, pp.201-284.

Manna Z. & Pnueli A. (1992) The temporal logic of reactive and concurrent systems - specification- Springer-Verlag.

Märtin C. (1996) Software Life Cycle Automation for Interactive Applications: The AME Design Environment. In: J. Vanderdonckt (ed.): Computer-Aided Design of User Interfaces. Namur University Press, pp. 57-74.

May J. & Barnard P. (1995) Towards supportive evaluation during design Interacting with Computers. **7**(2) pp. 115-143.

May J., Scott S. & Barnard P. (1996) Structuring Interfaces: a psychological guide. The ICS project, September. (http://www.shef.ac.uk/~pc1jm/guide.html)

McMillan K. L. (1992) Symbolic Model Checking: An Approach to the State Explosion Problem. Ph.D. Thesis, Carnegie-Mellon University, Tech report # CMU-CS-92-131.

Meyer B. (1988), Object oriented software construction, Prentice hall.

Milner R. (1989) Communication and Concurrency. Series in Computer Science. Prentice Hall International.

Moher T., Dirda V., Bastide R. & Palanque P. (1996) Monolingual, Articulated modelling of Users, Devices and Interfaces, 3rd EUROGRAPHICS workshop on "design, specification and verification of Interactive systems", Namur, Belgium, 5-7 june 1996, Springer Verlag.

Monk A. (1990) Action-effect rules: a technique for evaluating an informal specification against principles. Behaviour and Information Technology, 9(2), pp. 147-155.

Monk A., Wright P., Haber J. & Davenport L. (1993) Improving Your Human Computer Interface: A Practical Approach, BCS Practitioner Series, Prentice-Hall International, Hemel Hempstead.

Morgan C. (1990) Of wp and CSP, in A. Feijen, D. van Gasteren, D. Gries & J. Misra, eds, Beauty is our business, Springer-Verlag, chapter 36, pp. 319–326.

Moszkowski B. (1986) Executing temporal logic programs, Cambridge University Press.

Myers B. Ferrency A., McDaniel R., et al. (1996) The Amulet V2.0 reference manual. Carnegie-Mellon School of Computer Science Tech Report # CMU-CS-95-166-R1.

Myers B. & Rosson M. (1992) Survey on User Interface Programming. In: P. Bauersfeld, J. Bennett, G. Lynch (eds.): Striking a Balance. Proceedings CHI'92, New York: ACM Press, pp. 195-202.

Myers B. (1989) Tools for Creating User Interfaces: An Introduction and Survey, IEEE Software 6 (1), pp. 15-23.

Myers B. (1990) A new model for handling input. In ACM Transactions on Information Systems, volume 8 number 3, pp. 289-320.

Myers B. (1994) User interface software tools. Technical Report CMU-CS-94-182, School of Computer Science, Carnegie Mellon University.

Myers B. (1995) User Interface Software Tools. ACM Transactions on Computer-Human Interaction 2, 1, pp. 64-103.

Myers B. A., Giuse D. & Vander Zamiten B. (1992) Declarative programming in a prototype instance system: Object oriented programming without writing methods. In Proceedings of the ACM Conference on Object Oriented Programming: Systems, Languages, and Applications OOPSLA'92.

Myers B. et al. (1990) Garnet: Comprehensive support for graphical, highly interactive user interfaces. IEEE Computer volume 23 number 11, pp. 71-85.

Myers B., McDaniel R., Mickish A. & Klimovitski A. (1995) The Design for the Amulet User Interface Toolkit. Human Computing Interaction Consortium.

Naftalin M., Denvir T. & Bertran M., eds (1994), Proceedings, FME'94: Industrial Benefit of Formal Methods, number 873 in Lecture Notes in Computer Science, Formal Methods Europe, Springer-Verlag.

Nelson G. (1989) A generalization of Dijkstra's calculus. In ACM Transactions on Programming Languages and Systems, vol. 11, no. 4, pp. 517-561.

Netscape http://home.netscape.com

Nierstrasz O. Gibbs S. & Tsichritzis D. (1992) Component-oriented software development. In Communications of the ACM, vol. 35, no. 9, pp. 160-165, Sept.

Nigay (1994) Conception et modélisation logicielles des systèmes interactifs : application aux interfaces multimodales. PhD dissertation, University of Grenoble, France, 1994, 315 pages.

Nigay L. & Coutaz J. (1991) Building User Interfaces: A Cookbook for organising Software Agents. ESPRIT Basic Research action 3066, AMODEUS (Assimilating Models of Designers, Users and Systems).

Olsen D. (1990) Propositional production systems for dialogue description. In Human Factors in Computing Systems: Proceedings of CHI'90, pp. 57-63, ACM Press.

OSF/Motif (1991) Open Software Foundation, OSF/Motif Programmer's Reference, Revision 1.1.

Ousterhout J. (1994) Tcl and the Tk Toolkit, Addison-Wesley (Publ).

Palanque P. & Bastide R. (1994) Petri net based design of user-driven interfaces using the interactive cooperative objects formalism. Interactive Systems: Design, Specification, and Verification. F. Paternò (Ed.), Springer Verlag, pp. 383-400.

Palanque P. & Bastide R. (1995) Time modelling in Petri nets for the design of Interactive Systems. GIST workshop on Time, Glasgow and ACM SIGCHI bulletin, vol.28 n°2, pp. 43-47.

Palanque P. & Bastide R. (1995a) Verification of an Interactive Software by Analysis of its Formal Specification. Proceedings of the IFIP Interact'95 conference, Chapman et Hall.

Palanque P. & Bastide R. (1995b) Formal Specification and Verification of CSCW using the Interactive Cooperative Object Formalism. Proceedings of HCI'95, People and Computers X, Cambridge University Press.

Palanque P. & Bastide R. (1995c) Time modelling in Petri nets for the design of Interactive Systems. GIST workshop on Time modelling, Glasgow, U.K., July 1995.

Palanque P. & Bastide R. (1997) Modelling clients and servers in the Web using Interactive Cooperative Objects. (in this book).

Palanque P. (1992) Modelling interactive systems using the Interactive Cooperative Object formalism. PhD dissertation, University of Toulouse 1, September 1992.

Palanque P., Bastide R. & Dourte L. (1993b) Contextual help for free with the formal design of interactive systems. In proceedings of HCI International'93 conference, Elsevier Science Publ.

Palanque P., Bastide R. & Sengès V. (1994) Automatic Code Generation From a High-Level Petri Net Based Specification of Dialogue. In: Conference Proceedings EWHCI'94 (St. Petersburg, August).

Palanque P., Bastide R. & Sengès V. (1995) Validating Interactive System Design through the Verification of Formal Task Model and System Models. Proceeding of 6th IFIP EHCI'95 working conference, Chapman et Hall Publishers.

Palanque P., Bastide R., Sibertin C. & Dourte L. (1993a) Design of User-Driven Interfaces using Petri nets and Objects; CAISE'93. Lecture Notes in Computer Science n° 685, Springer-Verlag.

Palanque P., Paternò F., Bastide R., & Mezzanotte M. (1996) Towards an integrated proposal for interactive systems design based on TLIM and ICO. In F. Bodart & J. Vanderdonckt, eds. DSV-IS'96: Eurographics Workshop on Design, Specification and Verification of Interactive Systems. Springer Verlag.

Pangoli S. & Paternò F. (1995) Automatic generation of task-oriented help, Proceedings ACM UIST'95, pp.181-187, Pittsburgh, November 1995.

Parunak, H. & Van D. (1991) Don't link me in: set based hypermedia for taxonomic reasoning. In: Proceedings of Hypertext'91, San Antonio, TX, pp.233-242

Paternò F & Mezzanotte M. (1994) Analysing matis by interactor and ACTL. Technical Report System Modelling/WP36, CNUCE – C.N.R., September.

Paternò F. & Bucca F. (1997) Task-oriented design for interactive user interfaces of museum systems, Proceedings ICHIM Conference, Paris, September.

Paternò F. & Faconti G. (1992) On the Use of LOTOS to describe Graphical Interaction. In A. Monk, D. Diaper, & M. D. Harrison, editors, People and Computers VII– Proceedings of the HCI '92 Conference, pp. 155–173. Cambridge University Press.

Paternò F. & Mezzanotte M. (1995) Formal Analysis of the User and System Interactions in the CERD Case Study, Proceedings EHCI'95, IFIP Working Conference, Chapman&Hall Publisher, pp.213-226.

Paternò F. (1993) Definition of Properties of User Interfaces, Proceedings of Software Engineering and Knowledge Engineering '93 Conference, June, S.Francisco, pp.314-318.

Paternò F. (1994), A Theory of User-Interaction Objects, Journal of Visual Languages and Computing, 5, 3, pp.227-249, Academic Press.

Paternò F. (1994) A Formal Approach to the Evaluation of Interactive Systems. SIGCHI Bulletin, **26**, 2.

Paternò F. (1996) Critical Issues in User Interface Systems Engineering, Chapter 6: A Methodology for a Task-driven Modelling of Interactive Systems Architectures, pp. 93–108. Springer Verlag.

Paterno F. (1997) Formal Reasoning about Dialogue Properties with Automatic Support, Interacting with Computers, 1997, Elsevier Publisher.

Paternò F. (1997) The TLIM view of a Netscape-like Application. (in this book).

Paternò F., Mancini C. & Meniconi S. (1997) ConcurTaskTrees: A Diagrammatic Notation for Specifying Task Models, Proceedings Interact'97, Chapman&Hall, July.

Paternò F., Sciacchitano S. & Lowgren J. (1995) A User Interface Evaluation Mapping Physical User Actions to Task-driven Formal Specifications, Proceedings DSV-IS'95, pp.35-53, Springer Verlag..

Payne S. & Green T. R. G. (1989) The structure of command languages: an experiment on task-action grammar. International Journal of Man-Machine Studies, 30(2), pp. 213-234.

Pejtersen A.M. (1989) A Library System For Information Retrieval Based On A Cognitive Task Analysis And Supported By An Icon Based Interface. In ACM SIGIR Proceedings, ACM Press.

Pfaff G. & ten Hagen P. (eds.). (1985) User Interface Management Systems: proceedings of the Workshop on User Interface Management Systems, held in Seeheim FRG. Springer-Verlag, Berlin.

Pirolli P. & Card S. (1995) Information foraging in information access environments. Proceedings of CHI'95, ACM Press. pp. 51–58.

Plain S. (1994) Novell's visual appbuilder (sidebar to: "radical development"). In PC Magazine, **13**, 19.

Plotkin G. (1979) Dijkstra's predicate transformers and smyth's powerdomains. In Abstract Software Specifications, of Lecture Notes in Computer Science n°86, pp. 527-553, Springer-Verlag.

Pnueli A. (1986), Applications of temporal logic to the specification and verification of reactive systems: a survey of current trends, Lecture Notes in Computer Science n° 224, Springer Verlag, pp.510-584.

Potter B., Sinclair I. & Till D. (1991) An Introduction to Formal Specification and Z. Prentice Hall International, 1991.

Puerta A. (1996) The Mecano Project: Comprehensive and Integrated Support for Model-Based Interface Development. In: J. Vanderdonckt (ed.): Computer-Aided Design of User Interfaces. Namur University Press, pp. 19-36.

Puerta A., Eriksson H., Gennari J. & Musen M. (1994) Beyond Data Models for Automated User Interface Generation. In: G. Cockton, S. Draper, G. Weir (eds.): People and Computers IX. Proceedings BCS HCI'94. Cambridge University Press, pp. 353-366.

Quinn S., Ware J. & Spragens J. (1993) Tireless testers: automated tools can help iron out the kinks in your custom gui applications. In InforWorld, vol. 15, no. 36, Sept.

Ramamoorthy C.V.& Ho G.S. (1980) Performance evaluation of asynchronous concurrent systems using Petri nets. IEEE transactions on Software Engineering, 6(5), pp. 440-449.

Rice M. & Seidman S. (1994) A formal model for module interconnection languages. In IEEE Transactions on Software Engineering, vol. 20, no. 1, pp. 88-101.

Rivlin E., Botafogo R. & Shneiderman B. (1994) Navigating in hyperspace: designing a structure-based toolbox. CACM, 37(2):87-96

Roudaud B., Lavigne V., Lagneau O. & Minor E. (1990) SCENARIOO: A New Generation UIMS. In: D. Diaper, D. Gilmore, G. Cockton, B. Shackel (eds.). Proceedings INTERACT'90, Elsevier Science Publishers (North-Holland), pp. 607-612.

Rouff C. & Horowitz E. (1991) A system for specifying and rapidly prototyping user interfaces. in Taking Software Design Seriously, J. Karat(Ed.), Academic Press, pp. 257-272.

Rumbaugh J., Blaha M., Premerlain W., Eddy F. & Lorenson W. (1991) Objectoriented Modelling and Design. Englewood Cliffs: Prentice Hall.

Salton G., Allan J. & Buckley C. (1994) Automatic structuring and retrieval of large text files. CACM, 37(2):97-108

Schlungbaum E. & Elwert T. (1996a) Automatic User Interface Generation from Declarative Models. In: J. Vanderdonckt (ed.): Computer-Aided Design of User Interfaces. Presses Universitaires de Namur, pp. 3-18.

Schlungbaum E. & Elwert T. (1996b) Dialogue Graphs: a Formal and Visual Specification Technique for Dialogue Modelling. In: C. Roast & J. Siddiqi (Eds), BCS-FACS Workshop on Formal Aspects of the Human Computer Interface, Sheffield Hallam University. Electronic Workshops in Computing, Springer-Verlag, Booklet ISBN: 3-540-76105-5, URL: http://www.springer.co.uk/eWiC/Workshops/FAHCI.html.

Schlungbaum E. &. Elwert T. (1995) Modellierung von Graphischen Benutzungsoberflächen im Rahmen des TADEUS-Ansatzes. In: H.-D. Böcker (ed.): Software-Ergonomie '95 Mensch-Computer Interaktion Anwendungsbereiche lernen von einander. Stuttgart: Teubner, pp. 331-348.

Schlungbaum E. (1996) Modelling a Netscape-like browser using TADEUS Dialogue graphs. In: Handout of CHI'96 Workshop on Formal Methods in Computer Human Interaction: Comparison, Benefits, Open Questions. Vancouver, pp. 19-24.

Schlungbaum E. (1997) Individual User Interfaces and Model-based User Interface Software Tools. In: Proceedings of Intelligent User Interfaces '97 Conference (Orlando, January 1997), New York: ACM Press, pp. 229-232.

Schofield S. (1994) The UK Internet Book. Addison Wesley, Wokingham, United Kingdom.

Sears A. (1993) Layout appropriateness: A metric for evaluating user interface widget layout. In IEEE Transactions on Software Engineering, vol. 19, no. 7, pp. 707-719.

Shaw M. & Garlan D. (1995) Software Architecture. Perspectives on an Emerging Discipline, Prentice Hall.

Sibertin-blanc C. (1993) A client server protocol for the composition of Petri nets. In proceedings of Application and Theory of Petri nets Lecture Notes in Computer Science n° 691, Chicago.

Sibertin-Blanc C. (1994) Cooperative nets Proceedings of the 15th International Conference on Application and Theory of Petri nets, Lecture Notes in Computer Science n° 815, 1994

Singh G., Kok C. & Ngan T. (1990) Druid: a system for demonstrational rapid user interface development. Proceedings of the ACM Symposium on User Interface Software and Technology, pp. 167-177.

Siochi A., & Hartson H. R. (1989) Task oriented representation of asynchronous user interfaces. Proceedings of the ACM CHI'89 Conference on Human Factors in Computer Systems, pp. 325-330.

Sommerville I. (1992) Software Engineering. Addison-Wesley, fourth edition.

Spivey J. M. (1992) The Z Notation: A Reference Manual. Prentice Hall International, second edition.

Stotts P.D. Furuta R. & Ruiz J.C. (1992) Hyperdocuments as automata: trace-based browsing property verification. In: Proceedings of ECHT'92, Milano, December 1992. New York, ACM Press, pp.272-281

Sufrin B. & He J. (1990) Formal Methods in Human-Computer Interaction, Chapter 6 - Specification, analysis and refinement of interactive processes, pp. 153–200. Cambridge University Press, Cambridge.

Sufrin B. (1982) Formal Specification of a Display-Oriented Text Editor. Science of Computer Programming, 1, pp. 157–202.

Sutcliffe A. & Faraday P. (1994) Designing Presentation in Multimedia Interfaces, Proceedings ACM CHI'94, pp.92-98.

Systa K. (1994) Specifying user interfaces in DisCo. In SIGCHI Bulletin, (26), no. 2, pp. 53-58.

Szekely P., Luo P. & Neches R. (1993) Beyond interface builders: model-based interface tools. In: Ashlund S., et al. (eds.), proceedings of the ACM InterCHI'93 conference, New York: ACM Press, pp. 383-390.

Szekely P., Sukaviriya P., Castells P., Muthukumarasamy J. & Salcher E. (1996) Declarative interface models for user interface construction tools: the MASTERMIND approach. In: L. Bass, C. Unger (eds.): Engineering for Human-Computer Interaction. Proceedings of the IFIP TC2/WG2.7 working conference on engineering for human-computer interaction (Yellowstone Park, August 1995). London: Chapman & Hall, pp. 120-150.

Tauscher L. & Greenberg S. (1997) How people revisit web pages: empirical findings and implications for the design of history systems. International Journal of Human Computer Studies (forthcoming).

Telford A.J. & Johnson C. (1996) Viewpoints for accident analysis, in Formal Aspects of Computing, Vol. 3, n°1. ©1996 BCS.

Torres J.C. & Clares B.(1993) Graphic Objects: A Mathematical Abstract Model For Computer Graphics. Computer Graphic Forum, Vol. 12, N.5.

Torres J.C. & Clares B.(1994) A Formal Approach to the Specification of Graphic Object Functions, Computer Graphics Forum Vol. 13, N.3.

Torres J.C. & Clares B.(1994) Using an Abstract Model for the Specification of Interactive Graphics Systems. Paterno, F. (Ed.): Design, Specification and Verification of Interactive Graphic Systems. Springer Verlag.

Torres J.C., Gea M., Gutierrez F.L., Cabrera M. & Rodriguez M.L. (1996) GRALPLA: An Algebraic Specification Language for Interactive Graphic Systems. DSVIS'96. Namur.

Torres J.C., Gea M., Gutierrez F.L., Cabrera M., Rodriguez M.L. (1996) GRALPLA reference manual. http://Alhambra.uge.es/.

Tredoux G. (1992) Mechanizing execution sequence sematics in HOL. In South African Computer Journal, vol. 7, pp. 81-86. Also available as part of HOL distribution.

Viljamaa P. (1995) The patterns business: Impressions from PLoP-94. Software Engineering Notes, 20(1), pp. 74–78.

Visual Basic (1993) Microsoft Corporation, Microsoft Visual Basic Programmer's Guide.

Wang B., Holden T. & Hitchcock P. (1993) An Object Oriented Database Approach for Supporting Hypertext. In C. Rolland, F. Bodart, & C. Cauvet, editors, Advanced Information Systems Engineering 5th International Conference: CAiSE '93, pp. 601–628. Springer-Verlag.

Wang H. & Abowd G. (1994) A tabular interface for automated verification of event-based dialogs. Technical Report CMU-CS-94-189, School of Computer Science, Carnegie Mellon University, Pittsburgh.

Wasserman A. (1985) Extending state transition diagrams for the specification of human-computer interaction. IEEE Transactions on Software Engineering, SE-11(8), pp. 699-713.

Wellner P. (1989) Statemaster: a UIMS based on statecharts for prototyping and target implementation notation for specification. Proceedings of the ACM CHI'89 Conference on Human Factors in Computing Systems, pp. 177-182.

Wharton C., Rieman J., Lewis C. & Polson P. (1994) The cognitive walkthrough method: a practitioner's guide, in J. Nielsen and R. Mack, eds, Usability Inspection Methods, John Wiley, New York.

Wilson S., Johnson P., Kelly C., Cunningham J. & Markopoulos P. (1993) Beyond Hacking: a Model-based Approach to User Interface Design, Proceedings HCI'93, Cambridge University Press.

Wright P., Fields B. & Harrison M. (1996) Distributed information resources: A new approach to interaction modelling, in T. Green, J. Canas & C. Warren, eds, Proceedings of ECCE8: European Conference on Cognitive Ergonomics, EACE, pp. 5-10. URL:http://www.cs.york.ac.uk/~bob/papers/resource-ecce.ps

Yamada S., Hong J. & Sugita S. (1995) Development and evaluation of hypermedia for museum education: validation of metrics. ACM Trans. Computer-Human Interaction, 2(4):284-307

The Web Browser Case Study

The main objective of the case study is to offer a common ground for comparing different formal methods for the design of interactive systems. The case study is about the specification of a hypothetical NetScape-like web browser and a HTTP (Hyper-Text Transfer Protocol) server for HTML (HyperText Markup Language) documents.

These two components cooperate in order to allow users to retrieve and visualise HTML documents. The web browser is a graphical client requesting HTML documents over the internet from the web server. Servers are non graphical components storing HTML documents and providing those documents to clients on request. Clients and servers interact according to the HTTP Protocol.

1. Description of the Web Browser

Figure 1: A screen copy of the Netscape Web browser

The set of functions offered by a web browser can be classified in the following categories:

a) Visualise hypertext documents
    visualise information (text, images, ...)
    visualise links to other documents
b) Navigate over a hypertext
    retrieve a document (by acting on a link to this document)
    search for information over the hypertext
c) Management of documents
    provide history functions in order to come back to documents already visited
    provide functions for saving documents
    provide functions for loading local documents

2. Description of the Web Server

The web server is not graphically interactive as there is no graphical interface in order to trigger the functions it provides. The main function of a server is the function that allows clients to retrieve a page p from the server.

Other functions aims at providing information during a transfer in order to know the current state of the transfer process.

3. Requested Features

In order to compare the different specification techniques we have selected a set of features that must be taken into account in the specification and others that are optional.

3. 1. Specification

It is requested that the specification of the case study takes into account the following aspects:

a) History mechanisms
    The classical functions for accessing the history of the documents already retrieved such as Back and Forward are to be shown in the specification.
b) Browsability
    This includes the access to remote pages by using a link on the document currently displayed by the client as well as the access to a remote document by giving the complete address of the document.
c) Non-preemptiveness
    Some functions must be available at any time during the use of the web browser. The function Stop that cancels the process of retrieving a remote document must be available at any time when a document is being retrieved. The function Exit that closes the web browser must be available at any time whatever the current state of the browser.

d) Informative feedback about current state of the interaction

Information about the current state of the access to a remote document must be shown to the user. For example information such as "the system is currently downloading information", "the downloading of information has finished", etc. must be displayed in real time.

e) Concurrency among various servers and various browsers and dynamic instanciation of browsers

It must be possible for the user to follow concurrently various threads of dialogue using several instances of the web browser. Thus the specification must show how these instances are created and how the user can switch from the current one to another one. The server must be able to handle concurrently several requests for documents. This feature of the server must be shown on the specification of the case study.

3.2. Analysis of the specification

The specification will have to answer a set of questions such as:

a) Can you verify or disprove a number of usability properties on your specification?
b) How difficult is it to go from your specification to an implementation ?
c) What kind of constructs do you use in order to structure you specification ?
d) Does your specification cover all the aspects of the case study ?
e) How difficult will it be to modify your specification in order (for example) to add a new feature ?

4. Additional Features

Some other features that are classically encountered in web browsers can be integrated into the specification. However, in order to keep the specifications short, their integration in the specification is optional.

4.1. Bookmarks management

Bookmarks are a set of addresses to documents. The management of bookmarks allow users to store an address as a bookmark, to access a document using the bookmark and to organise the bookmarks in a hierarchy.

4.2. Browsing within a given html page

Netscape-like browsers display documents in a window. If the document is longer than the size of the window they scrolling is available to the user in order to visualise the whole document.

Index of Key Words

A

abstract 6; 29; 54; 94; 99; 106; 110; 141; 145; 157; 158; 160; 170; 198; 206; 221; 226-228; 236; 241; 242; 244; 246; 248; 249; 264; 279; 283; 284; 287; 290; 308

abstract interaction object 54

abstractions 32; 54; 79; 81; 97; 106; 145; 160; 272

action 12; 18; 21; 23; 25; 57; 61; 108; 110-112; 135; 152; 155; 169; 176; 178; 179; 181; 191; 234; 247; 249; 251; 256-259; 285; 287; 288; 289; 291; 292; 294; 295; 298; 303; 309; 313; 318-320; 327; 328; 331

ADEPT 220

agent 49; 50; 55-62; 65-73; 97; 104; 105; 159; 160; 170; 228

analogy 98; 99; 106; 114; 284

analysis 58; 60; 76-78; 82; 87; 88; 90; 95; 98; 110; 112; 121; 153; 155; 158; 159; 161; 169; 170; 175; 191; 193; 194; 197; 206; 214; 222; 223; 243; 244; 245; 279; 281; 283-286; 292-294; 296; 340

anchor points 4

application model 98; 190; 345

Arch 59

architecture model 49; 50; 51; 52; 73; 246

asynchronous 177; 180; 181; 228; 231-233; 235; 238; 240

attribute 77; 100; 101; 105; 142; 144; 146; 152-154; 168; 171; 172; 207; 208; 209; 212; 219

authoring tool 12

B

basic task 243; 250; 251

binding 39; 102; 104-108; 110; 114-116; 120; 318-320; 322

C

client server 175

code generation 118

cognition 303

cognitive 2; 192; 246; 297; 302

command 2-6; 8; 9; 11; 13-16; 18-22; 34; 38; 42; 43; 62; 65; 67; 68; 70; 71; 150; 189; 190; 262; 304; 313; 324; 325; 327-331; 333; 334; 337-339; 341; 342

commitment 107; 109; 273; 287

communication 31; 54; 57; 65; 67; 71; 96; 105; 107; 110; 157; 161; 175; 177; 178; 184; 189; 194; 229; 231; 254; 255

completeness 17; 18; 152; 196; 214; 226; 299

complex systems 45; 73; 169; 176

complexity 33; 43; 45; 49; 99; 161; 193; 199; 241; 279; 283

concept 31; 32; 34; 54; 59; 60; 61; 100; 123; 152; 221; 223; 242; 247; 251; 285; 296; 299

conceptual ideas 28

conceptual model 27; 28; 31; 54; 98; 284

Index of Authors